P9-AFR-219

STEPS TO LANGUAGE

TOWARD A THEORY OF
NATIVE LANGUAGE ACQUISITION

STEPS TO LANGUAGE

TOWARD A THEORY OF NATIVE LANGUAGE ACQUISITION

I. M. Schlesinger
The Hebrew University of Jerusalem and
The Israel Institute of Applied Social Research

LEA

Lawrence Erlbaum Associates, Publishers
1982   Hillsdale, New Jersey   London

Copyright © 1982 by Lawrence Erlbaum Associates, Inc.
  All rights reserved. No part of this book may be reproduced in
any form, by photostat, microform, retrieval system, or any other
means, without the prior written permission of the publisher.

Lawrence Erlbaum Associates, Inc., Publishers
365 Broadway
Hillsdale, New Jersey 07642

Library of Congress Cataloging in Publication Data

Schlesinger, I. M.
    Steps to language.

    Bibliography: p.
    Includes index.
    1. Language acquisition.   I. Title.
P118.S29   401′.9   81-17439
ISBN 0-89859-045-0   AACR2

Printed in the United States of America
10   9   8   7   6   5   4   3   2   1

P118
S29

*To Avigail
and to Shlomo, Ayala and Noam*

Contents

Preface

About 4 years ago it occurred to me that a collection of my previous articles might be published in book form. The articles I had in mind represented my work on the theory of language acquisition, spanning over a decade and including early presentations of my approach as well as later modifications of it. I had no idea then that I would end up writing a new book instead, containing a far more developed version of my theory. In retrospect, I find that most of the "blame" must be put on the man with whom I also published my previous book, Lawrence Erlbaum. When I laid before him my plans for the collection, he was encouraging as usual, but suggested that I do a little more than I had intended, to weld the papers together into a text. He also intimated that I might want to rewrite some of the papers or parts of them. That started it.

Not all of the material in this book is new, however. Chapter 3 includes one of my earliest papers on language acquisition and part of a later paper, almost without change. I could have reworked these, too, so as to reflect better my present views and integrate empirical findings that have become available in the meantime, but this would have meant losing some of the flavor of novelty, which attached to what is now sometimes called "the semantic revolution" at its inception. Furthermore, these papers contain at an embryonic stage some of the notions more fully developed in later chapters of this book, and their inclusion may serve, therefore, to give a good picture of how the theory developed. Chapter 4, which has also been published previously, treats one of the central themes of the book: the role of language learning vis-à-vis that of prior cognitive development.

Part I contains two background chapters dealing with previous approaches to language acquisition and the two just-mentioned chapters, and presents the main themes of the book. These are systematically expounded in Part II. I have tried to make each chapter self-contained as far as possible, so that each of the nine chapters can be read by itself as an independent study.

There are more people I am indebted to than I can enumerate here. In footnotes to some of the chapters, names of several persons whose comments were especially helpful are mentioned. I would like to express here my deep gratitude to Roger Brown, at whose invitation I spent several weeks in 1978 at the Department of Psychology and Social Relations, Harvard University. This gave me an invaluable opportunity to discuss various issues with him and with other colleagues, notably with Jill and Peter de Villiers and Stephen Kosslyn at that department, with John Macnamara (who was Visiting Professor at William James Hall at that time), and with Susan Carey, Jerry Fodor, and Merrill Garrett at MIT, Paula Menyuk and Jean Berko-Gleason of Boston University, Mathilda Holzman of Tufts University, and with Lise Menn of the Boston Veterans Administration Hospital. I am grateful to all of them for very stimulating discussions. I have learned much through correspondence with Sidney Greenbaum of the University of Wisconsin, Milwaukee. On my side of the Atlantic I want to mention my colleagues at the Psychology Department of the Hebrew University, Danny Frankel, Anat Ninio, Benny Shanon, and Moshe Anisfeld (who spent a year with us here), who patiently read drafts of some chapters and made many perspicacious comments.

My greatest debt, however, is to Mordechai Rimor, who meticulously read the entire draft of the manuscript and made innumerable comments and suggestions for its improvement. Almost every page of this book bears the imprint of his criticism. Very often he played the devil's advocate, challenging my opinions and impelling me either to modify them or to formulate them more clearly and, I hope, persuasively. I could have wished for no more efficient scientific superego.

Special thanks are due to Peggy Cykiert, our English typist, who with great virtuosity exercised two skills simultaneously with immaculate typing: deciphering my handwriting and copyediting.

Work on the manuscript and the study reported on in chapter 9 were supported by the Human Development Center of the Hebrew University, Jerusalem.

Some readers may feel I owe them an apology. To set their minds at rest, I hereby declare that I do not entertain the slightest doubts as to the ability of girls to acquire the art of talking. But that it is *only* girls who have this ability is also a false belief, which I avoided having imputed to me by refraining from using "she" throughout in referring anaphorically to "the child." An alternation between "she" and "he" I find rather confusing. The neologism "s/he" seems to suggest some uncertainty as to the child's sex, and commends itself neither to the eye nor to the ear. I hope, therefore, that I will not be accused of misogyny if I eschew such an androgynous term and resort instead to the expedient of using the shorter "he," subject to the stipulation that this pronoun is to be taken to refer to a child irrespective of her/his sex.

I. M. Schlesinger

Introduction

Currently there is a flurry of activity in the field of language development. Not only are new findings constantly being published, but the interests of researchers seem to keep moving from one problem area to another. Only a few years ago, one of the main concerns was the two-word stage, whereas nowadays much research is going on both on earlier stages—the one-word stage and prelinguistic precursors of language—and on later ones. Whereas previously syntax and semantics occupied the center of the stage, pragmatics is currently attracting an increasing amount of attention. Such shifts of focus may be a sign of vitality, provided that it does not result in a loss of all interest in a problem area after the first wave of sanguine activity has subsided. In the late 1960s and early 1970s various solutions were proposed concerning the problems raised in connection with early syntactic development, but no fully developed theory of the development of the child's grammar has been propounded yet. The present book is intended as a contribution toward such a theory.

The title of the book, *Steps to Language,* may be taken to refer not only to the steps taken by the child toward mastery of the linguistic system but also to those taken by the theorist trying to solve the enigma of how the child achieves this goal. I could aspire to laying no more than the groundwork for a theory; much further work will be needed to construct a full-fledged, testable theory of language acquisition. "First Steps" might therefore have been an even more appropriate designation; particularly so, because in this book I deal in most cases only with the earliest stages of the child's progress toward linguistic competence.

The steps taken by other theorists in the past few decades have been retraced, starting from the behaviorist approach and passing through the proposals made by adherents of the Chomskyan school, to the more recent semantically oriented approaches. Theories do not develop in a vacuum, and to appreciate properly any one approach, one must be clear about the insights afforded by those that preceded it as well as about their shortcomings. I hope therefore that my presentation of previous views, which takes up most of the first part of the book, will be conducive to a better understanding of the issues involved and to a fairer appraisal of the proposals presented in Part II.

These proposals concern the acquisition of words and the concepts underlying them (Chapters 5 and 6) and the development of the earliest syntactic constructions and the relational categories underlying them (Chapters 7–9). Many worthwhile topics have not been dealt with: the cognitive prerequisites of language, phonetic and pragmatic development, and the development of metalinguistic awareness among others. Rather than attempt an all-out attack on all aspects of language acquisition, I have concentrated on a few areas concerning which I was able to present, it is hoped, a coherent picture. As stated, my main concern here is with theory and not with a descriptive account of the available findings in the field.

The chapters of the book constitute a developing argument, in the course of which my sketch of a theory gradually unfolds. To give a bird'seye view of this sketch would be to little avail here. Instead a brief statement of a few recurrent themes will be made in the following section, which may serve for the reader's orientation.

Theory of Child Language, Linguistic Theory, and a Performance Model. These three areas of investigation deal with the following three questions: (1) How does the child acquire the linguistic system? (2) What is the structure of the linguistic system? (3) How does the mature linguistic system function in the speaker and hearer? The answers to these three questions will have to lean heavily on each other. Thus a theory of language acquisition will not be verisimilar if it fails to take into account what is known about the mature linguistic system. However, none of the just-cited three areas of endeavour may be accorded any priority over the others. All this would hardly be worth mentioning if it did not involve principles that have repeatedly been flouted. As shown in Chapter 1, behaviorists, to the extent that they concerned themselves with language acquisition and linguistic performance at all, did so without paying heed to certain basic facts about language revealed by linguistics. Later, the tables were turned, and sympathizers of the "Chomskyan revolution" chided behaviorists for being unable to provide a model of language acquisition that fits in tightly with their own views of language, which had been arrived at without any consideration for the way language is acquired or of how it functions in the hearer and speaker. This is about as reasonable as it would be for a theorist of language acquisition to lean back and expect linguists to tailor a grammar to the needs of the acquisition model he has concocted. By pursuing such a course one heads inevitably for theoretical shipwreck.

My own thinking about language was set off by some ideas I had about a performance model. The performance model, I held, contains rules that map underlying semantic relations into utterances. I therefore proposed that in learning the linguistic system, the child starts out with semantic relations in terms of which he perceives what is going on around him and learns the rules that map these into utterances (Schlesinger, 1971). Several writers then raised doubts as to whether the child's semantic relations even came near being as comprehensive as the relations that must be assumed to function in the adult grammar. It was therefore incumbent on me to show how the early semantic relations I had postulated and the rules mapping these into utterances develop into the mature linguistic system. In my book *Production and Comprehension of Utterances* (Schlesinger, 1977) this challenge was taken up, and a sketch was presented of a performance model that might have developed out of the rule system previously proposed for child language; naturally, this performance model implied a grammar of adult language (though only in its barest outlines). The present book is a complement to the former one. It shows in more detail how the child's early semantic relations and rules unfold into those of the adult (Chapters 8 and 9). In developing the argument, certain modifications have been introduced into the formulations of the previous book.

Conceptual and Linguistic Development.   The assumption is often made that the concepts expressed by language develop prior to their linguistic expression. The child, accordingly, learns to label those notions he has formed previously in the course of his cognitive development. The alternative approach accords to language acquisition a more central place in cognitive development. Concepts may be formed in the course of learning their linguistic expression. What is expressed and how it is expressed are two sides of a coin minted by the same process.

Contrary to what might be expected, there is little empirical evidence on this issue. It has been argued that the child's behavior prior to learning language (or before acquiring a certain type of linguistic expression) constitutes evidence that he construes the world around him intelligently, and that this implies that he has available to him some of the concepts he subsequently learns to express by means of language. To evaluate this argument, we must first be clear in what sense the term *concept* is being used here. The concepts expressed by language involve the possibility of making a distinction between instances and non-instances. Thus, one has the concept 'box' when one can distinguish between boxes and non-boxes. The concepts expressed by language, then, involve categorization. The foregoing argument from the way the child deals with his environment can now to seen to overlook an important distinction. As argued in Chapter 4, the child's interpretation of his environment must be distinguished from his imposing a categorization on it. What is going on may be interpreted by the child, ad hoc, without having recourse to any categories to which the interpretanda are assigned. That this possibility is so often overlooked may be due to our adult-centered view of the child. If the child interprets the environment appropriately, we tend to assume, this must be because he employs essentially those categories we ourselves employ in interpreting it. The first obvious question this raises is: Where would these categories come from? Would they not have to be attained in their turn by an interpretation of the environment? Construing the world around us must start somewhere, and the possibility cannot be ruled out that it starts with the child's dealing with each instance sui generis.

Categories, according to the latter view, come in later, possibly as a result of learning language. In Chapter 5 it is argued that there is little evidence for linguistically relevant categories being formed prior to language learning and a process is described by which the child learns a word and at the same time forms the category underlying it. Besides these categories, the semantic structure underlying a sentence includes also relational categories, which are expressed by various grammatical devices, such as word order and inflections. Here, again, it is argued, there is no evidence for the existence of relational categories prior to their linguistic expression (Chapter 7). Instead of sweeping the problem of conceptual development under the cognitive psychologist's rug, it is proposed here to view the task of the theorist of language acquisition as twofold: to account for the acquisition of concepts as well as of the linguistic means of expressing them. This proposal leads to a distinction between the semantic deep-structure level that underlies linguistic expression and a level of cognitive structures out of which the semantic deep structures are formed (see sections 3.4, 3.5, 9.5).

A Learning Approach.   There are writers who believe not only that the concepts underlying language antedate the acquisition of language but that they antedate experience. They argue that there is a stock of innate concepts, hypotheses, principles, or primitives that are responsible for organizing experience itself (and experience with language in particular). Thus the problem of accounting for the way language is learned largely vanishes: It boils down to the problem of what are the concepts and hypotheses, themselves unlearned, that make language possible. I have little sympathy with such a nativist approach. Not that the very thought of innate concepts is repugnant to me (as it seems to be to some), nor that I believe there to be any way of ruling out their existence on a priori grounds. In fact, in some areas, such as the categorical perception of phonemes, there seems to be good evidence for abilities that are not learned but innate. A nativist explanation, however, when advanced without any positive empirical evidence, seems to be an impediment to both theorizing and research, whereas an empiricist stance commends itself on purely heuristic grounds (Chapter 2). The spokesmen of nativism typically engage in brilliant verbal bouts but in little serious theorizing of their own.

The present book takes a learning approach. It attempts to show (sketchily, it should be admitted, and not yet in a sufficiently detailed manner) how the child acquires, through his experience with language, words (Chapters 5 and 6), grammatical word classes (Chapter 8) and rules (Chapter 7), and the concepts underlying these. No particular learning theory has been embraced; in fact, no new proposals have been made concerning such problems as the types of feedback or reinforcement made available to the language learner. On such issues I had nothing new to say and so they have been dealt with only in passing. What I have tried to show is the kinds of linguistic experiences that may be presumed to result in the child's acquiring, step by step, the linguistic system. Step by step— for acquiring language is not an all-or-none affair (as it is sometimes supposed to be by writers of a nativist persuasion, who, generally, adopt an a-developmental approach). There is no royal road to language. To learn about language we must be ready to follow the child as he is lolloping on his often circuitous way toward mastery.

REFERENCES

Schlesinger, I. M. Production of utterances and language acquisition. In D. I. Slobin (Ed.), *The ontogenesis of grammar*. New York: Academic Press, 1971.

Schlesinger, I.M. *Production and comprehension of utterances*. Hillsdale, N.J.: Lawrence Erlbaum Associates, 1977.

STEPS TO LANGUAGE

TOWARD A THEORY OF
NATIVE LANGUAGE ACQUISITION

PART I

1

The Behaviorist Approach and the Chomskyan Revolution

where mindless morphs stare vacantly with no other purpose than to be where they are.

—D. Bolinger

INTRODUCTION

Recent studies in child language are not in the behaviorist vein. The behaviorist approach to language acquisition has been superseded by others, and this book, too, expounds quite a different position. In beginning with a discussion of the behaviorist account of language development, I intend neither to praise it—for there is little reason to do so—nor to bury it, for there is little need for that. Rather, I believe that to appreciate the import of current theorizing, one must first understand what theorists in the behaviorist tradition tried to achieve and in what respects they failed.

After casting a parting glance at behaviorism, a critical evaluation is presented of what has been called the Chomskyan revolution, and its effects on thinking about language development. It was as a reaction to this school of thought that the semantic approach advocated in this book was developed. Chomsky started a new way of talking about the acquisition of syntax that was diametrically opposed to that of the behaviorists. In the fray that followed, little attention was paid to the acquisition of words. The present chapter, too, is concerned only with the acquisition of syntax, as are the succeeding ones, and only in Chapters 5 and 6 is the acquisition of words taken up.

1.1 THE INSUFFICIENCIES OF AN S-R ACCOUNT

It is common today to speak of learning the syntax of a language as of the internalization of rules. Knowing such rules, of course, does not imply awareness; rather, a rule is viewed as a construct underlying certain regularities of behavior, namely, that we understand sentences and utter them in accordance with the grammar (more or less). The fact that the child has internalized rules of grammar enables him to emit in accordance with these rules a large variety of different sentences, many of which he has never heard before. It is this *productivity* of language that has been stressed by Chomsky and his followers. They have asserted that behaviorist explanations of language acquisition cannot account for it. According to the behaviorists, to learn language is to learn a sequence of stimulus–response links. The child's internalized "rules" (the sneer quotes are the behaviorist's, who does not deign to use such language) are similar to the "rules" involved in motor sequences like brushing one's teeth and tying shoe laces, or in any other well-learned motor activity. Against this, Chomsky and his followers have argued that the child cannot be seriously maintained to have learned a different set of stimulus–response links for each utterance he makes. Life is too short for learning all the word strings we use (See Miller & Chomsky, 1963, p. 430).

This argument, however, does not invalidate all S–R theories of language learning. An S–R theory need not require that each sentence a child says (or understands) has been learned by him in its entirety. As Staats (1968, 1971) has shown, a relatively small number of S–R links may account for a large number of sentences. Suppose, for instance, that the child has heard the following word pairs, and has learned the links between the words in each pair:

    the ship
    the truck
    the house

Suppose, furthermore that he has heard, on different occasions, three words preceding "the"—say "made the . . . ", "built the . . . ", and "see the . . . ", each in its appropriate context—and established a link between each of these words and "the." Now, these six S–R links suffice to account for the emission of nine word strings:

    see the ship
    made the truck
    built the house
    built the ship,
    etc.

Some of these the child may never have heard before. Further, each additional link of a word with "the"—either preceding it or following it—adds (at least) three more word strings to his repertoire.

An S-R account thus allows of a certain amount of productivity. By resorting to the notions of *acquired stimulus equivalence* and *acquired response equivalence* (Jenkins & Palermo, 1964) an S-R model attains still more productive power. Suppose, for instance, that the just-discussed child is, in addition, exposed to

>one ship
>one truck

Because they have served as stimuli to the same responses ("ship" and "truck"), "one" and "the" come to form a stimulus equivalence class. As a result, the learner will be able to emit nine more strings, e.g.,

>see one ship
>made one truck
>built one house
>built one ship,
>etc.

These mechanisms, then, permit a large number of different sequences of words, all acceptable in adult language, on the basis of a limited number of learned connections between words.

A model of still greater productive power has been proposed by Braine (1963b). Although Braine did not espouse a classical S-R theory, his model is within the confines of behaviorism. Braine proposed that the child learns positions of words in phrases, and, later on, of phrases in sentences. He observed (as did several other investigators at the time) that at the two-word stage there is a small number of words that recur in many utterances, and always in a fixed position. In addition to these *pivot words*, there is a large number of words occupying the complementary position in the two-word utterance. An example of a pivot word that occurred in first position in one of the children studied is "allgone" (Braine, 1963a):

>allgone shoe
>allgone vitamins
>allgone egg
>allgone watch

What the child has learned is that "allgone" appears in first position. Hence any other word occurring together with "allgone" in the two-word utterance will—without further learning—take up the second position. Other first position pivots were, for example, "this," "that," "more," "other," "all," and "want." Among second position pivots reported are "off," "on," "there," "it;" for example:

boot off
shirt off
pants off
water off

Here, too, the child needs to learn merely the position of the pivot word; any word occurring with the pivot word will then automatically occupy the one remaining position.

That such constructions cannot be the result of mere imitation is shown by those cases where the utterances are unlikely to have been heard from an adult. Thus, the pivot word "allgone" gave rise to, for example, "allgone sticky" (after the child had washed his hands) and the pivot word "more" to "more high," "more wet," and "more page" (i.e., go on reading).

A pivot rule, that is, one that accords a position to one word in the two-word utterance, is productive: It enables the child to produce utterances he has never heard before, some of which sound as charmingly strange as those discussed earlier. Braine (1963b) has shown that this kind of position learning can occur also with artificially constructed "words" devoid of meaning. He suggests that position learning is a special kind of stimulus or response generalization, which he calls *contextual generalization.*

That the position-learning model has greater productive power than one based on stimulus and response equivalence can be seen by considering the hypothetical case of a child who has learned the S–R links in the following six word pairs:

one ship
one truck
one house
this car
this man
this box

By some chance, "this" has never been paired with "ship," "truck," or "house," nor has "one" been paired with "car," "man," or "box." Therefore, "this" and "one" will not form a stimulus equivalence class, and the Jenkins and Palermo model would not predict "this ship," "this horse," or "one car," "one man," and so on. Not so Braine's model, according to which the child has learned that "this" may come first with *any* word. It is a first position pivot word and hence permits the emission of "this ship," "this truck," and many other utterances of the pattern "this + ____" (and similarly for utterances of the pattern "one + ____").

Braine (1963b) also shows how the child may learn the positions of phrases, like "this man," within larger constituents, and the position of the latter within constituents still higher in the hierarchy—up to sentence level (e.g., "little Johnny" precedes "wants ice-cream"). He provides support for his model by experiments showing that children are capable of contextual generalization. It is not our purpose here to examine how well his model fits the now available data on child language (see section 7.3 for a discussion). The point to be made here is that Braine's model can account for productivity of language. (In fact, it has the productive power of a context-free phrase structure grammar, with the limitation that it fails to account for the acquisition of recursive rules [see McNeill, 1966]).

The fault of Braine's model, then, is not that it is not productive; rather, it is too productive in that it predicts word strings not permitted by the grammar. Thus, in the earlier example, "this" has been learned as a first position pivot word; it might accordingly occur before any other English word, whereas English grammar is more restrictive. If the child had nothing to go by but Braine's contextual generalization, he would therefore overgeneralize the use of pivot words and utter many ungrammatical sentences. Now, there is no doubt that children occasionally do overgeneralize (some examples have been given earlier). But the problem remains how they eventually learn to eschew such errors. This requires the incorporation of additional constraints into the system, but Braine's theory does not make it explicit how such constraints are learned.

Likewise, it can be shown that the less powerful Jenkins and Palermo model, and even that of Staats, are too productive; that is, they do not exclude strings not permitted by the grammar (see Ervin-Tripp, 1971, pp. 199–202).

Braine (1963b) has pointed out some of the limitations of his own approach. Some of the more advanced sentence structures cannot be acquired by the mechanism of contextual generalization. Further, Bever, Fodor, and Weksel (1965a, 1965b), starting from the assumption that the rule system of a language has the form of transformational grammar, have criticized Braine's theory on the grounds that it does not take us far enough: It cannot explain the acquisition of rules that can do what transformations can do. Their criticism does not take into account the possibility that the theory might furnish an explanation of the *first* stages of language learning, the rules learned according to the model being supplemented, and in part perhaps superseded, by subsequently learned ones (Schlesinger, 1967; see also Braine, 1965). The theory of rule learning outlined in section 7.5, in fact, incorporates Braine's notion of pivot words and views it as a steppingstone leading to the acquisition of more powerful rules.

Perhaps the most serious limitation of the models discussed so far is that they fail to deal with the correlation between the structure of a sentence and its meaning. Behaviorist theories are able to explain how the child learns to form the two sequences "dog bites man" and "man bites dog" (each by learning two stimulus–response links between adjacent words, or classes of words). What neither an S-R model nor that of Braine can explain is how the child learns which of these sequences is appropriate for describing a given situation. But children very early learn to express their meaning by word order; they do not confuse sentences like the aforementioned. This, then, is one of the facts any theory of child language must deal with.

The theorists mentioned earlier were presumably aware that they failed to account for the structure-meaning correlations (Braine [1963b], in fact, explicitly mentions this shortcoming). Their theories should be interpreted charitably as describing the constraints on the *form* of the linguistic output, an additional (yet to be contrived) component being needed to link this output to the intended meanings. Now, the semantic approach outlined in section 3.2 accounts for these structure-meaning links, and at the same time handles the problem dealt with by the theories just discussed: how the child acquires the constraints on the form of the utterance. Thus it supersedes the theories discussed earlier.

According to the semantic approach the child learns how different meanings are expressed by different sentence structures. One might have expected such an approach to be formulated very soon as a reaction against behaviorist explanations, with their complete neglect of meaning. But such was the stranglehold of behaviorism on theory construction that the semantic approach was not formulated for a long time. The behaviorist edifice succumbed only to the truculent attacks of Noam Chomsky. Chomsky's linguistic theory, transformational grammar, gave rise to an alternative approach to language development that is discussed in the following section.

1.2   THE TRANSFORMATIONALIST STANCE

The influence of Chomsky's linguistic theories on psychology has been enormous, and there is no exaggeration in speaking of a "Chomskyan revolution" in psychology, and particularly in psycholinguistics. One may regard the year 1959 as the date of onset of this revolution. This is the year Chomsky published his review of B. F. Skinner's book *Verbal Behavior* (Skinner, 1957). This review (Chomsky, 1959) has been characterized as "a virtuoso performance whose echoes are still reverberating in psychology and whose dust has still not settled after 10 years [MacCorquodale, 1970, p. 83]." Here we do not have to go into the question to what extent Chomsky's criticism of Skinner's behaviorism was justified (see MacCorquodale, 1970, for a refutation). The effect of this criticism was that most psychologists interested in language abandoned behaviorism—not only Skinner's behaviorism, but behaviorism *tout court*—and many more psychologists became interested in language. The revolution was an instant success.

Theorists who accepted Chomsky's theory of transformational grammar and dealt with child language from this vantage point made a clean break with behaviorist explanations. They argued that the child comes to master not only the surface structure of his language (as the behaviorists held), but also the deep structures revealed by transformational theory. In fact, the child was asserted to acquire, roughly speaking, a transformational grammar. For convenience, theorists taking this stance will be called *transformationalists*. The transformationalists argued that S-R theory should be dismissed as insufficient, because their methodological preconceptions debarred S-R theorists from dealing with those intangible deep structures that Chomsky had shown to be essential for the description of a language. For typical examples of transformationalist theorizing in the area of language development, see McNeill (1966), and more recently, Fodor, Bever, and Garrett (1974).

Chomsky's review also set the tone of much subsequent writing in linguistics and psycholinguistics. Concerning this, MacCorquodale (1970, p. 98) remarks: "The new look was a frown." Actually, this is an understatement, as a perusal of the writings of Chomsky's followers in the 1960s immediately shows. Revolutions are not good breeding grounds for tolerant attitudes. The transformationalists were wont to brush away disdainfully any divergent opinion, meeting it with a display of counter-examples or with the accusation that it disregarded the hallowed distinction between competence and performance. That this distinction was rather vague (see Schlesinger, 1971, for a critical examination) only added to its flexibility as a weapon. It was the great desert of the Chomskyan revolution that it upset the complacency of the behaviorist orthodoxy, thus paving the way for a renewed and vigorous effort in dealing with language development and language functioning. But before long the transformationalists established an orthodoxy of their own.

One of the unwholesome effects of the transformationalists' revolutionary zeal was the primacy accorded to linguistics vis-à-vis the psychology of language learning. Linguistics, it was believed, had settled *what* is learned and the task of the psychologist was therefore to show *how* it is learned (e.g., Postal, 1964, pp. 264–265). However, as pointed out elsewhere (Schlesinger, 1967), the fact that the problem of "what" is *logically* prior to the problem of "how" "does *not* entail the necessity of a neatly arranged research schedule according to which the question of 'what' is to be given a definite and final answer in the first place. The progress of science is more erratic than this; a makeshift statement regarding 'what' may serve for a while, and may have to be reconsidered in the light of research regarding 'how' [p. 401]." It took several years until it was realized that the direction of influence could be reversed: from psychology to linguistics (see, for instance, Watt, 1970). An interesting line of research is that of Culicover and Wexler (1977), who suggest that formal studies of learnability (under given conditions) can be used to decide between two linguistic theories: One theory might result in a language having a structure that can be shown not to be learnable under the postulated conditions.

Because transformationalist theories of language learning arose as a reaction to S-R accounts, one might have expected them to remedy the major deficiencies of the latter; particularly, one might have expected more attention to be paid to semantics and a different explanation of language learning to be proffered. Actually, the transformationalists did nothing less than that. Chomsky's (1965) model of grammar includes a semantic component that construes the meaning of the sentence from its deep structure. It would have been possible, therefore, to construct on the basis of this model a theory of language learning that shows how the child expresses meanings through sentence structures. But, in effect, theorists of child language working within this framework did not deal with the problem of how differences in meaning determine (via deep structure) differences in surface structure.

Closely related to this neglect of meaning was the tendency of transformationalists to view the development of grammar in isolation from other aspects of cognitive development. Recently it is being increasingly recognized that language learning does not take place in vacuo but may be based on previous cognitive attainments. This matter is taken up again in Chapter 4.

The third critical comment to be made about transformationalists' writings about child language is that they made no detailed proposal regarding the way the child learns the grammar of his language. As adherents of this school of thought correctly pointed out, the thesis that the child acquires a transformational grammar raises severe problems. The child receives surface structures as his input; the far richer deep structures, by contrast, are not directly observable. Hence, it was argued, an explanation of how deep structures are arrived at is in principle beyond the scope of learning theory (Katz & Postal, 1964, pp. 172–174; cf. also Bever, et al., 1965b). Here, Chomsky and his followers cut the Gordian knot: Certain aspects of deep structures—and certain other aspects of language—are argued not to be learned, but to be part of the innate knowledge the child brings with him to the language-learning task. Furthermore, this innate knowledge was claimed to be (at least in part), specifically linguistic; that is, it was *not* assumed to be part and parcel of the child's innate propensities to organize experience in certain ways.

This was a very audacious statement to make at a time when most psychologists were still deeply inured in the behaviorist tradition. Not too surprisingly, there were reactions of puzzlement, dismay, and acrimonious protest. But the transformationalists resolutely stood their ground. To drive the point home, they proposed to view the task of language learning as performed by what they called the Language Acquisition Device, or LAD, which takes as its input a corpus of speech and produces a grammar of the language as its output. It was claimed that the linguistic input was too impoverished to permit educing from it the grammatical system that underlies it. Hence, it was argued, if the child nonetheless arrives at a grammar on the basis of such input—and in a surprisingly short time, too—LAD must have a rather complex structure built into it, which determines in advance the kind of grammar the child arrives at (Chomsky, 1962, 1965; cf. Levelt, 1975, for a critical discussion). It was held that some insight into the structure of LAD can be obtained by a study of the properties common to all languages; these linguistic universals are presumably innate. What the child has to learn by scrutinizing the linguistic input is only the language-specific aspects of his native language (roughly, how deep structures are expressed by surface structures; although here, too, there were presumed to exist certain innate constraints [Chomsky, 1965, p. 65]). Thus the nativists.

The claims outlined here started a controversy between the transformationalists on the one hand and those linguists, psychologists, and philosophers who did not find this anti-empiricist stance acceptable, on the other. It is not our purpose here to go into the pros and cons of the nativist thesis; see Derwing (1973) for a cornucopia of criticisms and Hook (1969) for a philosopher's symposium. In Chapter 2 the issue is viewed from one specific angle: It will be argued there that the nativist approach is fruitless, as far as its potential for engendering research is concerned. Here one of the corollaries of this anti-empiricist approach should be pointed out. Instead of explaining how syntax is learned, workers in the field concentrated on a description of the grammars that were learned. Writing grammars of child language became the vogue (see, for instance, Bloom, 1970; Brown & Fraser, 1963; Menyuk, 1969). In the following section, the rationale for this endeavor is critically examined.

1.3 WANTED: A LEARNING APPROACH

The task of writing a grammar for a given corpus of speech is beset with serious methodological problems. It has been shown, Peters, 1970; (Peters & Ritchie, 1969), that a corpus of *any* language can be accounted for by a number of different grammars. A grammar, then, is underdetermined by the data. This methodological problem looms even larger when one sets out to construct a grammar of child language.[1] First, in dealing with child

---

[1]The following treatment of the problem of writing a child grammar follows largely that in Schlesinger (1976). Some of the problems of writing a grammar of child language have been elucidated by a methodological study of Brown and Fraser (1963). Matthews (1975), on the basis of a detailed examination of Brown's (1973) proposals, is also skeptical concerning the possibility of writing a child grammar.

language we are deprived of one of the main sources of data available to the linguist constructing a grammar of adult language, namely, the linguistic intuitions of native speakers. We have no direct access to the child's intuitions about his language, and there is no reason to assume that they match completely those of adults.

In writing a grammar of child language (for a given stage of linguistic development[2]), our only resources are therefore data on children's utterances. Now, one typically finds large individual differences between children at a given stage in respect to the types of regularities they observe. Investigators who have studied in depth the corpora of several children often had to propose a different grammar for each child (see, e.g., Bloom, 1970; Braine, 1976). It is unclear how one might transcend such individual grammars and write *a* grammar of child language. Obviously, one cannot simply include in this grammar every rule that appears in at least one of the corpora, because such a grammar would be quite unlike that of any individual child; that is, it would not portray the competence of anyone at that level of development. Likewise, it will not do to exclude any rule that does not appear in *all* the corpora, because, given the large individual differences, there would hardly be any rules left; such a strategy, then, would also not result in a grammar that captures what is known by children at the stage in question. One fares hardly any better by steering a middle course and deciding for each rule on the basis of some frequency criterion whether to include it in the grammar or not. Such a hybrid grammar, too, would describe a nonexisting language and fail to provide an insight into the linguistic knowledge attained by any individual child.

Note how the situation differs here from that of the linguist constructing a grammar of adult language. There one may plausibly assume that all native speakers of a given speech community share the same tacit knowledge about their language, and hence one is justified in generalizing from a limited sample of data (which includes, moreover, data on linguistic intuitions) to "the" grammar. In child language, on the other hand, we are barred from taking the same road because of the large individual differences, mentioned earlier, and because children's linguistic intuitions are not directly accessible. Hence, the attempt to construct grammars of child language can result only in "a naturalist's collection of schematic descriptions of what various children have uttered at various stages of their development. Unlike a grammar of an adult language which can be viewed—very roughly—as a theory of what kinds of utterances speakers of

---

[2]This is somewhat problematic because stage of linguistic development would have to be defined independently of the child's grammar. One might use a measure like mean length of utterance, which does not require formulation of the child's grammar (although it is obviously affected by the child's grammatical knowledge).

the language will find acceptable, such a collection is a theory of nothing at all [Schlesinger, 1967, p. 190]."

Instead of writing a grammar of "the" language of children, one might embark on a different venture: a descriptive study determining the proportion of children who have mastered a given rule at a given stage of their development. Here, too, complications arise, because a child's language is presumably continuously in a transitory stage; he acquires new structures, and incorporates new rules, following them often only imperfectly. Mastery of a rule is thus not an all-or-none affair. The situation here is similar to the "ongoing process of linked changes" in dialects, to deal   with which, Bickerton (1971) has proposed the introduction of "variable rules."

Although the grammars of child language presented so far are severely underdetermined by the data, they seem to have been constructed with at least one self-imposed constraint; namely, that the grammar should, as far as possible, be compatible with that of adult language. Because the child will ultimately develop an adult grammar, this seems to be a reasonable principle to follow. But it does not take us very far. Thus the occurrence of noun–noun constructions in child speech (expressing the agent of the action and its object—without the verb) induced Bloom (1970) to postulate a transformation not found in adult grammar, which deletes the verb node in the underlying structure (section 3.6). Those who propose to describe child language by a transformational grammar thus have to admit that the rules of child grammar may be not just a subset of those of adult grammar, and this conflicts with the aforementioned principle of compatibility.

It should be recognized, therefore, that the child may pursue a meandering path to adult grammar. Let me suggest that the task of a theory of child language is to plot this path, rather than to provide static portrayals of a continually changing system, which is what investigators writing child grammars have attempted to do. In plotting this path one will of course have to draw on corpora of children's speech, the problem to be dealt with being how the child moves from the knowledge exhibited in one corpus to that exhibited in a somewhat later one. To chart this route, then, involves dealing with the problem of learning: a consideration of *how* rules are learned, not only *what* rules are learned. Corpora of children's speech should be viewed as data bases for constructing a theory of language learning, not as an opportunity for displaying skill at writing embryonic grammars.

Chomsky's (1959) review of Skinner's book (section 1.2) resulted in a tendency by transformationalists of indiscriminate repudiation of all learning accounts. This is hardly justified. One may agree with Chomsky that there is more between stimulus and response than is dreamed of in Skinner's psychology, and still go on looking for an explanation of how language is learned. Such an explanation need not be confined to the theoretical apparatus of behavioristic theories.[3] The refutation of S-R theories need not lead to a condemnation of all possible language-learning theories due to guilt by association.

Consider that even if one accepts the thesis that there is a large innate component of language, there is no choice left to the transformationalist but to admit the need for a theory of how language is learned. Assuming that deep structures belong to our innate linguistic equipment, the problem remains to be dealt with of how the child acquires the specific rules that determine the ways these deep structures are realized in his native language. No nativist denies that these rules differ from language to language, and therefore cannot be innate. But regarding the way they are learned, the transformationalists have offered so far only the most general statements. The child, they argued, comes to the language-learning task with a very constrained set of innate hypotheses that he tests against the input (see Braine [1971] for a discussion of the problems attendant on this proposal). But no detailed accounts have been forthcoming as to what hypotheses are tested, what input data are relevant to these, and how these data are utilized and in what sequence.

Further, one may have doubts concerning the soundness of the transformationalists' claim that because they are not accessible to direct inspection, deep structures cannot be learned (section 1.2). This is a self-defeating line of reasoning. According to the standard theory of transformational grammar (Chomsky, 1965), deep structures are ordered, but this order is *not* universal. Because it is not universal, it cannot be innate, and hence we are faced with the problem of how this aspect of deep structure is learned (Bowerman, 1973, pp. 192-193; Schlesinger, 1971, p. 95). To deal with this problem, one of the claims made was that the child has the intuition that the subordinate clause order reflects the order in the deep structure of German (Roeper, 1973). Rather than resort to such far-fetched explanations, one should abandon the assumption that only what is directly observable can be learned. This is so only according to a simplistic S-R theory. Although theories of more advanced learning processes have not yet been developed in sufficient detail, there seems to be no obstacle in principle to developing an explanation of how the language learner infers from the input data structures and rules that cannot be observed directly. Note also that there are complex systems of underlying rules, besides language, which must ob-

---

[3]We have not dealt here with the neobehaviorist approach, because it concerns mainly the acquisition of words and not of grammar. The introduction of mediating responses seems to provide some of the apparatus needed for a theory of word learning (but see Chapter 5 and section 6.1) and possibly also of syntax learning. But so far only the scaffolding has been provided (see, e.g., Osgood, 1968); a full-blown theory would have to specify the nature of mediating links and their interrelationships.

viously be learned (one may learn the rules of checkers, for instance, by observing others play the game). In section 3.1, however, a different explanation is given of how deep structures are arrived at by the child beginning to learn his native language.

Finally, we note that the transformationalists' reluctance to have any trade with learning accounts has led to a neglect of dealing with the issue of motivation. Specifically, two questions may be raised: (1) What motivates the child to learn language? (2) What motivates the production of specific utterances on a given occasion? As for (1), it is now generally recognized that the child is not reinforced for talking grammatically (Brown, 1973, pp. 410–412), and the motivation for language learning must be sought elsewhere. Plausible candidates seem to be: the satisfaction of the exploratory drive; facilitation of communication; and the need for organizing information (see McNeill, 1966, pp. 62–65, for some speculations). The second question was dealt with in Skinner's *Verbal Behavior* (1957), but the effect of Chomsky's (1959) review of this book seems to have been not merely to discredit Skinner's answers but to silence the question.

The contribution of the transformationalists to the field of child language was twofold. Positively, they stressed that mastering a language implies mastering a system of rules, and impressed on us the need for distinguishing between the surface structure of the utterance and the deep structure underlying it, which carries among others the information relevant to the meaning of the sentence. Negatively, they undermined deeply entrenched behaviorist attitudes and clearly insufficient explanations of language learning. This achievement was bought at a heavy price. The question of how language is learned was neglected, as we have seen. Instead, writers in the transformationalist tradition occupied themselves with showing what had been learned by various children at certain stages of their development, that is, they embarked on the methodologically dubious enterprise of constructing grammars of child language. A penchant for arguing about the grammatical knowledge of children at various ages is also often found among investigators who have broken way from the transformationalist framework (e.g., Brown, 1973). Although there can be no objection in principle to this concern with an inventory of the child's knowledge as exhibited in his speech, when the methodological limitations of this endeavor are heeded, it should be subservient to a concern with what I view as the central problem of language development: how this inventory is acquired.

In this book an attempt is made to readjust our sights and focus on the learning problem. The position taken is that one should start from the assumption that language is learned—not only its language-specific aspects but also those presumably universal aspects that the transformationalists have claimed to be innate. This assumption is made because, unlike the nativist approach, it is expected to be heuristically fruitful. As far as a *innate*

theory of language development is concerned, the nativist approach is, in effect, an attempt to get something for nothing: Research on child language is curtailed by it. This argument is developed more fully in the following chapter.

REFERENCES

Bever, T. G., Fodor, J. A., & Weksel, W. Is linguistics empirical? *Psychological Review*, 1965, *72*, 493–500. (a)

Bever, T. G., Fodor, J. A., & Weksel, W. On the acquisition of syntax: A critique of "contextual generalization." *Psychological Review*, 1965, *72*, 467–482. (b)

Bickerton, D. Inherent variability and variable rules. *Foundations of Language*, 1971, *7*, 457–492.

Bloom, L. M. *Language development: Form and function in emerging grammars*. Cambridge, Mass.: MIT Press, 1970.

Bowerman, M. F. *Early syntactic development*. Cambridge, England: Cambridge University Press, 1973.

Braine, M.D.S. On learning the grammatical order of words. *Psychological Review*, 1963, *70*, 323–348. (a)

Braine, M.D.S. The ontogeny of English phrase structure: The first phase. *Language*, 1963, *39*, 1–13. (b)

Braine, M.D.S. On the basis of phrase structure: A reply to Bever, Fodor and Weksel. *Psychological Review*, 1965, *72*, 483–492.

Braine, M.D.S. On two types of models of the internalization of grammars. In D. I. Slobin (Ed.), *The ontogenesis of grammar*. New York: Academic Press, 1971.

Braine, M.D.S. Children's first word combinations. *Monograph of the Society for Research in Child Development*, 1976, *41*(1, Serial No. 164).

Brown, R. *A first language: The early stages*. Cambridge, Mass.: Harvard University Press, 1973.

Brown, R., & Fraser, C. The acquisition of syntax. In C. N. Cofer & B. S. Musgrave (Eds.), *Verbal behavior and learning: Problems and processes*. New York, McGraw-Hill, 1963.

Chomsky, N. Review of Skinner's *Verbal Behavior*. *Language*, 1959, *35*, 26–58.

Chomsky, N. Explanatory models in linguistics. In E. Nagel, P. Suppes, & A. Tarski (Eds.), *Logic, methodology, and philosophy of science: Proceedings of the 1960 International Congress*, Stanford, Calif.: Stanford University Press, 1962.

Chomsky, N. *Aspects of the theory of syntax*. Cambridge, Mass.: MIT Press, 1965.

Culicover, P. W., & Wexler, K. Some syntactic implications of a theory of language learnability. In P.E. Culicover, T. Wason, & A. Akmajian (Eds.), *Formal syntax*. New York: Academic Press, 1977.

Derwing, B. L. *Transformational grammar as a theory of language acquisition*. Cambridge, England: Cambridge University Press, 1973.

Ervin-Tripp, S. An overview of theories of grammatical development. In D. I. Slobin (Ed.), *The ontogenesis of grammar: A theoretical symposium*. New York: Academic Press, 1971.

Fodor, J. A., Bever, T. G., & Garrett, M. F. *The psychology of language.* New York: McGraw-Hill, 1974.

Hook, S. (Ed.). *Language and philosophy: A symposium.* New York: New York University Press, 1969.

Jenkins, J. H., & Palermo, D. S. Mediation processes and the acquisition of linguistic structure. In U. Bellugi & R. Brown (Eds.), The acquisition of language. *Monographs of the Society for Research in Child Development,* 1964, *29* (1, Serial No. 92).

Katz, J. & Postal, P. *An integrated theory of linguistic descriptions.* Cambridge, Mass.: MIT Press, 1964.

Levelt, W.J.M. *What became of LAD?* Lisse, Netherlands: Peter de Ridder Press, 1975.

MacCorquodale, K. On Chomsky's review of Skinner's *Verbal Behavior. Journal of the Experimental Analysis of Behavior,* 1970, *13,* 83–99.

McNeill, D. Developmental psycholinguistics. In F. Smith and G. A. Miller (Eds.), *The genesis of language: A psycholinguistic approach.* Cambridge, Mass.: MIT Press, 1966.

Matthews, P. H. Review of R. Brown. *A first language: The early stages. Journal of Linguistics,* 1975, *11,* 322–343.

Menyuk, P. *Sentences children use.* Cambridge, Mass.: MIT Press, 1969.

Miller, G. A. & Chomsky, N. Finitary models of language users. In R. D. Luce, R. R. Bush, & E. Galanter (Eds.), *Handbook of mathematical psychology* (Vol. 2), New York: Wiley, 1963.

Osgood, C. E. Toward a wedding of insufficiencies. In T. R. Dixon & D. L. Horton (Eds.), *Verbal behavior and general behavior theory.* Englewood Cliffs, N.J.: Prentice-Hall, 1968.

Peters, S. Why are there many "universal" bases? *Papers in Linguistics,* 1970, 2, 27-43.

Peters, P. S. & Ritchie, R. W. A note on the universal base hypothesis. *Journal of Linguistics,* 1969, *5,* 150–152.

Postal, P. M. Underlying and superficial linguistic structures. *Harvard Educational Review,* 1964, *34,* 246-266.

Roeper, T. Connecting children's language and linguistic theory. In T. E. Moore (Ed.), *Cognitive development and the acquisition of language.* New York: Academic Press, 1973.

Schlesinger, I. M. A note on the relationship between psychological and linguistic theories. *Foundations of Language,* 1967, *3,* 397–402.

Schlesinger, I. M. On linguistic competence. In Y. Bar Hillel (Ed.), *Pragmatics of natural languages.* Dordrecht: Reidel, 1971.

Schlesinger, I. M. Acquisition of grammar: What and how should we investigate? In W. von Raffler-Engel (Ed.), *Child Language-1975.* International Linguistic Association, 1976.

Skinner, B. F. *Verbal behavior.* New York: Appleton-Century-Crofts, 1957.

Staats, D. W. *Language, learning and cognition.* New York: Holt, 1968.

Staats, A. Linguistic-mentalistic theory versus an explanatory S-R learning theory of language development. In D. I. Slobin (Ed.), *The ontogenesis of grammar,* New York and London: Academic Press, 1971.

Watt, W. C. On two hypotheses concerning psycholinguistics. In J. R. Hayes (Ed.), *Cognition and the development of language.* New York: Wiley, 1970.

2 The Methodological Status of Chomsky's Rationalism

INTRODUCTION

In this book an attempt is made to deal with language development from an empiricist point of view. As argued in section 1.3, what we should strive for is a theory of how language is learned. I suggest that in constructing such a theory we should make as few assumptions as possible about specifically linguistic innate mechanisms, structures, and principles. Many psycholinguists will disagree with me on this point and follow Chomsky in arguing that without a rich innate component no account of language acquisition will be possible. If they are right, the approach taken in this book will turn out to lead to a dead-end. The present chapter therefore examines their claims critically and shows that, to the contrary, the innatist, or rationalist, approach is bound to be fruitless, whereas the empiricist stance holds promise for increasing our knowledge in this field.[1]

Over a decade ago Chomsky (1965) propounded his thesis of Rationalism. In the face of the prevalent empiricist viewpoint, he since has ably defended his claim that an explanation of the child's learning his native language is possible only by postulating innate "fixed and highly restricted schemata which come into operation under limited conditions of exposure to data,

[1] I am grateful to Moshe Anisfeld, Jerry Fodor, Etha Frenkel, and Benny Shanon for their perceptive critical comments on this chapter. Thanks to the careful reading of M. Rimor, I was able to correct many passages in which the exposition was unclear or the reasoning loose. I am indebted to Professors Dwight Bolinger, Eve Clark, David Crystal, Sidney Greenbaum, Hans Hörmann, Howard Kendler, John Macnamara, George A. Miller, Helmut Schnelle, and Walburga von Raffler Engel, who commented on the paper in writing. I made some revisions with these comments in mind, but do not delude myself into thinking that all these scholars will be pleased with the final result.

determine the interpretation of these data as experience" and lead to the development of an internalized system of rules, which is the knowledge of language (Chomsky, 1975, p. 154). It has been argued (Black, 1970) that "Nativism" would be a better name for this position than Rationalism (the name taken over by Chomsky from an old and respectable philosophical school, which in fact embraced a somewhat different doctrine). There is no need to go into this terminological issue here, and in deference to Chomsky I will use the label he prefers. Rationalism, then, is Chomsky's proposal of how one may account for "the child's discovery of . . . a deep and abstract theory—a generative grammar of his language—many of the concepts and principles of which are only remotely related to experience," a fact that, he claims, leaves "little hope that much of the structure of language can be learned by an organism initially uninformed as to its general character [Chomsky, 1965, p. 58]."

The heated debate that ensued is still going on. It seems, however, that the battle will be neither lost nor won by arguing the tenability of the rationalist approach or its implausibility. After all arguments have been marshalled, the proponents of Rationalism and Empiricism will remain just as firmly entrenched in their respective positions as before. With the amount of ingenuity already expended by proponents of the two camps, there would hardly seem to be any point in adding yet another chapter on the subject, particularly because there is no lack of well-balanced evaluations of the controversy (e.g., Ervin-Tripp, 1971; Levelt, 1974, 1975). Moreover, these latter-day Rationalists and Empiricists are actually less extremely opposed in their views than their often bitter verbal bouts make them appear to be. For, obviously, any empiricist today must acknowledge innate processing capacities that enable the organism to learn from the linguistic input, and even an extreme rationalist has to concede that language is not present at birth but requires a modicum of environmental support to develop. The issue thus seems to boil down to the question whether there is a little more to the environment than the rationalist, or a little more genetic determination than the empiricist, had thought. And surely, this is the kind of question one ought to entrust to empirical research. No new arguments are therefore presented in the following sections that bear on the issue whether Rationalism is right or wrong, plausible or not, philosophically respectable or not. Instead, what I try to show is that the empiricist approach is preferable on purely heuristic grounds. No progress will be made in theories and research in language development, unless one is ready to embark on an empiricist research program (perhaps suspending judgment as to the ultimate truth of Rationalism).[2]

---

[2]This chapter deals only with the rationalist thesis propounded by Chomsky. A different thesis, advanced by Fodor, is discussed in section 9.7.

2.1 THE RATIONALIST RESEARCH PROGRAM

Chomsky, in fact, has been insistent in claiming that Rationalism is just as much subject to empirical test as its rival, Empiricism (e.g., Chomsky, 1975, pp. 37, 137f, 223). Because so far no well-developed theory of an innate language faculty has been proposed, he accords to Rationalism the status of a "program of research" (Chomsky, 1968, p. 70). At the same time, however, he is at pains to persuade his readers of the futility of pursuing an empiricist research program. Now, I am convinced that following this advice would have a baneful effect on research in this field. In the following I therefore examine Chomsky's claim concerning the empirical status of Rationalism and evaluate its potential as a research program.

A research program leads to the formulation of a theory or of specific hypotheses. Disconfirmation of these does not necessarily lead to abandoning the program; instead, as Lakatos (1974) has pointed out, the typical reaction to such disconfirmation is to revise the theory (or hypotheses) and submit it to further empirical tests. Thus empirical refutation acts as a catalyst for further development of the program. Eventually, of course, there may come a time when the program has exhausted its heuristic value and then it should be abandoned for another one. These considerations apply also to the rationalist program. Disconfirmation of any specific rationalist hypothesis will generally not be sufficient ground for rejecting the program, but it is essential that it give rise to empirically refutable hypotheses.

To see whether the rationalist research program meets this requirement let us consider first the nature of hypotheses which will be formulated within it. The research that is discussed by Chomsky as taking place within this framework is largely linguistic: Languages are studied with a view to revealing their underlying grammatical principles. Take as an example the principle of structure dependence (Chomsky, 1975, pp. 31–33). A fuller discussion of this principle is presented later; suffice it to say here that according to Chomsky a study of the rules governing question formation in English leads to the conclusion that these are defined on sentences that have been analyzed into words and phrases. The latter are not necessarily physically marked. The fact that the child "unerringly makes use of the structure-dependent rule" cannot be explained in terms of experience, argues Chomsky, and it must therefore be assumed that this principle "is not learned but forms part of the conditions of language learning." This is confirmed by findings of other rules of English, which are also structure-dependent. Now, if this principle is innate, one may "conclude that other languages must have the same property on the assumption that humans are not specifically designed to learn one rather than another language, say English rather than Japanese." In other words, the principle of structure dependence is contained in what Chomsky calls *universal grammar*. Later, we discuss this example of Chomsky's line of reasoning and examine whether such a conclusion is justified.

Chomsky's claim of empirical status for Rationalism is based on the constraints that are imposed on the assignment of principles to universal grammar. He mentions both an upper and lower bound:

> The variety of languages provides an upper bound on the richness and specificity of the properties that he may assign to the universal grammar. The necessity of accounting for acquisition of particular grammars provides a lower bound [Chomsky, 1975, p. 153].

In the following I do not intend to refute Chomsky's Rationalism—there have been enough attempts to do that and Chomsky's thesis is still very much alive. My sole purpose is to show that the aforementioned constraints are insufficient for according empirical status to hypotheses formulated within the rationalist framework, because such hypotheses will typically not be falsifiable by counterexamples; hence Rationalism is not a fruitful research program. Further on, an empiricist research program is discussed that does lead to the formulation of refutable hypotheses.

2.2 CHOMSKY'S UPPER BOUND

Let us look first at Chomsky's upper bound. According to the foregoing quotation, Chomsky holds that a hypothesis that claims that a given principle belongs to universal grammar might be refuted by showing that this principle is violated in a single language. Crosslinguistic comparisons thus may lead to a revision of rationalist hypotheses. The notion of such an upper bound seems at first perfectly straightforward. On second thought, however, not all is well.

In the following, I discuss two possible forms of rationalist hypotheses, both of which meet this challenge: a weaker form, H_1, and a stronger form, H_2. Both forms specify which linguistic properties, or characteristics, or principles—for convenience I henceforth refer simply to principles—are innate.

Consider first the weaker form, H_1:

H_1: The principle P belongs to the innate set of
   principles L.

Now, showing that P is violated in any language does not falsify H_1, for the simple reason that H_1 does not claim that L is the *only* set of innate principles. It would be quite compatible with H_1—and quite adequate for a rationalist account of language acquisition—to assume that the language violating P employs a different set of principles, L', such that L' includes P' instead of P. According to this response to the putative counter-example to H_1, P and P' will be mutually exclusive alternatives, of which each language will include only one, but both P and P' are innate. As long as P and P' do not exhaust the set of logically possible alternatives, the child's chore of learning language is made easier by postulating that they are both included in the innate language-learning faculty: His task will be to find out whether P or P' applies to the specific language he is learning, and he will be exempt from considering other alternatives that are not in his innate repertoire. In other words, the challenge of accounting for language learning may also be met by a version of Rationalism according to which the innate language faculty may contain alternative, partially overlapping sets of principles.

Such a move would obviously vitiate the attempt to put an upper bound on hypotheses of the form of H_1. The lesson, then, would seem to be: Inflate your innate language faculty as much as you wish, and do not fear the pin-prick of counterexamples from another language. For each counterexample to H_1 there will be the same pat answer. In fact, H_1 has been formulated here so that it will not require any emendation, because it states only that P belongs to L and does not exclude the possibility that P' belongs to L', another set of innate principles.

It will be objected that Chomsky intended hypotheses of a stronger form. He speaks in terms of a universal grammar, to which evidence from other languages is relevant. The hypothesis he has in mind might be formulated as a conjunction of H_1 and the stipulation that L is common to all languages, or:

H_2: The principle P belongs to the innate set of principles L, and L is universal.

H_2 can obviously be falsified by a counterexample from a single language. The question is, however, why Rationalism should be wedded to H_2. When the move of postulating alternative Ls is resorted to, H_1 becomes in a sense less parsimonious than H_2, but parsimony is a criterion of choosing between theories that are *not* refuted by the data. The rational rationalist, who at first embraces H_2, would do well in case of a refutation to fall back on H_1, which permits him to postulate an alternative L, because, as stated, H_1 is equally well suited to an account of language learning (as P and P' are both innate).[3] That H_1 is not refutable by cross-linguistic

---

[3] As Professor Hörmann (personal communication) has pointed out, such a move would not be unproblematic. It would require a specification for whom H_1 is valid and why. It would indeed be difficult for the rationalist to give a principled account of why P and P' are distributed

evidence is not sufficient reason to foist on it a limitation not inherently required by the rationalist thesis. H_2 involves such a limitation: It would be prescribed by Rationalism cum Universalism, not by Rationalism. Whatever one may think of Chomsky's Rationalism, there is no denying that it was motivated by a real problem—how to account for the child's acquisition of the vastly complex system that language seems to be—and that it provides a possible approach to solving the problem. There is no such motivation for universalism.

This, then, is one of the weaknesses inherent in the rationalist program of research (though by no means the worst one, as we see later). Once alternative sets of principles are postulated, it becomes immune to empirical test by cross-linguistic research, and its fruitfulness is bound to be soon exhausted. But sooner or later this option is likely to be taken in order to survive in face of the conflicting evidence. The probability of discovering such evidence will increase as the number of putative linguistic universals increases, and the postulation of such universals is after all the whole point of the program. This is particularly so because the explanation of language learning, which is the raison d'être of Rationalism, seems to require increasingly richer hypotheses of what is innate (Chomsky, 1975, p. 207).

The aforementioned should of course not be construed as casting doubt on the usefulness of research on linguistic universals in its own right. Obviously, hypotheses concerning such universals are empirically meaningful because they are refutable by counterexamples. It should be evident, however, that such research does not have to be conducted within the framework of Rationalism. Rationalism makes claims over and above the existence of universals and it is the empirical status of these claims that is under scrutiny here.

Much of linguistic research, then, may properly be viewed as belonging to the universalist research program. Not one jot will be added to the hypotheses formulated within this program by additional assumptions as to the innateness of certain principles. Such assumptions are entirely gratuitous. This is because, for the time being, the only empirical evidence relevant to them will come from cross-linguistic research, the results of which, however, can corroborate only the universality of the principles and not its innateness (because such principles can be universal without being innate; see Cooper 1975, pp. 170–180; Sampson, 1978). There is no justification for Rationalism to hitch a free hike on Universalism.

---

among languages in the way they are, but he could always point out that this question might be asked about any difference between languages, and the fact that P and P' are claimed to be innate does not aggravate the problem. Note that the speakers of the two languages do not differ in their innate endowment; it is only the two languages that differ in their choice of (innate) principles.

The rationalist program of research thus can be shown to lack an effective upper bound. But what about the lower bound?

2.3 CHOMSKY'S LOWER BOUND

"The theories of universal grammar so far proposed . . . are still far from sufficiently rich and restrictive to explain acquisition of language; they do not sufficiently limit the class of admissable hypotheses [Chomsky, 1975, p. 207]." Such limitation is necessary if language learning is to be possible. This is Chomsky's (1975, p. 153) lower bound. A hypothesis of L can be faulted by showing that there is a principle P such that (1) P is not included in L; and (2) P cannot be acquired by the young child by usual learning strategies, unless he is assumed to be innately predisposed to discovering it.

But is this really a possibility of refutation? Note that it is not the discovered facts that count as refutation but only the inability to account for them in any other way. All will depend on who is to be the judge. The rationalist may regard his previous hypothesis as refuted by the recalcitrant principle, and he will promptly pronounce this principle innate. Those more empiricistically inclined may argue that an account of how the principle is learned will eventually be possible. They may turn out to be wrong—but when are we going to be certain that they are?

The disagreement between the rationalist and the empiricist, then, boils down to this: According to the rationalist, an account of how the principles revealed by linguistic study are learned is *not*, and according to the Empiricist—*not yet* in sight. Paradoxically, only by the empiricist admitting defeat can a rationalist hypothesis be *refuted*.

It appears therefore that rationalist hypotheses of the types H_1 and H_2 may be rejected in the absence of findings incompatible with them: by providing an empiricist explanation of the facts in question. Hence rationalist hypotheses may be viewed as mere repositories of principles, the learning of which is eventually to be explained. In this respect the relation between rationalist and empiricist explanations is not a symmetrical one. As long as it is not falsified by the data, an empiricist hypothesis of how a given principle is attained will not be superseded by a rationalist explanation (i.e., one which claims it to be innate).

This temporary status of innate principles is recognized by Chomsky (1975, p. 207) when he writes: "...theoretical progress in the explanation of language learning should be sought in the direction of richer theories of innate universals, at least, *until some other approach is suggested that has some degree of plausibility*" [emphasis added]. Chomsky has argued forcefully that attempts at showing how the principles underlying language are learned by induction from the observed data of language are bound to fail. Such arguments of infeasibility should be suspect. Before the advent of the airplane there were probably good arguments against the possibility of a steerable flying machine. The way to scientific progress is littered with such well-reasoned arguments.

Rationalism might be established by a collapse of its rival, Empiricism. But for this to happen there has first to be an empiricist research program that in the course of time is shown to be inadequate. It would be fatuous to cite Chomsky's (1959) famous rebuttal of Skinner as having succeeded in showing this (section 1.3). Skinner's learning theory is a highly restrictive one and other approaches to learning are possible. If to date no such well-developed theory has been proposed, this is due to the fact that the immensity of the problem became apparent only about a decade ago (thanks to Chomsky's work). This period of time has not been sufficient for developing an account of learning (just as it has not been sufficient for developing a definitive theory of what any single language is like: There is no complete generative grammar of English). As for the allegedly insurmountable obstacles a learning theory will have to cope with, I have more to say about them later on.

The lower bound suggested by Chomsky, then, does not ensure the falsifiability of a rationalist hypothesis. Instead, as the earlier discussion shows, it highlights an inherent weakness in the rationalist explanation: that it is based on what Putnam (1967) has called a "What Else" argument ("What else could it be but *innate*?"). Rationalism thus becomes the last refuge for those too tired to search any further.

Essentially the same comment applies to another claim made by Chomsky, namely, that many of the innate principles are specifically linguistic. Without this claim Rationalism would be much less interesting (and controversial), for, as Quine (1969) has put it, even "the behaviorist is knowingly and cheerfully up to his neck in innate mechanisms of learning-readiness." According to Chomsky (1975, p. 20) it is conceivable, but not very plausible, that the innate principles are common to language and to other cognitive domains. Against the suggestion made, for example, by Putnam (1967) that the innate predispositions necessary for learning language are those that underlie other complex skills, Chomsky (1975, pp. 18ff, 158-159) argues at length that this is highly unlikely. Whether this is so or not (and this question is examined later on), the merit of such a rider to a H_2-type hypothesis depends on the absence of evidence to the contrary. Here, again, the rationalist hypothesis serves as a repository of facts awaiting an alternative explanation.

The foregoing discussion should, I repeat, not be construed as implying any disparagement of linguistic research leading to the discovery of features common to many or all languages. Every science strives after significant generalizations, and linguistic universals certainly qualify for being such.

The issue here pertains to the origin of such universals. In principle several types of explanation seem to be possible, the rationalist explanation being one of them. The trouble with the latter, however, is that it spirits universals away into the realm of unassailable dogma.

As shown in the last two sections, what Chomsky calls the "upper" and "lower bounds" do not render rationalist hypotheses amenable to empirical refutation. Empiricist hypotheses, by contrast, are wide open to such refutation. In fact, Chomsky himself has been at pains to amass arguments to refute empiricism on empirical grounds. The validity of his arguments are questioned further on, but at any rate they suffice to show that the rationalist and the empiricist are not together in the same boat: The former, but not the latter, suffers from a dearth of refutable hypotheses.

That hypotheses formulated within the rationalist program are irrefutable does not mean that they are empirically meaningless (cf. Chomsky 1975, pp. 37-38). The claim that the other side of the moon is made of green cheese was an empirically meaningful (though false) statement even before a spacecraft could be designed to circle the moon. Likewise, rationalist hypotheses are empirically meaningful (and, conceivably, true) even at the present state of our knowledge. Major breakthroughs in neurology or in genetics may make it possible in the future to investigate which specific linguistic principles, if any, have an innate biological basis. Rationalism may then become a viable rationalist research program. But pending such a breakthrough there is nothing to keep such a rationalist program alive; for this purpose it is not sufficient that it gives rise to predictions that are testable in principle. What is needed are problems that can be studied empirically at the present time. In the following we see what kind of research a rationalist might conceivably embark on.

2.4   RATIONALIST PASTIMES

The rationalist thesis pertains to the human mind. Hence a rationalist research program cannot limit itself to linguistic investigations, but must also involve research with psychological variables in the areas of language learning and language behavior. Let us see now what possibilities are open to a rationalist to make contact with human psychology.

One avenue of approach has been pointed out by Chomsky (1975, pp. 29–30, 209). A rationalist hypothesis about innate principles leads to the prediction that in learning an artificial language violating any one of these principles, he "will have no cognitive structure available for dealing with this problem" and will therefore "not be able to find or construct a rich and insightful way to deal with the problem, to develop a relevant cognitive structure in the intuitive, unconscious manner characteristic of language learning [Chomsky, 1975, p. 24]."

This suggests an experiment comparing the learnability of two artificial languages, one of which conforms to the principles of Universal Grammar whereas the other violates them. If the latter is indeed not as easily learned as the former, this might be taken as corroboration of the rationalist hypothesis. But remember that the rationalist is interested in innate principles that are specifically linguistic; his thesis would have little interest if it were limited to general cognitive principles. The difficulty therefore is to find a violation of a putative innate principle that, intuitively, does not also make the language to be learned perceptually more complex, for example, by increasing the number of operations that must be memorized. For instance, Chomsky's (1965, pp. 55–56) example of a principle ruling out transformations mapping a string into its mirror image would not be an interesting principle to put to such an experimental test, because obviously such operations will be difficult to learn with linguistic as well as with any other materials. One possibility, explored by McNeill, Yukawa, and McNeill (1971) is the principle of object marking. In many languages only the indirect object is marked, whereas there are no known instances of a language with both unmarked indirect and marked direct objects. McNeill et al. were able to show that this principle is reflected in the way Japanese children understood sentences in which only one of the objects was marked (both the direct and the indirect objects are marked in Japanese). Cromer (1975), however, failed to replicate these corroborating results in an experiment with an artificial language. An attempt with a different type of transformation, with negative results, is reported in Scheslinger (1977, pp. 44–46).

It remains to be seen whether this experimental approach is going to be more fruitful in the future than it has been in the past 15 years since Chomsky (1965, pp. 55–56) first suggested it. The problem mentioned previously, of finding specifically linguistic principles, will not be easy to deal with. At any rate, it should be clear that a rationalist hypothesis cannot be refuted by a finding that violation of a putative innate principle has no effect on learnability, for it will always be possible to argue that in the absence of a specifically linguistic innate principle the learner proceeds by other means, for example, "trial and error, association, simple induction and generalization along certain available dimensions" (Chomsky, 1975, p. 24). Now, Chomsky (1975, pp. 29–30) holds that such learning will not be as effortless and as fast as learning through the innate language faculty. This argument is based on the assumption that whatever is innate will be attained fast, whereas whatever is not can only be acquired slowly and laboriously. Actually there is no necessary connection between innateness and rate of learning. An innately determined principle may require prolonged exposure to linguistic input for the child to find out how it is manifested in his native language. But a feature that runs counter to an innate principle, for example, one incorporated in an artificial language, may be mastered just in the way a puzzle is solved, and some puzzles may be solved very fast and easily. Moreover, as shown in the earlier discussion of Chomsky's upper bound, that a principle underlying one language is innate does not imply that it is a linguistic universal. There may be alternative sets of principles, one of which operates in the case of (inter alia) the artificial language. This, again, obviates the possibility of refuting a rationalist hypothesis experimentally.

It also obviates refutation of rationalist hypotheses by a study of errors children make in learning their native language. Should a child make errors violating a putative innate principle—contrary to what Chomsky (1975, pp. 173–174) would predict—the principle can still be "saved" by postulating alternative sets of principles. The absence of such errors, on the other hand, does not constitute strong confirmation of the innateness of the principle because it might be explained by the way the child learns the constructions in question. An example of such an explanation is given in the following section.

On the whole, the outlook for a rationalist research program does not seem too bright at present. There is the danger of such a program soon exhausting its usefulness, particularly in view of the lack of refutability of rationalist hypotheses. Most of the arguments suggested earlier for those cases in which expectations from rationalist hypotheses fail to come true can actually be found in the writings of Chomsky and others of similar persuasion. It is time now to recognize the consequence of providing the rationalist approach with such an array of escape clauses, namely, to deprive it of the status of an empirically refutable program.

2.5   A VIABLE RESEARCH PROGRAM

In the light of the foregoing, we now propose a viable research program that may contribute to our understanding of the structure of the human mind. Such a program would include three areas of research:

1. Linguistic research with the aim of discovering generalizations about the principles underlying human language (putative linguistic universals).
2. Psychological research aiming at the discovery of other cognitive domains in which the principles revealed in (1) operate.
3. Psychological research in which explanations are constructed and tested of how the principles revealed in (1) develop through interaction with the environment.

Linguistic research, (1), will provide the data that the research of (2) and (3) is intended to explain. The sources of environmental influence investigated may be of two, not mutually exclusive, kinds: (a) observation of the language of the child's elders and their responses to his utterances; (b) nonlinguistic experience that leads to the formation of general cognitive principles.

A complete research program, then, requires that one does not stop short after dealing with (1), as the rationalist would counsel us. For while (1) may suggest a possible solution, viz. innate linguistic principles, it fails, as shown earlier, to provide the means whereby to test this solution. Such a test is possible, if at all, only by a consideration of alternatives emerging from research in areas (2) and (3). This does not mean that (1), (2), and (3) must be pursued in this order. To the contrary, research in any one of these areas should influence that of the others. Psychological research in (2) and (3) should take its lead from the repository of findings revealed by the linguistic research of area (1). Take its lead from the findings, but not be subjected unquestioningly to the grammatical models that are based on them, for there is no merit to the requirement that (1) must completely determine the course of (3). The argument supporting this requirement runs roughly as follows: Linguistics has settled the question of *what* is learned, whereas psychology addresses itself to the question of *how* it is learned and the question of what logically precedes the question of how. But, as pointed out years ago (Schlesinger, 1967), psychological research may lead to a modification of linguistic theorizing so that these areas of investigation may ultimately converge on an overall theory. In Chomsky's recent work (1975, p. 248, note 19) such a possibility is admitted to—for the first time, to my knowledge. It is to be hoped that in the near future we will witness the mutually fecundating influence of these areas of endeavor.

According to the program outlined here, (1), which is the backbone of the rationalist research program, becomes valuable within a more comprehensive nonrationalist program encompassing also (2) and (3). It is of course legitimate to pursue a different course and to carry out purely linguistic research, isolated from any influence from psychology. After all, this is what generations of linguists have done. By espousing Chomsky's (1968, p. 76) claim that linguistics is a branch of cognitive psychology, one commits oneself to a wider scope of investigation, namely one that embraces (2) and (3) as well as (1). This implies the abandonment of the rationalist credo. The credo must be abandoned, not because it is inherently reprehensible (for such judgments are after all a matter of personal taste and hence unpersuasive), but because it would confine us to an ultimately fruitless research program. For Rationalism, as we have seen in the previous sections, does not stand on its own feet. Unlike scientific hypotheses, it is not vulnerable to facts it fails to explain; rather, its weakness lies precisely in that it can accommodate all possible facts within its province.

2.6   THE RATIONALIST AS PROPHET OF DOOM

It appears that the protagonists of Rationalism are not unaware of the inherent weakness of their position. This accounts for their attempts to bolster it by arguing that research in areas (2) and (3)—see the previous section—is not likely to be revealing. If this were correct, the proposed enlargement of the research program to include (2) and (3) would be inadvisable, and no other choice would remain but to limit all research effort to (1). Rationalism would win out by default. Recent developments, however, seem to show unequivocally that such misgivings regarding the promise of psychological research in areas (2) and (3) is unjustified.

First, with regard to (2), some beginnings have been made in explaining the first stages of language acquisition as based on cognitive developments in the sensorimotor stage (e.g., Edwards, 1973; Sinclair, 1971; cf. also Cromer, 1974, for a review of relevant research). There has also been some work tracing parallels between the development of linguistic and other cognitive skills (e.g., Greenfield, 1978). Further, Krashen (1973) has reviewed neurophysiological research showing a large overlap between the areas relevant to language functioning and those underlying other cognitive functions.

Now Chomsky does not deny that there may be cognitive parallels to the linguistic abilities possessed by the child. But he claims that on a priori grounds it is highly unlikely that these parallels go very far; in other words, language acquisition will remain largely unexplainable in terms of general cognitive abilities. His arguments (Chomsky, 1975, pp. 18–19, 158–159), however, remain unconvincing. For instance, he points out that there are species of animals that equal, and even surpass, humans in certain cognitively based skills, and still, although a human cannot run a maze as well as a rat, a rat is unable to acquire language. Such an argument suffers from the basic weakness that it treats an ability as either absent or as present to a given degree and does not allow for the possibility of an interaction of various cognitive abilities. Presumably, humans are able to combine various processes, in each of which animals may also be proficient, in a way that is beyond the capacity of animals. This, coupled perhaps with a superior memory capacity, may account for the fact that humans can acquire language whereas animals cannot. If it is a fact! Actually, this is beginning to be rather doubtful in view of recent success in teaching language to chimpanzees by a variety of methods (Fouts & Couch, 1976; Gardner & Gardner, 1975; Premack & Premack, 1974; Rumbaugh, Glasersfeld, Warner, Pisani, & Gill, 1974). The fact that in these experiments the chimpanzee still lags very much behind man with respect to ease of learning and final linguistic achievement should not be construed as an argument for the innatist position. First, research in this area is still in full swing, and it is therefore too early to say how large the disparity really is. Further, if it turns out, as it well may, that the differences may be viewed as a matter of degree, they can be put down to man's generally more powerful cognitive processing abilities, rather than to his specific linguistic endowment. These remarks are merely speculative and are only intended to counter Chomsky's no less speculative arguments against the reducibility of language-learning ability to other cognitive abilities. Most of the real work remains to be done.

Chomsky's major thrust, however, is against the claim that language learning can be accounted for by empiricist principles. Ever since his classic criticism of Skinner (Chomsky, 1959), he has reiterated his thesis that such an empiricist explanation stands no chance. Chomsky's insistence on this point seems to be motivated by his realization (1968, p. 79) that the rationalist program need not be undertaken if the empiricist program can be carried out. Because his rationalist thesis stands and falls with the feasibility of empiricist explanations, it is important here to examine at length the nature of Chomsky's arguments on this score. He discusses several syntactic phenomena for which, he claims, an empiricist explanation must be ruled out. I discuss here one of these in order to show where his underlying assumptions are faulty and that, therefore, an empiricist approach cannot be ruled out on a priori grounds.

The example concerns question formation with auxiliary verbs. In interrogative sentences the auxiliary of the verb phrase is moved to the beginning of the sentence. Thus, the interrogative forms of (1) are those given in (2):

1.   a. The man is in the room.
     b. The man is tall.
2.   a. Is the man in the room?
     b. Is the man tall?

Now, asks Chomsky (1975, pp. 31–32), what could be an empiricist explanation of the child's learning to produce sentences like (2)? Suppose the child somehow induces from examples like (1) and (2) the rule R:

R.   To form a question from a declarative sentence, take the first occurrence of "is" in the declarative sentence and move it to the first position.

But R will lead to the formation of the erroneous (4) out of (3):

3.   The man who is tall is in the room.
4.   *Is the man who tall is in the room?

In fact, however, children do not make mistakes like (4). Instead, they are able to form the correct question (5) without previous experience with sentences of similar structure.

5.   Is the man who is tall in the room?

The reason, argues Chomsky, is that the child operates on phrases, that is, his transformations are structure-dependent. In producing the question he respects phrase boundaries and grammatical categories, which are not, so he claims, physically marked. Because they are not physically marked, they cannot form the basis for learning from observation, and hence an explanation of language acquisition must, in cases like these, proceed from the postulation of innate structures. The principle of structure dependence is, according to Chomsky, one of the innate principles. It enables the child to master forms like (5) without previous trial and error. As mentioned at the beginning of this chapter, this conclusion is reinforced by the fact that other transformations are also structure-dependent.

It appears, however, that structure dependence does not present an unsolvable problem for an empiricist explanation. Observe, first, that Chomsky's argument rests on the assumption that the child proceeds immediately from (1) and (2) to (3) and (5). However, it is only reasonable to expect that before he learns to deal with (5), the child learns sentences like the following:

6.   The man smokes.
7.   Does the man smoke?
8.   The man in the blue jacket smokes.
9.   Does the man in the blue jacket smoke?

From there to (10) and (11) he has to make only one more step (how large a step it is will be discussed in a moment):

10.   The man who is tall smokes.
11.   Does the man who is tall smoke?

Finally, after mastering (11), the child can correctly produce (5) without first trying the erroneous (4).

In short, learning relatively complex structures like (5) is presumably made possible by a gradual building up of such structures. The child does not proceed from (1)–(2) immediately to (5); instead, he first learns the relations in sentences like (6)–(7), (8)–(9), and (10)–(11)—presumably in this order. Chomsky (1975, pp. 119–121) is, in fact, aware that "instantaneous learning" is an idealization. He takes pains to show why this idealization does not distort his presentation of the way language is acquired. One of his arguments is that we do not find any differences in the linguistic abilities of children as a consequence of differential order of presentation of data (Chomsky, 1975, pp. 121–122). In the present case, the child may encounter (10)–(11) before (8)–(9), and (5) before either of these; yet children do not seem to differ in their capability of producing (5). This argument, however, disregards the ample evidence that adults adapt the way they talk to a child to his level of comprehension (e.g., the studies quoted by Slobin, 1975), and that, should they fail to do so, the child seems to be able to filter out speech that is too difficult for him (Shipley, Smith, & Gleitman, 1969). Certainly, the child may encounter (5)–(11), or similar structures, in any order as speech directed at adults, and if he would try to process this he might get some queer ideas about language—but who listens?

In the present case, then, Chomsky's idealization of "instantaneous learning" is misleading. This objection may not be sufficient to refute Chomsky's argument concerning the impossibility of accounting for the acquisition of structure-dependent rules in empiricist terms. It has been suggested earlier that (11) may serve as a stepping stone to (5). But, a proponent of Rationalism might argue, (11) itself is an example of a structure-dependent rule. How does the child know that (10) is turned into a question by preposing "does", as in (11), and not, following the example of (2), by preposing the word "is"—which appears in (10)?

To meet this objection we must deal with another assumption that underlies Chomsky's argument, namely, that the rules acquired by the child operate on strings of words and on phrases divorced from their meanings. This assumption, that the acquisition of syntax (in the narrow sense that excludes semantics) proceeds independently of meaning, dominated the nativist theories of language acquisition rampant in the late 1960s. The language of the environment was taken to be the input to the "language acquisition device" and its output was the grammar of the native language. The question was raised of how a complex "abstract" system like a grammar can be inferred from an input consisting of strings of words, in which phrase boundaries and grammatical categories are not physically manifest, and the answer was thought to lie in the innate equipment of the language acquisition device (section 1.2).

This view of language acquisition has a serious flaw. It ignores the fact that adults usually talk to the young child about present objects and ongoing events. The child is therefore presented not merely with utterances but with utterances paired with their interpretation. He therefore learns how the relations he observes in the environment are expressed in the language. Transformationalists held that the child learns how to map into surface structures the transformationalists' deep structures, which are defined in terms of syntactic constructs (like noun phrase, verb phrase, auxiliary, and so on). These have no *direct* connection with the way the world is viewed, and are therefore, it was argued, unlearnable through experience with language. This led to the postulation of innate principles. Contrary to this view, the semantic approach to language learning—developed in the following chapter—holds that the deep structures that the child learns to express by utterances are semantic in nature, at least in the first stages of language learning, and reflect the way the child perceives the environment. The difficulty of how "abstract" syntactic deep structures are inferred from linguistic data does not arise when this semantic approach is adopted: Deep structures are not inferred from the utterance but are engendered by the way the child structures the world around him. No assumption of specifically linguistic innate concepts is required by this approach.⁴

According to this view, structure dependence is not a principle that the child must be supplied with so as to be able to learn language; rather, it characterizes the way language is learned. The child learns how phrases and other syntactic constructions (in the surface structure) express underlying semantic relations. If he understands a surface string at all, it is in terms of phrases. Thus, (3) is understood in terms of (1a) and (1b) and the corresponding underlying relations, and the rules of question formation operate on the underlying relational structures (the semantic deep structure), not on the physical manifestation of (3). Once (3) is understood, (5) may be formed correctly, because—stated rather loosely—the child intends to ask whether the man is in the room and not whether the man is tall. This embarrassingly simple explanation is a corollary of the semantic approach. Structure dependence is accordingly part and parcel of an explanation of how learning proceeds, and not an additional principle for which nativism needs to be invoked.

It appears therefore that Chomsky's claim that empiricism is unable to deal with the faultless performance of (5)—without previous trial and error, which would lead to uttering (4)—holds only for a certain brand of empiricist explanation, namely one that would limit the child to dealing with strings of words isolated from the underlying semantic relations. Such an explanation would indeed have to resort to a rule like R. If, as Chomsky demonstrates, such a rule does not work, this shows only that it is also possible to construe an empiricist explanation that is inadequate.

It might seem that the attack against empiricism could be launched also from another angle. Why is it, one might ask, that all languages have this

---

⁴One might hypothesize that the relations in terms of which one perceives the environment are innate. This would be a nativist hypothesis of the innocuous kind discussed earlier, because it does not involve specifically linguistic principles. Actually, however, alternative explanations are possible: The child may acquire these relations through interacting with his environment and/or via the native language he learns (Schlesinger, 1977, Chapter 2; section 3.4).

property of structure dependence? If a language without this property can operate equally well, then the fact that the property is universal shows that it is innate. Now even if we grant for the sake of argument the correctness of the antecedent clause, such a conclusion does not follow. Structure dependence is a universal feature of language for the simple reason that, as stated earlier, every language has a means of expressing underlying relations.

We note in passing that the fact that a linguistic feature is universal can never prove that it is innate. Katz's (1966, pp. 271–273) arguments to the contrary, perfectly plausible alternative proposals are possible in principle. To discuss these here would take us too far afield; a good presentation is to be found in Cooper (1975, pp. 170–180). Sampson (1978) has offered an empiricist account of the existence of certain universals. These, he argues, are actually predicted by an empiricist hypothesis, whereas a nativist hypothesis merely predicts *that* universals, not *which* universals exist. Further, as far as some of the universals discussed by linguists are concerned, it has been shown by Cooper that they reflect a particular way of analyzing data within a linguistic theory; they are imposed on the data, not discovered in them. An instance of this is the claim that the relations in deep structures are universal, which is either true by virtue of the way deep structures are formulated or else factually false (Schlesinger, 1971a). In all fairness to Chomsky, it should be added that his arguments for Rationalism are not based so much on the existence of universals but on the problem of accounting for language acquisition.

Note also that explaining universality by referring to innateness leaves the problem unsolved, because it still remains to explain how these principles became innate in the first place. This must have happened at some period in the dim past. Chomsky has no answer to this question and admits that it is "a total mystery" (Chomsky, 1968, p. 83). Indeed, it is such a mystery that one wonders why innateness should have been advanced as a solution to the learning problem in the first place. Because either these principles had to be learned in the period before they became innate—in which case we are again confronted with the learning problem, which the innateness hypothesis was intended to solve—or else they were selected because they were consonant with the operation of other cognitive processes. In the latter case the principles are not specifically linguistic, as Chomsky believes them to be, and Rationalism becomes the innocuous doctrine that (as claimed by Quine, who has been quoted earlier) even a behaviorist can embrace.

There are also principles of more limited application than structure dependence, which according to Chomsky qualify as universals. Consider the following example (Chomsky, 1976, p. 50):

12. Who did Mary believe that Bill wanted her to see?
13. *Who did Mary believe the claim that John saw?

Why is (12) grammatical whereas (13) is not? The principle at work is the complex noun phrase constraint: The word "who" (or any other word) cannot be moved from a sentence (here, "John saw who") that is embedded in a noun phrase ("the claim that . . .") to a position outside that noun phrase.[5]

If the knowledge of this principle would be evidenced early in the child's linguistic career, this might indeed present difficulties for an empiricst account of language learning. But here, again, we do not have a case of "instantaneous learning." It is only years after he has learned to speak fluently that the child will use sentences such as (12) and refrain from using constructions like (13). The same holds true for other examples cited by Chomsky as instantiations of universal principles—they are not the kind of simple expressions a child aged two, three, four (and sometimes even older) is likely to use. It is only by prolonged experience that the child finds the solution to the many special problems that languages pose for him. Perhaps he does so in the same way as he solves a puzzle (see section 2.4).

Now Chomsky argues that if the child would learn (12) from experience, he would be likely at first to generalize the extraction of "who" to (13), and the fact that he does not make errors like (13) disproves the learning account. But quite apart from the fact that evidence for the nonoccurrence of such overgeneralizations is not available, this argument proves nothing. Learning does not depend necessarily on the child's making an error and being corrected. Instead, he may learn passively by just observing how adults use language (see section 7.4 on passive learning of language). Thus he may notice that adults use constructions like (12) but never ones like (13). (Again, these observations must of course be made in terms of the underlying semantic relations.) By the time he ventures forth into utterances like (12), he has had ample time to learn the regularities in question by just listening.

In addition to arguments from abstract principles like those mentioned earlier, Chomsky (1975) repeatedly forwards a more general argument against the empiricist approach. The latter, he claims, is based on mechanisms like generalization and induction; however, no amount of generalization and induction will do the trick of leading the child from the input data to the abstract system of deep structures and transformation rules that underlie language. The validity of this argument depends on what the nature of the linguistic input is conceived to be. Once it is accepted that the input includes not only the utterance but also its interpretation (derived by the child from the situation in which it is uttered; see earlier discussion), the problem of learning appears in a different light. It is not solved thereby, of course, but it should be clear that one cannot rule out generalization and

---

[5]That this constraint is considerably more complex has been shown by Bolinger (1972).

induction on a priori grounds before a full specification of the learning process has been offered.

It now remains to comment on what Chomsky regards as insurmountable obstacles to an empiricist explanation. What needs to be explained, he argues, is how in a short period of time the child masters a highly complex system on the basis of limited and degenerate input data. Moreover, the rate of acquisition and the course of development are uniform across the species, which suggests the preponderance of maturational rather than environmental factors in linguistic development. All this augurs no good for learning theory, according to Chomsky.

In recent years, however, evidence has accumulated showing that these often-repeated arguments were based on insufficient knowledge of the facts. Let us review the evidence briefly here.

Degenerate and Limited Linguistic Input.   The rationalist argument here runs as follows. When adults speak they often hem and haw, they make false starts, and break off their sentences in the middle. Furthermore, their speech is often inundated by background noise that may make parts of it imperceptible. How, then, can the child conceivably induce the rules of grammar from such grammatically faulty input?

What is being overlooked here is the fact that adult speech directed at the young child differs considerably from that directed at older children and adults. Years ago Grewel (1959) observed that adults slow down in speaking to young children and make more pauses, thus, presumably, making it easier for the child to analyze the utterances. Further, there is plenty of evidence (e.g., Bolinger, 1969, p. 8; Brown & Bellugi, 1964; Buium, 1974; Moerk, 1974; von Raffler Engel, 1970; Vorster, 1975; and studies cited by the latter and by Slobin, 1975; see also Levelt, 1975, for a discussion of this issue) that the adult gears his speech to the child's level of comprehension; he uses shorter and simpler sentences and these are hardly ever grammatically incorrect. In fact, children as young as 4 years have been found to take the age of the listener into account and to speak differently to a young infant than to their elders or peers (Sachs & Devin, 1976). It appears that the child's responses to the speech of others serve as subtle cues for the interlocutor to adjust his speech to that of the child (Snow, 1976; von Raffler Engel, in press). But what of speech directed at adults, which also reaches the child's ears? As mentioned earlier, it seems that the child is capable of filtering out speech that appears to be beyond his ken (Shipley et al., 1969). Moreover, as Braine (1971) has shown, it is possible, at least for adults, to extract syntactic rules by listening to utterances in an unknown language that contain a considerable proportion of syntactic errors.

Degenerate input, then, is not the fearful monster that it has been made out to be. There is no need to throw our hands up in despair and forgo any attempt at an empiricist explanation. As for the claim that the data are too "limited" to lead the child to a correct grammar, Putnam (1967) has pointed out that in the course of the first 4 or 5 years the child has been exposed to his native language for a large number of hours, much larger in fact than that which the typical student of a foreign language has been exposed to; and moreover, the child, unlike the foreign-language student, does not have to combat intrusions from a previously learned language.

Uniformity of Development.   The rationalist claim here is based on the alleged fact that all children acquire language in the same way and pass the same landmarks in their development. This, it is maintained, indicates that the language acquisition device is preprogrammed, i.e., that it contains a rich innate structure. Some years ago, when few systematic data were available, one might indeed have surmised that in acquiring language, children are predestined to follow an unvarying routine. As more children were studied, however, more and more diversity was revealed amid this uniformity. For instance, some children do and some do not go through a phase that may be described in terms of pivot and open classes (Brown, 1973, pp. 101–104). Further, whereas the earlier view had been that all children first adopt a fixed word order—even those who learn a language in which word order is variable—it now seems that this is not invariably so (Slobin, 1973, pp. 197–198). Again, at the two-word stage some children do produce subject–object constructions, but some do not (Brown, 1973, p. 193–194). Note also that in her study of the language of three children, Bloom (1970) had to write a different grammar for each child. The problem of diversity is taken up again in section 7.7.

Speed of Development.   Language could not have been learned in such a short time, the rationalist argument goes, if it were not for innate structures. "Such a short time" was first taken to last until about age four (McNeill, 1966, p. 99), but later studies revealed that much of language learning goes on for several more years (e.g., Carol Chomsky, 1969).

The factual bases of the arguments against the feasibility of an empiricist theory appear thus to be rather shaky. The input is not as degenerate and learning is not as uniform and fast as was once believed.

A comment is in order now about the contention that language is so complex that it cannot be learned under the given conditions and rate of learning. That the conditions of learning are really not as adverse as Chomsky makes them out to be has been argued earlier. But besides this, it should be appreciated that this claim from complexity is almost vacuous. Is checkers a complex game or not? Is diplomacy? Or dominoes? Such questions are meaningless as long as they do not specify in respect to what the degree of complexity is to be assessed; they can be answered only in respect to a description of a mechanism of language learning. Complexity cannot be adduced as an argument against a theory of language learning that has not yet been formulated. To be sure, language appears to be an enormously complex system, but such a merely impressionistic judgment has no theoretical import. When what at first blush seems simple is revealed as being anything but that, we are struck with a sense of wonder, and this reaction is augmented by considering the acquisition problem. A sense of wonder and curiosity lie at the root of the scientific enterprise, and it would be unfortunate if they should be used instead as reasons to relinquish a field of investigation.

Suppose now for a moment that complexity in the impressionistic sense be taken seriously as an argument against empiricism. Then Rationalism would not be a solution to the complexity problem either. Language appears to be complex not only in its universal aspects, but no less so, though in different ways, in its language-specific aspects. The amount of information a speaker of English has to master does seem staggering indeed, and only part of this can conceivably be founded on universal linguistic principles. One has only to look at the intricate system of rules revealed by a careful study of a restricted area of English grammar, such as Greenbaum's (1969) investigation of adverbial usage, to realize the enormity of the task of acquiring the English language. These rules seem to be specific to English. If, as seems likely, most of them turn out not to be reducible to universal linguistic principles, a foreknowledge of universal grammar would do little to alleviate this task.

What Chomsky has tried to do is to establish Rationalism by default, for lack of an alternative theory. He argues against the prospects of an approach that would trace the acquisition of linguistic principles through experience with language and solely on the basis of general cognitive strategies. However, as we have seen, his arguments rest on faulty factual foundations, and are partly launched against a particular, clearly inefficient, type of empiricist explanation. This does not imply, of course, that the alternative approach proposed at the beginning of the previous section has been vindicated. Obviously, psychological research in those areas has still a long way to go; in fact, it has barely started, and it is still far from engendering a well-substantiated theory. Chomsky's writings on this topic aim to bury such a theory prenatally.

Chomsky's work in linguistics has had a tremendous impact on psychology. It was through his writings that a renewed interest in the psychology of language was sparked, and that psycholinguistics, as we know it now, has become possible. Our indebtedness to his fecundating influence should not lure us into a credulous acceptance of his more questionable doctrines. The thesis that linguistic structures need not be learned because they are innate can only stifle research, not promulgate it. Instead we should continue to concentrate on psychological research in areas (2) and (3) of section 2.5. The pertinacious rationalist who would choose to elevate his search after linguistic universals to the status of a theory of the human mind will soon be faced with the prospect of embracing a dogma immune to empirical test.

The examination of a priori objections to the research program sketched here thus leaves us with our hands free to attempt a learning account of linguistic development. It is shown in the following chapters that such an account is feasible if one adopts a semantic approach to language learning, which tries to show how the child builds up his knowledge of language by matching his perception of the environment with the linguistic input. There is no telling beforehand how far the framework outlined in this book will take us, but there is no ground for giving up the venture before its possibilities have been thoroughly explored.

REFERENCES

Black, M. Comment [on N. Chomsky: Problems of explanation in linguistics]. In R. Borger & F. Cioffi (Eds.), *Explanation in the behavioral sciences.* Cambridge, England: Cambridge University Press, 1970.

Bloom, L. *Language development: Form and function in emerging grammars.* Cambridge, Mass.: MIT Press, 1970.

Bolinger, D. Genericness: A linguistic universal? *Linguistics,* 1969, *53,* 5-9.

Bolinger, D. *What did John keep the car that was in? *Linguistic Inquiry,* 1972, *3,* 109-114.

Braine, M.D.S. On two types of models of the internalization of grammars. In D. E. Slobin (Ed.), *The ontogenesis of grammar.* New York: Academic Press, 1971.

Brown, R. *A first language: The early stages.* Cambridge, Mass.: Harvard University Press, 1973.

Brown, R., & Bellugi, U. Three processes in the acquisition of syntax. *Harvard Educational Review,* 1964, *34,* 133-151.

Buium, N. An investigation of the word order parameter of a parent-child verbal interaction in a relatively free order language. *Language and Speech,* 1974, *17,* 182-186.

Chomsky, C. *The acquisition of syntax in children from 5 to 10.* Cambridge, Mass.: MIT Press, 1969.

Chomsky, N. Review of Skinner's *Verbal Behavior, Language,* 1959, *35,* 26-58.

Chomsky, N. *Aspects of the theory of syntax.* Cambridge, Mass.: MIT Press, 1965.

Chomsky, N. *Language and mind.* New York: Harcourt, Brace, 1968.

Chomsky, N. *Reflections on language.* New York: Pantheon, 1975.

Chomsky, N. On the nature of language. *Annals of the New York Academy of Sciences,* 1976, *280,* 46-57.

Cooper, D. E. *Knowledge of language.* London: Prism Press, 1975.

Cromer, R. F. The development of language and cognition: The cognition hypothesis. In

B. Foss (Ed.), *New perspectives in child development*, Harmondsworth, England: Penguin Books, 1974.

Cromer, R. An experimental investigation of a putative linguistic universal: Marking and the indirect object. *Journal of Experimental Child Psychology*, 1975, *20*, 73–80.

Edwards, D. Sensory-motor intelligence and semantic relations in early child grammar. *Cognition*, 1973, *2*, 395–434.

Ervin-Tripp, S. An overview of theories of grammatical development. In D. I. Slobin (Ed.), *The ontogenesis of grammar: A theoretical symposium*. New York: Academic Press, 1971.

Fouts, R. S., & Couch, J. B. Cultural evolution of learned language in chimpanzees. In M. E. Hahn & E. C. Simmel (Eds.), *Communicative behavior and evolution*. New York: Academic Press, 1976.

Gardner, B. T., & Gardner, R. A. Evidence for sentence constituents in the early utterances of child and chimpanzee. *Journal of Experimental Psychology—General,* 1975, *104,* 244–267.

Greenbaum, S. *Studies in English adverbial usage*. London: Longman, 1969.

Greenfield, P. M. Structural parallels between language and action in development. In A. Lock (Ed.), *Action, gesture and symbol: The emergence of language*. London: Academic Press, 1978.

Grewel, F. How do children acquire the use of language. *Phonetica*, 1959, *3*, 193–202.

Katz, J. J. *The philosophy of language*. New York: Harper & Row, 1966.

Krashen, S. D. Mental abilities underlying linguistic and non-linguistic functions. *Linguistics*, 1973, *115*, 39–55.

Lakatos, I. The role of crucial experiments in science. *Studies in the history and philosophy of science*, 1974, *4*, 309–325.

Levelt, W.J.M. *Formal grammars in linguistics and psycholinguistics* (Vol. 3), Psycholinguistic applications. The Hague: Mouton, 1974.

Levelt, W.J.M. *What became of LAD?* Lisse, Netherlands: Peter de Ridder Press, 1975.

McNeill, D. The creation of language by children. In D. Lyons & R. J. Wales (Eds.), *Psycholinguistics papers: The proceedings of the 1966 Edinburgh Conference*, Edinburgh: Edinburgh University Press, 1966.

McNeill, D., Yukawa, R. & McNeill, N. B. The acquisition of direct and indirect objects in Japanese. *Child Development*, 1971, *42*, 237–249.

Moerk, E. Changes in verbal child–mother interaction with increasing language skills of the child. *Journal of Psycholinguistic Research*, 1974, *3*, 101–116.

Premack, D., & Premack, A. J. Teaching visual language to apes and language deficient persons. In R. L. Schiefelbusch & L. L. Lloyd (Eds.), *Language perspectives—Acquisition, retardation and intervention*. Baltimore: University Park Press, 1974.

Putnam, H. The "innateness hypothesis" and explanatory models in linguistics. *Synthese*, 1967, *17*, 12–22.

Quine, W. V. Linguistics and philosophy. In S. Hook (Ed.), *Language and philosophy*. New York: New York University Press, 1969.

Rumbaugh, D. M., von Glasersfeld, E. Warner, H. Pisani, P. & Gill, T. V. Lana (chimpanzee) learning language: A progress report. *Brain and Language*, 1974, *1*, 205–212.

Sachs, J., & Devin, J. Young children's use of age-appropriate speech styles in social interaction and role playing. *Journal of Child Language*, 1976, *3*, 81–98.

Sampson, E. Linguistic universals as evidence for empiricism. *Journal of Linguistics*, 1978, *14*, 183–206.

Schlesinger, I. M. A note on the relationship between psychological and linguistic theories. *Foundations of Language*, 1967, *3*, 397–402.

Schlesinger, I. M. The grammar of sign language and the problem of language universals. In J. Morton (Ed.), *Biological and social factors in psycholinguistics*. London: Logos Press, 1971. (a)

Schlesinger, I. M. Production of utterances and language acquisition. In D. Slobin (Ed.), *The ontogenesis of grammar*, New York: Academic Press, 1971. (b)

Schlesinger, I. M. *Production and comprehension of utterances*. Hillsdale, N.J.: Lawrence Erlbaum Associates, 1977.

Shipley, E., Smith, C., & Gleitman, L. A study in the acquisition of language: Free responses to commands. *Language*, 1969, *45*, 322–342.

Sinclair, H. Sensorimotor action patterns as a condition for the acquisition of syntax. In R. Huxley & E. Ingram (Eds.), *Language acquisition: Models and methods*. London: Academic Press, 1971.

Slobin, D. I. Cognitive prerequisites for the development of grammar. In C. A. Ferguson & D. I. Slobin (Eds.), *Studies in child language development*. New York: Holt, Rinehart & Winston, 1973.

Slobin, D. I. On the nature of talk to children. In E. H. Lenneberg (Eds.), *Foundations of Language development: A multi-disciplinary approach* (Vol. 1), New York: Academic Press, 1975.

Snow, C. Mothers' speech. In W. Von Raffler Engel & Y. Lebrun (Eds.) *Baby talk and infant speech*. Amsterdam: Swets & Zeitlinger, 1976.

von Raffler Engel, W. The LAD, our underlying unconscious, and more on "felt-sets." *Language Sciences*, 1970, *13*, 15–18.

von Raffler Engel, W. The non-verbal adjustment of adults to children's communicative style. In D. Lance (Ed.), *Proceedings of the Mid-America Linguistic Conference*, (in press).

Vorster, J. Mommy Linguist. The case for Motherese. *Lingua*, 1975, *37*, 281–312.

3 The Semantic Approach

INTRODUCTION

In the first chapter, it was shown how the earlier behaviorist accounts of language learning were displaced by descriptions of the child's linguistic development in terms of transformational grammar. In the late 1960s, several investigators began independently of each other to pursue what is now commonly referred to as the semantic approach to child language. The importance of semantics for an understanding of language acquisition was pointed out by Slobin (1966) in his discussion of McNeill's nativist approach. At about that time, Ruth Clark, Paul van Buren, and Renira Huxley, of the Nuffield Language Development Research Project in Edinburgh, began to analyze child language in terms of case grammar. Their work, described in several mimeographed papers bearing the date of 1967, went largely unnoticed. The same year, I first circulated a paper suggesting that the child learns to express in his speech underlying semantic structures that reflect the way he perceives his environment; this paper was published years later (Schlesinger, 1971b). Melissa Bowerman's doctoral thesis, in which she also proposes case grammar as a model for child speech, was submitted in 1970, and subsequently published in book form (Bowerman, 1973a). Bloom's (1970) well-known study, in which she takes account of the semantic relations expressed in child speech, was apparently carried out in the same period, as were the studies by Antinucci and Parisi (1973) and Schaerlaekens (1973), who also adopt a semantic approach.

Although there are important differences between the positions of these investigators, they all share the view that an understanding of child language is possible only by relating what the child says to the meanings he presumably tries to express. This was hardly a new discovery. Earlier in the century, the Sterns (Stern & Stern, 1928/1968), for instance, had looked at the relations the child expresses in his speech, and although their terminology is syntactic, they were actually concerned with semantic relations. Later, Werner and Kaplan (1963, ch. 11) discussed early child speech in terms of Identifying Predications, Agents, Actions, and Attribution. Earlier writers, then, recognized that child speech should be viewed from the vantage point of meaning, but during the time behaviorism held its sway this approach could not come into its own. Its eclipse continued when accounts of language development within the transformationalist framework were propounded. Only after a long hiatus did investigators return to the homely truth that children's speech is best described by the meanings it expresses.

3.1 MOTIVATIONS FOR THE SEMANTIC APPROACH

Although most writers today agree on the need for describing child language in semantic terms, there are various versions of the semantic approach. My own version, presented in outline in the next section, differs in many aspects from those of other writers. The differences in outlook between various investigators adopting the semantic approach becomes clearer when we consider what prompted them to abandon transformational grammar as a model for the description of language development.

Writers on child language working within the transformationalist framework focused on the gradually emerging deep structures, and these were formalized in syntactic terms (such as noun, noun phrase, verb, verb phrase). The fact that the child expresses certain meanings in his earliest utterances was of course never denied, but it played no important role in theorizing. This neglect could not go unnoticed very long. It should not be thought, however, that a transformational account is in principle unable to accommodate meaning: In Chomsky's (1965) Standard Theory a semantic component interprets the deep structure of the sentence, which contains all the information pertinent to its meaning. In fact, Bloom (1970), one of the first researchers to analyze child utterances in terms of their meanings, nonetheless ascribed to them syntactic deep structures of transformational grammar. These two kinds of analysis, then, may be complementary.

A major disadvantage of representing the child's competence within the framework of transformational grammar is that the child is credited thereby with too much knowledge. This conclusion was arrived at by the investigators of the Nuffield Research Project, mentioned earlier. They first used transformational grammar as their model, but as stated in their Annual Report for 1966-1967, they soon noted that thereby "grammar was implicitly attributed to the child which we could not verify [Ingram, 1966-1967, p. 3]." Unlike Bloom, they therefore abandoned the transformational model for Fillmore's (1968) case grammar, which had just become known at that time. Likewise, Bowerman (1973a, pp. 176-194; 1973b) concludes on the basis of a careful study that syntactic categories like subject and predicate are not needed for the description of early child language (see also section 3.4).

A further difficulty with the transformationalist approach to child language is that it raises the problem of how the child could have attained the deep structures that are held to underlie his utterances (and it will be remembered that this led to the controversial thesis of innate linguistic structures; see section 1.3). Deep structures are related to surface structures through often complex transformations, but only the surface structure is exhibited directly in speech. The question this poses is how the child can have access to a deep structure that is several removes from his experience. This problem is avoided if one assumes that the structures underlying the child's speech are not divorced from experience; rather, they reflect the way he conceives of what he talks about. The input to the child is not merely the speech of others, as was assumed by workers adopting the transformationalist model, but utterances each of which is paired with a representation of the situation talked about. The child perceives certain relations in the situation, and these figure in the underlying semantic structures (see the following section). The underlying structures are thus directly given in the child's experience of what the utterances are about. This is how I proposed to meet the challenge to a learning account of child language (Schlesinger, 1971a, 1971b). This challenge is not met by Bloom, who retains syntactic deep structures in her theory. She therefore points out that she has no answer to the question of how language is acquired (Bloom, 1970, p. 233; see also Brown, 1973, pp. 114-118 for a comparison of Bloom's and Schlesinger's approaches).

My proposal that the deep structures underlying speech are semantic was also motivated by considerations about the nature of a performance model. In learning our native language, we develop a mechanism for speaking and comprehending langauge; a theory of language acquisition must therefore ultimately be integrated with a theory of linguistic performance. Even in the first stages of theorizing about early child language, one should keep in mind that what is learned by the child must eventually lead up to an adult performance model. This model must account for the way meanings are mapped into utterances. Within the framework of Chomsky's Standard Theory (1965), such a mapping would have to be an indirect one; it would have to be routed through deep structures, which in themselves are not semantic. The difficulties involved in explaining how this is achieved have not been solved completely to this day (see Fodor, Bever, & Garrett, 1974, Chapters 6 & 7, for a recent discussion). These difficulties led me to propose semantic deep structures that are mapped directly into surface structures (Schlesinger, 1971b). A presentation of a performance model was subsequently given in Schlesinger (1977), and further developments of the latter are discussed in Chapters 8 & 9.

My vesion of the semantic approach was first presented in detail in Schlesinger (1971b).[1] A shorter and less often quoted essay (Schlesinger, 1971a) is presented in full in the following section. Some problems that the proposal made in this work gave rise to, and some further developments are discussed in the sections that follow it.[2]

3.2 I-MARKERS AND
RELATION RULES: 1971

The Onslaught On A Learning Theory Approach

For some time now, a nativist view of language acquisition has had some vigorous spokesmen. Their claim is essentially that the language acquisition device cannot be assumed to operate merely on the basis of known principles of learning theory, because the linguistic input to the device is not sufficiently rich to yield a grammar by applying these principles. Therefore, it is argued, the device (alias the child acquiring a grammar) must be equipped with powerful innate constraints that determine the form of the grammar that is acquired.

What is objectionable about such an explanation is that it is no explanation at all. Even if the nativist were right that the learning-theory approach is untenable—and I argue further on that he is not—this would not constitute any support whatsoever for his own approach. To see that this is so, imagine a learning theorist using the same type of argumentation. He first enlarges on the difficulties attendant on any attempt to provide a genetically

---

[1]At the time I developed my proposal, I was unaware of the then ongoing work in generative semantics. However, after reading a first draft of this paper, in 1967, the late Yehoshua Bar Hillel pointed out to me an early paper on case grammar by Fillmore that was just then being circulated, containing ideas later presented in Fillmore (1968), and this was influential in further developing my thinking.

[2]Footnotes have been added referring to sections in this book discussing or modifying the statements made. The paper was prepared for presentation at the Study Group on Mechanisms of Language Development, held at the Ciba Foundation, London, May 1968. It is reprinted here, with minor, mainly stylistic, changes, from R. Huxley and E. Ingram, *Language Acquisition: Models and Methods* (1971) with the kind permission of the publishers.

based explanation for language acquisition. After having proved to his satisfaction that genetics is "in principle" incapable of explaining how deep structures are handed down from generation to generation, our learning theorist smugly concludes that, therefore, deep structures must be inferred by the child from the corpus of speech he encounters. Such an argument would of course not be accepted. It would be correctly pointed out that the task of learning theory does not end here; rather, it begins here and the learning theorist must show *how* deep structures are inferred from the corpus. I submit that the nativist is in the same position as this imaginary learning theorist: His claim is not strengthened by merely pointing out the weaknesses of an empiricist position.

Further, the arguments advanced so far by the proponents of nativism do not seem to me to disparage the view that grammar is learned. Their arguments are based on generalities and amount to little more than saying: "I dare you to show me how a child can learn deep structures that are hidden so well that it takes a linguist to find them!" Of course there could hardly have been anything but such general pronouncements because there is no well-developed learning account of the acquisition of grammar (except for the initial phases of learning). In the absence of a theory that can be criticized, nothing is left but to forestall attempts to construct such a theory by declaring these to be out of the question "in principle." This way of argumentation has been refuted convincingly by Crothers and Suppes (1967), and I do not enlarge on it here.

What we need, then, are not war cries but theories. There is no sense in ruling out on a priori grounds either a nativist or a learning theory. If someone suggests a theory based on innate constructs and rules, we should ask *which* constructs, or rules, or ways of inference are innate, and *how* they are inherited; just as the onus is on the learning theorist to state what is learned, and how it is learned. The convenient formula, "This could not have been learned, therefore it must be innate," cannot be accepted in lieu of theorizing. Let us then not look for ways of succeeding in theorizing without trying; instead, let us try.

In the following, I intend to sketch the bare outlines of an explanation of how grammar is learned. The details remain to be filled in, and this can be done only after much further study.

A Different Conception Of Deep Structure

Let us start by examining the alleged difficulties of a learning theory approach to acquisition of grammar. These have to do with the concept of deep structure as developed by Chomsky (1965). According to this view, the surface structures that the child is exposed to are derived from deep structures by means of transformations. The child cannot understand an utterance unless he recovers the deep structure that underlies it. Now it is hard to see how some of the information contained in the deep structures could have been obtained by the child from the utterances he is exposed to. Specifically, the problem arises in regard to the following aspects of deep structure:

1. The branches of the P-marker (phrase-marker, i.e., the deep structure of transformational grammar) that represents the deep structure are ordered, and this order may differ from that in the surface
2. In the deep structures there appear major categories—like NP, VP,, etc.—that are highly abstract entities, and are nowhere apparent in the surface structure.

So far, no explanation has been forthcoming of how the child arrives at such deep structures, which does not assume that something or other is due to his innate capacity. But, unless it is substantiated by positive evidence, the claim that something is innate does not amount to an explanation; it amounts to throwing your hands up before the complexity of the phenomenon to be explained. The following proposal is based on the assumption that the deep structures that the speaker and listener operate with are not exactly those which currently figure in generative grammar. In particular I suggest that they contain neither information about grammatical categories nor about order. This information is introduced through transformations that convert the deep structure into the surface.

This changed conception of deep structures makes it possible, as I now try to show, to give a learning account of language acquisition. But this is not the only motivation for introducing such a change. The necessity for hypothesizing a somewhat modified form of deep structures became apparent in considering a model for the production of utterances. Elsewhere (Schlesinger, 1971b) I have argued that the linguistically relevant aspect of the speaker's intentions must serve as input to such a model. These may be formalized as input-markers or I-MARKERS. The I-marker contains concepts, and the relations holding between these concepts; the speaker realizes the concepts in the form of words and the relations holding between them by grammatical means, such as word order and inflection.

Now, the notion of relations between words is not novel. Chomsky (1965, pp. 68 ff.) has shown that functional relations can be defined in terms of category symbols appearing in the P-marker of deep structure. Thus, the object of a VP is the relation holding between the NP of this VP and the whole VP, and so on. But note that the reverse is also true: Information regarding grammatical categories (NP, VP, etc.) can be extracted from the relational notions. I suggest therefore that it is these relations that appear in the I-marker. Because relations and categories can be retrieved from each other, I-markers and P-markers are similar to each other. The main difference is not in the information they contain, but in the form in which this information appears. The reason why I have proposed I-markers rather than P-markers for the performance model is that in I-markers the information appears in a form that seems to be closer to the speaker's intentions. When he says "John built this mobile," the speaker intends to express the fact that the goal of the building action is the mobile (and not John). It makes less sense to state that he intends "mobile" to be the NP of the VP. We think about our environment in terms of relations, not of noun and verb phrases, and therefore relations should figure as hypothetical constructs in a model of the speaker and the hearer.

Suppose for a moment that the foregoing argument is wrong, and that it is the grammatical categories that appear in the performance model. Then the question arises as to how they got there. For lexical categories, such as N and V, there is little difficulty because these can be viewed as classes of words. No similar solution is possible for the major categories, like NP and VP, which appear higher up in the phrase structure tree. By contrast, the relations in the I-marker present no obstacle for an account of how grammar is learned. When Johnny builds a mobile, the situation is perceived in such a way that Johnny is the agent of the activity of building and the mobile is its object. This way of viewing the world—which finds its expression in the I-marker—is the only thing that must be claimed to be innate.[3] Surely this is a far cry from the claim that specific linguistic constructs are innate. The latter assumption is far stronger than the former, and the former should therefore be preferred.

Let us look at a much simplified example of an I-marker in Fig. 3.1. The figure is simplified through omitting some information (viz. the fact the "Johnny" is singular, "build" occurs in the past, etc.), all of which must be assumed to be contained in the speaker's intentions and in the I-marker.

Two important points must be mentioned in connection with this I-marker. First, the I-marker is hierarchically arranged just as the corresponding P-marker is. This is so because the concepts in question are also hierarchically arranged in the speaker's intentions. In the I-marker of Fig. 3.1, the mobile and not John is modified in a certain manner (which is expressed in speech by "this"). Similarly, in "Tommy eats a big apple," it is the apple that is big and not Tommy. The second point is that the I-marker does not contain any information as to the temporal order in which the words appear in the utterance. There is of course a logical order of elements, in the sense that the relations in question are not symmetrical; the mobile is the object of the building activity, and not vice versa.

---

[3]But see sections 3.4 and 7.1 for an alternative view.

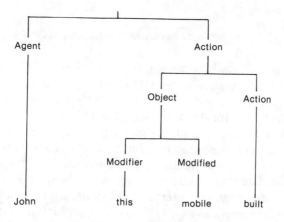

FIG. 3.1 A simplified diagram of the I-marker of "John built this mobile."

But the speaker's intentions in themselves do not determine the temporal order of words or concepts, and therefore this order has no place in the I-marker. In the resulting utterance, order of words will be determined by a rule of grammar, which has to be learned. Formally, this rule is a transformation, but to avoid confusion I prefer to call it a REALIZATION RULE.[4] The realization rule states, for example, that in Fig. 3.1 the branches of the Action node are to be realized in the order Action + Object: "built" is uttered before "this mobile." It may be helpful, therefore, to look at the I-marker as a mobile rather than as a tree (this has been suggested to me by Dan Slobin): The branches can revolve freely around the node, as it were.

Speaking is the process of realizing an I-marker through speech sounds. Understanding is the process of assigning an I-marker to the heard utterance. Both are based on rules that pair meanings with utterances, and it is these rules that the child must learn. Learning takes place when the child hears utterances in a meaningful situation. He perceives the situation in terms of concepts and relations, that is, in terms of an I-marker, and associates it with the heard utterance.

In some nativist discussions of language acquisition, a model is described, the input of which are the linguistic data, that is, utterances, and the output is a grammar, that is, a set of rules relating utterances to meanings. It is argued that the linguistic input does not contain the deep structures that are the bearers of semantic information, and that this raises the problem for

---

[4]This statement is imprecise: There are important formal differences between the two (see section 8.2). The realization rules responsible for the linguistic expression of I-marker relations are called *relation rules* (see Schlesinger, 1977, section 2A). The development of these rules is dealt with in Chapters 7 and 8. The treatment there supersedes the account of learning realization rules given later in this section. The term "Object" introduced in the following has been rightly criticized as being a syntactic term. "Patient" would have been more appropriate. It should be appreciated that these rules are not only involved in production, but also in comprehension (see Schlesinger, 1977, Chapter 6; and section 8.2).

learning theory of how the acquisition model arrives at the meaning-utterance rules from such an input. The present proposal suggests that the input contains not only utterances, but utterances coupled with their meanings. The task of the model is to derive from these meaning–utterance pairs a set of rules that show how utterances and meanings are paired. Surely this should not be beyond the scope of learning principles. If the input would be no more than linguistic data, there might indeed be a problem. But children do not learn grammar by listening to speech without reference to the situation, just as they do not learn the meaning of words by listening to a mere list of words.

There are differences between I-markers and P-markers in addition to those mentioned earlier; because these do not affect the main argument of this presentation, I mention some of these only in passing (see Schlesinger, 1971b, for a discussion). It seems to be necessary for the functioning of the production model that the I-marker should not contain words, but rather concepts that are neutral as to grammatical category. The terminal string in Fig. 3.1 should be conceived of as consisting of such concepts.[5] Thus, "build" stands for a class of words that includes also "building" (gerund noun), and "built" (past form). A realization rule determines which one of the words belonging to this class is chosen for the utterance. Syntactic features, such as "count," "common," "animate," and "human," also belong to the concepts as they appear in the I-marker, and presumably some selectional rules belong to the I-marker. (But "John frightens sincerity" is ruled out by the speaker's intention and not by an acquired realization rule.)

Note also that there is no one-to-one correspondence between P-markers as currently conceived of and I-markers. In "I smell the flower" we have an Agent-Action relation, but this is not true of every case where the sentence consists of a noun-phrase followed by a verb-phrase. For instance, "the flower smells" exemplifies a different relation. Fillmore (1968) has discussed this problem at length, and has arrived at a linguistic solution that has influenced the present formulation.

Instead of going on to discuss I-markers, let me try to show how the child learns to map these into utterances, that is, how he acquires realization rules. I limit myself here to the learning of word order because I have nothing new to contribute to the learning of other aspects of grammar.

Learning Realization Rules

The realization rule that the child finally comes to use must accord a relative position to the terms of a relation. If A is the object of B, the English-

---

[5]The acquisition of these concepts, called *protoverbal elements*, is discussed in Chapters 5 and 6.

speaking child must learn that the corresponding words, *a* and *b*, are to be uttered in the order b + a. However, such a rule is probably not learned directly but by some detours. Here I want to suggest one plausible route by which the child may arrive at the rule that functions in the adult speaker.

My suggestion is that before he acquires realization rules, the child makes use of concepts, such as Agent or Object, and these concepts figure as pivots in his two-word utterances. In other words, the English-speaking child learns that the word representing the Agent appears in the first position, the Object-word in the second position, and so on. And, of course, if one word acts as a pivot in the two-word utterance, the position of the second word is also determined thereby. For example, the child says "Tommy eat," rather than "eat Tommy," because he has learned that the word expressing the Agent ("Tommy") comes first, without having had to learn any rule concerning the position of the Action word.

Concepts like Agent and Object are rather abstract, and one might question whether a small child is able to master these. However, there is plenty of evidence that the child perceives his environment not just in concrete terms. Thus, "more" is a word that appears very early in many children; but what is its concrete reference? In the literature on child language you find "more apple," but also "more wet," "more outside," and many others. The child seems to refer by this word to something that has been and is no more, and/or something that he has had and wants still more of. The verbal definition here is very complex, but apparently the environmental and external cues that trigger the response "more" are not too complex for the child. Likewise, the child will have no trouble in identifying the agent or the source of an action. From examples in adults' speech, he then learns that the word referring to the agent always comes first.

The pivots suggested by Braine (1963) refer to individual words. It may be the case that conceptual pivots—like Agent, Object, Modifier, and others—that I am proposing here have their origin in Braine's pivots. The child first learns that several words are P_2.[6] Next he observes that these words figure as Object, and generalizes from these instances to the rule that all Objects are P_2. This would be an instance of concept formation. If this is so, we should predict that, at a certain stage, when the child learns a new word and then uses it as an object of an action, this word will appear in the second position. (Braine's pivot theory would predict this for newly learned word only if it appears together with a P_1 word.) Further, if the *same* word is used as agent it will appear in first position. To test this prediction one would have to analyze an extensive and fairly exhaustive corpus of the child's speech. At any rate, the assumption seems plausible that pivots of in-

---

[6]That is, second-position pivot; see section 1.1 for a discussion of Braine's theory.

dividual words are learned first, and that conceptual pivots are generalized from them: The latter will be called, therefore, *generalized pivots*, or GPs.

GPs are operative only in two-word utterances. "Tommy eat" may result from the rule that agent is a GP_1, "eat apple" may be due to the rule that object is a GP_2. But these two rules are not sufficient to determine the word order in "Tommy eat apple." For structured utterances of three words or more, the rule must be such as to relate two terms to each other, and these are the realization rules of the mature speaker. Realization rules are learned on the basis of GPs. For instance, after having learned that the Agent comes in first position, the child learns the rule that the Agent precedes the Action belonging to it. Figure 3.2 illustrates how "Tommy eat apple" may result from two such realization rules. These rules may be applied in either sequence, and at present we do not know anything about the sequence of steps in the performance model.

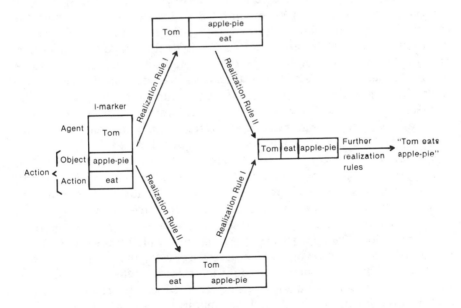

FIG. 3.2   Schematic representation of two alternative ways of realizing an I-marker.

Note. Rule I orders the Agent before the Action, Rule II orders the Action before the Object. The elements in the I-marker are unordered—shown by vertical arrangement—and realization rules introduce order—shown by left-to-right arrangement. The figure shows that the rules can be applied in any sequence. The model assumes a hierarchical organization of the I-marker; see Fig. 3.1, and section 8.2–8.3 for a more detailed treatment.

Some Illustrative Data

In conclusion, let us consider some data that seem to accord with the explanation that has been sketched here. But first notice one important point about GPs. Among the GPs we find Agent, Object, Modifier, Location, and possibly some others; but "Action" cannot be a GP because in the two-word utterance it sometimes comes in the first place—when coupled with an Object—and sometimes in the second place—when coupled with an Agent.

Table 3.1 presents translations from the Hebrew of two-word utterances of a boy between the ages 1:8 and 1:11. I used to jot down his utterances sporadically, usually not more than five to eight a day, and often much less. Such a small corpus cannot of course provide conclusive evidence, but the data are suggestive. At least my recording was not biased by my hypotheses, because at the time they were made, though I had some ideas about realization rules, I had none about GPs.

The relations that are expressed by utterances in Table 3.1 are Agent with Action (in the left column), Agent with Object, and Action with Object (in the middle and right columns, respectively). In this period I recorded many more utterances that did not express any one of these relations, and these are not presented here. A full Agent–Action–Object combination first appeared in the 11th week and such utterances are also not included in the table. Utterances that do not follow the adult word order are marked with an asterisk. Further, Introducers, like "Mummy," "Daddy" (i.e., the name of any person whom the child addresses), have been omitted. (The utterance on "Week 1" actually occurred about 3 weeks before that of "Week 2.")

The Agent–Object combinations deserve special mention. It seems that we have here a stage which precedes that of the Action–Object combinations. Although there are few such utterances reported by other writers, I have found many Agent–Object combinations also in another Hebrew-speaking child.[7] The appearance of Agent–Object utterances supports the notion of generalized pivots, which according to the present proposal are the basis of the development of realization rules. For the mature speaker there is no place for a realization rule Agent + Object. Instead of assuming that the child learns such a rule and then unlearns it, it seems more plausible that the child learns a GP_1. In the present case, 'Agent' appears as GP_1 in

---

[7]Since this was written, various other writers have reported Agent–Object utterances; see, for instance, Bowerman (1975, p. 272) and Brown (1973, p. 174), but these apparently do not always precede Action–Object combinations (see Leopold, 1949, pp. 48–49). Section 3.6 presents alternative explanations of the Agent–Object combinations.

(1) utterances constituted of an Agent and its Action; and (2) in utterances where the Agent appears in combination with an Object.

Looking at the words that exemplify the various GPs, we first of all note that the Agents that appear in the Agent–Action utterances are for the most part the same as those appearing in the Agent–Object utterances: "Daddy," "Eve," "Jimmy," etc. Likewise, largely the same Objects occur with the Agent (middle column) as with the Action (right column). This is in line with the claim that the child learns the concepts *Agent* and *Object* as GPs. By contrast, none of the Action words that appear with an Object occurs also with the Agent: The left column contains mainly intransitive verbs and some vocal mimicry that serves instead of verbs, whereas the right column contains transitive verbs, or combinations like "give-me," "put-on," which always appear as a unit at that period. There is no single *Action* class apparent in these data; this is to be expected because, as stated, *Action* cannot be a GP because it must appear sometimes before an Object and sometimes after an Agent.

In Table 3.1 there is hardly any overlap between the class of nouns that serve as Agents and the class of nouns that serve as Objects. The latter are inanimate (water, tea, slippers, radio, etc.), whereas the former are mostly animate (Daisy, Mummy, Daddy; a "car" is perhaps also animate for the child). Perhaps the child first acquires two classes—animate nouns and inanimate nouns—instead of one noun class, and thus learns from the outset to make a distinction that is essential in the grammar of the mature speaker. In general, it may turn out that the first grammatical categories are learned as classes of words that are associated with a given GP, like Agent, Modifier, or Location. Other categories, like "verb," cannot be learned in connection with the GP, and would have to await the appearance of a realization rule like Agent + Action.[8]

Earlier I made a plea for more work on explicitly formulated theories. Now I would like to add another plea: What we need just as urgently are extensive transcripts of utterances made available to workers in the field, against which theories can be tested. The data published so far may be sufficient to support the respective writers' explanations, but they certainly do not suffice to evaluate these against rival explanations. If the transcripts are to be useful for testing the explanation presented here, which involves semantic concepts and relations, then the child's utterances must be accompanied by a description of the situation and a guess at the meaning of the utterance.

---

[8]The acquisition of word classes is dealt with in section 8.1.

TABLE 3.1

Some Two-Word Utterances of a Child Aged
1:8–1:11 (translated from Hebrew)

Week	Agent with Action	Agent with Object	Action with Object
1		Daddy water (Daddy has given me water)	
2	Eve sh . . . sh . . . (Eve sleeps)		Give-me grapes
3		*tea, Daddy Daddy (Daddy shall give me tea)	
5	Daisy bye-bye	*tea Eve, Eve tea (Eve drinks tea)	
6	Daddy noo . . . noo . . . (Daddy threatened me saying "noo, noo") Daisy bye-bye Eve hee . . . hee . . . hee. . . (Eve laughs)		
7		Daisy dessert (Daisy shall give me some dessert)	
8	Eve comes		
9	Mummy comes Daddy hit	water, Jimmy water (Jimmy drinks water) [?]	

10	Mummy, Jimmy, Eve, all bye-bye (they are all going away)
	car drive (the car is driving)
11	Daddy hit
	house fall (when playing with building blocks)
	Eve juice (Eve gave me juice)
	Mummy, Eve . . . all bye-bye
12	*beigel don't want
	give-me, give-me cookie
	*cookie give-me
14	*tea give-me
	put-on slippers
	put-on sweater
	switch-off radio
	*pants take-off
15	Daisy comes
	bring-me car
16	*ahhn . . . car (mimics noise of car)
	car fell
	yes, who comes?
	Daisy comes
	put-on shoes
	Daddy, take paper?
	*Daddy, paper take, yes?

Note: An asterisk indicates that the utterance does not follow adult word order.

57

3.3 SUPPORT FOR THE
SEMANTIC APPROACH

Analyses in terms of semantic categories have been performed for children's utterances in various languages: English (e.g., Bloom, 1970; Bowerman, 1973a; Brown, 1973; Nelson, 1975); Hebrew (Baine, 1976); Italian (An tinucci & Parisi, 1973); Spanish (quoted in Brown, 1973); German (Miller, 1975); Dutch (Arlman-Rupp, van Niekerk de Haan, & van der Sandt-Koenderman, 1976; Schaerlaekens, 1973); Swedish (Lindhagen, 1976); Samoan (Kernan, 1969); Finnish (Bowerman, 1973a); and Luo (spoken in Kenya [Bowerman, 1975b]). In his cross-linguistic comparison of semantic relations in child language, Slobin (1970) also analyzed some examples from Luo and Russian. The semantic relations in the speech of mothers to their young children have been discussed by Snow (1977). The semantic approach also serves as a basis for a recent remedial language program for retarded children (Miller & Yoder, 1974).

As pointed out in an earlier discussion, the input to the child learning language is not only the speech he hears but speech coupled with an internal representation of the relations perceived in the situation referred to. Everyday observation confirms that adults normally speak to very young children about things occurring at the moment, so that the child can infer what is being talked about (cf. Macnamara, 1972). True, the child also overhears much talk that is not directed at him, and which may be unconnected with what he perceives, but it appears plausible that he simply does not attend to most of this (cf. section 2.6). It has been observed that hearing children of deaf parents, whose only experience with spoken language was through listening to the radio or TV, failed to learn to speak (Ervin-Tripp, 1973, p. 262). Experimental evidence for the crucial role of correlated semantic input in language learning has been provided by Moeser and Bregman (1972, 1973). They found an artificial miniature language to be learned best when each "sentence" in the language referred to a constellation of figures, so that there was a systematic relationship between the structure of the sentence and that in the referent constellation (which is analogous to the situation in natural language), whereas a semantically empty language failed to be learned (see also Moeser & Olson, 1974). In Braine's (1971) experiment, college students did manage to master the syntax of a meaningless contrived language by passive listening, but it is highly unlikely that small children can perform such a feat, if only because, presumably, they will hardly listen long enough to such meaningless talk. It should be noted that the miniature language in this experiment and those in the Moeser and Bregman experiment involved only rewrite rules and no transformations. It is difficult therefore to generalize from the results obtained by these investigators to the learning of a natural language, which makes use of transformations mapping deep structures into surface structures. The theoretical studies to be described presently, on the other hand, deal specifically with languages involving transformations.

Work on language development that followed in the wake of the Chomskyan revolution paid very little attention to semantics. Chomsky (1962, p. 531) had argued that possibly semantics does no more than "provide the motivation to language learning, while playing no necessary part in its mechanism." Doubt on this conclusion is cast by Gold's (1967) investigation of the learnability of various types of languages, the sentences of which are presented to the learner under various conditions, but without information as to their meaning. Gold gave a formal proof that certain types of languages, including that to which natural languages belong, cannot be learned at all, unless the learner is told not only what sentences are well formed but also what sentences are not well formed (see also Levelt, 1974, pp. 148–152). It appears, therefore, that for a language to be learnable, the learner either must also be told what sentences are unacceptable, or else he must have access to the meaning of the sentences presented. Now, the child is typically provided with very little information of the former type (Braine, 1971, pp. 159-161; Brown, 1973, pp. 410-412). Gold's results suggest strongly, therefore, that semantic information is indispensable for language learning. Likewise, Wexler, Culicover, and Hamburger (1975) conclude from their formal study of the learnability of languages that the learner must have access to the meaning of the linguistic input (cf. also Culicover & Wexler, 1977; and see section 3.5). Anderson (1977), in his computer simulation of language learning, also assumes that the learning program "takes as its basic input *pairs* consisting of sentences and representations of their meanings [p. 320]."

Whereas there is thus agreement among recent researchers concerning the importance of semantic information for language learning, opinions are divided as to the formalism appropriate for representing the underlying semantic structures. Several investigators of child language have adopted one or another linguistic model: case grammar (Bowerman, 1973a; Kernan, 1969; Lindhagen, 1976); generative semantics (Antinucci & Parisi, 1973); and Chafe's (1970) theory of semantic structures (Nelson, 1975). Miller (1975, pp. 176–179) developed his own system of categories, based on predicate logic, and Bloom (1970), Slobin (1970), Schlesinger (1971b), and Braine (1976) also used terms of their own. In his computer simulation of language learning, Anderson (1977) uses networks of propositions previously developed by him for the representation of knowledge. The differences are not merely terminological but substantive as well: What one investigator regards as a single category is often subdivided by another into a number of categories. Thus, Bloom (1970) has three different kinds of negation (which she calls *non existence*, *rejection*, and *denial*), where some other investigators posit one general *negation* category, and Slobin (1970) lists a category *demand*, *desire*, which most other writers do not consider a separate category. (See Brown, 1973, pp. 116–118, for a comparison of the classifications of Bloom and of Schlesinger, and Howe's [1976] comparison of those of Bloom, Schlesinger, and Slobin [1970].) As Brown (1973, p. 118) has pointed out, relations could be much more finely subdivided than either Bloom or Schlesinger proposed. Bowerman (1976b, pp. 143–146) also shows that there are indefinitely many ways of categorizing relations.

How, then, should one arrive at a decision between various possibilities of ascribing relations to a child? An answer to this question was attempted in my paper published in 1974 (Schlesinger, 1974), excerpts of which are reproduced in the following section. This work contains, germinally, many of the ideas subsequently developed and presented in Chapters 4, 7, 8, and 9. Some comments intended to update it are made in section 3.5.

3.4   THE ORIGIN AND NATURE OF
I-MARKER RELATIONS: 1974

Syntactic Versus Semantic
Relational Categories

In recent theories of first-language acquisition, there have been two approaches to relational concepts.[9] Under the influence of the newly emerged school of transformational grammar, investigators first held that the child learning language must master those structures and rules specified by the grammar. This meant transformational grammar of the Chomskyan type, in 1965, when this view was promulgated by its most prominent spokesman, David McNeill (1966). The relational concepts underlying the child's language are, according to McNeill, the concepts of the deep structure as specified in Chomsky's grammar; that is, such syntactic concepts as "subject," which is the noun phrase directly dominated by "sentence" in the deep structure and "object," which is the noun phrase of the verb phrase.

[9]This section is excerpted, with minor changes, from (Schlesinger, 1974), and reproduced by kind permission of the publishers. A previous version of the paper was presented at a conference on language intervention held in June 1973 in Wisconsin Dells, Wisconsin, and sponsored by the Mental Retardation Branch of the National Institute of Child Health and Human Development. The discussion which followed that representation, and notably Melissa Bowerman's comments, helped me in writing the present version. I am also indebted to the late Yehoshua Bar Hillel and to Charles Greenbaum, Sidney Greenbaum, Lila Namir, and Mordechai Rimor for valuable comments. The paper was prepared within the framework of a study supported by the Human Development Center of the Hebrew University.

These are specifically linguistic concepts, and the fact that they are not exhibited in the surface structure of adult speech raised the problem of how they can be learned. The alternative approach outlined in section 3.2 is that the relational categories underlying child speech are semantic in nature and reflect the way the child perceives the world. Learning grammar takes place by observing how the adult expresses these relations in speech. Whereas McNeill and others held that the input to the child's language acquisition device is merely the linguistic productions of adults, Schlesinger (1971b; see also section 3.2) pointed out that these are paired with the situation that the adult talks about and that is perceived by the child in terms of certain semantic relations. The situation is directly accessible, and learning the grammar involves finding out how the situation connects with adult sentences referring to it. There are, then, according to this approach, no specifically linguistic relational categories hidden away in the deep structure, which, as mentioned, pose a severe problem for learning theory. Instead, there are semantic relational categories, such as Agent and Action, Possessor and Possessed, Location, etc., in terms of which the child perceives his environment. The attainment of these is dependent on the child's general cognitive development and not on any innate syntactic concepts.

It has been argued that by positing relational categories that are semantic in nature, the link connecting child grammar with adult grammar is broken, because the latter is formulated in terms of syntactic categories. But in principle this presents no problem. It should be remembered that the deep structure of Chomskyan grammar is interpreted by a so-called "semantic component," which, roughly speaking, assigns meaning to it. Thus, in certain sentences, the noun phrase dominated by "sentence" in deep structures (i.e., the subject) and the main verb may be interpreted as standing in the Agent-Action relation. In the classic transformational model we have two systems of rules: one mapping deep structures into their semantic interpretations and one mapping the same deep structures into surface structures. In principle one can formulate for each pair of rules applying to a given deep structure—one rule from each of the above two systems—a single rule connecting the semantic structure with the surface structure directly. It is therefore possible that the grammar underlying the child's speech as well as that underlying adult speech consists of such rules mapping semantic relations directly into surface structures.

This, then, is one way of viewing the relationship between the child's grammar and that of the adult: Both are basically similar in that they are formulated in terms of semantic relational concepts. Another possibility has been proposed by Melissa Bowerman (1973a, pp. 176–187; 1973b). Bowerman critically evaluated the two rival claims concerning the nature of the concepts underlying child language. She pointed out that a syntactic category like "subject of"—in deep structure—does not coincide with any one semantic category but rather subsumes a number of these. Experiencers of States, Agents of Actions, and Instruments can all be deep structure subjects, as in "John wants bread," "John cuts bread," and "The knife cuts bread," respectively. The usefulness of the "subject" category is that it permits us to subsume under one rule linguistic phenomena pertaining to sentences expressing all the above semantic relations. "It is bread that John wants" and "It is bread that John—or the knife—cuts" are synonymous with the aforementioned sentences. There is a virtue, then, in not disposing of syntactic categories as far as adult grammar is concerned, according to Bowerman. On the other hand, she concluded, after examining child speech for categories like "subject of," that there is no evidence that such syntactic relations are operative.

Bowerman therefore advanced the following solution. The child learning language operates at first with semantic categories. These he learns to express verbally. For instance, he learns that (in English) the word for the initiator of an action precedes the word for the corresponding action, as in "Danny runs." Somewhat later he learns that the word for person affected precedes the verb describing how the person is affected, as in "Danny wants . . .," and, similarly, the "instrument" precedes its action ("The knife cuts"). Eventually he comes to realize that the nouns expressing these semantic relations follow similar rules in respect to position in the declarative sentence and to transformational possibilities. This leads to the abstraction "subject" that henceforward functions in his system of rules. A similar pattern may be followed for some other syntactic categories.

This is a very plausible account of how the child may acquire "abstract" syntactic relational categories. It elegantly solves the problem of preserving the simplicity of the rule system made possible by syntactic categories without paying the price of forgoing a learning approach in favor of innate knowledge. There is, however, an alternative solution to the problem of simplicity which does not necessitate the assumption that the child abandons semantic relational categories for more abstract syntactic ones.

It seems possible that in the course of learning language the child restructures his cognitions so that one semantic category is taken to be a special instance of another. For instance, when the child realizes that "Danny wants," "Fred sees," and similar constructions involving Persons Affected follow the same rule as the previously learned one for the Agent-Action construction ("Danny runs," "Fred plays"), he comes to regard "want" and "see" as denoting a kind of Action. And the fact that in active sentences the words for the instruments, like those for Agents, precede the words for the corresponding Actions ("the knife cuts," like "the dog barks") leads him to treat Instruments as a kind of Agent. It is this extended Agent category that in the more mature system of adult rules plays a role parallel to that of what the linguists call *subject*. (For some qualifications of this account see section 9.4.) It is by no means only the terminology that is at issue here, because the postulation of an extended Agent has empirical consequences. It implies that when the Person Affected appears in *subject* position, it is in some sense viewed as having the character of an Agent. Likewise, by subjectivizing the Instrument it receives some connotations of an instigator of an action. Nothing of the sort follows if Person Affected and Instrument are subsumed, together with the Agent, under the higher order concept *subject*. These are therefore empirically meaningful alternatives.

Is there any evidence for such an assimilation of Person Affected and Instrument? There seems to be some support, at least in the case of the Instrumental. This comes from the observation that Instruments cannot always be subjectivized. Thus we have:

> The brush paints flat surfaces.
> The brush scratches the picture.

but not

> The brush paints the picture.

The reason seems to be that when the Instrumental is subjectivized it is invested with characteristics of the instigator of an action. It then seems possible to regard the brush, somewhat metaphorically, as scratching or painting flat surfaces on its own. However, where a work of art is concerned this would mean stretching the notion of an Agent too far: Painting a picture requires an artist who holds the brush. In general, when the action requires deliberation, the Instrumental cannot function as subject. Thus it would be strange to say:

> This pen writes poetry.
> The pencil sketches the plan.
> Ivory pieces play chess.

Compare this to:

> This pen draws thin lines.
> The pencil draws a circle.
> Ivory pieces move on the chess board.

This goes to show that the subject partakes of the nature of an Agent, as in the foregoing sentences. What apparently happens is that the category of the Instrumental is absorbed into that of the Agent. Thus one can coordinate not only Agents and Agents or Instruments and Instruments, as for example:

> The area was ravaged by floods and by storms.
> The area was ravaged by mercenaries and by guerilla forces.

But in certain cases one can coordinate also Agents and Instruments:

> The area was ravaged by floods and by guerilla forces.
> [Quirk, Greenbaum, Leech, & Svartvik, 1972, p. 325].

This assimilation of the concept of Instrument to that of the Agent seems to occur in the ontogenesis of grammar as well as in phylogenesis. The case of ontogenesis has been argued earlier: The child forms extended agent categories. As Greenfield, Nelson, and Saltzman (1972) showed, the 11-month-old child wielding a cup views it as an extension of his own hand, and somewhat later "by connection with the child's hand the cup becomes 'animate' and therefore an actor . . . ." As for phylogenesis, the foregoing examples seem to show that the Agent concept at some point in the development of the English language came to accommodate the Instrumental. There seems to be a very general principle at work here. Semantic relations create a syntactic mold, and subsequently other semantic relations are cast into it, but not without a certain amount of reinterpretation. The Agent–Action relation may have been an example of this. A certain sentence structure was made to serve this relation, and the Instrumental was later viewed as a special kind of Agent. Consequently, it could be expressed by means of the existing structure.

Similar processes may have been at work when other cases are realized as subjects. Thus, "see," "hear," and "receive" may be treated as Actions of Agents, just like "look," "listen," and "accept," respectively. In fact, it is not easy to convince college students that "see" is not an action in the usual sense (Sidney Greenbaum, personal communication). Sentences with some verbs that appear to be not at all like actions cannot be passivized, for example:

> The truck weighs five tons.
> The bottle contains vinegar.
> He had a good time.

Here one of Bowerman's principal motivations for positing a subject category does not apply.

The discussion in the following sections is based on the assumption that relational categories underlying language are semantic in nature. The next question to be dealt with concerns ways in which such categories can be inferred.

Inferring Relational Categories

Several studies have recently been made of small children acquiring various languages. In a review of this work Slobin (1971) listed available material in 30 languages. For some of these, data have been recorded in sufficient detail to permit a comparison of the semantic relations underlying children's speech in various languages. Crosslinguistic universals of language acquisition have recently come into the focus of interest, and there have been interesting attempts to formulate such universals (Slobin, 1971). In a comparison of the acquisition of four unrelated languages—English, Finnish, Samoan, and Luo—Bowerman (1975b) found a number of semantic relations occurring in the speech of all the children studied in what she called early stage I (i.e., MLU's of up to 1.3–1.50). Bowerman's list of universal relations is as follows (some of the terms here differ from those she used):

1. Agent–Action (e.g., "Mommy push").
2. Action–Object (e.g., "bite finger").
3. Possession (e.g., "aunt car").
4. Demonstratives (also called Introducer + X, Ostensive sentences, Nomination, e.g., "there cow").
5. Attribution (sometimes called Modifier + Noun, e.g., "big bed"). Bowerman reported that only constructions in which an adjective serves as modifier are found in all speech samples and those in which nouns are modifiers, like "animal book," appear only in some of them.

In addition, some relational concepts occurred in some, but not all, speech samples, and are therefore probably not universal:

6. Agent–Object (e.g., "Kendall spider," with "looked at" implied). Not all writers would agree that this is a separate relation (section 3.6).
7. Location of object ("car garage") and of action ("sit bed").
8. Negation.
9. Recurrence (e.g., "more nut").
10. Notice (e.g., "hi spoon").

In late stage I (i.e., MLUs up to 2.00 morphemes) three-word strings appear, combining two of the just-listed relations, e.g., Agent–Action–Object of Agent–Action–Location. Negation appears in all samples, and in addition there is one new relational concept:

11. Dative (or Recipient of action, e.g., "show me book").

Brown (1973) identified yet another relational category in early child speech:

12.   Affected Person (or, Experiencer), State, and Source (e.g., "hear horn," "Adam see that," "I like jelly").

Although the linguistic expression of this relation is like that of the Agent–Action–Object relation, it should be distinguished from the latter, because verbs like "want," "like," "see," and "hear" do not refer to actions instigated by agents. Relation 12 appears in late stage I of all five children included in Brown's analysis.

This list of relations seems to raise some questions. Why, for instance, should (1) and (2) be both represented here as dyadic relations, whereas (12) is expressed as a triadic relation? Could one not just as well say that there is one Agent–Action–Object relation, or else an Affected Person-State alongside a State-Source relation? Should (7) be considered as one relational concept, Location, or as two different ones, Location of object and Location of action?

One way of dealing with questions such as these is by referring to the child's speech that exhibits these relational categories. If two items in a list of possible relations begin to appear in children's speech simultaneously, and if they use the same syntactic patterns to express these, there is good reason to regard them as belonging to one and the same underlying relational category (provided of course that these relations are intuitively sufficiently similar to warrant such collapsing). According to this test one may be reasonably confident about treating (1) and (2) as separate relational categories and (7) as a single one. I am uncertain, however, about the status of (12). Clearly, many problems remain even with these criteria for defining relations. In a later section we return to them.

Another approach is to deal with the child's relations within the framework of a grammar. In contrast to Bloom (1970) and Schlesinger (1971a, 1971b), who inferred semantic relations from corpora on an intuitive basis, most recent analyses of child speech have followed more or less closely one of the semantically based grammatical models: Fillmore's (1968) case grammar (e.g., Bowerman, 1973a) or generative semantics (e.g., Antinucci & Parisi, 1973). Such analyses seem to be on somewhat firmer ground, although the question is still open as to which is the best grammar for the representation of child language. Even if it were settled which grammar is more elegant and simple by linguistic criteria, this would not necessarily mean that the same grammar is operative in the child acquiring language. Further on I will show that inferring from adult grammar to that of a child may indeed lead to incorrect analysis of his speech.

Perhaps the most reliable conclusions would be those based not exclusively on the child's corpus of utterances but also on what is known independently about his cognitive development. Some attempts in this direction have already been made. Both Brown (1973, pp. 198–201) and Sinclair (1971) have argued that early language is based on the achievements of the sensorimotor period.

Brown suggested that the ability to recognize objects acquired in the sensorimotor period is a precondition for the child's expressing Demonstratives—(4): "this . . .," "that . . .," and Recurrence—(9): "more . . ." When the 4- to 8-month-old child sees a familiar object, he sometimes performs the habitual action schema in abbreviated form (e.g., when he sees a rattle he "shakes" his hands), and this may be regarded as the nonverbal precursor of demonstratives (and, we may add, of "Notice"—[10]). At this period the child also develops procedures to make interesting sights last, which forms the basis for the verbal expression of Recurrence.

Further, Brown argued, the child's ability to express nonexistence ("all gone . . .," "no more . . ." subsumed in the list under Negation) presupposes his ability to anticipate objects on the basis of signs and notice when anticipations fail to be confirmed, and this ability is also attained in the sensorimotor period. Finally, object permanence is required for the child's posing questions about location ("where . . ."): The child now knows that an object does not cease to exist when it disappears from sight.

Sinclair (1971) has argued that there is a similarity between certain aspects of Chomskyan deep structures and those structures that, according to Piaget, are the outcome of the sensorimotor period. At the end of the sensorimotor period the child can: (1) order temporally and spatially, which corresponds to concatenation of elements in base structure; (2) use a whole category of objects for the same action, which corresponds to categorization of major categories in the base, (e.g., noun–phrase, verb–phrase); and (3) embed one action pattern into another, which corresponds to the recursive rules of embedding in the base.

A more elaborate study of the underpinnings of early child language has been carried out by Veneziano (1973). On the basis of Piagetian theory she attempted to trace the development of agent and action schemas and their expression at the one-word stage.

An experimental approach that seems to hold much promise for the investigation of the cognitive basis of linguistic development is that of Greenfield, Nelson, and Saltzman (1972). In an experiment on the manipulation of nesting cups they found a developmental sequence of strategies that has a parallel in the developmental sequence of two linguistic structures: conjunction of sentences by "and" and sentences with relative clauses. They concluded that it is the same cognitive organizations that make possible motor behavior and linguistic behavior.

Inferences From Speech To Cognitive Development

As far as adult language is concerned, it is generally recognized that, as Sapir put it, "it would be naive to imagine that any analysis of experience is dependent on pattern expressed in language [Sapir & Swadesh, 1946]." English has a word for dead people and for dead animals but not for dead plants, but this and similar lexical gaps do not indicate a corresponding lack of concepts in the cognition of speakers of the language. The fact that a primitive language may be "capable of expressing a multiplicity of *nuances* which in other languages must be expressed by clumsy circumlocutions [Jespersen 1964, p. 427]" is in itself no evidence of parallel differences in the ability to conceptualize the world. Some deaf people use a language of signs in which the subject and the object of the sentence can usually not be distinguished by grammatical means, but this lack of certainly does not in-capacitate them from dealing with the world (Namir & Schlesinger, 1978). It is possible, then, to perceive relations that are not incorporated in the gram-mar of a language. There seems to be no reason why this should not be true also of child language. If it were not, we would have to conclude that struc-turally ambiguous utterances in child speech invariably reflect a lack of distinction between the relations in question. For instance, when a noun + noun sequence is used for indicating possession ("Mommy sock" = Mommy's sock) as well as Agent and Object of the Action ("Mommy sock" = Mommy puts on the sock [see Bloom, 1970, pp. 1–14]), this would indicate that the child confuses the notion of a Possessor with that of the Agent of an action. But this seems to be quite implausible. Imagine how the child would react if mother would put on her sock instead of handing it to the child!

Although conclusions drawn from a lack of distinction in child language as to the immaturity of his cognitions often seem to be compelling, one should never accept unquestioningly the evidence of child language alone. There seem to be three factors that may cause linguistic development to lag behind cognitive development:

1. Complexity of the linguistic expression. This factor has been stressed by Slobin (1971), who has formulated the principle that "new functions are first expressed by old forms." When a child has matured to the point that he wishes to express a semantic intention for which he as yet has no linguistic means, he uses existing forms until he gradually acquires those accepted in adult language. The order of acquisition of linguistic forms is dictated in part by their relative complexity and hence may be out of pace with the maturing of concepts the child is ready to express. Slobin cited the case of a bilingual child who at a certain age verbalized certain locative rela-

tions in Hungarian while failing to express them in Serbo-Croatian In the latter language the linguistic realization is more complex.

2.   Communicative needs. Certain relational concepts may remain unexpressed because it is not important for him to communicate about them or because there are others that are more important. Admittedly, such explanations are ad hoc and to an extent even circular. They seem to indicate, however, that caution should be exercised in inferring from speech to cognitive structure.

3.   Saliency. This factor is closely related to the preceding one. Owing to the limitations on length of utterance, the child will presumably tend to express only the most salient features of the situation. That he omits mention of others does not imply that he is unaware of them or unable to deal with them conceptually. Bowerman (1975b) wonders why the instrumental does not appear in early child language despite the obvious importance of this relation for the child: He uses spoons and playthings to reach, hit, and otherwise act on other things. The reason may be that it is usually the effect attained by the use of these tools that is most salient to the child and not the tools themselves. As mentioned, the latter may be perceived as an extension of the child's hand (Greenfield et al., 1972).[10]

These, then, are possible reasons why the child may fail to express relational concepts that are operative in his cognition. Occasionally the reverse situation may hold: The child expresses linguistically relations that are left unexpressed in adult language. The difference between durative and non-durative actions is not invariably and unequivocally grammatically marked in English, but some children have been reported to use—for some time—the present tense for the former while reserving the past tense for the latter; e.g., "wash" on the one hand and "broke" or "dropped" on the other, irrespective of the time the action took place (Sinclair, 1971, pp. 75–76).

Cognitive Structures And I-Markers

The aforementioned considerations lead to the conclusion that cognitive structures must be distinguished from I-Markers, the deep structures that

---

[10]Bowerman also raised the question of the scarcity of datives (indirect objects) at the earliest stages. But datives apparently do occur in many of the children studied (see Brown, 1973). Perhaps their relatively low frequency reflects the fact that the small child more often receives than gives—just as he usually omits to mention himself as agent, he tends not to mention himself as receiver.

underlie the production and comprehension of sentences. We are capable of organizing the world around us in innumerable ways, perceiving any number of relations between objects, attributes, states, actions, etc. We are also capable, in principle, of talking about any one of these perceived aspects. But many of them are not linguistically relevant; that is the grammar provides no rules for tying them to surface structures of sentences. For instance, the durative–nondurative distinction mentioned earlier is one which the speaker of English may be aware of, but it is not a distinction made in the grammar of his language. It would be a mistake to assume that any relation perceived must ipso facto figure in the deep structure underlying the sentence pertaining to this situation. Some of the relations are provided for by the grammar and many more are not.

Our cognitive structures, then, are infinitely richer and more variegated than the I-markers that function in language.[11] Given sufficient verbal skill, one can talk about everything that appears in the cognitive structures, but grammar does not always pave the way for us. Which aspects of cognitive structures are represented in the I-markers depends on the particular language. Some of them, like the Agent–Action and the Action–Object relations, appear in the I-markers of the speakers of almost all languages (see, however, Namir & Schlesinger, 1978), but others, like the durative-nondurative distinction, only in some languages.

It follows, then, that the child must learn which of the multifarious aspects of the world around him are included in the I-marker, and hence expressed in speech. However, I-markers are not acquired as an independent system. Rather, the child learns the system of I-markers together with its relationships with syntactic constructions. As already pointed out, this does not present an unsurmountable obstacle for a learning approach as I-markers are part and parcel of the child's cognitive structure.

The distinction between cognitive structures and I-markers made here also provides a basis for answering a question posed by Brown (1973) concerning relational concepts. Brown argued that "ultimtely *each* utterance expresses a distinct relation which is the meaning of that utterance [p. 118]." This raises the question as to the criteria for categorizing these relations; or, in Brown's words, "how finely should the abstractions be sliced? [p. 146]." As far as cognitive structures are concerned, this question certainly stands; these may contain infinitely many relations, and at present there even seems to be no evidence for the psychological reality of any classification of these relations. But if the question is asked about I-markers, the answer may be suggested that there should be as many relations as are necessary to account for the rules that map them into surface

---

[11]By "cognitive structures" we refer here to structures operative at the time an utterance is made and leading to it, and *not* the more permanent aspects of cognitive organization.

structures. In other words, a relation in an I-marker is one which makes a difference, linguistically.

To illustrate this principle, take the development of negation in child speech, as described at length by Bloom (1970). She discussed three categories of negation: nonexistence, rejection, and denial. Intuitively it seems clear that when the child utters a negation, he intends *either* nonexistence *or* rejection *or* denial; cognitively there is presumably no confusion among these categories (although one might well ask whether there are not still finer cognitive distinctions to be made). The question examined by Bloom is whether these categories are differentially expressed in the child's speech. She concluded that at first all three categories are expressed by the same syntactic structures, and only subsequently are different semantic categories of negation expressed differentially. In the above terminology, in the first stages there is no distinction between types of Negation in the child's I-markers and only subsequently is such a distinction attained. Here, too, cognitive structures mature before I-markers.

In the earlier discussion, we have seen that when deep structures are assumed to be semantic in nature there is no need to postulate that the child is born equipped with specifically linguistic structures. It might be argued, however, that this is a spurious advantage, because all that is achieved thereby is to push the problem of innateness one step back since now semantic relations must be assumed to be innate, as I had argued in 1971 (see section 3.2). This is incorrect, however, according to the aforementioned view of the relationship between I-markers and cognitive structures. The question of how much innate structure there is in cognition is left entirely open. The soundest approach would be to make as few assumptions as possible, that is to impute to the child's cognition at the outset as little categorization of relations as possible. He probably comes into a world that is a booming and buzzing confusion, rather than into one that is neatly parceled into Agents, Actions, and so on. At first he perceives only that his mother takes him up, his father takes him up, his mother moves away, etc., and he does not lump all this together into one Agent–Action relation. Relational concepts gradually become crystallized. The child forms I-markers that are the schematic representation of a motley world. Language presumably plays a major part in this: By hearing sentences in which all agents are treated the same way, he acquires the Agent concept with rules for realizing it in speech. It is of course true, but trivial, that the capability for forming such concepts must be innate.

In contrast to "cognitive determinism," which postulates a one-way influence from cognitive to linguistic development, I propose therefore an interactionist approach (further discussed in the next chapter). Language builds on the developing cognitive repertoire and in turn shapes it. In regard to the development of words and concepts such a view of a two-way effect has long since been well known: By learning the meanings of words the child learns how to categorize the entities these words stand for. It seems plausible that the learning of sentence structures similarly leads to a certain manner of "slicing up" experience.

However, the acquisition of I-markers does not imply that previously existent distinctions in cognitive structure are obliterated. The child as well as the adult may continue to be aware of relations not expressed in the I-markers of his language. Examples are the previously discussed distinction between durative and nondurative and the instrumental case discussed in the first section. The Instrumental is of course a relation in cognitive structure notwithstanding the fact that its linguistic expression in English and in some other languages may be by means of that surface structure that is commonly used for the Agent–Action relation; for example, "The knife cuts bread" like "The boy cuts bread." One way of putting this is that the same I-marker is operative in the two cases. By viewing two cognitive notions as similar in some way, they can be treated identically in the I-marker. Consequently they are expressed identically in the surface structure. This is one way of formulating the principle discussed earlier, that different functions are perceived as similar so that they can be expressed in the same linguistic form.

Two Fallacies

The distinction between cognitive structures and I-markers discussed in the preceding section seems to be especially important in the investigation of child language. It implies, on the one hand, that one should not infer without further evidence from immature features of a child's speech to a comparable immaturity of his cognitive development. On the other hand, it is also possible to fall into the opposite error of inferring from the child's cognitive development to the development of his I-markers. This is the first fallacy to be dealt with here: attributing relations presumably existing in a child's cognitive structures to his I-markers without independent confirmation from the child's speech.

Related to this is what one might call the anachronistic fallacy, namely, that of viewing the child's linguistic development from the vantage point of adult grammar. In much recent research on child language the goal has been an explanation of how the child acquires adult grammar. This approach may result in a tendency to work backward from adult grammar and credit the child with as much of it as possible. The child's speech is interpreted in terms of relations that are known to be represented in adult grammar. It is sounder methodology to ascribe as little as possible to the child's I-markers and to show how he builds these up by gradually augmenting them.

Although writers in the field have not been completely blind to the danger of incurring these fallacies, they have sometimes not been sufficiently aware of it. Let us exemplify this with a mild case of affliction due to the joint operation of both the above fallacies: recent analyses of child language by Antinucci and Parisi (1973, 1975).

Antinucci and Parisi present an interesting approach to the description of child language that leans heavily on notions taken from generative semantics. They are the first to have introduced the concept of *performative* into the field of language learning. The "semantic configurations" that they impute to the child at the stage when he utters his first two- or three-word sentences are impressive in their complexity. Thus, when Italian-speaking Claudia says "mamma da" (= mommy give), commenting on the fact that mother gave her something, the semantic representation, according to Antinucci and Parisi, contains:

1. A proposition stating that (a) for something (b) mother (c) causes this something to be close to (d) Claudia.
2. A "descriptive" performative expressing the fact that by making this utterance something is described or stated. When the same two words are uttered in order to ask mother to give her something, the performative is "requestive."

All this, Antinucci and Parisi argue, must be in the structure realized by the child, because she obviously understands all this. Although Claudia utters only the two words standing for the agent—"mamma"—and for the action "da," she obviously knows that she is the recipient and that the intention of the utterance is "descriptive" rather than "requestive."

Antinucci and Parisi are undoubtedly right about the child's understanding, but what their argument establishes is that this information is contained in the child's cognitive structures and not that it is represented in his I-markers. The latter, by definition, contain only what the child expresses in his speech. It seems that at that stage Claudia did not express all the information contained in (1) and (2). By inferring directly from what the child "obviously knows" to her grammar, Antinucci and Parisi commit the first fallacy. The distinction between I-markers and cognitive structures insisted on earlier is designed to guard against this error.

Antinucci and Parisi point out that "da" is a three-place verb (X gives Y to Z). To argue that therefore all three arguments, X, Y, and Z, must be represented in the child's grammar would be to commit the anachronistic fallacy, unless it can be shown that not only adult grammar but also the child treats it as a three-place verb. In fact, Claudia at this stage never mentions all three arguments in a single utterance. Antinucci and Parisi, however, believe that they can prove that "da" functions as a three-place verb by showing that through adequate prompting the various elements can be brought to the surface one at a time (e.g., Claudia: "doll" Mother: "Where is the doll?" Claudia: "here-is") or two at a time (e.g., "eat Mummy" and then "eat noodles"). They conclude therefore that the semantic structure is all there and the child lacks only the ability to express more than part of it.

But does this really follow? Could it not be that the child attends only to one or two aspects of the situation at a time and tries to realize these verbally? The effect of prompting might be merely to induce the child to change his focus from one aspect to another. To return to "da," it is possible that in the child's I-marker it appears on one occasion with the Agent only, on another with the Object only, and on the third with the Recipient. To argue otherwise on the grounds that there are no such constructions in adult grammar (and no such I-markers in adult speech) would be to commit the anachronistic fallacy. The same applies to the agentless passive and to transitive verbs without the appropriate object, which occur in child language and apparently result from I-markers different from those of the adult (see also section 3.6). The possibility cannot be ruled out that an I-marker may contain elements that are not realized in the utterance, but in each case evidence for such a claim would have to be based on linguistic behavior (see also the discussion by Bowerman, 1974b).

To conclude my criticism of Antinucci and Parisi's approach, I submit that the only meaningful way of representing the child's underlying structures must be based on what he actually utters, not on what he may be assumed to know to be the case.

In this section I have touched on various methodological issues in the investigation of relational concepts underlying children's language. The discussion revolved mainly around the relation between linguistic and cognitive development. After a period of attempts to study the development of the grammatical rule system without relating it to the child's general development, and even without viewing his utterances in relation to the situation in which they occur, there has recently been growing recognition of the close links between the child's linguistic and cognitive structures. The error now to be guarded against is insufficient distinction between these structures. In the future, a careful examination of their interaction may be expected to lead to a better understanding of child development.

3.5   THE ORIGIN AND NATURE OF
I-MARKER RELATIONS: POSTSCRIPT 1979

Inferring Relational Categories

The preceding section discussed criteria for deciding which I-marker relations appear in the child's language. More than that was done in my 1971
work (Schlesinger, 1971b): To illustrate my approach, a list of eight relations was presented that were exhibited in the few data on child language
published at the time the paper was written. I hold no brief, however, for
either that list or the one presented in the preceding section. Many of the
specific critisims that have been launched at one item or another are probably
justified. My main objective is to explain how relational categories
originate and develop.

Here it should be noted that the child's relational categories presumably
change in the course of his linguistic development; they may gradually expand in scope, or else may become more finely differentiated. Braine (1976)
has argued for categories of a much more limited scope than the ones proposed earlier, which are subsequently extended (see section 7.6). Moreover,
there may be individual differences between children in respect to the
categories employed (see section 7.7).

To forestall possible misunderstandings, it should also be pointed out
that in setting up a list of relational categories and stating realization rules
no claim is being made that these amount to a "grammar" accounting for
corpora of children's speech. Occasionally there will be utterances that defy
description by realization rules (see section 7.3). Furthermore, many utterances do not exhibit any one of the relations appearing in one of the proposed lists, and there are many more which cannot be unequivocally
categorized. In fact, the whole enterprise of writing a grammar for all
children at a given stage, or even for a single child, must be regarded as
problematic (see section 1.4).

Statements about the child's early relational categories become possible
only by going beyond his utterances: We must infer what he means by them.
Here one must rely on what Brown (1973) calls "rich" interpretation; that
is, account must be taken of the child's ongoing activity, the immediate
situation, and the order of words in the utterance (the importance of the latter is argued by Brown, 1973, pp. 147–151, following Bloom, 1970). The rationale of "rich" interpretation has recently been challenged by Howe
(1976). She shows that word order and other syntactic criteria do not permit
an unequivocal classification of children's utterances into any of the sets of

relations proposed by Bloom (1970), Schlesinger, (1971b), and Slobin (1970). The criterion proposed in the preceding section that an I-marker relation is one that makes a linguistic difference might be appropriate for adult language; but as far as children's speech is concerned, surface cues are too impoverished, according to Howe, to furnish us with a means for revealing the underlying relations. Neither do the child's activities and other situational cues permit us to arrive at firm conclusions. In particular, Howe points out that there is no assurance that the child perceives reality in the same way adults do, and this may vitiate our attempts at inferring the relations underlying his utterances.

Howe's work should serve to caution us against drawing conclusions from child speech in too facile a manner. On the whole, she seems to be overcautious, however. Braine's (1976) exemplary study of early child speech, which had not yet appeared when Howe's paper was written, has done much to develop the methodology of inferring relational categories on the basis of surface cues and shows how fairly well-founded conclusions can be arrived at by a painstaking, minute analysis of corpora. Howe's warning not to impute to the child our adult way of conceiving reality has some justification; further, no one would deny the importance of cognitive development for theorizing about child language. But there is no reason to assume that the child's conception of the world differs so radically from ours that one has to relinquish all attempts to figure out what he means. In fact, Howe's suggested remedy for child language research, that we "begin by specifying the situations children can conceive of and investigating how they refer to these situations [p. 45]," ultimately also depends on adult interpretation, as Rodgon (1977) has pointed out. In short, our interpretations of child speech are anything but incontrovertible, but to study child language at all one must risk making interpretations that are rich and wrong. Theorizing is precarious, but if we want to get anywhere we have to theorize.

Syntactic Versus Semantic Relational Categories

Recently, Braine (1976) has shown that children's speech data do not justify crediting them with syntactic categories (like 'subject'). As Bowerman (1976a) points out, his evidence is stronger than that previously advanced by herself (Bowerman, 1973b; see section 3.4). Here a comment is in order concerning some misunderstandings that have arisen in connection with the claim that early child language is semantic in nature. No one ever thought of denying that the child's surface structures exhibit certain regularities, like word order; and there can be no objection to calling this knowledge syntactic (Bowerman, 1975a, p. 85). What is being claimed is that the relations underlying children's speech are semantic.

Now, this claim has been debated. In her first book, Bloom (1970), although recognizing that the child expresses semantic relations, analyzed her data within the Chomskyan framework, and in later writings (e.g., Bloom, Miller, & Hood, 1975) she continues to hold that very early the child attains superordinate, syntactic categories. The evidence marshalled for this is that he expresses different semantic functions by the same word positions; for instance, both Agents and Possessors appear in initial position, whereas Objects and Possessions appear in final position (Bloom, Lightbown, & Hood, 1975, p. 19). But, as Bowerman (1975a, pp. 87-90) convincingly argues, sameness of position in itself is insufficient for inferring identity of deep structures in adult language (because a given surface structure may have been derived from either one of two different deep structures); and likewise it does not imply that the child views different semantic notions "as functionally equivalent at some higher level of abstraction [p. 88]." When the Agent and the Possessor are accorded the same position, this may be due to different rules, resulting in similar surface structures.

Bowerman (1974a) agrees, however, that ultimately the child switches to syntactic categories, because these exist in adult grammar. The view, outlined in section 3.4, is that the so-called syntactic categories result from semantic assimilation, that is, an extension of semantic categories. This thesis has not gone unchallenged. The issue will be discussed in sections 9.1–9.4, where a more fully developed theory of semantic assimilation is to be presented.

The crucial question here is how the linguistic system of the child develops into an adult system. There is a large gap between the lists of semantic relations proposed by various writers and the more comprehensive syntactic relations, like subject and predicate, which according to many linguists figure in adult grammar. It might be thought that case grammar can bridge this gap, because it also posits semantic relations and is believed by its adherents to be suitable as an adult grammar. But case grammar, as formulated by Fillmore (1968), has some drawbacks as a model of early child language (Braine, 1976, pp. 82-85). In particular, it assumes certain word classes (notably the verb), which the child cannot be credited with from the outset. This would leave us therefore with the question of how the child's early system develops into a case grammar.

The last two chapters of this book attempt to sketch a model of the adult linguistic system (based on Schlesinger, 1977) and to show how this is acquired by the child. Specifically, I discuss the acquisition of word classes (section 8.1), the operation of relation rules (a subclass of realization rules) in the production of more complex utterances (sections 8.2–8.3) and of so-called "transformations" (section 8.4), and the organization of the lexicon (sections 9.6–9.7).

Cognitive Structures And I-Markers

One of the main themes developed in section 3.4 was the distinction between two levels: cognitive structures and I-markers. A similar distinction has been independently arrived at by Bloom (1973, p. 119; her terms are *cognitive categories* and *grammatical categories*). Writers in the field have often neglected to differentiate between these levels, as will be repeatedly seen in the following chapters. In my original paper (Schlesinger, 1974), I accused Antinucci and Parisi of such neglect, but as Parisi (1974) pointed out in his reply, this was not quite justified (see also Bates, 1976, pp. 79–84). (In accordance with some of Parisi's clarifications, portions of my original discussion of Antinucci and Parisi have been omitted in section 3.4.)

Parisi explains that by "semantic structure" Antinucci and he mean "cognitive structure which is construed with the intention to communicate it. Therefore semantic structures are a subclass of cognitive structures [p. 102]." However, as Bowerman (1974b) cogently observes, on this view of semantic structures, "certain steps which the child must take between his early attempts to communicate verbally and his final adult understanding are lost, not being representable within this system." What is missing in this system is "the level at which the nonsystematic and redundant aspects of the cognitive apprehension of events are filtered out and those which are systematic and play special semantic and syntactic roles within a language are recognized, retained, sharpened and organized in relation to each other." These "systematic" aspects are taken care of by the I-marker, which, unlike cognitive structures, consists of categories (see section 7.2). The distinction between cognitive structures and I-markers, then, is not merely one of scope, but is a qualitative one. This becomes clear in chapters 7 and 9 (see especially section 9.5), where the development of I-marker relations is dealt with (see also Schlesinger, 1977, Chapter 5).

Parisi also gives a detailed account of criteria for deciding what aspects of the situation that are left unexpressed in the child's utterance are included in his semantic structure. I still doubt whether these criteria are nearly strong enough. The child's early utterances typically omit constituents expressing aspects of the situation he is presumably aware of (see also Brown, 1973, pp. 147–156). As Parisi observes, Antinucci and Parisi's (1975) approach parallels that of Greenfield and Smith (1976) to one-word speech. (A discussion of the Greenfield and Smith approach in my 1974 paper has been omitted in section 3.4.) Both impute to the child an underlying structure that is richer than warranted by his utterances. There are important differences between the structures inferred by Antinucci and Parisi on the one hand and Greenfield and Smith on the other; the former posit structures that are much more abstract and extremely powerful, as discussed by the latter authors (Greenfield & Smith, 1976, pp. 203–205). Greenfield and Smith's thesis has given rise to considerable controversy (see section 7.3). The question to what extent imputing a richer structure is justified at the two-word stage is discussed in the following section. But first we must discuss briefly an alternative model, which also makes a distinction between cognitive and semantic structures.

In a recent paper, Wexler and Culicover (1974) proposed a model that includes, in addition to surface structures and deep structures, two levels: Semantic Representations (SRs) and the World-as-Perceived. The latter seems to correspond to our cognitive structure level. The SR level is motivated by the following considerations of learnability. Previous work (e.g., Hamburger & Wexler, 1973) had shown that a theory of language learning is possible if the child can be assumed to construct from the input utterance its interpretation and from the interpretation the deep structure underlying it (see also section 3.1). What stands in the way of making such an assumption is that deep structures, as currently conceived of in generative grammar, are not universal because languages have been shown to differ in respect to the order assigned to deep-structure constituents. An SR level is therefore postulated that differs from the deep structure only in that its constituents are unordered, and that can be presumed therefore to be universal. SRs, thus, differ from I-markers: They include deep structure categories, like subject of and object of, which, as Wexler and Culicover point out, are not simply translatable into semantic relational categories, like Agent and Patient. The correspondence between the former and the latter is language-dependent. In ergative languages, for instance, the Agent may be the underlying object rather than the subject, according to their analysis.

Wexler and Culicover believe that a language described by this model is learnable in principle, under the assumption that there are certain universal constraints on possible derivations of deep structures from SRs; and they in fact provide evidence for the universality of these constraints. It appears, however, that their model poses two serious problems for a theory of language learning:

1. Wexler and Culicover must assume that the child masters somehow the mapping from the World-as-Perceived to the SR level. But because SRs are conceived of as containing abstract categories, whose correspondence with semantic notions, like Agent and Patient, is language-dependent, it is hard to see how a child could learn such a mapping.

2. They assume that the order of constituents in the deep structure is discovered by the child on the basis of an input that consists of a string of lexical items, each of which is paired with an SR. They show that on the basis of the order of the lexical items he can find out how the SR constituents are ordered in the deep structure, if it is assumed that categories of lexical items (presumably parts of speech) can serve as cues to SR categories. In view of the abstract nature of the latter, it remains obscure how the child might have learned how they correspond with lexical items.

Both these problems stem from the abstract nature of SR categories, and, as far as I can see, could be solved only by fiat, namely, by postulating that the mappings in question are innate. This would be a specifically innate endowment, postulated ad hoc, just to keep the theory afloat. As argued in the previous chapter, the strategy of multiplying innate entities without independent justification can result only in stultifying research.

Now, by waiving the stipulation that SRs consist of abstract categories, an empiricist solution to these problems becomes attainable. In effect, this is the solution proposed in this chapter. I-markers, which are constituted of semantic categories, are constructed out of the World-as-Perceived, and the order of constituents is discovered from the lexical string that serves as input. That such semantic categories can form the basis of the adult model is shown in the last two chapters.

3.6   THE PROBLEM OF MISSING CONSTITUENTS

In the child's early utterance, at the two-word and three-word stage, one of the constituents that is mandatory in adult speech is often missing. Some examples are:

Cindy bottle
(= Cindy   is   bringing   a   bottle;   Braine,   1974,   Table   1)
Mummy cool
(= Mummy's   soup   is   cool;   Brown,   1973,   p.   208)
Put truck window
(the   Agent   is   missing;   Brown,   1973,   p.   205)

Brown (1973, p. 205) concludes on the basis of his corpora that any major constituent of the sentence may be missing in the child's speech. This does not seem surprising. The child is a novice in the field of language; compiling a somewhat complex utterance may involve considerable mental effort and therefore he tends to manage with as little work as possible. But this explanation from laziness raises the question of the level at which the saving takes place. One possibility would be that he tends to construct only a very simple I-marker, perhaps one that contains only a single relation, and as a consequence the utterance is truncated. Several investigators—as, for instance, Antinucci and Parisi (1973) [see section 3.4]—have advocated a different explanation. The brevity of the utterance, in their view, disguises the fact that the underlying structure is more rich, and might perhaps even suffice for producing a syntactically complete adult utterance. It is only in realizing this underlying structure that the child omits certain constituents.

The latter approach has been argued forcefully by Bloom (1970). Utterances like those in the aforementioned example are held by her to result from a "reduction transformation" that deletes a node in the underlying deep structure. The reason such a transformation is applied is a "cognitive limitation in handling structural complexity [p. 165]." But how do we know that the deep structure before deletion was in fact richer than is apparent from the utterance? Perhaps the limitation on structural complexity extends to the deep structure as well? Bloom presents evidence discrediting this alternative account. One of the cases she examines is Agent–Object constructions, like "Cindy bottle," mentioned earlier. These constructions are frequent in the speech of many, though not all, children (Bowerman, 1975b). Adult grammar, of course, does not permit such constructions: There must always be a verb connecting the subject (the agent) with the object. In the deep structure, the verb–phrase node, which dominates the object noun phrase also dominates a verb node. The child, argues Bloom, must therefore have constructed the full deep structure and subsequently deleted from it the verb node. Observe that here Bloom's evidence is based on adult grammar, and hence open to the objection that it involves the 'anachronistic fallacy' (see section 3.4). Perhaps more convincing is the fact pointed out by Bloom that at the time the child uses Agent-Object constructions, he also uses Agent-Action and Action–Object constructions. This shows, according to Bloom, that he is capable of formulating at a deeper level the full Agent-Action-Object structure, and only because of the complexity constraint he rarely expresses all three constituents in his utterance.

Various criticisms against Bloom's hypothesis have been advanced by, among others, Bowerman (1973a, pp. 90–94), Braine (1974, 1976, pp. 78–82), Brown (1973, pp. 231–239), Matthews (1975), and Miller (1975, pp. 97–103). Some of these have been met by Bloom, Miller, and Hood (1975). They carried out a statistical analysis of child speech and showed how various factors contribute to the probability of any one constituent being emitted in speech.

A somewhat different view of the Agent-Object construction has been proposed by Bowerman (1973a, pp. 94–102, see also Bowerman, 1976a, pp.

100–101), who presented arguments to the effect that the underlying structure contains not merely a verb node, as suggested by Bloom, but also a specific verb, which is subsequently deleted. There are also differences of opinion concerning the reason for the deletion. According to Bloom it is a complexity constraint, as we have seen. On the other hand, Brown (1973, pp. 239–242) has proposed that the child may observe how adults use elliptical speech, and overgeneralizing from this, feel free to drop *any* constituent from his utterance.

These investigators all assume that the child's underlying structure is richer than is revealed by his utterances. I do not think, however, they have presented compelling evidence that this is so. My arguments in the previous section against the Antinucci and Parisi hypothesis seem in part to be applicable also in the present context. It is certainly almost self-evident that the child who says "Mummy cool" has, at some level, a representation of the fact that it is Mummy's soup that is cool; what needs to be clarified is whether that level is the one which directly underlies speech (the I-marker level) or the deeper lying cognitive level. The fact that the child is capable to form Possessor–Possession constructions (e.g., "Mummy soup") and does so on other occasions does not prove that at the time of producing the just-cited utterance he entertained a Possessor–Possession relation in his I-marker. He may simply have been attaching names to two aspects of the situation. Even in those instances when various two-word combinations are uttered on the same occasion—for example, "Lois read," "read book," and "Lois book" (Brown, 1973, p. 236)—there is no assurance that all the constituents mentioned (i.e., those underlying "Lois," "read," and "book") appear in one I-marker; instead, the child may have been focusing first on one relation then on another, and in each instance a different I-marker may have been realized.

This alternative proposal leaves us with the task of explaining the occurrence of Agent–Object constructions, like "Cindy bottle." If these are not derived from a more explicit underlying structure containing also an Action term, we must show how they originate. The explanation given earlier for "Mummy cool" that the child is merely allocating two words relevant to the situation cannot be applied to Agent–Object constructions, because in the latter a particular word order tends to be observed: The Agent precedes the Object. Such a regularity is evidence that a rule is being applied, and the question is, what is the underlying I-marker relation the rule is applied to?

One possible answer, implied in Schlesinger (1971b), is that there is indeed an underlying relation Agent–Object. As Brown (1973) remarks: "consider a child kicking a ball or turning a key. The agent and object seem to be in direct interaction; a person initiates a movement in a thing [p. 194]." The child may have observed such a relation being expressed in adult speech and have formed the appropriate realization rule: Agent + Object (the intervening verb in adult speech having gone unnoticed, just as various function words and grammatical morphemes do). This explanation has the drawback that it assumes a cul de sac: The child forms a relation and learns a rule that he must subsequently discard for more mature ones.

Another solution, based on generalized pivots, has been suggested in section 3.2. According to still another approach, which at present seems to me to come nearest to the truth, our analysis of Agent–Object constructions is in fact erroneous, as these are really Agent–Action constructions in disguise. Observe first that the child at that early stage has not yet mastered fully the rules according to which parts of speech are selected. An adjective may under certain conditions do duty for a noun (as when a child says "allgone sticky"; Braine, 1963) and a noun as a verb (see also section 8.1). In the utterance "Mommy sock," "sock" may stand for the action of putting on the sock, and in "Cindy bottle," "bottle" may mean the bringing of a bottle.[12] This interpretation at the first blush does not seem to be applicable to all putative Agent–Object constructions, however. Consider "Betty head," said by Steven when Betty moved a tractor near his head (Braine, 1974; Table 1). It seems implausible that the word "head" had come to mean for Steven the action of moving-near-head. Similarly, to interpret "bear" as signifying an action of giving-to-bear in "Kathryn bear" (Braine, 1974, Table 1) might seem a bit strained.

Not so strained, though, if viewed in a somewhat different light. Braine (1974) has recently proposed that there is a continuity between one-word utterances and certain types of utterances with missing constituents. Most one word utterances stand for a whole event or situation (see section 7.3); to refer to the event, the child hits on one of its salient aspects, for which he happens to know a word. Likewise, in the two-word stage, the child may utter a word for the Agent and a word that expresses one salient aspect of the action event. Thus, "head," though it has for the child a meaning similar to the one it has for the adult, may on that particular occasion have been the one word chosen to express the whole event of moving a toy tractor close to the child's head. According to Braine, then, these utterances are not due to an error in word class, but to "holophrastic insertion" of one word for the whole verb phrase.[13] Sometimes this word is a verb, and we obtain a regular Agent–Action construction. On other occasions it is a noun, with the result of what, superficially, looks like a construction linking an Agent to an Ob-

---

[12]This explanation was first suggested to me by Susan Ervin-Tripp in a discussion of the Study Group on Mechanisms of Language Development at the Ciba Foundation, London, May 1968.

[13]Recall in this connection that the I-marker is hierarchically organized, Action and Object belonging both to a higher Action constituent; see Figs. 3.1 and 3.2 and section 8.3 for discussion.

ject. This explanation has the merit that it accounts not only for the latter type of constructions but also for other noun + noun combinations, like those where the second noun stands for the location (as in "Betty head") or for the recipient (as in "Kathryn bear").

Braine's proposal does not require an underlying structure that is richer than what is revealed by the utterance. Because he has shown how the data can be adequately accounted for without such an assumption, there seems to be no justification for crediting the child at that stage of development with an attainment for which there is sufficient evidence only at a later stage.

REFERENCES

Anderson, J. R. Computer simulation of a language acquisition system: A second report. In D. Laberge & S. J. Samuels (Eds.), *Basic processes in reading: Perception and comprehension*. Hillsdale, N.J.: Lawrence Erlbaum Associates, 1977.

Antinucci, F., & Parisi, D. Early language acquisition: A model and some data. In C. A. Ferguson & D. I. Slobin (Eds.), *Studies of child language development*. New York: Holt, Rinehart & Winston, 1973.

Antinucci, F., & Parisi, D. Early semantic development in child language. In E. Lenneberg & E. Lenneberg (Eds.), *Foundations of language development: A multidisciplinary approach*, New York: Academic Press, 1975.

Arlman-Rupp, A.J.L., van Niekerk de Haan, D., & van de Sandt-Koenderman, M. Brown's early stages: Some evidence from the Dutch. *Journal of Child Language*, 1976, *3*, 267-274.

Bates, E. *Language and context: The acquisition of pragmatics*. New York: Academic Press, 1976.

Bloom, L. *Language development: Form and function in emerging grammars*. Cambridge, Mass.: MIT Press, 1970.

Bloom, L. *One word at a time: The use of single word utterances before syntax*. The Hague: Mouton, 1973.

Bloom, L., Lightbown, P., & Hood, L. Structure and variation in child language. *Monographs of the Society for Research in Child Development*, 1975, *40* (2, Serial No. 160).

Bloom, L., Miller, P., & Hood, L. Variation and reduction as aspects of competence in language development. In A. Pick (Ed.), *Minnesota Symposium on Child Psychology* (Vol. 9). Minneapolis: University of Minnesota Press, 1975.

Bowerman, M. F. *Early syntactic development*. Cambridge, England: Cambridge University Press, 1973. (a)

Bowerman, M. Structural relationships in children's utterances: Syntactic or semantic? In T. E. Moore (Ed.), *Cognitive development and the acquisition of language*. New York: Academic Press, 1973. (b)

Bowerman, M. Development of concepts underlying language: Discussion summary. In R. L. Schiefelbusch & L. L. Lloyd (Eds.), *Language perspectives: Acquisition, retardation, and intervention*. Baltimore: University Park Press, 1974. (a)

Bowerman, M. Learning the structure of causative verbs: A study in the relationship of cognitive, semantic and syntactic development. In E. Clark (Ed.), *Papers and Reports on Child Language Development, No. 8.* Stanford: Linguistics Committee, 1974. (b)

Bowerman, M. Commentary [to Bloom, L., Lightbown, P., & Hood, L., Structure and variation in child language]. *Monographs of the Society for Research in Child Development,* 1975, *40* (2, Serial No. 160). (a)

Bowerman, M. Cross-linguistic similarities at two stages of syntactic development. In E. Lenneberg & E. Lenneberg (Eds.), *Foundation of language development: A multi-disciplinary approach,* New York: Academic Press, 1975. (b)

Bowerman, M. Commentary [to Braine, M.D.S., Children's first word combinations]. *Monographs of the Society for Research in Child Development,* 1976, *41*,(1, Serial No. 164). (a)

Bowerman, M. Semantic factors in the acquisition of rules for word use and sentence construction. In D. Morehead & A. Morehead (Eds.), *Directions in normal and deficient child language.* Baltimore: University Park Press, 1976. (b)

Braine, M.D.S. The ontogeny of English phrase structure: The first phase. *Language,* 1963, *39,* 1–13.

Braine, M.D.S. On two types of models of the internalization of grammars. In D. I. Slobin (Ed.), *The ontogenesis of grammar.* New York: Academic Press, 1971.

Braine, M.D.S. Length constraints, reduction rules, and holophrastic processes in children's word combinations. *Journal of Verbal Learning and Verbal Behavior,* 1974, *13,* 448–456.

Braine, M.D.S. Children's first word combinations. *Monographs of the Society for Research in Child Development,* 1976, *41*(1, Serial No. 164).

Brown, R. *A first language: The early stages.* Cambridge, Mass.: Harvard University Press, 1973.

Chafe, W. L. *Meaning and the structure of language.* Chicago: University of Chicago Press, 1970.

Chomsky, N. Explanatory models in linguistics. In E. Nagel, P. Suppes, & A. Tarski (Eds.), *Logic, methodology, and philosophy of science: Proceedings of the 1960 International Congress.* Stanford, Calif.: Stanford University Press, 1962.

Chomsky, N. *Aspects of the theory of syntax.* Cambridge, Mass.: MIT Press, 1965.

Crothers, E., & Suppes, P. *Experiments in second language learning.* New York: Academic Press, 1967.

Culicover, P. W. & Wexler, K. Some syntactic implications of a theory of language learnability. In P. E. Culicover, T. Wasow, & A. Akmajian (Eds.), *Formal syntax.* New York: Academic Press, 1977.

Ervin-Tripp, S. Some strategies for the first two years. In T. E. Moore (Ed.), *Cognitive development and the acquisition of language.* New York: Academic Press, 1973.

Fillmore, C. J. The case for case. In E. Bach & R. T. Harms (Eds.), *Universals in linguistic theory.* New York: Holt, Rinehart & Winston, 1968.

Fodor, J. A., Bever, T. G., & Garrett, M. F. *The psychology of language.* New York: McGraw-Hill, 1974.

Gold, E. M. Language identification in the limit. *Information and control,* 1967, *10,* 447–474.

Greenbaum, S. Personal communication.

Greenfield, P. M., Nelson, K., & Saltzman, E. The development of rulebound strategies for manipulating seriated cups: A parallel between action and grammar. *Cognitive Psychology,* 1972, *3,* 291–310.

Greenfield, P. M., & Smith, J. H. *The structure of communication in early language development,* New York: Academic Press, 1976.

Hamburger, H., & Wexler, K. Identifiability of transformational grammars. In J. Hintikka, J. Moravczik, & P. Suppes (Eds.), *Approaches to natural language.* Dordrecht, Holland: Reidel, 1973.

Howe, C. J. The meaning of two-word utterances in the speech of young children. *Journal of Child Language,* 1976, *3,* 29–48.

Huxley, R., & Ingram, E. (Eds.). *Language acquisition: Models and methods.* London: Academic Press, 1971.

Ingram, T.T.S. *Annual Report to the Nuffield Foundation 1966-67.* Edinburgh: Language Development Research Project in the Department of Child Life and Health, University of Edinburgh, 1966-1967.

Jespersen, O. *Language: Its nature, development and origin.* New York: Norton, 1964 (Originally published 1922).

Kernan, K. T. The acquisition of language by Samoan children. Unpublished doctoral dissertation, University of California, Berkeley, 1969.

Leopold, W. F. *Speech development of a bilingual child: A linguistic record* (Vol. 3). *Grammar and general problems in the first two years.* Evanston, Ill.: Northwestern University Press, 1949.

Levelt, W. J. M. *Formal grammars in linguistics and psycholinguistics* (Vol. 3). *Psycholinguistic applications.* The Hague: Mounton, 1974.

Lindhagen, K. *Semantic relations in Swedish children's early sentences.* Acta Universitatis Upsaliensis, Studia psychologica Upsaliensa, Uppsala, 1976.

Macnamara, J. The cognitive basis of language learning in children. *Psychological Review,* 1972, *79,* 1–13.

McNeill, D. Developmental psycholinguistics. In F. Smith & G. A. Miller (Eds.), *The genesis of language: A psycholinguistic approach.* Cambridge, Mass.: MIT Press, 1966.

Matthews, P. H. Review of R. Brown, *A first language: The early stages. Journal of Linguistics,* 1975, *11,* 312–343.

Miller, M. M. *Zur Logik der frühen Sprachentwicklung.* Deutsches Seminar der Universität Frankfurt am Main, April, 1975.

Miller, J. F., & Yoder, D. E. An ontogenetic language teaching strategy for retarded children. In R. L. Schiefelbusch & L. L. Lloyd (Eds.), *Language perspectives—Acquisition, retardation and intervention.* Baltimore: University Park Press, 1974.

Moeser, S. D., & Bregman, A. S. The role of reference in the acquisition of a miniature artificial language. *Journal of Verbal Learning and Verbal Behavior,* 1972, *11,* 759–769.

Moeser, S. D. & Bregman, A. S. Imagery and language acquisition. *Journal of Verbal Learning and Verbal Behavior,* 1973, *12,* 91–98.

Moeser, S. D., & Olson, A. J. The role of reference in the acquisition of a miniature artificial language. *Journal of Verbal Learning and Verbal Behavior,* 1974, *17,* 204–218.

Namir, L., & Schlesinger, I. M. The grammar of sign language. In I. M. Schlesinger & L. Namir (Eds.), *Sign language of the deaf: Psychological, linguistic and sociological perspectives.* New York: Academic Press, 1978.

Nelson, K. The nominal shift in semantic-syntactic development. *Cognitive Psychology*, 1975, *7*, 461–479.

Parisi, D. What is behind child utterances? *Journal of Child Language*, 1974, *1*, 97–105.

Quirk, R., Greenbaum, S., Leech, G. & Svartvik, J. *A grammar of contemporary English*. New York: Harcourt Brace Jovanovich, 1972.

Rodgon, M. M. Situation and meaning in one- and two-word utterances: Observations on Howe's "The meanings of two-word utterances in the speech of young children." *Journal of Child Language*, 1977, *4*, 111–114.

Sapir, E., & Swadesh, M. American Indian grammatical categories. *Word*, 1946, *2*, 103–112.

Schaerlaekens, A. M. *The two-word sentence in child language development*. The Hague: Mouton, 1973.

Schlesinger, I. M. Learning grammar: From pivot to realization rule. In R. Huxley & E. Ingram (Eds.), *Language acquisition: Models and methods*. London: Academic Press, 1971. (a)

Schlesinger, I. M. Production of utterances and language acquisition. In D. I. Slobin (Ed.), *The ontogenesis of grammar*. New York: Academic Press, 1971. (b)

Schlesinger, I. M. Relational concepts underlying language. In R. L. Schiefelbusch & L. L. Lloyd, (Eds.), *Language perspectives—acquisition, retardation and intervention.* Baltimore: University Park Press, 1974.

Schlesinger, I. M. *Production and comprehension of utterances*. Hillsdale, N.J.: Lawrence Erlbaum Associates, 1977.

Sinclair, H. Sensorimotor action patterns as a condition for the acquisition of syntax. In R. Huxley & E. Ingram (Eds.), *Language acquisition: Models and methods*. London: Academic Press, 1971.

Slobin, D. I. Comments on "Developmental Psycholinguistics." In F. Smith & G. A. Miller (Eds.), *The genesis of language: A psycholinguistic approach*. Cambridge, Mass.: MIT Press, 1966.

Slobin, D. I. Universals of grammatical development in children. In G. B. Flores d'Arcais & W.J.M. Levelt (Eds.), *Advances in psycholinguistics*. Amsterdam: North-Holland, 1970.

Slobin, D. I. Developmental psycholinguistics. In W. O. Dingwall (Ed.), *A survey of linguistic science*. University of Maryland, 1971.

Snow, C. E. Mother's speech research: From input to interaction. In C. E. Snow & C. A. Ferguson (Eds.), *Talking to children: Language input and acquisition*. Cambridge, England: Cambridge University Press, 1977.

Stern, C., & Stern, W. *Die Kindersprache: Eine psychologische und sprachtheoretische Untersuchung*. Darmstadt: Wissenschaftliche Buchgesellschaft, 1968. (Originally published 1928.)

Veneziano, E. Analysis of wish sentences in the one-word stage of language acquisition: A cognitive approach. Unpublished Master's thesis, Tufts University, 1973.

Werner, H., & Kaplan, B. *Symbol formation: An organismic-developmental approach to language and the expression of thought*. New York: Wiley, 1963.

Wexler, K., & Culicover, P. W. The semantic basis for language acquisition: The invariance principle as a replacement for the universal base hypothesis. *Social Science Working Papers*, 50, School of Social Sciences, University of California, Irvine, 1974.

Wexler, K., Culicover, P., & Hamburger, H. Learning-theoretic foundations of linguistic universals. *Theoretical Linguistics*, 1975, *2*, 215–253.

4 Cognitive Development and Linguistic Input

*But the student will remember that the Sciences . . . advance
by zig-zagging from one absolute formula to another which
corrects it by going too far the other way.*
—William James, *Principles of Psychology*

INTRODUCTION

The transformationalist view of language development, which dominated
the scene in the mid- and late 1960s, gave rise to two countermovements.
The neglect of semantics in work on language development carried out
within the Chomskyan framework was opposed by investigators who
espoused an approach reinstating semantics as a central facet in the description of child language, as described in the preceding chapter. The Chomskyan emphasis on the independence of language of other cognitive functions, on the other hand, was countered by a spate of studies designed to
reveal the close relationship between linguistic and cognitive development
and the dependence of the former on the latter. This trend, sometimes
characterized by the slogan "cognition leads language," is closely allied to
the semantic approach: Both lines of thought impugn the splendid isolation
of language, and both diminish the plausibility of the claim of an innate
component of specifically linguistic knowledge.

Piagetian theory provided the groundwork for several writers who began
to view language learning as based on general cognitive development. In
section 3.4 some of the proposals made by Sinclair (1971; see also Sinclair-
de Zwart, 1973) and Brown (1973) concerning the sensorimotor roots of
early child language were briefly reviewed. Among studies based on Piaget's
work are Veneziano (1973), Morehead and Morehead (1974), Greenfield
and Smith (1976), and Carter ([1975], who subtitles her paper "The
Transformation of Sensorimotor Morphemes into Words"). Particularly
relevant to the problem of the development of relational categories (discussed in the preceding chapter) is a study by Edwards (1973). Affinities with

the Piagetian viewpoint are also evident in the thesis of Rodgon, Jankowsky, and Alenskas (1977) that "language arises in conjunction with overt action [p. 42]," and in McNeill's (1975) research showing how the child's early sentences have structures that follow the patterns of his actions (see also Greenfield, Nelson, & Saltzman, 1972, described briefly in section 3.4). An emphasis on perception rather than action is prevalent in the work of Eve Clark, carried out outside the Piagetian framework, on the acquisition of relational words ("more" and "less," "tall" and "short," "come" and "go," and "on," "in," and "under"), which she shows to be determined by the child's way of structuring his environment (reviewed in Clark, 1977).

This accentuation of cognitive development was a wholesome reaction against previous approaches of language acquisition that focused almost exclusively on the contribution of linguistic input to the child (a notable exception being Von Raffler-Engel [1964, pp. 30-31, 50-51], who stressed the role of cognitive development; for a tempered approach see Brown [1965].

It is not my purpose to discuss this work in detail here. (Excellent critical reviews are those by Cromer [1974] and Bowerman [1976]). Instead, this chapter examines in general the thesis of cognitive primacy in language development.

Two types of claims are implicit, but not always clearly distinguished, in writings on the primacy of cognition:

1. The abilities that underlie the learning of language are attained in the course of cognitive development.
2. The specific structures, categories and processes implicated in language functions have been either prepared for, or—according to a stronger version—acquired in the course of cognitive development.

Of these two assertions, (1) appears to be the more moderate and immediately plausible one. It could be argued, however, that some abilities develop fully only through exercising the functions employed in language learning. But our main concern in this chapter is with (2). Here, in turn, various versions of the claim made are possible, the most extreme being that *all* the structures, categories, and processes are acquired through cognitive development. Such a conception accords only a minor role to language learning: All that remains to be done after the achievements of cognitive development is to establish links between these and the corresponding linguistic notions. By contrast, it is argued here that there is much more to learning language than just this.

In the following, an attempt is made to clarify the role of linguistic input in language learning vis-à-vis that of cognitive development by discussing two extreme positions.[1] According to one of these, language development is wholly determined by the child's cognitive development attained through interacting with the extralinguistic environment, whereas the other claims that it is solely the linguistic input to the child which accounts for acquisition of language. Presumably, none of these positions is likely to find a spokesman among present-day theorists when stated in this extreme form. They are stated here in this manner only for the purpose of exposition, in order to examine various arguments for and against them. After discussing these points, an integrated middle-of-the-road approach is advocated.

4.1   COGNITIVE DETERMINISM

The view that linguistic development is completely determined by cognitive development may be termed *cognitive determinism* (CD). CD claims that the child attains the concepts expressed by the language through maturation and interaction with the extra-linguistic environment, and subsequently these concepts are associated with their suitable linguistic expression. As stated, we are concerned here with CD in its 'pure' form, which does not accord any role to the child's linguistic interaction with the adult. It is doubtful whether such an extreme position is embraced by anyone at present. But this is a convenient way to start, and in the following I try to show how CD must be qualified to become plausible.

It seems obvious that there are two restrictions that must be imposed on CD. First, there are linguistic concepts, such as gender in some languages, which are uncorrelated or only very imperfectly correlated with semantic concepts. Many grammatical rules, such as agreement phenomena, are such that communication would not be impaired by their nonobservance. There are, then, complexities in language beyond those required for expressing the concepts and relations attained by cognitive development. These are surface

---

[1]The following sections (to the end of the chapter) are reprinted here with a few slight adaptations from my paper which appeared in *Journal of Child Language* (Schlesinger, 1977). Permission of the publishers, Cambridge University Press, is gratefully acknowledged. A shorter version of this paper was presented at the National Council for Research conference on "The Effects of the Environment on Cognitive Functioning" (chaired by Charles Greenbaum), held in Arad, Israel, in October 1974. I have benefited from helpful criticism by Daniel Frankel, Charles Greenbaum, Anat Ninio, and Edy Veneziano, and comments by Jerome Bruner and Walburga von Raffler-Engel. Special thanks are due to Mordechai Rimor and Etha Frenkel for their perceptive reading of drafts of the paper and their many suggestions for improvement in presentation. The original paper referred to Bloom, Lightbown, and Hood (1975, p. 30), and charged that they failed to distinguish between interpretation and formation of concepts. As Lois Bloom has since pointed out to me, this was a misinterpretation, as can be seen from the same page in their paper, and I therefore omit this passage here, with apologies to the authors.

phenomena, the acquisition of which depends entirely on linguistic input, and the CD hypothesis is not applicable here. Only the underlying structures that are the bearers of meaning may be claimed to be cognitively determined.

A further reservation regarding CD is as follows. As shown by Slobin (1973), factors of linguistic complexity determine the rate at which structures are learned. For a notion to be linguistically expressed, two requirements have to be met. The child must not only have achieved the degree of cognitive maturity necessary for conceiving the notion but he must also be able to deal with the complexity of the linguistic expression. Of course, the latter ability is also dependent on his cognitive development. Cromer (1974, pp. 239–246), however, has discussed findings about linguistic development that appear to depend neither on changes of meaning nor on changes in cognitive complexity or the growth of cognitive abilities of the child. In addition to the complexity there may be, in the early stages of language learning, factors of saliency and communicative importance that determine which of the cognitive notions available to the child are expressed in language (see section 3.4). It appears, then, that cognitive development may at times outstrip linguistic development.

The CD hypothesis should therefore be reformulated so as to claim merely that concepts and relations that underlie language and constitute the meaning of what is expressed by it are *formed* by cognitive development. The manner of expressing these notions and the rate at which the child learns to express them are determined in part by linguistic factors such as complexity of the linguistic construction. The import of this reformulated hypothesis lies in what it negates: The underlying notions are *not* formed by the child's experience with language, but rather by his experience and interaction with the environment independently of learning language. Stated in this form, the hypothesis seems to correspond to Cromer's (1974) weak version of the cognition hypothesis. But even this formulation leaves much to be desired, as is shown presently.

4.2 THE CATEGORIZATION PROBLEM

Cognitive development in itself cannot be sufficient for the formation of a concept that underlies language. This becomes evident when we distinguish two problems that have to be dealt with by the child in learning such a concept; we call these the *interpretation problem* and the *categorization problem*.

To function effectively, the child must attain certain cognitive skills that enable him to interpret what is going on in his environment. This interpretation problem can be solved without the aid of language; in fact its solution is itself a prerequisite for learning language. But language learning depends in addition on a categorization of objects and events, which is needed solely for the purpose of speaking and understanding speech. It is argued later that the categorization problem cannot be dealt with independently of language: Its solution is part and parcel of the language learning process.

The child copes with the interpretation problem in interacting with the environment. At a certain stage of development he begins to understand that there are various agents carrying out a variety of actions: There is daddy picking up the bottle, mummy handing him the bottle, and perhaps himself dropping the bottle. At first he does not yet perceive these in terms of actions being carried out by different agents and only in the course of his cognitive development does he attain the ability to interpret the world in this manner. But now the question must be raised: Given that he has solved this interpretation problem, can he then be said to have acquired an agent *concept*?

The tacit assumption made by some writers seems to be that to interpret the environment is, ipso facto, to form concepts or schemata. (For a contrary approach see Bloom [1973, p. 121].) In the following, I argue that this assumption is unwarranted. The fact that the child interprets the environment does not imply that he categorizes the various states, processes and events.

Consider first that a concept has been acquired only to the extent that one knows what belongs to it and what does not.[2] Now, what are the boundaries of the agent concept? Mummy handing the bottle to the child is no doubt an event where an agent is performing some action, but what about mummy just holding the bottle? To take one further step, can the bottle be said to be an agent 'containing' the milk in the same way that mother is an agent holding the bottle? Clearly there are gradations here of 'agentiveness.' In our adult judgment of what does and what does not fall under the agent concept, we are very much influenced by what our language expresses as an agent. Cognitive development gives us no clue to the solution of this *categorization problem*. The world is not presented to us in neatly arranged discrete categories. The nature of the solution may differ according to the language learned by the child. Witness, for instance, the tense systems of different languages that carve up temporal concepts in different ways.

The categorization problem must be solved by the child also when he learns the concepts underlying words. Nelson (1974) has argued that the concept is first acquired independently of the word as part of the child's extra-linguistic experience. Her proposal does not deal with the categorization problem, because the child still has to learn what the boundaries of the word are, and these boundaries are dependent on the language. The bound-

---

[2]*Concept* will be used here to denote a class or category.

aries of the concept *uncle* depend on the kinship terminology employed by the language in question. An Israeli mother would either express delight or correct her child if he were to use the same Hebrew word for both a hairbrush and a painter's brush, an occurrence that would be considered normal by an English-speaking parent; and examples of such cross-linguistic differences are legion. This issue is taken up in the following chapter.

Now, just as there is no inherently 'correct' or 'natural' way to group objects into concepts, so there is no one way to group grammatical relations. The problems of delimiting the Agent relation have been discussed earlier. Similar considerations are pertinent in regard to the Patient concept. In discussing the acquisition of the notion of transitive verb, Macnamara (1972) argues that the child must perceive that something happens to the object, that the object is affected by the action denoted by the verb. But how much affected does it have to be if it is to be considered the object of a transitive verb? Suppose you hit a wall with your head, is the wall 'affected' without showing it? And when you sit on a bed that has just been made and the bed shows it very much, should it be considered a patient (and hence "sit" as a transitive verb), contrary to what is suggested by the sentence "I sit on the bed"? Cognitive development will not furnish the clue to this problem of where the boundaries are to be drawn. There seems to be nothing in the child's extra-linguistic interaction with the environment showing him where the boundaries are to be drawn.

But let us assume for a moment that there is a solution to this difficulty and that in some unexplained way the events interpreted by the child fall into some predestined categories. What would such a spontaneously formed system of categories be like? If it is to be a key to language learning, this system must cover every relation which appears in any one of the languages of the world. But, as is well known, languages differ in the distinctions they observe. Thus, what is treated in English as one relation may turn out to be two relations, each expressed in a different way, in some other language. Take the relation of Possession, for instance. In English, alienable and inalienable possession are expressed in the same way: we say "John's book" just as we say "John's arm" or "John's father," although the book obviously does not belong to John the same way as his arm or his father does. There are languages that make these distinctions, and in other languages still other distinctions are made (Cassirer 1953, pp. 263–264).

In order to account for the categorization problem, CD would have to maintain that all these distinctions are acquired through extralinguistic experience; in fact, it would have to make the implausible claim that the child organizes his experience as a large hierarchy of categories (like possession) and subcategories (like alienable and inalienble possession), of which a smaller set is ultimately employed in his grammar depending on the language he happens to learn. If, instead, only the general distinctions at the top of the hierarchy are cognitively predetermined, any other distinctions used by a particular language community would have to be learned through linguistic interaction—a possibility denied by the extreme CD hypothesis.

Further, there is a difficulty even with the claim that higher-order distinctions are acquired solely through cognitive development. If there is any operational meaning to the concept of 'concept' it is this: For someone to have a concept entails that all instances of the concept elicit a common response. The child may understand that there is an agent performing an action, but he does not have the concept *Agent* until he responds in some distinguishable way to the various occurrences of agents. In the case of the concepts *dog*, *uncle*, and *brush*, there are obvious common responses. Some of these are linguistic, that is, the word by which the child labels the various instances of the concept, and others are extralinguistic: He may avoid all dogs and approach all uncles, or vice versa.

Consider now grammatical concepts such as the Agent concept. Is there any response divorced from linguistic interaction that is common to all occurrences of an agent? In a Piagetian vein one might argue that the child acquires the Agent concept by abstracting a specific, customary actor from the action and when he realizes that for any action he wants performed there are several alternative people who might carry it out. Once he has reached the stage where he considers any person a potential 'fulfiller' of his wishes for actions, one may be justified in speaking of a common (nonlinguistic) response to all agents: There will be a set of alternative characteristic behaviors in cases of the child wanting to have some action performed.

Now note that the child (ultimately, though perhaps not at the beginning) expresses the Agent-Action relation not only in situations like these. If someone opens a box without the child having asked for it and perphaps even having expected it, one cannot ascribe to the child an analysis of the situation as involving one-out-of-many box-openers and the opening of a box; and still less so as one-out-of-many agents and an action. Presumably, he views this, very concretely, as an occurrence involving the specific relation between so and so and the opening of a box. There is nothing that impels him to de-center: Why should he generalize the concept obtained in situations where he wishes actions to be performed to the latter situation? Only to the extent that the exigencies of the situation demand this—that is, when he looks for someone to help him—will he come to consider anyone as a potential doer and not when no such demand is built into the situation. In the latter case, then, there is no conceivable nonlinguistic response in common with all other 'agent–action' situations.

Similar considerations apply to other relations expressed in speech. Most of these have their origin in cognitive growth of the sensorimotor period, but, as some recent research shows, the relations expressed in language are almost invariably much more inclusive than the concepts the child can be credited with on the basis of his extralinguistic experience. Hence the CD hypothesis is inadequate for explaining how the agent relation and other relations appear in the child's speech in such situations. The common response in all situations where these relations are realized must be a *linguistic response*. And this brings us to the linguistic input hypothesis.

4.3   THE LINGUISTIC INPUT HYPOTHESIS

The *linguistic input* (LI) *hypothesis* asserts, in contradiction to the CD hypothesis, that the child's linguistic development is determined by his experience with language. We have already seen that the extreme version of CD must be modified so as to accord to linguistic input the responsibility for the acquisition of certain surface phenomena. The LI hypothesis claims, in addition, that the child's linguistic experience accounts for acquisition of concepts underlying language. This offers a solution to the categorization problem. The child learns what counts as "doggy" by observing what goes by this name. Similarly, he forms the Agent concept by observing that different events—daddy picking up the bottle, mummy handing him the bottle, himself dropping it, etc.—are expressed linguistically by certain structures in which the agent is realized by means of word order or inflection (section 3.4). The question of what belongs to the Agent concept is settled by the linguistic form expressing it. Likewise, it is the linguistic form of the expression that determines that in "I hit the wall" the wall is the patient of the action of hitting, whereas the bed is *not* the patient in "I sit on the bed." There is nothing in nature which prescribes this categorization, as shown by observations of Gvozdev's Zhenya (quoted in Bowerman 1973, p. 208), who at first used the accusative case (which marks the object) only "to mark those direct objects which designated the objects of action, particularly those occurring with verbs referring to the transfer or relocation of objects . . . ." Zhenya, then, had to utilize the linguistic input to learn how to form the patient category resulting in grammatically correct utterances.

The linguistic input, then, imposes order on the many unique occurrences of objects, events, and relations. The common response through which he acquires concepts of these is educed by the child from the linguistic input, which may be either a word (or collocation) that labels the object or event, or else a syntactic form that 'labels' the relation. This notion is further developed in sections 7.2–7.5.

It may be expected that this categorization will be in agreement with the cognitive organization the child brings with him to the language-learning task. Events that are in all obvious respects dissimilar are unlikely to be categorized in the same manner. The evolution of the language was presumably dependent on the way speakers perceived similarities (see section 5.6). The work of Rosch (1973) has shown that there may often be a cognitive 'core' of a concept. In general, this core will be respected by all languages, but the categorization of what lies outside the core will be determined by each particular language (e.g., how much of what lies outside the core of red belongs to "red" rather than to the adjoining colors—"orange," "yellow," etc.—will vary with the language spoken).

An analogous situation may be expected to hold for grammatical relations. Brown (1973, p. 195-196) shows that in child language a syntactic construction does not at first express the full range of semantic meaning that it expresses in adult language. Thus the possessive construction in child speech is at first used mainly for alienable possession and not for inalienable possession. He later learns that inalienable possession is also regarded (for the purpose of speaking) as a kind of possession, but this learning cannot be put down to cognitive maturation. There is nothing in nature or in the structure of the human mind that decrees that these two belong together; in fact there are languages that distinguish between the two. It is the linguistic input that shows the child whether or not to collapse these cognitively distinguishable relations into one. Earlier (section 3.4; also sections 9.3–9.4) I presented some linguistic evidence for such semantic assimilation operating in the utterance-producing mechanism. Recently, several writers have independently observed such extensions: In addition to Brown there are Bloom, Miller and Hood (1975), Braine (1976), and Edwards (1976). McNeill (1975, 1978) discusses a similar phenomenon, which he calls *semiotic extension*.

It should be noted that the LI hypothesis makes assertions only about linguistic development, and in itself does not entail anything about the way linguistic development reflects back on cognition. However, a weak version of the linguistic relativity hypothesis is, if not entailed, at least made plausible by it. "See" and "hear" are treated by language in a way similar to words expressing action, such as "hold" and "kick," and hence one may be easily led to view the person who sees as a kind of agent carrying out the 'action' of seeing (Waismann, 1962). It has indeed been observed that college students need a great deal of convincing to agree that there is a difference between active verbs on the one hand and stative ones, like "see," on the other (Sidney Greenbaum, personal communication). The effect of the verbal input seems to make itself strongly felt here. Likewise, verbal input has been found effective in experimental situations where discriminability of figures could be enhanced by providing them with unique verbal labels (De Rivera 1959; Katz 1963). Also relevant in this connection is the effect of labeling on memory found in the classical Carmichael, Hogan, and Walter (1932) experiment, in which a given figure presented to subjects would be recalled either as dumbbells, for instance, or as eyeglasses, depending on the verbal label supplied. This experiment and its replication (Herman, Lawless, & Marshall, 1957) measured recognition; Daniel (1972) found similar results in a recall task as well.

These considerations concerning the possible influence of linguistic structure on cognition suggest that we explore the possibility that the effect of linguistic input is not limited to categorizing: We must reconsider the interpretation problem.

4.4 THE INTERPRETATION PROBLEM

By interacting with his environment and by observing others interact with it the child learns to structure the world cognitively. One of the ways others relate to the environment is by commenting on it verbally, and it seems plausible that already at the earliest stages of language development the child learns from these comments to interpret what goes on around him. (A similar view is held by Bruner and his co-workers [Bruner, Olver, & Greenfield, 1966].) One of the ways that this may happen is that the adult's way of talking about ongoing events draws the child's attention to certain aspects of them, which otherwise would have remained unnoticed or at least less salient. This point has been made repeatedly; thus, Brown (1958, pp. 206–207) speaks of the word as a "lure to cognition" (see also Slobin, 1966, p. 89; Wells, 1974, p. 254). In other words, the linguistic input may direct the child to interpret the environment and not only to categorize those notions that he has already attained extra-linguistically. Earlier it was proposed that the function of linguistic input is to deal with the categorization problem: After he has constructed a map of the world through his extra-linguistic experience, the child utilizes linguistic input to draw in the borders between adjoining categories. Now we suggest that linguistic input may also be responsible for constructing certain parts of the map itself. Perhaps he is helped in this venture by the adult, who unconsciously modifies his speech "in a way which facilitates the child's initial search for consistencies in the expression of semantic concepts and which perhaps even suggests to him which semantic concepts he should consider important." (Bowerman, 1973, p. 213). The role of joint activities of mother and child in early language acquisition has been in the focus of recent research by Bruner (1975). See also Bowerman (1976) for a discussion of recent work pointing in this direction.

This does not mean that the child is wholly dependent on linguistic input. Presumably, most concepts would have been attained by him in any case in the course of cognitive growth, albeit with some delay. What is claimed here

---

[5]Studies showing deaf children to have intellectual abilities comparable to those of hearing children (Furth & Youniss, 1971) do therefore not conflict with this hypothesis.

is merely that in effect the formation of a given concept may be triggered off by linguistic input, not that the latter is indispensable for it.[3]

To illustrate, take the distinction between proper and common nouns. This distinction has an obvious semantic correlate. Macnamara (1972; Katz, Baker, & Macnamara, 1974) therefore holds that the child's extralinguistic experience makes him aware that persons and dogs are individuals in a way chairs and toy blocks, for instance, are not, and this enables him to learn the distinction between proper and common nouns. There is another possibility, however, which has been discussed by Quine (1960, p. 95 ff.). The child observes how different nouns are treated linguistically, notably in respect to the use of articles ("a boy" vs. "John"), and thereby arrives at the classification of nouns as proper and common. In addition, there is also the possibility of the child's benefiting from direct instruction. For instance, when he uses his sister's name in talking about another girl, the adult corrects him by saying, for example, "This is not Susie, this is Carol; only she [pointing] is called Susie." Such linguistic experiences may alert him to the difference between humans (liberally interpreted to include dogs above the rank of street dogs), who are equipped with proper-noun names, and everything else, which can have only common-noun labels.

Two experiments by Katz et al. (1974) with girls under two years of age are relevant here. When a nonce word preceded by an article (e.g., "a/the zav") was used to refer to a doll, this word was taken to refer to any doll, whereas when the nonce word was used without an article (e.g., "zav") it was treated as a proper noun referring only the particular doll for which it was introduces. By contrast, no such distinction was made when nonce words were used to label toy blocks. From these results, Katz et al. infer, correctly, that these children had acquired the distinction between individuals and things already before the experiment. What the experiment does not show, however, is how it is acquired. Whereas the suggestion made by these authors that the distinction is brought about the extralinguistic experience is quite plausible, there is nothing in the findings to rule out alternative explanations like that of Quine, which would accord to the linguistic input a role in the attainment of this distinction: The differential linguistic treatment may have primed the child to notice the difference between persons and dogs, on the one hand, and things like tables, chairs, and spoons, on the other.[4]

In proposing this LI explanation I do not intend to argue that this is the whole truth; in fact, in the following section I argue that it is only a partial

---

[4]The fact that the girls disregarded the linguistic cues in connection with the naming of blocks does not argue against this explanation for two reasons: (1) the priming effect depends on its being correlated with a cognitive difference; (2) in any case, the subjects' experience in the course of the experiment was presumably too short to have led to the learning of the distinction.

answer and present an approach that integrates the LI and CD hypotheses. My discussion of proper and common nouns only shows that linguistic input should not be ruled out as a possible factor in the formation of cognitive categories.

As another illustration let us look at a cross-linguistic comparison of the passive voice by Hartmann (1954). On the basis of his thoroughgoing investigation of the passive in old and new Irish and in certain other languages, Hartmann concludes that in these languages the passive is reserved for actions and processes that are carried out through the influence of a power that leaves no choice to the agent. He links this finding to a particular way of viewing the world in traditional Irish culture, which differs from that of, for example, the ancient Greeks, where the passive was not used in this manner. Assuming this explanation to be correct, we may now raise the question of how the child born into Irish culture absorbs this particular mentality that correlates with the passive voice.

The obvious answer is of course that the child learns to view the world in the way adults do by communicating with them about what happens (or by just hearing adults communicate with each other). This explanation is based on the effects of linguistic input. Imagine for a moment that all adults in the Irish child's environment turned mute. It is very doubtful that much of their worldview could be imparted to the child through their nonverbal behavior. But I would go one step further and argue that it may not only have been the way events were explicitly explained to the child which imbued him with their mentality. A less direct, but nonetheless very potent influence may have been exercised by the linguistic form in which adults talked about these events. In other words, their consistent use of the passive voice for certain kinds of events and processes to the exclusion of others may have served to show the child that these form a class apart, and this may have precipitated the formation of the Irish mentality.[5]

In a recent paper, Marion Blank (1974, see also 1975) has argued forcefully for the importance of LI: "The skills gained in mastering some of the more complex language structures are vital to the child's cognitive development [1974, p. 243]." Particularly, she claims that the cognitive skills acquired in the sensorimotor period will not enable the child to understand questions of "how" and "why." When confronted with such questions there is nothing in the situation which provides the child with a clue to their meaning. Blank shows that the only way the child can figure out the meaning of "why" is through trying the word out by using it in questions, even without understanding these questions himself. From the

---

[5]Of course, this can have been true only of the Irish child, not of Irish culture as a whole. Irish deities should not be credited with imposing a language with a special kind of passive on their subordinates so as to inculcate in their mind the proper worldview.

adults' responses to these questions, he gradually determines the meaning of the verbally expressed concept. Blank accedes that understanding of "why" may presuppose additional cognitive skills, 'such as some primitive notion of purpose or a burgeoning sense of curiosity [p. 242].' These, however, 'remain undeveloped until called upon in situations using higher level language formulations [p. 242].'

Let us consider now possible objections to the LI hypothesis. Studies showing that linguistic development keeps pace with cognitive development and that stages in the acquisition of certain constructions can be predicted from their relative complexity (Slobin, 1973) do not conflict with the hypothesis. Rather, what they show is that for a distinction to emerge, a certain level of maturity is indispensable, and this leaves open the possibility that this distinction is triggered off by linguistic input. An apparent difficulty stems from the evidence that a linguistic form may begin to appear in children's speech a considerable time after the semantic notions expressed by it have been mastered (Slobin, 1973. p. 184). This, however, does not invalidate the LI hypothesis, because the data in question pertain to speech production and it is quite possible that long before they were actively produced by the child the new forms were heard by him and helped in shaping the relevant cognitive notions.

In her recent study of gesture language created by deaf 2- to 4-year olds who had no previous experience of a conventional sign language, Susan Goldin-Meadow (1975) obtained findings which she interpreted to the effect that these children express various "roles," that is, grammatical concepts, such as agent, patient, and recipient. This seems to show that the appearance of these relations is not dependent on linguistic input. Note, however, that the mere fact that a child refers by signs to what the investigator classifies as, for example, the Agent does not prove that the child has formed an agent concept. He can be credited with such a concept only if there is a systematic way in which he expresses it linguistically. A consistent rule for the signing of the various concepts was in fact found by Goldin-Meadow. She reports, first, that the children did not always refer to all roles—agent, action, recipient, and so on—explicitly, and there were certain roles whose expression was preferred to that of others. Further, these preferences were related to the order of signs: That role "more likely to be produced . . . occupies the initial position of the two-gesture phrase, and the less likely sign occupies the second position." This 'rule' has a close parallel in the tendency of speaking children to utter first the word denoting the more salient aspect of the situation (Schlesinger, 1976). The "role more likely to be reproduced" is presumably that which is more important and salient for the child. It appears therefore that the children are not adhering to any grammatical rule but are just following their natural tendency to express important things first. No concepts like Agent or Recipient are therefore needed to account for the observed sequence of signs.

Another argument is based on Sinclair-de Zwart's (1967) experiments on the effect of language on conservation in children. She found that French words that might be used to express the principle of conservation verbally were mastered by conservers much more than by nonconservers. In her experiment she tried to find out whether nonconservers could be taught conservation by supplying them with these linguistic tools. In several training sessions, nonconservers learned the language of conservation to a criterion. When retested on a conservation task, only 10 out of the 28 who were initially nonconservers achieved complete conservation. (1967, pp. 53–68).

These findings are sometimes cited as evidence that language training has only negligible effects on a cognitively central operation, and that therefore 'cognition leads language' rather than vice versa. Such a sweeping generalization is of course unwarranted on the basis of a failure to influence a certain type of 'cognition' by a certain type of 'language' skill. Besides, note that the experiment proves only what you want it to prove. Those committed to the CD hypothesis in its stronger or weaker version may be cheered by the fact that linguistic training had so little effect. The sceptic may rightly point out that ten of the children did improve in their conservation performances; so linguistic input does have an effect after all.

Trying to decide what this experiment 'really' proves is rather like deciding whether a glass of water is half-full or half-empty. Instead, let us look at another experiment that, though described in the same book, I have not seen much quoted in connnection with the CD issue. This is an experiment on seriation conducted on much the same lines as the conservation experiment. Children who performed poorly on seriation were given linguistic training presumably relevant to seriation. The results strikingly differed from those in the conservation experiment: 18 out of 23 subjects showed improved performance, and 10 of these achieved 'true' seriation (Sinclair-de Zwart 1967, pp. 126–127). Evidently, the linguistic input did have an appreciable effect on this type of cognitive functioning.[6] Of course, these results do not entitle us to any extravagant claims, such as that 'language precedes cognition,' but they may certainly be regarded as a point in favour of the LI hypothesis.

It seems, then, that there is no good argument so far against the claim that in interpreting the environment the child is guided by linguistic input from adults, just as there is no good argument against a mitigated CD hypothesis. We thus have two rival hypotheses for the interpretation problem (with the LI hypothesis perhaps having a slight edge over its rival, in view of Sinclair-de Zwart's seriation experiment). But are they really rivals?

---

[6]Sinclair-de Zwart (1967) points out that (contrary to the conservation experiment) training sessions in the seriation experiment involved elements essential to seriation behavior, and that this may account for the difference in experimental findings.

4.5 AN INTEGRATED APPROACH

The CD and LI hypotheses need not be viewed as incompatible. First, extra-linguistic experience may be responsible for the emergence of one relation and linguistic experience for another. In particular, it seems that in respect to some of the earliest relations expressed in the two-word stage there is little plausibility to the claim that these are engendered by the linguistic input. Presumably, the child has too little linguistic material available at this stage to help him form the Agent relation, for instance. It makes little sense, intuitively, to say that only through observing how people talk about events is the child's attention drawn to the fact that there may be an agent performing an action, as this is one of the first relations to be expressed in his speech. In fact, a very plausible account within the Piagetian framework has been offered of how this relation develops through the child's interaction with his environment (Veneziano, 1973). A modicum of cognitive development must precede any learning of language, because language remains meaningless unless referring to some already interpreted aspect of the environment. However, once some structuring of the environment has occurred and some primitive utterances can be understood in accordance with this structure, there is room for an influence of the form of these utterances on the child's cognitive development: They may direct him toward further interpreting events and states referred to and toward categorizing the relations.

Second, there is no a priori reason why acquisition must be uniform over children. Conceivably, one child may learn a given distinction through extra-linguistic experience, as claimed by the CD hypothesis, whereas another child tends more to utilize linguistic input.

Finally, the two processes may operate even within a single child acquiring one particular distinction. As already pointed out, the interpretation of the environment by linguistic input must be *prepared* for by cognitive development, as a certain level of cognitive maturity is a prerequisite for such interpretation to occur. Linguistic input in its turn may, as we have seen, *prime* the perception of cognitive distinctions. What I am suggesting now is that on first dealing with a certain aspect of his surroundings the child may understand it only vaguely and imperfectly: The manner of talking about it then points the way for the child to gain a firmer grasp of the distinction in question. Alternatively, cognitive development may *facilitate* the operation of linguistic input. The lessons learned by the child in his interaction with the environment subsequently converge on those he learns from the language describing this environment. To use a metaphor of Quine's (1960, p. 93): "The child scrambles up an intellectual chimney supporting himself against each side by pressure against the other."

To illustrate, take again the case of proper and common nouns. The three possible sources of the child's acquiring the notions underlying these categories have already been discussed earlier: (1) the child may learn to individuate people and dogs through his experience with them; (2) he may learn the distinction via that between two (linguistically defined) classes of nouns, viz. those that are preceded by articles (" a boy," "the boy") and those which are not ("John"); and (3) he may learn the distinction between these two classes by direct instruction. According to the cognitive viewpoint, learning proceeds by means of (1), whereas the LI hypothesis would ascribe learning of the distinction to (2) and/or (3). A further possibility is that learning occurs through the interplay of (1), (2), and (3). The child is alerted to noticing the formal distinctions of (2) through his extralinguistic experience, which has already led him toward individuating people and dogs, and conversely, the linguistic distinctions of (2) reinforce his extralinguistic experience. Cognitive development and linguistic input may thus be mutually supportive.

A similar example is the distinction between mass and count nouns. This may have been mastered by the linguistic cues that differentiate between them, as pointed out by Quine (1960, p. 90 ff.). Extralinguistic cues are correlated with these; thus, "sugar," "water," and "flour" on the one hand differ from "apple," "candy," and "horse," on the other. Either of these sets of cues may serve to teach the child the underlying semantic distinction, but there may also be a convergence of these two types of cues.

In German, where proper nouns may be preceded by the definite article, linguistic cues, (2), may be much less effective for learning the proper/common noun distinction, and in Russian and other languages that have no articles, (2) will not operate at all. The relative contribution of extralinguistic and linguistic experience may thus differ from language to language. Moreover, it may differ even for different children learning the same language. Conceivably, one child may learn the distinction between common and proper nouns primarily, or even exclusively, through extralinguistic experience, whereas another child learns the same distinction in the same language primarily through the linguistic input from adult speakers. How the interpretation problem is solved will depend therefore (1) on the distinction learned; (2) on the language learned; and (3) on the individual child.

CONCLUSION

In psychological theorizing, as in most endeavors, it is usually not wise to side with the extremists. An extreme standpoint may serve to clarify a possibility, but in general an either/or approach will turn out to be unwarranted. Thus, after a largely sterile debate on the nature–nurture issue, the either/or approach was abandoned. I therefore propose that it is not *either* cognitive development *or* linguistic input that determines linguistic growth but an interaction between these factors, which will almost certainly reveal itself to be much more complex than the foregoing discussion makes it appear.

This chapter closes Part I in which some basic themes have been presented on which the theory of language-learning theory—or, rather outlines for such a theory—developed in Part II are based. In Part II we do not concern ourselves with the undoubtedly important issue of cognitive development that precedes language learning and makes it possible, but concentrate, instead, on the actual acquisition processes. It is shown how these processes lead not only to the mastery of rules governing speaking and understanding but also—and as a concomitant of rule learning—to the formation of underlying categories on which these rules operate. The first two chapters of Part II deal with the formation of categories underlying words, and the succeeding chapters with the formation of relational categories that are realized in speech by various grammatical devices.

REFERENCES

Blank, M. Cognitive functions of language in the pre-school years. *Developmental Psychology*, 1974, *10*, 229–245.

Blank, M. Mastering the intangible through language. In D. Aaronson & R. W. Rieber (Eds.), *Developmental psycholinguistics and communication disorders*. Annuals of the New York Academy of Science, 1975, *263*, 44–58.

Bloom, L. *One word at a time: The use of single-word utterances before syntax*. The Hague: Mouton, 1973.

Bloom, L., Lightbown, P., & Hood, L. Structure and variation in child language. *Monographs of the Society for Research in Child Development*. 1975, *40* (2, Serial No. 160).

Bloom, L., Miller, P., & Hood, L. Variation and reduction as aspects of competence in language development. In A. Pick (Ed.), *Minnesota symposia on child psychology*, (Vol. 9) Minneapolis: University of Minnesota Press, 1975.

Bowerman, M. Structural relationships in children's utterances: Syntactic or semantic? In T. E. Moore (Ed.), *Cognitive development and the acquisition of language*. New York: Academic Press, 1973.

Bowerman, M. Semantic factors in the acquisition of rules for word use and sentence construction. In D. M. Morehead & A. E. Morehead (Eds.), *Normal and deficient language*. Baltimore: University Park Press, 1976.

Braine, M.D.S. Children's first word combinations. *Monographs of the Society for Research in Child Development*, 1976, *41*, (1, Serial No. 164).

Brown, R. *Words and things*. Glencoe, Ill.: Free Press, 1958.

Brown, R. *Social psychology*. New York: Free Press, 1965.

Brown, R. *A first language: The early stages*. Cambridge, Mass.: Harvard University Press, 1973.

Bruner, J. S. The ontogenesis of speech acts. *Journal of Child Language*, 1975, *2*, 1–19.

Bruner, J. S., Olver, R. R., & Greenfield, P. M. *Studies in cognitive growth*. New York: Wiley, 1966.

Carmichael, L., Hogan, H. P., & Walter, A. A. An experimental study of the effect of language on the production of visually perceived form. *Journal of Experimental Psychology*, 1932, *15*, 73–86.

Carter, A. L. The transformation of sensorimotor morphemes into words: A case study of the development of "more" and "mine." *Journal of Child Language*, 1975, *2*, 233–250.

Cassirer, E. *The philosophy of symbolic forms. Vol. I: Language*. New Haven: Yale University Press, 1953.

Clark, E. Strategies and the mapping problem in first language acquisition. In J. Macnamara (Ed.), *Language learning and thought*. New York: Academic Press, 1977.

Cromer, R. F. The development of language and cognition: The cognition hypothesis. In B. Foss (Ed.), *New Perspectives in child development*. Harmondsworth, England: Penguin, 1974.

Daniel, T. C. Nature of the effect of verbal labels on recognition memory for form. *Journal of Experimental Psychology*, 1972, *96*, 152–157.

De Rivera, J. Some conditions governing the use of the cue-producing response as an explanatory device. *Journal of Experimental Psychology*, 1959, *57*, 299–304.

Edwards, D. Sensory-motor intelligence and semantic relations in early child grammar. *Cognition*, 1973, *2*, 395–434.

Edwards, D. Constraints on actions: A source of early meanings in child language. Unpublished paper, 1976.

Furth, H. G., & Youniss, J. Formal operations and language: A comparison of deaf and hearing adolescents. *International Journal of Psychology*, 1971, *6*, 49–66.

Goldin-Meadow, S. J. The representation of semantic relations in a manual language created by deaf children of hearing parents: A language you can't dismiss out of hand. Technical Report 26. Philadelphia: University of Pennsylvania, 1975.

Greenfield, P. M., Nelson, K., & Saltzman, E. The development of rulebound strategies for manipulating seriated cups: A parallel between action and grammar. *Cognitive Psychology*, 1972, *3*, 291–310.

Greenfield, P. M., & Smith, J. H. *The structure of communication in early language development*. New York: Academic Press, 1976.

Hartmann, H. *Das Passiv*. Heidelberg: Winter, 1954.

Herman, D. T., Lawless, R. H., & Marshall, R.W. Variables in the effect of language on the reproduction of visually perceived forms. *Perception and Motor Skills*, 1957, *7*, 171–186.

Katz, P. A. Effects of labels on children's perception and discrimination learning. *Journal of Experimental Psychology*, 1963, *66*, 423–428.

Katz, N., Baker, E., & Macnamara, J. What's in a name? A study of how children learn common and proper names. *Child Development*, 1974, *45*, 469–473.

Macnamara, J. The cognitive basis of language learning in children. *Psychological Review*, 1972, *79*, 1–13.

McNeill, D. Semiotic Extension. In R. L. Solso (Ed.), *Information processing and cognition*: *The Loyola Symposium*. Hillsdale, N.J.: Lawrence Erlbaum Associates, 1975.

McNeill, D. Speech and thought. In I. Markova (Ed.), *The social context of language*. Chichester: Wiley, 1978.

Morehead, D. M., & Morehead, A. From signal to sign: A Piagetian view of thought and language during the first two years. In R. L. Schiefelbusch & L. L. Lloyd (Eds.), *Language perspectives—Acquisition, retardation and intervention*. Baltimore: University Park Press, 1974.

Nelson, K. Concept, word and sentence. Interrelations in acquisition and development. *Psychological Review*, 1974, *81*, 267–285.

Quine, W. V. *Word and object*. Cambridge, Mass.: MIT Press, 1960.

Rodgon, M. M., Jankowski, W., & Alenskas, L. A multi-functional approach to single-word usage. *Journal of Child Language*, 1977, *4*, 23–43.

Rosch, E. H. On the internal structure of perceptual and semantic categories. In T. E. Moore (Ed.), *Cognitive development and the acquisition of language*. New York: Academic Press, 1973.

Schlesinger, I. M. Is there a natural word-order? In W. von Raffler-Engel & Y. Lebrun (Eds.), *Baby talk and infant speech*. Amsterdam: Swets & Zeitlinger, 1976.

Schlesinger, I. M. The role of cognitive development and linguistic input in language acquisition. *Journal of Child Language*, 1977, *4*, 153–169.

Sinclair-de Zwart, H. *Acquisition du langage et développement de la pensée: Sous-systèmes linguistiques et opérations concrètes*. Paris: Dunod, 1967.

Sinclair, H. Sensorimotor action patterns as a condition for the acquisition of syntax. In R. Huxley & E. Ingram (Eds.), *Language acquisition: Models and methods*. London: Academic Press, 1971.

Sinclair-de Zwart, H. Language acquisition and cognitive development. In T. E. Moore (Ed.), *Cognitive development and the acquisition of language*. New York: Academic Press, 1973.

Slobin, D. I. Comments on "Developmental Psycholinguistics." In F. Smith & G. A. Miller (Eds.), *The genesis of language: A psycholinguistic approach*. Cambridge, Mass.: MIT Press, 1966.

Slobin, D. I. Cognitive prerequisites for the development of grammar. In C. A. Ferguson & D. I. Slobin (Eds.), *Studies in child development*. New York: Holt, Rinehart & Winston, 1973.

Veneziano, E. Analysis of wish sentences in the one-word stage of language acquisition: A cognitive approach. Unpublished Master's thesis, Tufts University, 1973.

Von Raffler-Engel, W. *Il prelinguaggio infantile*. Brescia: Paideia, 1964.

Waismann, F. The resources of language. In M. Black (Ed.), *The importance of language*. Englewood Cliffs, N.J.: Prentice-Hall, 1962.

Wells, G. Learning to code experience through language. *Journal of Child Language*, 1974, *2*, 243–269.

PART II

5 Acquisition of Words: The First Steps

When they named any thing, and as they spoke turned towards it, I saw and remembered that they called what they would point out by the name they uttered . . . . And thus by constantly hearing words, as they occurred in various sentences, I collected gradually for what they stood.

—St. Augustine, *Confessions*

INTRODUCTION

In chapter 3 we introduced the notion of I-marker, the relational structure that underlies speech. An I-marker consists of protoverbal elements between which certain semantic relations hold. The protoverbal elements are expressed by words, and the relations by various grammatical means, such as word order, inflections, and function words. The relationships involved here can be summarized by the formula: protoverbal element is to word as I-marker is to sentence. The development of relational categories that figure in I-markers has been outlined briefly in Chapter 3, and the issue will be taken up again in the last three chapters. We now turn to the problem of the origin of protoverbal elements—the 'concepts' that underlie words.[1]

[1]Two previous versions of this chapter were circulated. I am grateful to the following persons for their valuable comments on these versions: Moshe Anisfeld, Marion Blank, Roger Brown, Eve Clark, Herbert Clark, Jerry Fodor, Etha Frenkel, Howard Kendler, Hilary Putnam, Charles Osgood, John Macnamara, Lise Menn, Katherine Nelson, Anat Ninio, Willard Quine, Walburga von Raffler Engel, Benny Shanon, and an anonymous reviewer. I have learned from all of them, but naturally, none of them will be pleased with all that appears in this final version.

One view, which has recently been advocated by various writers, is that these concepts antedate the acquisition of words. Huttenlocher (1974, pp. 355-356), for instance, writes about "unitary cohesive elements of experience," which subsequently are linked to a word. This is in accord with the general thesis of the primacy of cognitive development, which has been discussed in the previous chapter. In this chapter it is argued in further detail that there is not sufficient evidence for the assumption that the child learns words by linking a sequence of speech sounds to a previously existing concept. (Here and in the following, *concept* is used in the sense of category). Instead, it is proposed that the formation of these concepts is a concomitant of learning words.

Learning words can occur in two quite different ways. One is that outlined by St. Augustine in the quote that heads this chapter: The word is heard in connection with what it refers to. This is how the child's first words must be learned. Only after he has mastered a stock of words in this manner will the child be able to acquire additional words by hearing them uttered in a verbal context, as when the word's meaning is explained to him, or when he figures out from the context what the word means. This further stage is dealt with in the next chapter.

This reference to the Augustinian view of language acquisition may seem strange to those acquainted with the attacks made on it. And, indeed, this classical view is insufficient in at least two respects. First, it does not deal—nor does it purport to deal—with the acquisition of those words that do not refer to anything the adult caretaker might "turn toward." These words will have to be learned from the verbal context, and the discussion of the processes involved here is deferred to the next chapter. The view is insufficient also in that it ignores a fundamental aspect of acquisition. Words do not stand for specific referents but for classes of things, of actions, or of properties, and so on. What needs to be explained, then, is how words come to refer, not to what philosophers call particulars, but to universals: How "dog" comes to mean not a certain dog, but any dog. The short passage from St. Augustine does not deal with this at all.

Still, the Augustinian observation is basically correct, as far as it goes: The child's first words are learned by being linked to their referents. The first section of this chapter discusses this process briefly. The next three sections then explain how the word comes to stand for a universal, a concept—or, in our terminology, for a protoverbal element. The explanation given does not require the assumption of any prelinguistic concepts. A comparison with other approaches follows in section 5.5. The final section then examines critically the thesis that there are prelinguistic concepts to which words are linked. In the following chapter we discuss further stages in the acquisition of words.

Our account in this chapter does not start from scratch. Before the child uses words he may engage in "conversations" with others through actions and gestures; these interchanges may be viewed as a preparatory stage for the acquisition of language, as shown by Bruner (1975). Furthermore, the child may also express internal states and react to ongoing events by making sounds that cannot be considered words that refer, as described by Dore, Franklin, Miller, and Ramer (1976). These precursors to the use of words, important as they are, are not dealt with here.

5.1   REFERENT PAIRING

The earliest words acquired by the child are mostly those he hears in conjunction with their referents. We call this REFERENT PAIRING. The term "referent" is used here and in the following not only for objects denoted by words, but also for actions ("kick"), states and properties ("big"), events and social situations ("hi," "goodnight"). (This classification is not meant to be either exhaustive or mutually exclusive; see Bowerman [1976, p. 127] on the vague boundaries between these classes). Although for convenience of exposition most of our examples will pertain to the acquisition of words for objects, the claims made will also be applicable, mutatis mutandis, to other words that are acquired through referent pairing.

It is proposed, then, that the first step of learning a word is by pairing it with a referent (i.e., a specific object, person, action, event, etc.); we call this a PAIRED REFERENT. As a result, the word will be stored in memory alongside the paired referent. To be precise we should say, alongside an internal representation of the paired referent, but for convenience the less cumbersome formulation is used here occasionally. When the sound of the word is then heard on another occasion, this internal representation will be activated (in neo-behavioristic terms, the word gives rise to the mediated response associated with it). At this stage the child cannot yet be said to "understand" the word (in the usual sense of "understand"), because the latter is still linked to a specific previously experienced referent, and not, as in the adult speaker, to a category. In other words, the word does not yet stand for a concept, but only for a particular instance of a concept. Referent pairing is therefore only the first step in learning the meaning of a word; further steps are discussed in the next two sections.

One of the results of referent pairing is, as stated, that on hearing the word, the child may be reminded of its referent. Another possibility is that when the child once again comes across the paired referent, he will utter the word it was paired with (or an approximation to this word). In doing so, he may be using the word to label the referent, or else he may use it in lieu of a sentence: to say something about the referent, to ask for it, etc. (see section 7.3).

Nothing new can be added here concerning the mechanism that makes such learning possible: how the child is reinforced, whether he learns by imitation or passively (see, however, section 7.4). Nor do I intend to plot here the rate and course of learning, or discuss the disuse that words, once learned, often fall into (Stern & Stern, 1928/1968, pp. 177-178; Bloom, 1973, pp. 79-80). Our concern in this chapter is with certain problems with which the theory of word acquisition is beset. The first of these problems, to be considered in the following, is raised by the notion of referent pairing itself: How does one pair a word with a particular referent?

That this is indeed a problem becomes clear through the following consideration. The notion of referent pairing implies that when the adult utters a word in a given situation, the child will single out an aspect of the situation as paired referent. How does it come about that he chooses precisely the aspect intended by the adult? After all, "cookie" might refer to the act of eating it, or, perhaps to mother's hand that holds it, or to the coating on the cookie. If nothing is to go awry, there must be some sort of tacit understanding between adult and child on this point. Presumably, one aspect of the situation will stand out more saliently than others, for the adult as well as for the child, and this is what the word spoken by the adult refers to. When approaching the child with food, the mother will mention either the food or the action of eating because this is what is salient in the situation to both of them; it would be a rare mother who would name instead the child's ear or the sleeve of her own dress. Again, there is natural preference for attending to whole objects rather than to their parts (e.g., to the whole cookie rather than to its coating), as is suggested by the observations of Ninio and Bruner (1978; cf. also Quine, 1973, p. 54, on body-mindedness). Child and adult must have a shared view of the world, as pointed out by Bruner (1974/1975), who also presents some speculations of how this shared view is attained.

Furthermore, the adult tends to facilitate the referent pairing process: When he pronounces the name of an object it will usually be one at which the child is already looking (Newport, Gleitman, & Gleitman, 1977, pp. 139-140). Often he will indicate what he is talking about by pointing at the referent or by looking at it—"turning toward" it, in St. Augustine's words. But this does not yet solve our problem; for, one may go on to ask, how does the child come to construe the pointing gesture correctly? In this connection it has been suggested by Quine (1973) that pointing involves movement and contrast, and thereby heightens the salience of the referent: "The scene is enlivened by the conspicuous intrusion of a finger in the foreground of a chosen object, or by the motion of a finger outlining a chosen region" [p. 44; see also Price, 1962, pp. 169-173].

Now it may appear to us that in many cases of referent pairing the available clues for disambiguating the referent may fail. The pointing finger may be off the mark (especially when an action, a part of an object, or one of its properties is intended), and occasionally what is salient for the child at the moment is not what is salient for the adult. This may be so; but note that the child need not learn a new word on its first occurrence. Typically he will hear it again and again, and the repeated occurrence of pointing and the repeated operation of saliency will have a chance to correct the occasionally occuring mistake. Further, the child not only hears the word, but eventually produces it, and his usage either is or is not approved by adults. As a consequence, his usage eventually converges on the accepted one.

Here, however, a new problem arises. If the child is dependent on repeated experiences of a word, how does he recognize the word when he hears it again? After all, the adult will not always repeat the word with the same intonation and pitch. The child, then, must learn to regard various different sounds as instances of one and the same word. In learning the physical aspect of the word he faces a task parallel to that faced in learning its meaning, namely, how to move from the particular to the universal, from a specific sound experienced on a given occasion to the word in its various physical manifestations (as pointed out to me by John Macnamara in personal communication, 1978).

Presumably, categorization of sounds is in its turn facilitated by referent pairing; that is, sounds that are sufficiently similar to each other will be classified as belonging to the same word when they are linked to the same referent. But note that "the same" is imprecise here. Often the word is paired with referents of the same kind, and even if it is the same object that is referred to on various occasions, it will look a little different (due to differences of lighting, angle at which it is viewed, and so on). Referents of a word are never quite the same, just as the physical aspects of a word are never quite the same. If the child is to learn from repeated experiences with the word-referent combination, he must recognize similarity *both* in the situations the words are uttered in and in the acoustic aspects of the word. These two tasks are mutually supporting; to borrow Quine's (1960, p. 93) metaphor, "The child scrambles up an intellectual chimney, supporting himself against each side by pressures against the others."

The child, then, must solve two problems simultaneously: categorization of referents and categorization of sounds. Categorization of referents is a central problem in word acquisition that occupies us in the following two sections; here we have drawn attention to and outlined a solution of, the seemingly minor problem of categorization of sounds.

5.2   INITIAL GENERALIZATION

As a consequence of referent pairing the child may tend to produce the word on meeting with an object (event, situation, etc.) that is in some way similar to those which the word was first paired with. The mechanism at work here is generalization. What may lead to generalization is some perceived similarity to the situation in which referent pairing first occurred. (Clark [1974] has reviewed findings on perceptual dimensions that are salient to the young child and which may therefore form the basis for such generalization.)

But, interestingly, children may also generalize on the basis of contiguity, that is, when something in the situation has been experienced previously in association with the paired referent (Anglin, 1977). The child who sees mummy's clothes may say "mummy", and "nose" may be said in response to a handkerchief. The reason for this may be that the word had been linked not to a single aspect of the situation (mummy), but to several such aspects (mummy and clothes) (Bloom & Lahey, 1978, p. 120), or to the situation as a whole. Consequently, whenever something is perceived by the child as similar to *one* of the aspects of this situation, he will utter the word. Another possibility is that the child is "commenting rather than naming" (Anisfeld, in press, ch. 4). The word serves the child as a primitive means of expressing a relation, as Greenfield and Smith (1976, p. 215) have proposed (see section 7.3). Thus, "mummy" may have been intended to mean "These clothes are mummy's."

Here and in the following we speak of generalization both when what is responded to by a word was experienced in contiguity with a paired referent and when generalization is based on similarity. The modifying adjective in the term "initial generalization" intends to impress on us that this is only a step in the process of learning the meaning of the word. For not only is it patently incorrect to identify the meaning of a word with a specific paired referent; it is also incorrect that the word means simply everything that somehow resembles the paired referent or was experienced in contiguity with it. To learn the meaning of a word does not involve merely linking it to certain particular referents, but rather linking it to a category of referents (that is, a concept). This means that the child must be able to tell apart (at least in most cases) what belongs to the category from what does not belong to it, what merits the use of the word and what does not. Although similarity may be the basis for categorization, perception of similarity in itself does not constitute categorization. Note that anything may at one time or another be perceived as similar in some aspect to the paired referent. Hence, similarity by itself does not provide sufficient means for distinguishing between instances and noninstances of a category.

In fact, initial generalization will often result in using a word in a way that differs from adult usage. The most frequently reported errors are those in which the child overextends the use of a word (Leopold, 1949, pp. 147-150; Clark, 1973), as when he calls a donkey "rabbit." Underextensions also occur, as when the child uses "hot" for hot objects but not for hot weather (Leopold, 1949, pp. 150-152; further examples are quoted in Anglin, 1977, pp. 105-106; and Bowerman, 1976, p. 117); and sometimes there is partial overlap between the child's extension and that of the adult (Schlesinger, 1974, p. 138). Recently it has been contended that at first the child goes through a short period in which underextension is the rule (Bowerman, 1976, p. 129; Nelson, Rescorla, Gruendel, Benedict, 1978; for contrary claims see Anglin, 1977, pp. 124-128; Bloom, 1973, pp. 76-77; and Nelson & Nelson, 1978). This is understandable if we remember that generalization on the basis of similarity is a matter of degree and that, presumably, the child's tendency to say a word is at first much weaker than later, when he has had more practice with it. As a consequence, he may use the word only for instances resembling a paired referent very closely. Moreover, increasing experience and familiarity with his surroundings presumably makes him more alert to those aspects in new instances in which they are similar to a paired referent. This may lead to extending the use of the word to these new instances (which may be in accordance with adult usage, but sometimes may constitute an overextension, from the adult viewpoint). An explanation of early underextensions and overextensions within the Piagetian framework has been proposed by Anisfeld (in press, ch. 4).

A further characteristic of the child's early generalizations is that they may result in a word being used not for a single concept (as it typically is in adult language), but for a number of notions loosely related to each other. Bowerman (1976, 1978) reports on the frequent occurrence of so-called associative complexes. Her daughter Eva, for instance, learned the word "kick" when kicking a ball, and at 17-20 months of age used it on various occasions, when seeing a fluttering moth or a picture of a kitten with a ball in its paw, before throwing something, or when pushing her stomach against a mirror. Each of these instances has something in common with the original referent of "kick," but some of them seem to have nothing in common with the other referents: The basis of generalization changes from occasion to occasion. Similar findings have been reported by Thomson and Chapman (1977). Such instability of word use was also observed under experimental conditions by Nelson and Bonvillian (1973).

To summarize, initial generalization often leads to incorrect word use. Generalization may not go far enough, and then we have underextension, or else it may go too far, with the result of overextension of word use.

Generalization is a prerequisite for categorization, but to achieve that categorization which makes for acceptable use of words, additional processes have to occur.

The next section deals with the step that follows initial generalization: The child learns to link the word to a relatively stable category in correspondence to adult usage.

5.3 CATEGORIZATION

After a word has been linked to one or more paired referents, the limits of its applicability must be established. In part this is achieved by the process of referent pairing discussed in the foregoing. When the child does not generalize a word sufficiently (i.e., he underextends), he may hear the word paired with additional referents, and thus come to extend the use of the word. However, in other cases the process of referent pairing does not suffice to solve the categorization problem. In the following, a solution is proposed which does not presuppose that the child has formed concepts prior to learning words. The proposal involves two processes. One is the familiar process of discrimination learning. The other process is hypothesized here following work by Posner and Keele (1968, 1970); Rosch (1977; Rosch & Mervis, 1975); Tversky (1977); Smith, Shoben, and Rips (1974); and Clark (1973), and may be called POSITIVE CUE EXTRACTION. The account given in this and the following section has also been influenced by Price (1962).

Let us now look at these two processes, each in its turn.

Discrimination Learning

Discrimination learning ensues when adult use of a word conflicts with that of the child. The process will be somewhat as follows: (1) the child encounters something that reminds him of a paired referent, whether because it resembles it or because it was previously experienced in contiguity with it; (2) the adult uses for this new instance a word which differs from that learned for the paired referent; and subsequently (3) the child notices certain salient attributes in which the new instance differs from the paired referent. For instance, (1) the child sees a horse that reminds him of the referent of the previously learned word "doggie"; (2) the adult calls it "horse"; and (3) the child notices that the horse, unlike doggie, has a mane. The latter property may henceforward operate as a discriminating cue: It will be a NEGATIVE CUE for the word "doggie", and a POSITIVE CUE for the word "horse".

Discrimination learning thus acts as an antidote to overextension: The child learns for certain referents that they do not fall under the province of "doggie". (Kendler and Kendler [1975, pp. 228-230] have recently suggested that this development involves the child's transition from a single-stage paradigm to a two-stage, mediational paradigm). As the aforementioned example shows, discrimination may occur without the child actually committing an overextension by uttering the word he is reminded of: He may not actually say "doggie," for instance, but merely notice a resemblance with previously encountered paired referents (dogs), and hear the adult use a different word. Alternatively, he may actually exclaim "doggie" and be told the correct name by the adult; and again both a positive and a negative cue will be acquired. When the adult merely rejects the child's use of the word without offering an alternative, there will be only a negative cue (when there is a mane, it is not "doggie").

To forestall a possible misunderstanding, I want to point out that this earlier discussion is intended to explain how the child delimits the use of *words*, and not how he acquires distinctions between things. That is, the previously discussed process is not claimed to lead to his distinguishing between, for example, dogs and horses. On the contrary, the ability to make such a distinction—on the basis of differentiating properties, such as the horse's mane—is presupposed here (for, otherwise, how could he ever find out when to use "doggie" and when to use "horse"). The child may become aware of the difference between a horse and a dog—or between two different dogs, for that matter—without adult prompting. The issue here, however, is the child's use of words: To learn the correct use of a word it is not sufficient just to perceive differences between referents, but the child must also observe how these differences correlate with the applicability and nonapplicability of the word. (Conceivably, the differences the child becomes alerted to by the adult's use of a word may be those that might have been overlooked otherwise; but this is inconsequential for the issue under discussion).

Cues And Properties

The notion of cue is in need of some elaboration here. Cues may originate in perceptual configurations (e.g., a mane and hoofs), including dynamic characteristics (such as the specific gait of a horse) and various structural relations (such as the spatial relations of the animal's eyes, ears, and nose). Moreover, functional aspects may serve as cues: The child may notice what someone does with a referent (e.g., rides a horse) or what he himself does with it.

In our terminology, a cue is a property that serves for the classification of referents into a category. Accordingly, not all properties of an object (or an action, event, state, etc.) are cues. But a property x may become a cue for membership in category C. As a result, when something is perceived as having property x, it may be taken to belong to category C. In other words, I propose that a distinction be made between aspects of the environment—which may be called "properties," "attributes," or "characteristics"—and the psychological construct involved in categorization, for which the term "cue" is to be reserved. Such a distinction has usually not been observed by writers on the subject.

An important qualification has now to be made to the claim that perception of property x which is a cue for category C leads to classifying the bearer of the property as belonging to category C. Categorization is based on similarity of properties, not their identity. Consider that the child who has isolated a property as a discriminating cue will normally not encounter any instance with a property that he perceives as exactly identical to the property of a previously encountered instance. Thus, on each further occasion of seeing a horse he may see a mane or hoof which is similar to those seen at the time of discrimination learning, or observe a gait similar to that noticed originally, etc. Such resemblance is sufficient for the cue to operate, and the greater the resemblance, the more potent the cue will be for the purpose of categorization. Note the parallel to the process of initial generalization after referent pairing. The adult use of a word in association with a property gives rise to generalization—to bearers of similar properties.

But, it might be objected, in talking about similarity between such complex properties one leaves open the question of how similarity is to be defined. Recent attempts to come to grips with the notorious problem of similarity employ the notion of feature. Features are elementary attributes, and the degree of similarity between x and y is taken to be the degree to which their features match (Tversky, 1977). It appears, in fact, that as far as certain verbs and adjectives are concerned, such elementary features are useful constructs for the description of the learning process (see, e.g., Clark, 1973, and section 6.2). Specifically, the child learns to discriminate between complementaries (like "give" and "take") and opposites (like "big" and "little") by finding out which single elementary feature distinguishes between them.

It is significant, however, that such distinctions, based on a single elementary feature, are precisely those mastered by the child rather late in the course of language acquisition. Among the words he learns early are those denoting objects, and here the discriminating properties are much more global ones. There hardly seem to be any two objects for which the small child will usually have to learn two names and which differ only in that one of them is, say, round whereas the other is square, or that one is red and the other is green. The child may of course learn to discriminate between such objects—for instance, between red, edible apples and green ones for cooking—but there are few instances in which he will have to learn separate names for objects differing in only a few such features. Nor will he learn names for objects differing in more than one such dimension (e.g., a red and round vs. green and square one); such discriminations are common in the laboratory experiment, not in language learning. The object categories he learns to name normally differ in a large number of dimensions, and not only that but these are interrelated in complex ways. The child learning to discriminate between a dog and a horse presumably is not helped by attending to their overall color (a dog and a horse may even not differ in color), but to their ears, feet, snouts, and tails, each of which has a particular shape and coloring (see Thomson & Chapman, 1977). Or else he observes that a dog brings the slippers and is petted, whereas the horse is involved in quite different kinds of events. It is these global perceptual configurations that become cues for categories. Ultimately, such properties will be reducible into complex structures of elementary features, and this should make it possible, in principle, to extend to them Tversky's (1977) formalization of the concept of similarity. At any rate, it seems beyond question that the properties of two objects (or even of the same object) perceived at different points in time will normally be not identical, but only similar.

Extraction Of Positive Cues

Discrimination learning is presumably not sufficient for learning the extension of a word. The process cannot take place unless the child encounters things (actions, properties, etc.) which are sufficiently similar to the original referent for generalization to occur and which are moreover sufficiently important to merit the adult's naming them. These conditions are not always met. Suppose that a child has had much experience with a particular word and has heard it applied to various instances, but has had no chance to delimit its boundaries by discrimination learning. Still, it is hardly to be expected that, when the opportunity arises, perhaps years later, he would overextend the use of the word in the manner typical of the child beginning to acquire a vocabulary. Instead, we may assume that by dint of his experience with the word he registers those properties that appear repeatedly in its referents. These properties then become cues. We call this process POSITIVE CUE EXTRACTION.

That one can extract positive cues without discrimination learning is attested to by the observation that we may form a category without having a name for it, by mere exposure to various instances. Suppose I do not know the word for seashells but have the opportunity of observing, all by myself, many seashells on the beach. No doubt there will come a time when I unfailingly recognize a new instance as being a seashell, even if it differs in shape and color from any seashell I have ever observed. In this case there was no conflict with linguistic norms that might have led to discrimination learning. It is just that different seashells have enough in common to set them off from pieces of seaweed, pebbles, dried-up jelly fish, etc., so that I do not mistake a new seashell for the latter (even if I also do not know the names of the latter).[2]

What this story suggests is that mere exposure to instances may at times be sufficient for the formation of categories, at least as far as adults are concerned. Let us now change our hypothetical example somewhat and suppose that often when I observe a seashell there is a biologist at hand who informs me: "This is another seashell." Further, suppose that, mysteriously, the biologist is never present when I stumble on seaweed, a pebble, or the like; that is, I am not afforded an opportunity for discrimination learning (because, for all I know, the biologist, had he been present, might have mumbled "seashell" also in the case of what, as a matter of fact, is a pebble). Even so, the fact that each new instance of the category is paired with a name will be very helpful to me; it will facilitate the process of extracting positive cues and, thereby, the process of categorization. (On the role of words in concept formation see Vygotsky [1962] and Stones [1970].)

Note now that the child beginning to learn words is amply provided with this kind of assistance: Very often, when he perceives a new instance of a category, the adult will name it. The name serves as a reminder of one or more previously experienced paired referents, which are then compared with the new instance. The child may then notice properties of the new instance as being similar to those of a previously paired referent, and these properties may then become cues. (Of course, not all these processes need to be carried out intentionally or with full awareness.) For example, after having learned the word "horse" through referent pairing, the child may see another horse and hear the adult say "horse". This name reminds him of the horse with which the word had been paired before (either the first time "horse" was paired with a horse, or on one of the later occasions of such referent pairing). As a result he may notice—perhaps for the first time—say, the hoofs that both these instances have in common. This then

---

[2]That there are clusters of attributes that set off categories of objects is the burden of Rosch's (1977) research.

becomes a positive cue, which on any further occurrence will lead to assigning to its bearer the word "horse".[3]

This process may then be repeated. The next time the word is paired with a referent, the same cue may be noticed again, and this cue will be strengthened as a consequence (see the discussion of cue values further on). Another, no less important consequence of repetition may be that a new positive cue is extracted. Positive cues may thus accrue gradually through successive comparisons of paired referents. Now, each such comparison may be with only one previously experienced paired referent. This has the following important implication: Once an encounter with a new instance has resulted in extraction of a positive cue, there is no need to remember that particular instance, because the process of cue extraction may be repeated with any other previously stored paired referent. A single paired referent is sufficient. The cue may be stored and the instance leading to its extraction discarded.

The earlier description of positive cue extraction is an explication of the traditional notion of abstraction. According to one classic view, a universal, or concept, is formed by abstracting from particular instances those elements or attributes that are common to all of them. This view has been criticized as involving an unduly large load on human processing capacity and being too time-consuming (Nelson, 1974). This is indeed so, if abstraction of common elements is conceived of as involving a process which requires that all relevant exemplars are stored and later compared at one go. If, however, abstraction is viewed as a process based on successive comparisons—as suggested here—this objection loses its force. As stated, each such comparison is performed between only a few—perhaps only two—exemplars at a time, and there is thus no need to store all exemplars.

To recapitulate briefly, we have argued that learning words involves categorizing, and categorizing is based on the formation of cues. Cues may be formed by two processes. One is discrimination learning, which results from a clash between the child's tendency to generalize and adult usage, and the other is the less obtrusive process of positive cue extraction, resulting from repeated pairing of a given word with a referent.

The notion of discrimination learning is of course the stock-in-trade of experimental psychologists. Positive cue extraction, too, has had its share of investigation in the psychological laboratory. It presumably accounts for schemas or prototypes that have been amply demonstrated with a wide variety of materials. Thus, Posner and Keele's (1968, 1970) experiments

---

[3]Extraction of positive cues may also occur when the adult does not utter the name but the child utters it, or even only thinks it. And even this may not be necessary: The mere experience of the new instance may lead to positive cue extraction, as suggested by the seashell example. By providing a name, however, the adult greatly facilitates the process, as stated.

show that one can abstract a schema from various instances of a concept (dot patterns that are distortions of the schema), and these findings have held up under replication (Peterson, Meagher, Chait, & Gillie, 1973; Strange, Keeney, Kessel, & Jenkins, 1970). Similar results with different materials were obtained in several studies (Edmonds & Evans, 1966; Edmonds, Mueller, & Evans, 1966; Franks & Bransford, 1971; Reed, 1972; see also Klatzky & Stoy, 1974). The process of schema abstraction does not require consciousness and occurs even in animals (Posner, 1973).

When a property is isolated as a cue—through discrimination learning or positive cue extraction—its internal representation is stored along with the corresponding word. Then, when this property is subsequently observed in an object, action, event, etc., it may serve as a cue for categorizing the latter. For example, a property of a car, say, the noise of the motor, may have been isolated as a cue and its internal representation be stored with the word "car." When the noise of a motor is subsequently heard it may serve as a cue for "car," as it matches that internal representation. Henceforward, we sometimes use the term *cue* for the observable property (e.g., the noise made by the motor) as well as for its internal representation. As the context will make it clear in what sense the term is used, no confusion between these two related senses should result.

Cue Values

Referents are assigned to categories on the basis of their cues. In the next subsection, category assignment is expounded further; here we must first clarify the notion of CUE VALUE (or cue validity, as it is sometimes called).

Cues may differ in the degree they are correlated with a given category. As already noted, after a property has been singled out as a cue by positive cue extraction, the child may encounter additional exemplars of the category in question and notice the same property. The process of cue extraction will then be repeated, and each such repetition will strengthen the positive cue. Likewise, the potency of negative and positive cues will increase through repeated discriminations.

The value of a cue, x, for a given category C increases with the frequency with which it has been associated with category C. Suppose now that a property has been isolated as a cue both for category C and for category C'. The efficiency of the cue will be lowered thereby: By being associated also with C', it is a less valid predictor of C. Thus, the fact that not only horses but also lions are observed by the child to have a mane makes the cue mane a less certain indication for membership in the category 'horse.' (Perhaps he then goes on to distinguish between horses' manes and lions' manes, thus developing, again, two highly efficient cues; but this is another story.) The cue value of cue x for category C, then, decrease with the frequency with which x has been associated with categories other than C (cf. Rosch, 1977; Rosch & Mervis, 1975).

It should be noted that it is not the objective frequency of a property that determines cue value, but the frequency with which the property has been identified as a cue. Of course, these two variables are positively correlated, but the correlation is far from perfect as the child may often fail to notice a property in a referent.

Cue value is a function not only of frequency, but also of saliency. During discrimination learning, the more salient a property is at the moment for the child, the greater its value as a negative and positive cue; and similarly for positive cue extraction. This variable of saliency is not readily quantifiable and has therefore not been included in the definitions of cue validity, such as that of Rosch and Mervis (1975), although these writers recognize its importance in categorization. Experimental evidence that some cues are given preference over others in categorization is reported by Bruner, Goodnow, and Austin (1956, pp. 196-216). In addition to saliency there will presumably be other factors affecting cue value, which have to do with the conditions obtaining at the time the word is paired with the referent.

As stated, presence of a property that has previously been isolated as a cue is indicative of a category. However, assignment to a category is dependent also on other factors, such as the degree of similarity of the property noticed to the internally represented property, as becomes clear in section 5.4.

The foregoing exposition implies that cue values change as the child encounters additional instances of the category to which a word refers. These changes are not restricted to the early age at which the child learns his native language; they may continue throughout the individual's life. They may involve not only increases but also decreases of cue value, as when one finds out that what was previously held to be a positive cue is absent in an instance of the category, or is actually a negative cue (i.e., a cue found in discrimination learning to be associated with a different category; see the earlier discussion of "Discrimination Learning").

So far, we have clarified the notions of cue and cue value, and have dealt with the ways cues are arrived at. In the following section we must examine the role played by cues in the use of words.

5.4   PROTOVERBAL ELEMENTS

As pointed out before, a word does not stand for particular referents but for a category of referents. But when we use a word in speaking we often do not intend at all to refer to a category but to a specific instance of it. Thus we may intend to speak about the chair right in front of us (and not about chairs in general, or the concept of chair, or any category that includes chairs). The mapping from the specific instance to the word is therefore not a direct one. In a model of word use we therefore introduce a construct that mediates between what is to be expressed by the word and the production of the word: the PROTOVERBAL ELEMENT.

We have already had occasion to mention protoverbal elements and have described them, rather loosely, as the concepts that underlie words. Somewhat more precisely, we may now state that the protoverbal element of a word is the internal representation of what has been stored as a result of experience with referents paired with this word. Let us use single quotes for protoverbal elements; for example, for the protoverbal element associated with the word "chair" we write 'chair'. The protoverbal element 'chair', then, is all that the child has learned about what the word "chair" refers to (i.e., about the meaning of "chair"). The protoverbal element, then, contains all the cues that have been isolated through discrimination learning and positive cue extraction (and not only that; but more about this later). In our internal lexicon there is a LEXICAL ENTRY that lists the pair 'chair'-"chair", that is, a protoverbal element and the word that goes with it.

The role of the protoverbal element in word use can be briefly described as follows. In speaking (or writing), (1) what is to be referred to is ASSIGNED to a protoverbal element, and (2) a lexical look-up finds the word that corresponds to the protoverbal element (hence the term protoverbal element: to designate that out of which the word is formed). When speaking about a particular chair, we assign what we have in mind to the protoverbal element 'chair' and find the word "chair" by means of the lexical entry that lists 'chair' with "chair". (Of course, this two-stage process does not require awareness, and it may be instantaneous). Conversely when we hear (or read) a word, its protoverbal element is retrieved from the lexical entry—we understand its meaning.

It will be recalled that, in our model, the semantic structure that underlies an utterance—the I-marker—consists of protoverbal elements and the relations between them, and that this structure is mapped into an utterance by realization rules (section 3.2). Accordingly, what has been called here lexical entry is a kind of realization rule. More will be said about lexical entries in later chapters (e.g., sections 8.1, 9.2 and 9.6). Here we must deal with the question of how, in speaking, we assign what is to be expressed by a word to a protoverbal element.

Assignment To A Protoverbal Element

Our discussion of cue values in the preceding section has dealt with one of the ways an instance that is to be named is assigned to a category. The terms introduced earlier now lead to the following formulation. When one intends to name a certain instance, properties may be noticed in it which are similar to cues isolated previously in the course of learning a word. The instance will then be assigned to the protoverbal element that contains these cues.

A property noticed in the particular instance may have varying degrees of similarity to a cue (see section 5.3). The mane of a particular animal I now see before me may be more or less similar to the mane that I observed when isolating the property mane as a cue for "horse." The greater the similarity of the property now noticed to the cue, the more the latter will contribute to the assignment of its bearer to the protoverbal element that includes that cue.

Furthermore, when a property has been previously isolated as a cue, it has a cue value. Cue values have been defined above as the degree to which a property is indicative of membership in a category, and we may now state that the cue value of a property is the degree to which the latter contributes to the assignment to the protoverbal element. Negative cues (section 5.3) will counteract assignment to the protoverbal element. In other words, assignment to a protoverbal element will be a function of both negative and positive cues, each weighted by its cue value.

Note that according to this account there will not necessarily be any cue that is criterial for assignment to a protoverbal element; rather, it is the totality of cues which determine how a given exemplar is assigned. There is a traditional view according to which a concept is defined by necessary and sufficient attributes or properties. The foregoing treatment, by contrast, is in line with the view that a concept may be defined by a disjunction of attributes, and that for a given concept there may be not one single attribute common to all instances (cf. the Wittgensteinian notion of 'family resemblance').[4] It is also in accord with the approach of Rosch (1977; Rosch & Mervis, 1975), that membership of an exemplar in a category is a matter of degree.

The properties of an instance that is to be named may often provide conflicting evidence. One way such a conflict may come about is through the presence of properties that pertain to negative cues alongside those that pertain to positive ones. Assignment to a protoverbal element will then be made as a function of all cue values, as stated earlier. Two other possible sources of conflict should be mentioned:

---

[4]Of course, there may also be concepts that do have criterial attributes (or "defining attributes" [Smith, Shoben, & Rips, 1974]). In these cases, the cue in the protoverbal element is tagged as being criterial: In the absence of a property similar to it, assignment to this protoverbal element cannot be made. I suspect that such protoverbal elements are to be found mainly among those acquired later, through learning words in a linguistic context (see section 6.1) rather than by direct experience with exemplars. See Putnam (1975) for an illuminating discussion of this whole issue.

1. A given property may be a cue for more than one protoverbal element. For instance, upright ears may have been noticed to occur with dogs as well as with horses, and as a consequence, upright ears are a cue both for both 'dog' and 'horse.' When the property upright ears is then noticed in an animal, both these cues will be activated.

2. A given property may resemble two different cues. For instance, a dog's gait may have been isolated as a cue for 'dog' and a horse's gait—for 'horse.' An animal may then be observed to have a gait which is not quite like that of a dog and also not quite like that of a horse.

The outcome of such conflicts will be decided by the factors of similarity and cue value, discussed earlier, and of course it will depend on the totality of cues activated. The conflict need of course not be a conscious one. But sometimes, when the sides are almost even (that horse really looks very much like a pony, or vice versa), we may begin to waver in assigning a protoverbal element to the instance. We may then try to obtain more information about the instance to be named; for example, we may take a closer look so as to find additional properties that might be cues.

Note that the conflicts discussed here are between two categories for which there is a word (for it is such categories that protoverbal elements stand for). There may also be cases where an instance to be named resembles something for which the child knows no word. He may then assign that instance to the "nearest" protoverbal element, even though the similarity between the instance and the unnamed entity is much greater. (Essentially this is what often happens in initial generalization; see section 5.2). An adult may be more wary, and hesitate in his assignment, but when the discrepancy becomes too great, the child, too, may hesitate and inquire after the correct name. All this goes to show that assignment to a protoverbal element is dependent, among others, on the available alternatives (see also Barrett, 1978). When other protoverbal elements are good candidates, finer discriminations must be made.

So far we have discussed the role of cues in the assignment to a protoverbal element. We now come to an additional factor. Consider that when a word has been paired with a referent, the internal representation of the latter may be stored along with the word. In fact, this is presupposed by the process of initial generalization (section 5.2): The child is reminded of a previously paired referent. Likewise, those processes by which cues are formed—discrimination and positive cue extraction (section 5.3)—involve comparison of a new exemplar with the internal representation of a previously stored paired referent.[5] It is proposed that these internal representations are constituents of the protoverbal element. An instance, then, may be assigned to a protoverbal element on the basis of its resemblance to one or more previously stored paired referents.

Let us illustrate this. Suppose a child sees an animal that reminds him of a certain dog, or of several other dogs, in association with which he had heard the word "dog." The resemblance of the animal in front of him with that other dog (or those other dogs) may lead him to call it "dog"; in our present terminology, he may make the assignment to the protoverbal element 'dog.' Now, this is precisely the process of initial generalization that has been introduced in the description of the early stages of word learning (section 5.2). What I am suggesting now is that such a process may also occur at much later stages, in fact all through our lives.

There is a difference between assigning an exemplar to a protoverbal element on the basis of its resemblance to previous paired referents and doing so by means of cues. That this is so becomes clear on considering that not all properties of a paired referent will have become cues. To return to our example, suppose that of all the properties of dogs, the child has isolated (through discrimination or positive cue extraction) two cues: barking and the typical shape of a dog's snout. Suppose, further, that he now is only afforded a rear view of the particular exemplar of a dog (its snout is not seen) and the animal does not bark at the time. In other words, the previously isolated cues do not operate. Then the child may still note a resemblance to a previously seen dog (i.e., to its internal representation) in respect to other properties (e.g., gait, overall shape, etc.), and as a result make an assignment to the protoverbal element 'dog.'

Assignment to a protoverbal element, then, may be made by comparing an instance to be named to a paired referent in toto. Even though some of the information pertaining to the latter may be forgotten (see, e.g., Paivio, 1977), it will typically contain more information than the sum total of cues. If a property of an exemplar that is not a cue is similar to a property contained in the internal representation of a paired referent, this may be a factor in assigning that exemplar to the protoverbal element in question. (This does not necessarily involve awareness of having previously encountered the paired referent).

---

[5]The claim that a paired referent may be stored is supported experimentally by a study of Posner and Keele (1968), in which subjects not only abstracted a schema from dot patterns but also stored specific instances of patterns they had been exposed to. Similar findings with digit and letter strings were obtained in a study by Reitman and Bower (1973); see also Bourne and O'Banion (1969). See the discussion of a similar notion by Brooks (1978), see also Garner (1978).

Constituents Of A Protoverbal Element

In the light of the preceding discussion we must now amplify our description of protoverbal elements. A protoverbal element contains (1) cues isolated through previous experiences with a word and with the referents paired with it; and/or (2) the internal representations of (some or, at times, even all) previously encountered paired referents.[6] Note that (1) and (2) may each by themselves provide a basis for assignment to a protoverbal element. For a given protoverbal element all cues may have somehow been lost (faded from memory, we might say, but keeping in mind that no conscious memory of cues need be involved), or no cues at all have been isolated in the first place; the protoverbal element then consists only of internal representations of paired referents. Alternatively, it may be the case that no paired referents have been stored, or they may have been subsequently forgotten, and the protoverbal element consists only of cues. When (1) and (2) are present, however, they will operate jointly in the assignment of instances. Positive cues will indicate which properties of the internal representation of the paired referent are important. In other words, cues function as "footnotes" to the paired referents, stating to what degree their properties are central to the protoverbal elements (the degree being determined by the cue value).

Our discussion thus far has viewed cues and paired referent as two completely different kinds of constituents of protoverbal elements. On reflection, however, we will realize that the difference between them is mainly one of scope. Recall that a cue is an internal representation of a proper part of a paired referent, or of some aspect thereof. A cue is like an internal representation of a paired referent in that both give rise to generalization: Remember that a property noted in an exemplar resembles to a greater or lesser extent the property (of a previous paired referent) that has been isolated as a cue. Consider further that cues, like paired referents, may be subject to discrimination learning. A bushy tail may have become a cue for 'fox', but when it later turns out that animals called by other names have bushy tails, discrimination learning may set in. That is, the child will note properties that distinguish the different kinds of bushy tails—those that are cues for 'fox' and those that are not. Note now that these properties will be, in effect, cues for classifying the cue tail. When finer discriminations are subsequently made, cues of a still lower order may be called for. In short, a

---

[6]To forestall misunderstandings, let me state that the aforementioned is not intended as a full explication of word meaning; such an explication requires a much longer treatment (see Miller & Johnson-Laird, 1976). Among the issues not dealt with is the distinction (if there is one) between lexical knowledge and knowledge of the world.

protoverbal element may be conceived of as a hierarchical structure of cues, with the internal representation of a paired referent at the top of the hierarchy.

Protoverbal Elements And Images

In talking about what the child remembers as a result of referent pairing, I have clung fastidiously to the term 'internal representation'. What is the nature of these internal representations? It is tempting to conceive of them as images. However, the status of images is at present a matter of debate (see Anderson [1978] for a critical evaluation of recent arguments concerning this issue). I have therefore refrained from committing myself on this point. But our discussion seems to throw an interesting sidelight on one of the aspects of the imagery controversy, and concerning this, a few comments are made here.

There is a classic argument against the view that we think in images, which goes as follows. Much of our thinking is about concepts: We think, as we speak, of cabbages and kings, and not only of a particular cabbage or king. By contrast, an image, as Berkeley argued, is always of a particular. We can have an image of a right-angled triangle, of an obtuse one, of an equilateral or a scalene triangle, but there can be no image of a triangle which combines all these incompatible properties.

Now, this problem seems to arise only if we posit that the concept is a single unanalyzed image. If, however, we allow for the possibility that it comprises several images (which was basically Hume's proposal), the aforementioned objection does not hold. On our account, a protoverbal element may contain representations of several paired referents, and of parts and aspects of such referents (viz. cues). If each of these constituents is considered to be an image, the protoverbal element as a whole will be anything but a single unitary image, because the various hierarchically arranged paired referents and cues (see earlier discussion) will not merge into one single picture.[7] This complexity entails the advantage that the problem raised by the view of concepts as images is avoided. (Whether there is an abstract representation beyond such images is another issue that need not concern us here.)

A different solution of the Berkeleyan problem has been offered by Galton (1907), who likened the generic image to a kind of composite photograph resulting from repeated exposures of the same plate to many

---

[7]For a related view see Price (1962, pp. 287-294) who proposed that there are "inchoate" images, that have undetermined properties and may stand for universals. Compare also the Kantian schema, which is a rule for providing an image for a concept.

instances of a concept. This, however, can at best be only a partial solution. A composite photograph of various kinds of triangles would probably look like a mess, not like a triangle (see Brown, 1958, pp. 83-89; Price, 1962, pp. 284-287, for critical discussions). This notion of composite photograph is related to that of a prototype that reflects the central tendency of various instances (e.g., Posner & Keele, 1968). Such a central tendency applies only to cases (such as the abstract patterns used in their experiment) where instances differ quantitatively along one or more dimensions, not where the differences are of a more qualitative nature, that is, when discrete properties are involved. Suppose, for instance, that a child has experience with some dogs with flapping ears and others with upright ears. What would be the meaning of "central tendency" here—ears jutting out at right angles from the skull? An explanation in terms of cues accounts for this case as one where two (mutually incompatible) cues are included in the protoverbal element: A dog may have either kind of ears.

Development Of Protoverbal Elements

The formation of a protoverbal element begins as soon as the child begins to learn a word. The word is paired with referents, and the internal representations of these referents (to the extent that they are stored) constitute the protoverbal element. Then cues are isolated, and these, too, become part of the protoverbal element. Even after the child already uses a word in the way an adult does, the protoverbal element does not remain fixed and frozen. Further experience may change cue values, subjoin additonal cues and representations of paired referents, or lead to their fading out of memory. In fact, a protoverbal element may continue to change throughout the individual's lifetime, as he encounters more and more instances to which the word in question refers and as he hears or reads the word in different contexts (see section 6.1). We may speculate, however, that the greater the amount of experience which already went into the formation of a protoverbal element, the less any single additional experience will be likely to influence it, and hence the most rapid and extensive changes may be expected to occur normally in the early stages of acquiring a word.

Children will differ in their experiences that lead to the formation of a given protoverbal element. It follows (as has been pointed out to me by Deena Bernstein) that the cues, cue values, and internal representations of paired referents that constitute the protoverbal element of one person will normally differ somewhat from those that constitute the corresponding protoverbal element (i.e., the one associated with the same word) of another person. For one person, 'cat' may be an internal representation of a black cat and the cues whiskers and claws, whereas for another person it is the internal representations of spotted cats, and the cat's tail and ears may be the cues with the highest cue value. But such is the redundancy of cues that both will agree on what is and what is not to be called "cat." Their intensions may differ, whereas the extensions do not.

As the child grows older, his protoverbal elements presumably solidify to an extent, thus keeping in check the ever-present tendency to generalize words beyond accepted usage. The result is beautifully illustrated by a 27-month-old who said "a Band Aid is like a spider" (Nelson, Rescorla, Gruendel, & Benedict, 1978, p. 965). At a somewhat earlier stage the girl might have generalized from the paired referent and simply have called a band aid "spider"; but in the present instance, the protoverbal elements in question had already been well established, and so no error of classification occurred (see Winner [1979] on a differentiation between metaphors and early overextensions along similar lines).

The process of generalization never quite subsides, even after the pro-toverbal element has become firmly established. This is shown by the ubi-quitous use of metaphor (see Gardner, Kircher, Winner, & Perkins, 1975; Winner, 1979). Occasionally newly created metaphors and metonymies become incorporated into the language (particularly when the language is flexible and rapidly developing, an extreme case being the Israeli Sign Language; see Cohen, Namir, & Schlesinger, 1977).

Our discussion of protoverbal elements is resumed in the final chapter, in which the organization of the lexicon is dealt with.

5.5 A COMPARISON WITH OTHER APPROACHES

Precedence Of Concept Or Word

The present proposal differs from those of several other writers (e.g., Fodor, 1975; Huttenlocher, 1974) in that it does not assume that the child comes to the language learning task equipped with certain concepts for which he has to find verbal labels. In section 5.6 we discuss the question whether there is any independent evidence for such prelinguistic concepts. Here it should be observed that postulating such concepts does not present a solution for the problems of word acquisition, because it does nothing to clarify how the child deals with the delimitation of verbal concepts: As noted, the child may start out with rather outlandish notions, from the adult viewpoint, about the use of a word. Conversely, as we have seen in section 5.3, an explanation of how the child goes about delimiting word meanings does not require the assumption of a link between a word and a previously established concept; instead, the word may be linked to a paired referent, and the boundaries of its applicability be established subsequently through further experience with the word.

The view espoused here is, then, that learning a concept (a protoverbal element, in my terms) is a concomitant, not a prerequisite, of learning the use of a word. This is in accord with Brown (1965, pp. 315-317), who has pointed out that learning word use is a sufficient condition for learning concepts. A modified position is that of Bowerman (1976), who claims that some of the child's early words may be tags for his previously formed concepts, whereas others serve as a "lure to cognition", in Brown's (1958, p. 206) happy phrase, and lead to the formation of a concept. Nelson (1974; Nelson et al., 1978) has suggested that there is a developmental trend, the child's first words being preceded by concepts whereas at a later stage concepts may be acquired through words.[8] By contrast, the present theory posits a single acquisition process, the formation of a concept (or protoverbal element, in the present terminology) being concomitant to the acquisition of a word. (This should, of course, not be taken to deny the possibility of the child forming concepts for which no words are learned [see section 5.6]).

The view that the acquisition of words is not based on previously formed concepts is also that of Anglin (1977). Taking his lead from Posner (1973), Anglin holds that the child abstracts from particular instances a prototype or schema, which represents the central tendency of the particular instances. The prototype of a dog would be, accordingly, the "average" dog. But what could this be? As pointed out earlier, such a Galtonian approach is inapplicable to 'dog' and to many other concepts comprising a heterogeneous set of instances.

Whereas Nelson (1974) and Huttenlocher (1974) view prelinguistic concepts as arising out of the child's interaction with his environment, it has recently been claimed by Fodor (1975) that these concepts are not learned at all. The child, says Fodor, maps words into items of an internal code that is innate. Fodor believes that the empiricist approach, which views the child as constructing concepts out of primitive elements, is bound to fail. His claim, if valid, would demolish existing theories of word learning: Nelson's, Anglin's, the one presented in this chapter, and Clark's feature theory (discussed later on). I believe, however, that his arguments can be faulted. A detailed examination of Fodor's thesis would take us too far afield here, and is postponed to the final chapter (section 9.7), in which the organization of the lexicon is discussed.

---

[8]Katherine Nelson speaks about concepts that precede words. However, as she has clarified in personal communication, there is no irreconcilable difference between our views on this point because, according to her, a concept may at first be constituted of a single referent. Later experience may then modify the concept.

Hypothesis Testing

Currently, the acquisition of language as well as other learning processes are often described as hypothesis testing (already Brown's [1958, ch. 6] "original word game" was described in these terms). Although it does not exclude such a possibility, the present approach does not require the assumption that the child actively forms hypotheses or engages in a search for confirming or disconfirming evidence, as Clark (1974, p. 107), for instance, suggests. Of course, if "hypothesis testing" is used without implying awareness and intention, this whole issue dissolves into one of terminological preference.

Clark's Feature Theory

Some writers (e.g., Clark, 1973; Menyuk, 1971) conceptualize word meaning as a set of semantic features, and consider the acquisition of a word as an establishing of connections between it and such features. The affinity of this approach to the one advocated here is obvious. It will be instructive to point out the differences between my theory and Clark's feature theory.

In her theory of word acquisition, Eve Clark (1973, 1974, 1975, 1977) follows linguists like Katz (1966) and Bierwisch (1970), who hold that word meanings are decomposable into elementary semantic elements or features. For her, too, there is a "universal set of semantic primitives" (Clark, 1973, p. 76; see also Clark, 1974, p. 109), a subset of which the child links to each word. The status of the universality claim is not quite clear. On one interpretation, this claim is incorrect. As argued previously, the cues the child comes to associate with a word usually originate in perceptual configurations like a hoof, a mane, a flapping ear, and a particular gait. Thomson and Chapman (1977) also found that categorization depended on such molar properties: "The presence of eyes and nose were necessary to the word for an animate referent (both people and animals). The presence of mouth and upright posture (rather than all-fours) appeared to be additional perceptual features necessary to the overextension of words denoting people [p. 374]." Such cues can hardly be universal. They apply to dogs and horses, and not to, say, camels and kangaroos, for the recognition of which different cues are needed. In general, the cues pertinent to the concepts members of one culture are familiar with will differ from the cues that are pertinent to concepts of members of another culture. One might, of course, hold fast to the universality hypothesis by arguing that there is an indefinitely large universal set of such cues, and each speech community utilizes only a subset of these. But such a stratagem obviously renders the universality hypothesis empirically vacuous (cf. Schlesinger, 1971).

Now Clark (1973, p. 86; 1974, p. 109, footnote 2) points out that such complexes as 'canine' and 'four-legged,' which figure in feature descriptions, are really only a shorthand for perceptual and cognitive primitives. Clearly, if these primitives are taken to be very fine-grained, as those elements our perceptual apparatus works with, then they are indeed universal. On this interpretation the universality hypothesis is obviously true. Each perceptually distinguishable attribute then may become a "feature," as it may have a part to play in some perceptually complex cue. (Such a overwhelmingly large set of features will of course not be anything like the feature list of manageable proportions that linguists have in mind.) However, as argued earlier, it is not these atomic perceptual attributes that are functional in the delimitation of most early concepts but rather complex configurations of them. As stated, these configurations are, in part, specific to a culture and may even differ to some extent from one child to another within a culture.

The isolation of cues has been hypothesized here as being a somewhat advanced process, taking place in the wake of initial generalization. Clark's presentation makes it appear that features are abstracted from the beginning (Clark & Clark, 1977, p. 458). Moreover, she states that the meaning of a word *is* the features abstracted from it (Clark, 1973, p. 72; 1974, p. 108; 1977, p. 151). One way of interpreting this statement (and I am not at all certain whether Clark would subscribe to this interpretation) is that, except for the salient features, all aspects of the referent are forgotten, or at least are not functional as far as the learning process is concerned. Now, this would be a very strong and not well-motivated assumption. By contrast, the present theory posits, in addition, the storing of a representation of referents themselves. If this were not the case, positive cue extraction could not take place, because the latter process requires a comparison of the exemplar with previous ones. On the above interpretation, then, Clark's theory would therefore leave the small child with only discrimination learning to help him acquire the correct use of the word. But as shown earlier, it is rather implausible that discrimination learning is sufficient to this end.

Two further points on which the present theory differs from that of Clark should be mentioned here: (1) Unlike Clark, I have introduced negative as well as positive cues (see also Barrett, 1978); (2) Clark speaks of features always as binary—as either present or absent. By contrast, I conceive of cues as being operative to a greater or lesser degree. Similarity of properties, rather than their identity, has been claimed here to play a role both in positive cue extraction and in the assignment of an instance to a protoverbal element. But in principle an adaptation of Clark's theory is possible in which features would be present to different degrees.

Instability Of Word Use

Any theory of word acquisition must account for the many shifts that the child's word use undergoes. As shown in section 5.2, the child's use of a word may be overextended or underextended, or it may partially overlap that of the adult, or he may engage in associative complexes, etc., and these uses not only vary between children but even within a single child. Such instability is to be expected on our account, that in the early stages of word acquisition the child has not yet a concept but rather applies the word in each single case on the basis of initial generalization. Naturally, such generalizations are subject to momentary influences and the child will not adhere to them steadfastly. Within Clark's framework, these phenomena must be dealt with in terms of addition and deletion of features. To get rid of overextension the child adds features, underextension necessitates deletion of features, and partial overlap—both addition and deletion. Associative complexes are taken to be "partial overextensions" in which "the child might pick out only some of the criterial properties he has identified with the meaning of a word when he overextends it [Clark, 1975, p. 80]."

It might be admissible to have features that are fickle; it seems less sound to hypothesize inconstant concepts. The instability of early word use creates a problem for a theory that links words to previously existing concepts, because these phenomena apparently indicate that "a concept [is] undergoing constant change [Nelson, Rescorla et al., 1978]." Let us see how such a theory might deal with the facts.

One common approach to the problem is to argue that early word use may fail to reflect what the child really knows about the word's meaning. Overextensions, on this account, are merely the child's way of getting along with a very limited vocabulary. For lack of a word he, like Humpty Dumpty, pays a word extra and makes it do a lot of work. In fact, Thomson and Chapman (1977) report that children who overextended a word in production tended not to do so in comprehension. At the first blush, this seems to indicate that children knew the "correct" meaning of the word and, for lack of an alternative, took the liberty to apply it to additional referents. However, to appreciate the implications of this finding, we must note what the experimental procedure was. Thomson and Chapman first ascertained for a given child in what way he overextended words in production. Suppose that a child would call a tomato "apple." They then presented him with two pictures of objects—say, a picture of an apple and one of a tomato—and asked him for the object the name of which had been overextended in production ("Show me the apple!"). A statistically significant preference for the appropriate picture was found (i.e., the picture of the apple tended to be chosen). Note now that this finding does not corroborate the above hypothesis that overextensions in production are merely due to production deficiency. For suppose the child had no inkling that "apple" might be an inappropriate name for tomato; that is, he had overextended "apple" through initial generalization, as suggested in section 5.2. When asked to show an apple he would then prefer the picture of an apple over that of a tomato, because the former is more similar to the object that the word "apple" had originally been paired with. That the child refrained from overextension in this experimental task thus does not show that he had acquired a concept of apple with boundaries coinciding with those of the adult concept.

To prove that overextension is due merely to production deficiency, one would have to show that, when asked for an apple, the child refuses to choose the picture of a tomato even when not given the picture of an apple as an alternative (cf. Huttenlocher, 1974, p. 359). Thomson and Chapman included an experimental condition in which the child had to choose between the overextended exemplar (tomato) and an unrelated one (e.g., a bottle). If the child had already drawn the boundary between what is and what is not an apple, we would expect no preference for either one of these pictures: Either he would refuse to choose any one, or else he would choose between them randomly. This did not happen. Thomson and Chapman found that in 80% of the cases the overextended exemplar (tomato) was preferred, and "the only other responses were refusals to choose [p. 371]." Moreover, sometimes the child overextended in comprehension when the choice was between an appropriate instance (apple) and one for which overextension had been noted in production (tomato). These findings show that overextension reflects, at least in some cases, the meaning that the word has for the child.

It is true, however, that there are some cases of overextension, that must be explained as being consequences of production deficit. Nelson, Rescorla, Gruendel, and Benedict (1978, p. 963), for instance, report on a child who had the word "strawberry" in his comprehension vocabulary, but called a strawberry "apple." Thomson and Chapman (1977) and Gruendel (1977) also report on overextensions of words to referents for which the child knew the appropriate name. But these cases are the exception rather than the rule. In many cases, as we have seen, production deficiency does not explain overextension. Theories claiming the precedence of concepts, then, will have to explain what makes these concepts shift and stir rather than hold still when words are fitted to them.

Another attempt to reconcile the phenomenon of overextension with the claim that words are linked to already existing concepts is due to Nelson et al. (1978; see also Bloom, 1973, p. 79). Overextensions, they argue, result from the child's active exploration of the boundaries of the word concept. Nelson et al. consider cases where the child first uses "moon" and "clock" correctly, and later overextends these words to things each of which share only one feature with the moon or a clock (e.g., a crescent shape or a buzzing sound, respectively). They regard it as implausible that the child should regard these things as "appropriate instances of the underlying concept MOON or CLOCK [p. 964]." Instead, they suggest, the child intends to indicate that the object in question is somehow *like*—but isn't really—a clock or the moon; he uses words for familiar objects "to classify and crossclassify features of other objects and events" [p. 964]. This is due to his "emerging fascination with similarities and differences between things, which may be useful for assigning things to old concepts and for forming new ones [p. 965]."

Note that Nelson et al.'s hypothesis is similar to the production deficiency hypothesis in that both assume that, when overextending, the child already has attained a concept (of, e.g., clock). A distinction is made between objects that clearly belong to this category and those that possibly belong to it (e.g., because they are attended by a buzzing sound). The results of Thomson and Chapman's experiment, quoted in the foregoing, indicate that it is often not the case that the child who overextends has already formed a category. My theory does not make such an assumption. It posits that the child generalizes from, for example, a clock to a buzzing telephone in just the same way that he generalizes from one clock (the paired referent) to another one. In both cases some similarity is perceived. Because no concept of clock is presupposed, no additional process of active exploration needs to be hypothesized.

5.6 THE PROBLEM OF PRELINGUISTIC CONCEPTS

In the preceding sections, an explanation of word acquisition has been offered which does not assume that the child forms concepts through experience before he learns words. It now remains for us to examine whether there is any independent evidence for such prelinguistic concepts.

A cautionary remark is in order here concerning a potential source of confusion. The term *concept* is often used in a sense different from the one intended here. Thus, in speaking of an object concept, or the concept of causality, one refers to the way the child organizes the continually changing influx of sensory stimuli into coherent wholes. When taken in this sense, it is all but self-evident that some conceptualization must precede language, and this particular use of the term *concept* seems to account for at least some of the appeal of the view that words are linked to previously formed concepts. It has been argued, for instance, that the child must have an object concept if he is to learn names for objects, and although this assertion has been debated (see Bloom, 1973; Corrigan, 1977; Huttenlocher, 1974; Quine, 1960, pp. 90-95), this is a question of the cognitive prerequisites of language learning, which we do not deal with here. 'Concept' is used here in the sense of category the possession of which implies the ability to distinguish between instances and noninstances. The point at issue is, then, not how the child interprets the environment, but how he categorizes it (cf. section 4.2). For, as Neisser (1976) has remarked, "perceiving is not a matter of assigning objects to categories. . . . I will probably not categorize [the perceived chair] at all unless the situation requires that I do so. I can sit down in it, avoid it, move it out of the way. . . without ever naming it at all, to others or to myself. While some of these activities might be said to categorize it 'implicitly,' each does so in a unique and different way [pp. 74-75]."

Now, there can be no question that we can form concepts, in the sense of categories, for which we have no words. The seashell example presented earlier (in "Extraction of Positive Cues," section 5.3) serves to illustrate this possibility, and there is experimental evidence to this effect, some of it reviewed further on. The question is not whether concepts can be formed independently of word acquisition but whether the child in fact does form concepts before he learns words and whether he makes use of them in learning words, as claimed by some theorists (see previous section). This is indeed a tempting view because it appears to simplify the child's arduous task of learning words. If words were learned without previously existing concepts to which they can be attached (as argued by the theory presented in this chapter), the child would have to grope after concepts with nothing to guide him but the way others use words. But, as some researchers have remarked (Anglin, 1977; Nelson & Bonvillian, 1973), not very much groping appears to be going on: The child applies most words immediately to their correct referents. So it might seem that when he begins to learn the meaning of words, he already has available to him a world parcelled up into concepts. (The occasional overextensions and underextensions would remain a nagging problem, of course, but these might perhaps be dealt with as exceptions to the rule.)

Let us formulate a hypothesis that expresses this point of view:

PRELINGUISTIC CONCEPTS HYPOTHESIS:
The child forms categories on the basis of his experience with the environment, and the acquisition of a word involves forming a link between it and such a previously attained category.

In the following, I deal with the pros and cons of this hypothesis. Let me emphasize again that what we are dealing with primarily is not the claim that the child forms concepts independently of language but the much stronger claim embodied in the aforementioned hypothesis, viz. that it is these concepts that words become attached to. It should be noted that this hypothesis is allied in spirit to the Cognitive Determinism approach, which has been examined and found wanting in Chapter 4.

Criteria For Prelinguistic Concepts

It might appear that the protagonists of the Prelinguistic Concepts Hypothesis can cite some research findings in support of their view and can proffer an explanation of how these concepts are attained. The child, so goes this line of thought, perceives similarities in his environment. Further, he notices that various things are responded to in the same way. By noting these resemblances, it might be argued, concepts are formed.

But consider that noticing similarities, although necessary for the formation of concepts, is not a sufficient condition for their formation. Remember that between any two things there will be some similarity along some dimension. "Having" a concept, in the sense of category, implies that one has a way of judging what is an instance of the concept and what is not. True, the boundaries of many concepts are fuzzy, but a fuzzy boundary is still a boundary; there will always be some cases that are clear instances of the concept and some that are clearly not. In examining the evidence for the Prelinguistic Concepts Hypothesis we therefore have to employ the following criterion:

> CRITERION 1: A category has been attained only if there is a way of distinguishing between instances belonging to it and noninstances.

Suppose now that a child's behavior evinces the attainment of a category by Criterion 1, but there is no evidence that he has somehow internally represented this category so that it is available for further use. Clearly, we will then have no evidence for the Prelinguistic Concepts Hypothesis, which claims that a word may later be attached to this category as a label. This consideration leads to formulating

> CRITERION 2: Only a category that is stable and available for further use can figure in word acquisition.

(Whether a category that fails to meet this criterion ought to be called "category" or "concept" at all is a terminological issue that need not concern us here.)

A third criterion relevant here is:

CRITERION 3: A category will be useful for word acquisition to the degree that it is coextensive with a category labeled by a word.

Obviously, when the child learns a word for a category that does not match with that employed in adult language, the result may be misapplication of the word. The child would have to readjust the boundaries of the category in order to use the word appropriately.

In the following, we examine the evidence for the Prelinguistic Concepts Hypothesis. It is shown that what evidence can be marshalled fails on at least one of the aforementioned criteria. After that, some arguments against the hypothesis are considered.

Early Sorting Behavior

When given small objects to handle, even very young children may put some of them together in a group, either spontaneously or when asked to do so. Ostensibly, these children are categorizing. Often such sorting follows principles quite unlike those according to which the concepts labeled by words are organized (see Vygotsky, 1962, pp. 59–69). Incidentally, this may be true even of older children (Weigl, 1927; quoted in Werner, 1957, pp. 227–228) and adults (Weigl, 1927, p. 26; Luria, 1976). Sometimes, however, the child appears to group together objects on the basis of a common property, in the way educated adults do. Could this kind of behavior be construed as evidence for the attainment of prelinguistic concepts?

An experiment by Ricciuti (1965) has sometimes been cited as evidence for early categorization behavior. Ricciuti observed the spontaneous play behavior of children with sets of eight objects, where the objects in each set belonged to two subsets differing in size, form, or in several dimensions. Children as young as one year were found to observe these distinctions: They tended to manipulate several objects of one subset before manipulating those of the other and they also would put together several objects belonging to the same subset. Incidentally such behavior is not limited to humans. Premack (1976, pp. 217–218) found that young chimps, when given blocks differing in both form and color, sorted them into two boxes on the basis of color.

Note, first, that there is nothing in these findings showing that the sorting behavior of these children satisfied criterion 2. When a child manipulates two or more similar objects sequentially, or when he puts them together, he responds to a perceived similarity. But it does not follow necessarily that the category he responds to is stored in memory and is available for later use. One of Premack's chimps, in fact, spontaneously shifted criteria after sorting blocks according to color, and sorted them according to shape. This experiment therefore does not support the Prelinguistic Concepts Hypothesis (and Ricciuti, who was not concerned with language learning, never claimed that it does).

A further point to be noted is that in three of the experimental conditions each subset contained objects of identical shape, size and color. This is quite unlike the situation the child finds himself in when learning words, because there he has to assign a common name to referents differing from each other in many respects. The word learning task is more analogous to Ricciuti's fourth experimental condition (Task III), where the two subsets were distinguished by size, and the objects in each subset varied in shape and color with no two objects being identical on these two dimensions. In this condition, unlike the three others, hardly any one of the 12-month-olds engaged in object grouping, and less than a fifth of them evidenced selective ordering of object manipulation. The 18-month-olds did much better in this experimental condition, but at that age the child usually has command of a considerable number of words.

Criterion 2 is also not met by the behavior observed in an experiment by Rosch, Mervis, Gray, Johnson, and Boyes-Braem (1976, experiment 8). Three-year-old children were given an "oddity problem": They were shown sets of pictures of three objects and asked which two of a set were alike. When the pictures were of "basic objects"—for example, a cat, a (different looking) cat, and a car—performance was perfect. Because their ability to name the objects in the pictures was much lower, they could not have relied wholly on naming when solving the task. These results were replicated in a sorting task (experiment 9). There is nothing in these results, however, to show that the product of the pairing task remains available as a category. Further, their subjects operated on the basis of similarity—a cat is more similar to another cat than it is to a car—and reacting to such similarity is no evidence for the possession of a concept, with a boundary between instances belonging to the concept and those not belonging to it. If the same children would have been given a set of three cats, two of which are very much alike whereas one is very dissimilar to the others, they would presumably also have been able to pick out the two similar ones. In other words, the behavior elicited in these experiments also fails to satisfy our criterion 1. A child may perceive similarity and yet not form a concept. For why should he?

Categories Based On Common Responses

One possible reason why a child should form a category consisting of various things is that these require a common response. According to Nelson (1974), a word becomes attached to a previously formed "functional core.'' The "functional core" of "ball," for instance, is formed as the child "synthesize[s] over time the various relations into which the ball enters [p. 277]," that is, the various actions and events in which it is involved. Brown (1965, pp. 318–322) discussed the possibility that concepts are learned on the basis of nonlinguistic responses. The role of function in word learning has also been stressed by Anglin (1977), and Pylyshyn (1977, p. 44) has suggested that "an *internal* naming or referencing act is performed when a set of objects is susceptible to common actions [emphasis added]."

Assuming for the moment that nonlinguistic responses may establish categories that meet our criteria 1 and 2, we note that they often fail to meet criterion 3. The child's functional categories may be orthogonal to those adopted by adult language. For example, a Swedish-speaking child used one word (cake) for any food he could put into his mouth himself, and another one (eat) for all other food (Segerstedt, 1947). Even if these functional categories had been formed before the corresponding words were acquired (for which there is no evidence), their utility for word acquisition is dubious: Ultimately the Swedish words for "cake" and "eat" have to be reassigned to other categories. Such divergence between the way the child divides up reality on the basis of function on the one hand, and the categorization reflected in the language on the other seems to be usual in the domain of food and eating. Thus Ament (1899, p. 78) reports on a 20.5-month-old girl who called all solid food by the word used for bread, while using another word for all beverages—except milk, for which she had still another word. Some 5 months later an additional distinction emerged—between milk drunk out of a bottle and all beverages, including milk drunk out of a cup. Similarly the daughter of one of my students (Gina Shimborsky, personal communication, 1977) had one word for milk drunk when in bed and another one for food eaten with a spoon.

Furthermore, it is very doubtful whether commonality of the child's responses will often lead to categories with relatively clear boundaries. For this to be the case, each instance of the category would have to be associated with a unique, or almost unique, response or set of responses. In actual fact, however, the first objects for which the child learns names typically give rise each to a variety of responses by the child. A spoon is used not only for eating, but also to bang the table with, to drop on the floor (so as to be picked up by the parent), and so on. Banging on the table and dropping on the floor, on the other hand, can be achieved with other objects too, and these objects in turn will be used in a variety of ways: some may be rolled, some are malleable, etc. If any one of these responses defines a category of objects, the latter will not be one to which the child later attaches a word. Only gradually does the child come to respond to objects in conformity with their standard use—but by that time his acquisition of language is already quite far advanced. A possible objection to this argument might be that prelinguistic concepts are defined not over single responses but over complex profiles of responses. But in view of the fact that, as mentioned, profiles for different concepts partially overlap, it seems farfetched to assume that in the short time before the child understands words such complex concepts have had time to crystallize.

As an alternative to the proposal that prelinguistic concepts are defined by the child's responses one might consider the possibility (pointed out to me by Mordechai Rimor, personal communication, 1978) that they are defined by those of the adult. After all, the adult is much more consistent in his responses to objects, than the child is. Mother may roll a ball, but hardly a bottle, and she will use a spoon only for eating and not to bang the table with. Perhaps, then, the Common Response Hypothesis may be salvaged by pointing out that the child disregards his own happy-go-lucky responses to objects and focuses on the staid routines employed by adults.

There is, however, some evidence discrediting the notion of functional information playing a central role in the acquisition of words. Anglin's (1977, p. 25) finding that function rarely serves as a basis for overextension does not square well with the thesis that words are attached as labels to concepts defined on the basis of common responses.

I conclude therefore that considerations pertaining to the commonality of responses to objects do little to bolster the Prelinguistic Concepts Hypothesis. Let us see now whether this hypothesis becomes more plausible if we approach objects from the stimulus end.

Clusters Of Attributes

Studies by Rosch (1977; Rosch et al., 1976) have shown that the clusters of perceptual and functional attributes serve to chunk the environment into information-rich bundles. These are the so-called "basic objects", (e.g., chair, dog, as distinguished from superordinates like furniture, animal, and subordinates, like Morris chair and collie). Could the child form prelinguistic concepts by capitalizing on the existence of such clusters of attributes? There is indeed some evidence that experience with certain perceptual invariants can be utilized for the formation of categories even in the absence of feedback (Edmonds, Mueller, & Evans, 1966). The process responsible for this is presumably positive cue extraction. One might argue therefore, that the child observes the regularities in the environment, uses these to form representations of 'basic objects,' and, equipped with these, approaches the language learning task. In fact, this is the way the concept of *seashell* was formed in our example in section 5.3.

One question left open by Rosch's work is how pervasive such 'basic objects' are. There is certainly no guarantee that her findings concerning certain objects may be generalized to actions, states, and properties. But even apart from this question Rosch's findings do not constitute evidence for pre-linguistic concepts, because it is far from clear that basic objects are iden-tified by the child *prior* to learning language. Given the large amount of data which presumably have to be processed in making use of the correla-tional structure of perceptual attributes, and given the early age at which the child learns words (see e.g., Nelson, Rescorla, et al. 1978), this seems rather implausible. And in fact, in those cases where the child still overex-tends or underextends the use of a word he provides us with evidence that he does not yet have 'basic objects' to hitch the word on to. In those rare cases where language acquisition is begun at a much later age, previously iden-tified basic objects may be capitalized on. Genie, who due to extreme social isolation, began to learn language only in adolescence, did not overextend; rather, her use of words "reflected categorizations that were already well developed [Curtiss, 1977, p. 200]." At an earlier age, we may add, categorizations are not yet well developed, which explains why children in their second year, unlike Genie, are prone to overextend.

The Case Against The Prelinguistic Concepts Hypothesis

So far we have seen that there is no conclusive evidence for prelinguistic concepts that might be usefully employed in acquiring words. But can we go further and adduce arguments *against* such a possibility? In the following, we deal with an argument to this effect, based on cross-linguistic com-parisons.

If a child's concepts stem indeed from his prelinguistic experience, we ought to expect a marked uniformity in the way children belonging to dif-ferent speech communities categorize the material world around them, at least as far as early childhood experience is concerned. But if this is the case, then these prelinguistic concepts will be a poor guide to the language learner. As already noted in section 4.2, languages differ among themselves in the categorizations they adopt. A child of French-speaking parents must learn one word for paint brush ("pinceau") and another one for other kinds of brushes ("brosse"), and so must the child learning German or Hebrew, whereas English decrees that all these kinds of brushes belong to the same concept. Or, to give another pedestrian example, consider the way various languages label a foot and a leg. In English there are two separate words for these—and what, apparently, could be more "natural" than this distinc-tion? But in fact there is only one word for both of these in Hebrew, and the same is true of such widely differing languages as Hungarian and Polish (though Polish has a different word for sole of the foot), and according to Miller and Johnson-Laird (1976, p. 299), one Papuan language. German, Italian, and Czech, again, are like English in this respect. (They further resemble English in that they metaphorically extend "leg" to the leg of a chair; unlike the French, for whom a chair has no leg but a foot.) If there is any prelinguistic concept, it must be either *foot* or *leg and foot*, and in either case it can be of use only for a part of the world's children.[9] For such linguistic differences cannot all be traced to cultural ones that might be reflected in children's prelinguistic experience (See also Brown, 1965, pp. 315–317; and see Bowerman, 1976, p. 109; 1978, note 2 for further examples of cross-linguistic differences).

The cross-linguistic data should teach us a lesson, but they should not be taken to prove too much. First, examples of conflicting classifications adopted by various languages are anything but easy to procure. At least as far as words normally belonging to children's earliest vocabularies are concerned, there seems to be a large degree of consensus among languages, and only marginal differences. The possibility cannot be dismissed out of hand, therefore, that in learning words, children rely on prelinguistic concepts most of the time. Moreover, even in those cases where his language gives the lie to his prelinguistic concepts, the child may have merely to adjust his categorization. Suppose that on the basis of his experience he has formed a concept 'leg and foot'. His encounter with words then requires the introduction of an additional distinction. Or, conversely, a prelinguistic concept may have to be subsequently broadened (or both broadened and narrowed) in the light of linguistic experience. Anyhow, the child would not have to start from scratch. Instead of having to construct his protoverbal elements from paired referents, in the manner proposed in this chapter, he is given a headstart, and begins with concepts that are gradually brought in line with those used by the speakers of the language.

But note that even if this account is correct (and as we have seen earlier, there is so far no good evidence for the Prelinguistic Concepts Hypothesis), our theory of word acquisition would have to resort to all those processes that have been hypothesized above for learning a word's limits of applicability. Overextension and underextension would have to be combatted, and to do so, cues would have to be isolated. Prelinguistic concepts may entail some saving of labor for the child, but none for the theorist; the same theoretical apparatus will be required. Furthermore, there seem to be instances where children learn words for referents with which they had no

---

[9]Curiously, Werner (1957, p. 279) views the fact that "foot and leg, or arm and hand are considered to be a single unit" for the child, as an example of "childish thinking." Here he seems to commit the not too uncommon fallacy of regarding the categorization imposed by the languages known by the researcher as in some sense "correct," and all other categorizations (in this case, the one adopted by, e.g., Hebrew) as "primitive." Furthermore, he makes an unwarranted inference, because, as far as these examples go, there is nothing showing that children differ from adults in *interpreting* the environment.

previous experience.[10] In these cases there can have been no question of relying on prelinguistic concepts attained through experience; that is, the whole course of acquisition, from paired referent to protoverbal element, must be transversed.

A theory of word learning based on prelinguistic concepts is therefore not an alternative to the theory outlined in this chapter. The assumption of prelinguistic concepts can only introduce an additional ramification into the theory, namely, that the child sometimes may take a shortcut and link the word to an already existing concept. The question remains, however, whether this assumption is correct. In the preceding subsections we have seen that there is no evidence for it. There are also arguments against it. Thus, Anisfeld (in press, ch. 4) claims on the basis of Piagetian theory that, by the time the child begins learning words, he has not yet developed to the point of being able to represent concepts internally.

To recapitulate, introducing the notion of prelinguistic concepts into a theory of word acquisition is justified only if at least one of the following is the case: (1) there is independent evidence for the Prelinguistic Concepts Hypothesis; (2) the theory of word acquisition can be simplified by the introduction of this hypothesis; (3) the relative ease with which children seem to learn the meaning of most words and their errorless performance on most words makes it implausible that this is accomplished without the benefit of previously formed concepts. The above discussion has shown that neither (1) nor (2) is the case. As for (3), we see in a moment that it is not wellfounded. That the child cannot avail himself of a shortcut via prelinguistic concepts does not mean that he must organize an entirely random world by means of language alone. Rather, as shown in the following subsection, there are perceptual regularities in the world which operate with the linguistic regularities in a mutually reinforcing manner. This facilitates the child's task, and thus (3) is done away with; no sufficient motivation for the introduction of prelinguistic concepts is left.

Texture Versus Prelinguistic Concepts

Our perceptual world is structured. Unlike laboratory experiments on concept formation, where every attribute is equally likely to appear, there are,

---

[10]An example related to me by Lise Menn is of a boy who was taken for a walk. There was a fire hose lying on the sidewalk, and the accompanying adult dutifully supplied the word "hose" (this being almost certainly the child's first experience with a hose). After a short while, he came across another hose on the sidewalk and said "hose."

in our everyday experience, as Rosch has shown, correlations between the attributes perceived in the environment, and these predispose us to form certain concepts rather than others. It dos not follow, however, that our categorization of the world is completely determined by this correlational structure. True, certain categorizations will be difficult, or even impossible, for the child to attain, just as it is difficult to carve wood against the grain. But such categorizations will also not be required by the lingustic system: Language classes like with like. Conversely, just as there are many ways of carving wood without going against the grain, the structure of attributes allows for alternative categorizations. Our perceptual world has what may be called *texture*, which constrains but does not fully determine the formation of concepts. The languages of the world reflect this texture each in a different way. And the child avails himself of the texture and finds it echoed in the native language.

Texture suggests concepts; it does not create them. Whenever we sort, classify, recognize, and note similarities, we do so in conformity to texture. However, after the sorting and noting is done, the singled out elements may tend to fall back into their previous mold. The concepts that the child eventually acquires are not so evanescent. He singles out objects, actions and properties from reality, but for the results to be permanent, they must be firmly anchored to relatively invariant linguistic responses. Texture and linguistic input must converge on the formation of a conceptual system.

According to the foregoing account it is possible to account for the similarities between languages as well as for the differences between them. The similarities between language—which, at least at the basic object level, outweigh the differences between them—are due to their dealing with domains of the same, universal texture. That there are also differences is due to the fact that, as stated, texture does not completely determine categorization. If it did, we would hardly expect the child to err in using words (i.e., to underextend or overextend the use of words). On the other hand, the fact that the perceived world is not textureless and random explains why children do not go on searching blindly for the meaning of a word. On the contrary, a child acquires words, on the whole, rapidly and easily, and with most words his performance is errorless from the beginning (as pointed out at the beginning of this section). Without the guidance of texture his progress would be much more laborious, and communication with adults would at first be excruciatingly difficult. Luckily, both he and the adult perceive some texture in the world around them.

We have followed the child through the first stages of word acquisition. In the next chapter some processes occurring at later stages are dealt with.

REFERENCES

Ament, W. *Die Entwicklung von Sprechen und Denken beim Kinde*. Leipzig: Wunderlich, 1899.

Anderson, J. R. Arguments concerning representation for mental imagery. *Psychological Review*, 1978, *85*, 249-277.

Anglin, I. M. *Word, object, and conceptual development*. New York: Norton, 1977.

Anisfeld, M. *The origins of symbols and the beginning of language*. Hillsdale, N. J.: Lawrence Erlbaum Associates, in press.

St. Augustine, [*The Confessions*] (E. B. Pusey, trans.). New York: Pocket Books, 1952.

Barrett, M. D. Lexical development and overextension in child language. *Journal of Child Language*, 1978, *5*, 205-219.

Bierwish, M. Semantics. In J. Lyons (Ed.), *New horizons in linguistics*. Harmondsworth, England: Penguin, 1970.

Bloom, L. *One word at a time: The use of single-word utterances before syntax*. The Hague: Mouton, 1973.

Bloom, L., & Lahey, M. *Language development and language disorders*. New York: Wiley, 1978.

Bourne, L. E., Jr., & O'Banion, K. Memory for individual events in concept identification. *Psychonomic Science*, 1969, *16*, 101-102.

Bowerman, M. Semantic factors in the acquisition of rules for word use and sentence construction. In D. Morehead & A. Morehead (Eds.), *Directions in normal and deficient child language*. Baltimore: University Park Press, 1976.

Bowerman, M. The acquisition of word meaning: An investigation into some current conflicts. In N. Waterson & C. Snow (Eds.), *The development of communication*. New York: Wiley, 1978.

Brooks, L. Nonanalytic concept formation and memory for instances. In E. Rosch B. B. Lloyd (Eds.), *Cognition and categorization*. Hillsdale, N.J.: Lawrence Erlbaum Associates, 1978.

Brown, R. *Words and things*. Glencoe, Illinois: Free Press, 1958.

Brown, R. *Social Psychology*. New York: Free Press, 1965.

Bruner, J. S. The ontogenesis of speech acts. *Journal of Child Language,* 1975, *2*,1-19.

Bruner, J. S., Goodnow, J. J., & Austin, G. A. *A study of thinking*. New York: Wiley, 1956.

Clark, E. What's in a word? On the child's acquisition of semantics in his first language. In T. E. Moore (Ed.), *Cognitive development and the acquisition of language*. New York: Academic Pess, 1973.

Clark, E. Some aspects of the conceptual basis for first language acquisition. In R. L. Schiefelbusch & L. L. Lloyd (Eds.), *Language perspectives-Acquisition, retardation and intervention*. Baltimore: University Park Press, 1974.

Clark, E. Knowledge, context, and strategy in the acquisition of meaning. In D. P. Dato (Ed.), *Georgetown University round table in language and linguistics 1975*. Washington, D.C.: Georgetown University Press, 1975.

Clark, E. Strategies and the mapping problem in first language acquisition. In J. Macnamara (Ed.), *Language learning and thought*. New York: Academic Press, 1977.

Bruner, J. S. From communication to language. *Cognition,* 1974-1975,*3* 255-287.

Clark, H. H., & Clark, E. V. *Psychology and language: An introduction to psycholinguistics*. New York: Harcourt Brace Jovanovich, 1977.

Cohen, E., Namir, L., & Schlesinger, I. M. *A new dictionary of sign language*. The Hague: Mouton, 1977.

Corringan, R. *Synchrony between task domains: Object permanence and language*. Paper presented at the Symposium on Sequence and Synchrony in Cognitive Development, 1977.

Curtiss, S. *Genie: A psycholinguistic study of a modern-day "wild child"*. New York: Academic Press, 1977.

Dore, J., Franklin, M. B., Miller, R. T., & Ramer, A. L. H. Transitional phenomena in early language acquisition. *Journal of Child Languge*, 1976, *3* , 13-28.

Edmonds, E. M., & Evans, S. H. Schema learning without a prototype. *Psychonomoic Science*, 1966, *5*, 247-248.

Edmonds, E. M., Mueller, M. R., & Evans, S. H. Effects of knowledge of results on mixed schema discrimination. *Psychonomic Science*, 1966, *6*, 377-378.

Fodor, J.A., *The language of thought*. New York: Crowell, 1975.

Franks, J. J., & Bransford, J. D. Abstraction of visual patterns. *Journal of Experimental Psychology*, 1971, *90*, 65-74.

Galton, F. *Inquiries into human faulty and its development*. London: Dent, 1907.

Garner, H., Kircher, M., Winner, E., & Perkins, D. Children's metaphoric productions and preferences. *Journal of Child Language*, 1975, *2*, 125-141.

Garner, E. R. Aspects of a stimulus: Features, dimensions, and configurations. In E. Rosch & B. B. Lloyd (Eds.), *Cognition and categorization*. Hillsdale, N. J.: Lawrence Erlbaum Associates, 1978.

Greenfield, P. M., & Smith, J. H. *The structure of communication in early language development*. New York: Academic Press, 1976.

Gruendel, J. M. Referential extension in early language development. *Child Development*, 1977, *45*, 1567-1576.

Huttenlocher, J. The origins of language comprehension. In R. L. Solso (Ed.), *Theories in Cognitive Psychology: The Loyola symposium*. Potomac, Md: Lawrence Erlbaum Associates, 1974.

Katz, J. J. *The philosophy of language*. New York: Harper & Row, 1966.

Kendler, H. H., & Kendler, T. S. From discrimination learning to cognitive development: A neobehavioristic odyssey. In W. R. Estes (Ed.), *Handbook of learning and cognitive processes (Vol. l): Introduction to concepts and issues*. Hillsdale, N. J.: Lawrence Erlbaum Associates, 1975.

Klatzky, R. L., & Stoy, A. M. Using visual codes for comparison of pictures.*Memory and Cognition,* 1974, *2*, 727-736.

Leopold, W. F. *Speech development of a bilingual child: A linguist's record. (Vol. 3.)* Evanston, Ill.: Northwestern University Press, 1949.

Luria, A. R. *Cognitive development: Its cultural and social foundations*. Cambridge, Mass.: Harvard University Press, 1976.

Menyuk, R. *The acquisition and development of language*. Englewood Cliffs, N. J.: Prentice-Hall, 1971.

Miller, G. A., & Johnson-Laird, P. N. *Language and perception*. Cambridge, Mass.: Harvard University Press, 1976.

Neisser, U . *Cognition and reality*. San Francisco: Freeman, 1976.

Nelson, K. Concept, word, and sentence: Interrelations in acquisition and development. *Pychological Review*, 1974, *81*, 267-285.

Nelson, K., & Bonvillian, J. D. Concepts and words in the 18-month-old: Acquiring concept names under controlled conditions. *Cognition*, 1973, *2*, 435-450.

Nelson, K. E., & Nelson, K. Cognitive pendulum, and their linguistic realization. In K. E. Nelson (Ed.), *Children's language*, (Vol. 1). New York: Gardner Press, 1978.

Nelson, K., Rescorla, L., Gruendel, I., & Benedict, H. Early lexicons: What do they mean? *Child Development*, 1978, *49*, 960-968.

Newport, E. L., Gleitman, M., & Gleitman, L. R. Mother, I'd rather do it myself: Some effects and non-effects of maternal speech style. In C. A. Ferguson,& C. E. Snow, (Eds.), *Talking to children*. New York: Cambridge University Press, 1977.

Ninio, A., & Bruner, J. The achievement and antecedents of   labelling *Journal of the Child Language, 1978, 5,* 1-15.

Paivio, A. Images, propositions, and knowledge. In J. M. Nichols (Ed.), *Images, perception and knowledge*. Dordrecht, Holland: Reidel, 1977.

Peterson, M. J., Meagher, R. B., Jr., Chait, H., & Gillie, S The abstraction and generalization of dot patterns. *Cognitive Psychology*, 1973, *4*, 378-398.

Posner, M. I. *Cognition: An introduction*. Glenview, Illinois: Scott, Foresman, 1973.

Posner, M. I., & Keele, S. W. On the genesis of abstract ideas. *Journal of Experimental Psychology*, 1968,*77*, 353-363.

Posner, M. I., & Keele, S. W. Retention of abstract ideas. *Journal of Experimental Psychology* 1970, *83*, 304-308.

Premack, D. *Intelligence in ape and man*. Hillsdale, N. J.: Lawrence Erlbaum Associates, 1976.

Price, M. M. *Thinking and experience* Cambridge, Mass.: Harvard University Press, 1962

Putnam, H. The meaning of "meaning." In K. Gunderson (Ed.), *Language, mind and knowledge (Vol. 7) Minnesota Studies in the Philosophy of Science* Minneapolis: University of Minnesota Press, 1975.

Pylyshyn, Z. What does it take to bootstrap a language? In J. Macnamara (Ed.), *Language learning and thought*. New York: Academic Press, 1977.

Quine, W. V. *Word and object*. Cambridge, Mass.: MIT Press, 1960.

Quine, W. V. *The roots of reference*. La Salle, Ill.: Open Court, 1973.

Reed, S. K. Pattern recognition and categorization. *Cognitive Psychology*, 1972, *3*, 382–407.

Reitman, J. A., & Bower, G. H. Storage and later recognition of concepts. *Cognitive Psychology*, 1973, *4*, 194–206.

Ricciuti, H. N. Object grouping as selective ordering behavior in infants 12 to 24 months old. *Merrill Palmer Quarterly of Behavior and Development*. 1965, *11*, 129–148.

Rosch, E. Human categorization. In N. Warren (Ed.), *Advances in cross-cultural psychology*, (Vol. 1). London: Academic Press, 1977.

Rosch, E., & Mervis, C. B. Family resemblances: Studies in the internal structure of categories. *Cognitive Psychology*, 1975, *7*, 573–605.

Rosch, E., Mervis, C. B., Gray, W. N., Johnson, D. M., & Boyes-Braem, P. Basic objects in natural categories. *Cognitive Psychology*, 1976, *8*, 382–439.

Schlesinger, I. M. The grammar of sign language and the problem of linguistic universals. In J. Morton (Ed.), *Biological and social factors in psycholinguistics*. London: Logos Press, 1971.

Schlesinger, I. M. Relational concepts underlying language. In R. L. Schiefelbusch & L. Lloyd (Eds.), *Language perspectives—Acquisition, retardation and intervention*. Baltimore: University Park Press, 1974.

Segerstedt, T. T. *Die Macht des Wortes: Eine Sprachsoziologie*. Zurich: Pan Verlage, 1947.

Smith, E. E., Shoben, E. J., & Rips, L. J. Structure and process in semantic memory: A featural model for semantic decisions. *Psychological Review*, 1974, *81*, 214–241.

Stern, C. & Stern, W. *Die Kindersprache: Eine psychologische und sprachtheoretishe Untersuchung*. Dramstadt: Wissenschaftliche Buchgesellschaft, 1968. (Originally published 1928)

Stones, E. Verbal labeling and concept formation in primary school children. *British Journal of Educational Psychology*, 1970, *4*, 245–252.

Strange, W., Keeney, T., Kessel, F. S., & Jenkins, J. J. Abstraction over time of prototypes from distortions of random patterns: A replication. *Journal of Experimental Psychology*, 1970, *83*, 505–510.

Thomson, J. R., & Chapman, R. S. Who is "daddy" revisited: The status of two-year-olds' over-extended words in use and comprehension. *Journal of Child Language*, 1977, *4*, 359–375.

Tversky, A. Features of similarity. *Psychological Review*, 1977, *84*, 327–352.

Vygotsky, L. S. *Thought and language*. Cambridge, Mass.: MIT Press, 1962.

Weigl, E. Zur Psychologie sogenannter Abstraktionsprozesse. I. Untersuchungen über das "Ordnen." *Zeitschrift für Psychologie*, 1927, *103*, 1–45.

Werner, H. *Comparative psychology of mental development*. New York: International Universities, 1957.

Winner, E. New names for old things: The emergence of metaphoric language. *Journal of Child Language*, 1979, *6*, 469–491.

6

The Acquisition of Words: Further Steps

And when tweetle beetles
battle with paddles in a puddle,
they call it a tweetle beetle puddle paddle battle.
—Dr. Seuss

INTRODUCTION

In the previous chapter we have seen how the child acquires his first stock of words—those denoting "basic objects," actions, social situations, and some properties. In the following, we deal with the processes involved in the acquisition of certain other kinds of words.

The simple process of referent pairing described in section 5.1 is not sufficient to account for the acquisition of many of the words the child comes to know. The first section of the present chapter discusses additional mechanisms through which the link between a word and its referent may be established. The section after that plots the progress of word acquisition and deals with some special problems, such as the acquisition of superordinates, subordinates, and spatial adjectives. Up to that point we deal with words that have a relatively fixed meaning. This is not true of all words: The meaning of deictic words ("this," "here," "how," etc.) and of many verbs depends on the situational or verbal context in which they are used. This issue is discussed in the final section.

6.1 PAIRING MECHANISMS

Verbal Ostension

In section 5.1 we discussed the process of referent pairing. The child learns a word by hearing it uttered and having his attention drawn—through pointing or by other means—to its referent; thus a link is established between the

151

word and an internal representation of its referent. As the child grows older he gains an understanding of verbal expressions (that were themselves learned previously, in other verbal contexts): "This is . . .," "Look at . . .," "Take the . . .," etc. When the child's attention is drawn to a referent by means of such expressions, we may speak of VERBAL OSTENSION. At first, verbal ostension will usually be accompanied by pointing to, handling, or looking at the referent, and this may be one of the ways the child learns the meaning of the above phrases that are used for verbal ostension. Later on, expressions may be used without such nonverbal ostension, for example, "The . . . is on the table," "Watch mummy . . . ing in the kitchen." An example of such referent pairing through verbal ostension is to be found in Susan Carey's (1978, pp. 271-272) report of word acquisition in a nursing school. The investigators introduced a new name for a color, "chromium," by means of simple instructions, like "Bring me the chromium tray, not the red one!" when there were only two trays around. Presumably, adults teach a child many words in such an incidental manner, often without intending to teach him.

Learning by verbal ostension involves the process of referent pairing. But not all words are learned through referent pairing, as is seen in the following.

Learning In The Absence Of The Referent

The child frequently hears the meaning of a word explained to him, when the referent is not actually present, or else he "picks up" its meaning from the context. We must now consider the process that is at work here: How does the child form a protoverbal element (section 5.4) in the absence of the referent?

A solution to this problem was proposed years ago by Osgood (1953, pp. 697-698), who described a process of "assign" conditioning. His example was the word "zebra," the meaning of which might have been explained to the child as denoting a horse with stripes. The mediating response (meaning) of "zebra," according to Osgood, is parasitic on those of "horse" and "stripes." This example, however, is potentially misleading, because it might suggest to us that all words acquired through verbal explanation can be learned in this way. But whereas the addition of stripes to a horse may yield a tolerable replica of a zebra, there are many cases where such a simple additive operation is inadequate. Suppose the adult explains to the child that "stool" means "a chair without a back." The child must now subtract somehow his internal representations for "chair" and "back" from one another. He has to take into account the function word "without" so as to perform the appropriate operation. There are only a few objects that are like a zebra in that they can be viewed as a simple superimposition of other, named elements. For the meaning of other words to be explained verbally, the child must be able to make sense of whole utterances, and among others of those that include words denoting relations, like "without," and relations indicated by syntactic means.

Suppose now we say, instead, that when a word is explained to the child, in the absence of a referent, he links the word to the verbal definition given. Thus, "zebra" would be linked not to the internal representation of a zebra seen when the word was uttered, but to the verbal expression "horse with stripes," or, better, to the I-marker (the semantic structure) underlying it. However, whereas it may occasionally happen that a child remembers merely the definition of a word, this does not seem to be at all typical. Suppose the adult explains to a child that "A hospital is where sick people stay." The child will not just store this sentence (or the corresponding I-marker), but he will presumably elaborate on it: He may imagine a situation of sick people lying in a room, with a doctor walking in and out, applying his stethoscope and writing prescriptions, and so on. Sometimes this elaboration may in fact involve a misunderstanding, as was the case with the little boy who was afraid to go to the country because of the dangerous wild animals roaming there, after he had heard that the country is where there are few houses and many animals. At any rate, the definition serves as a starting point for an imagined experience, and it is to this experience that the word becomes attached.

Further encounters with the word may enrich and modify this experience. Thus, the child may hear about somebody coming out of a hospital being very weak, or about somebody who is sick and yet does not go to the hospital. The situation here is essentially similar to that in which a word is learned by pairing it directly with referents (sections 5.1-5.3), except that instead of the referents we have now the various experiences gleaned from utterances that include the new word. From these experiences cues are extracted, which are included in the newly formed protoverbal element (see sections 5.3-5.4).

Verbal explanation is one way of learning words. Often, however, we learn a word without having it defined for us, merely by hearing it repeatedly in various contexts. There is no intention of others to explain its meaning to us. To what extent do children also pick up words in this manner? This has been the subject of a study by Werner and Kaplan (1950). They presented to children aged 9 to 13 years nonce-words embedded in sentences. One set of sentences, for instance, included the nonce-word "hudray":

1.   If you eat well and sleep well you will hudray.
2.   Mrs. Smith wanted to hudray her family.
3.   Jane had to hudray the cloth so that the dress would fit Mary.

4.   You hudray what you know by reading and studying.
5.   To hudray the number of children in the class there must be enough chairs.
6.   You must have enough space in the bookcase to hudray your library.

Note that no definition of "hudray" is given. The child can only infer its meaning from the context. ("Hudray" means, according to Werner and Kaplan's gloss, "grow, increase, expand, etc.")

Werner and Kaplan found that 9-year-olds were only rarely successful in learning the meaning of the nonce-words from context (the overall proportion of correct solutions at that age level was 0.067). Success increased with age (reaching 0.477 at age 13). Their experiment seems to indicate that the achievement of picking up words from verbal context alone is rather difficult, and is attained at a relatively late age. However, in real life situations, the context in which a word is learned is presumably richer than that supplied in their experiment, and conditions may be more favorable to learning in other ways;[1] caution is therefore in order in generalizing from these experimental findings.

It seems reasonable to assume that the process whereby a word is learned from the verbal context, is similar to that by which a word is learned from a definition. Note that the context may after all be an (inadvertently given) definition of sorts ("hudray," for instance, being defined as something that happens if you eat well and sleep well, in sentence 1 above). The verbal context, like the definition, gives rise to an imagined experience, and the word is learned by pairing it with this experience or some aspects of it. Hearing a sentence containing the new word leads to imagining a situation. That aspect of the situation that is described by the new word is supplemented by the hearer on the basis of what he is led to expect. When the new word is encountered again in another context, one tries to make it fit there.

But the fit is often far from perfect. Let us illustrate this by the responses of one of the subjects in Werner and Kaplan's (1950, p. 16; see also p. 57) experiment. The word "hudray" in the first sentence was construed by him as "feel good." Sentence 2 was accordingly glossed as "Mrs. Smith wanted to make her family feel good." Note that "hudray" is interpreted as a noncausative verb in sentence 1 and as a causative verb in sentence 2. This is quite in accord with the way language works: A verb may have both a noncausative and a causative meaning (e.g., the "Flowers grow" and "He

---

[1]Not always, though. Von Raffler-Engel (1972) reports on a small girl who was afraid of "it," without knowing whether an "it" was a disease, a dangerous monster, or some other punishment. It turned out that the child had been repeatedly threatened: "You get it!"

grows flowers"). But when the child comes to sentence 3, the meaning of "hudray" is foisted on the sentence without much regard to syntactic structure; he explains: "Jane makes the dress good to fit Mary so Mary feels good." The child connects "hudray" with Mary and not, as prescribed by the structure of the sentence, with the cloth. The sentence is suffused, as it were, with the meaning construed for "hudray," and this is done without adequate syntactic analysis. In other cases, the meaning construed for the whole phrase in which the nonce-word is embedded is ascribed to the nonce-word. Thus, given the sentence "Philip asked John to help him protema his homework," one 9-year-old proceeded to fit the concept of homework to subsequent sentences (Werner & Kaplan, 1950, p. 23).

Occasionally a word is given a somewhat different meaning in each of the contexts it is encountered in. The situation then parallels that of a word paired with various referents which are all instances of the same concept. In such a case the meaning is determined through a process of positive cue extraction (section 5.3). One of Werner and Kaplan's subjects interpreted a nonce-word in a different way for each of the three sentences presented to him: hit back, lie, holler at (p. 31). He thereupon decided that the word meant "not respect your elders"—the common denominator of the previous solutions.

Werner and Kaplan's protocols also show that the interpretation given to a word may change somewhat from sentence to sentence. Thus a word is understood as "dirty" in one sentence and as "burnt" (explaining: "burnt is dirt-like") in another one (p. 33), "plant" in one sentence and "pot" in the next (p. 39), or "safety" and "safety rules" (p. 39), "honor" and "guts" (p. 41). Interestingly, these are the kinds of change of meaning which words often undergo in their history (Werner, 1954).

Werner and Kaplan's subjects were asked to explain the nonce-word after reading each sentence. In this respect, the experimental situation differed from real-life situations, in which no such overt responses are normally made. This feature of their experiment may have led the child to learn the meaning of the word in a more conscious and deliberate manner than is usual in real life. At any rate, the requirement to formulate the meaning after each sentence did not result in the child's equating the meaning with that of any single known word, as the numerous quotes from Werner and Kaplan's protocols attest (see, e.g., p. 38).

Sometimes the child may be able to figure out the meaning of a word even without any context, from the morphemes constituting it. Knowledge of the noun "hammer" may be sufficient for him to construe the meaning of the like-sounding verb. Once he has internalized the rules of word formation, he may use these to compound the meaning of "movement" from that of "move" and his knowledge of the function of the suffix "-ment." These rules may even enable him to form new words himself: "untie"from "tie," "movable" from "move," and so on. In all these cases, new protoverbal elements are formed on the basis of existing ones (and there will be certain links between these protoverbal elements [see section 9.6]). But the latter are elaborated on, not taken over as they are. In this respect the situation here differs from that discussed in the following.

Pairing With Existing Protoverbal Elements

An examination of the referents assigned by Werner and Kaplan to the nonce-words in their study shows that these are of two kinds. The meaning of "hudray" in the example presented earlier was glossed as "grow, increase, expand, etc." No single English word corresponds in meaning to this word. Most other nonce-words used in their study, however, differed from "hudray" in this respect: They were translatable by a single word. Thus, "sackoy" was translated as "courage," and "lidber" as "gather." (Recall that the subjects in this experiment were 9-13 year olds, who presumably knew these words.) This distinction is not discussed by Werner and Kaplan, but it seems to be an important one to make in dealing with pairing mechanisms. In the case of "hudray," the child had to form a new protoverbal element; this is the situation dealt with in chapter 5. By contrast, in the case of "sackoy" the child merely had to find for the new word a protoverbal element already in his repertoire, namely, that which goes with the word "courage."

The latter situation is also quite frequent in native-language learning. The child often learns two names for the same thing. When mother is called "mummy" by the child, whereas father addresses her by her first name, no confusion need ensue: The child learns both names and knows in which situations each is appropriate. Often the child learns a word for some referent (e.g., "dog") and subsequently learns a superordinate term ("animal"), in connection with the same referent (a dog). The two words will then be linked for some time with the same protoverbal element. Subsequently the child will realize that the superordinate term stands for many more things than the previously learned term "dog" denotes: not only dogs, but cats and mice as well, for each of which the child may already have learned a word, and hence have a protoverbal element available. A new protoverbal element will be fashioned on the basis of existing ones. The situation is similar when subordinate terms are learned (e.g., when "poodle" is learned after "dog"). The acquisition of superordinate and subordinate terms is briefly discussed in section 6.2.

6.2   THE PROGRESS OF CATEGORIZATION

In this section I discuss some later developments, following those described in Chapter 5. First, the acquisition of superordinate and subordinate terms, already touched earlier are dealt with. Next, I take a brief look at the way word meanings change, that is, how protoverbal elements are modified. Then some views regarding the course of word acquisition are presented.

Superordinates And Subordinates

The names by which a thing may be called form a hierarchy: A certain dog may also be a poodle, and of course he is a mammal and an animal. In his classic paper, Brown (1958) has discussed the question of which name in the hierarchy is first used in adult speech to the child. His proposals have been borne out by recent research (Anglin, 1977). Here we are concerned with the learning of additional words in the hierarchy for the same referent, that is, with the learning of a superordinate term after the subordinate term has been learned (e.g., "animal" after "dog" has been learned) or vice versa (e.g., learning "poodle" after "dog"). (In the following, the reader should keep in mind that whereas "superordinate" and "subordinate" are relative terms—a given word may be both a superordinate in respect to one word and a subordinate of another one—we reserve these two terms for words acquired *after* the "basic" level words.)

Suppose the child knows the word "sandwich," and on some occasion hears it referred to as "food" (perhaps by verbal ostension: "Finish your food"). "Food" may now become for him a synonym for "sandwich," which means that the gradual delimitation of the concept that may have gone into the acquisition of "sandwich" need not be repeated. The child will not underextend the use of "food" to refer to only a certain kind of sandwich, nor will he "overextend" it, as long as he has not learned that "food" applies to other things as well. This is because, as stated in section 6.1, the new word is linked to an already existing protoverbal element, not merely to a particular referent. The protoverbal element, (as we have seen in section 5.4) contains a set of cues: properties that were found to be common to various instances of the category. This has consequences for the acquisition of superordinate terms, as is seen presently.

To learn the meaning of "food," the child must of course hear the word paired with other things as well, say, with milk, apples, and cereal. And he must be able to generalize the word to further instances of food in connection with which he may never have heard the word uttered before. The process at work here is positive cue extraction (section 5.3): The child notices what is common to sandwiches, milk, apples, and cereals, and the common properties (functional ones, in this case) become the cues of the word "food." But in the present case, positive cue extraction is a somewhat different process from that which occurred when "sandwich" or "apple" was first learned. To learn "sandwich" he had to note the properties of various sandwiches, to isolate these properties, and thereby the relevant cues were generated. When he later learns "food," however, the properties in question have already been isolated before, and the child can utilize the cues already formed for "sandwich," "milk," "apple," and "cereal."[2]

Presumably, cue extraction is a difficult process for the child. When cue extraction is based on the referents themselves (as discussed in section 5.3) there will often be only a very few properties isolated at a time. Not so when cue extraction is based on protoverbal elements. Comparing the already isolated cues of various previously existing protoverbal elements may be in a sense easier than analyzing the properties of various referents and storing these as cues. (Remember that the account of forming cues given in section 5.3 is not based on the assumption of a universal set of innate features or cues which the child brings with him to the language-learning task). Perhaps we may expect therefore that the typical process of cue extraction from protoverbal elements results in retrieving most of the common cues. This would explain the finding by Saltz, Soller and Sigel (1972) that underextension is the rule in learning superordinate terms, like "toy" and "food." These authors point out that their findings contradict those of other studies of word acquisition, in which overextension was found to occur. But there is such a contradiction only on the assumption that learning superordinates involves the same process as the previous learning of the subordinate terms. On our account the processes differ. The child who hears the word "food" applied to staple food eaten at the table at mealtime will extract all, or most of the cues common to these kinds of food, and hence will not regard things like cookies as belonging to the category food, that is, he will underextend. It is suggested, then, that superordinate terms, are learned primarily by a process of positive cue extraction. (However, findings contradicting those of Saltz et al. have been reported by Nelson [1974], Neimark [1974], and Anglin [1977, pp. 128–129].)

The situation is different when the child learns a subordinate term after he already knows a name higher in the hierarchy; for example, "poodle" after he already knows "dog," "marshmallow" after he knows "candy," or when he learns a more precise term like "stroll" after a more general one, like "walk." At first the new term may here function merely as a synonym ("poodle" may be just another name for "dog" for the child). But soon he finds out that the new term is of more restricted applicability. Discrimination learning sets in. The child isolates cues that distinguish dogs called "poodle" from other dogs and strolling from just walking.

In the foregoing we have considered only the acquisition of superordinate and subordinate terms by means of referent pairing. This is not the only

---

[2]Actually, "food" will often be applied to items for which the child has no other name as well as to those for which he has learned a word previously. The statements made here should therefore be accordingly qualified, but this does not undermine the following argument.

possibility, however: The new word may be explained to the child (see section 6.1). He may be told, for instance: "Dogs, cats, horses and cows are animals." No dog, or other animal is present when the word "animal" is uttered, but the word is paired with other protoverbal elements. Positive cue extraction will take place, utilizing the cues included in these protoverbal elements. The cues common to the protoverbal elements of "dog," "cat," "horse," and "cow," for instance, will be incorporated in a new protoverbal element for "animal." (There will be links between the lexical entries for "animal" and those for "dog," "cat," "horse," etc. [see section 9.6 and the beginning of section 9.7].)

For further discussion of the acquisition of superordinate and subordinate terms the reader is referred to Miller and Johnson-Laird (1976, pp. 293-298).

Modification Of Protoverbal Elements

At the end of section 5.4 we have already seen that protoverbal elements are subject to changes. As a result of further experiences with a word there may occur changes in the boundaries of the concept associated with it, that is, in the protoverbal element. As we see in a moment, these changes are also the result of the two learning processes responsible for the first steps in vocabulary acquisition: discrimination learning and positive cue extraction (section 5.3).

As the child increases his vocabulary, there will be more and more distinctions in the things talked about which he must take into account in expressing himself: The space covered by his stock of words becomes more and more crowded, so to speak. The various words may therefore have to accommodate to each other, and the boundaries of their applicability may have to be redefined. Occasionally this results in the sudden appearance of errors in word use after a long period of correct use. Bowerman (1976) reports that her two daughters substituted, for instance, "take" for "put" or "bring," "put" for "take," "bring," "give," etc., and "give" for "put," after variable lengths of time in which all of the words involved had been used frequently and appropriately. Bowerman's explanation is best given in her own words: "The words had begun to move into semantic proximity after a period in which they had led relatively independent lives [p. 60]." She suggests that, presumably, each of these words was used correctly only in relatively specific contexts, and as their use began to spread "over an increasingly wide and varied semantic terrain . . . [they began] to bump up against each others' territories [p. 62]." (See Bowerman [1978] for further discussion.)

The process of making successively finer discriminations has been studied mainly in the "lexical field" of spatial adjectives. Children usually learn first the meaning of "big" and "little"; other adjectives denoting size con-trasts—"long" and "short," "high" and "low," "thick" and "thin," etc.—come in only later (see, e.g., Bartlett, 1976; Clark, 1972). "Big" and "little" first serve the child as all-purpose words for length, height, thickness, and width, and subsequently he must learn to draw additional distinctions (Sinclair-de Zwart, 1969). One way of conceptualizing the for-mation of these additional protoverbal elements is due to Herbert Clark (1973) and Eve Clark (1973). They suggest that spatial adjectives differ in the number of semantic features which define them, and that the more features required for the definition of a word, the later will it be learned. Thus, "high" differs from "big" in having the additional feature + ver-tical, and consequently it is acquired later than big. Feature analysis has also been applied to verbs of possession ("give," "take," "spend," "buy," "sell," etc.), and here, too, complexity in terms of features has been shown to predict the order of acquisition (Gentner, 1975).[3] Note now that the feature account is readily accommodated by the processes described in sec-tion 5.3. The addition of features may be conceptualized as the acquisition of additional discriminating cues as a result of discrimination learning.

A different process must be involved, however, according to the modification of feature theory suggested by the work of Susan Carey (1978). Carey found that a child may give evidence of knowing the meaning of a more complex word, for instance "tall," for some tasks and for some objects, but not for other tasks and for other objects. If the child had registered merely some of the semantic features of "tall," argues Carey, we would find no such variation. She suggests, therefore, that the child learns, "object by object . . . what spatial adjective applies to what variation [p. 286]." His lexical entry for "tall" for example, may include the informa-tion that the word applies to buildings—and then it describes their extension from the ground up—and to people, and then it describes their extension from head to toe. The child may know what "deep" means when applied to swimming pools, but not when applied to, for example, holes and bowls. What information is stored with the word will be "a reflection of the child's haphazard encounters with the word [p. 287]." Gradually, as he learns how the word is used with many objects, the child abstracts from these object-specific "features" and forms genuine, semantic features. Note that this is the process of positive cue extraction discussed in section 5.3: Similarities

---

[3]For a feature analysis of German pronouns see Deutsch and Pechmann (1978). The Clarks have also claimed that the polarity feature is one of the child's latest acquisitions in this area, and this manifests itself in the confusion of antonyms, for example, of "wide" (positive pole) with "narrow" (negative pole). Several studies have disconfirmed this, however (see Carey, 1978; de Villiers and de Villiers, 1978, pp. 136-143, and Carey, 1978, pp. 275-289, present useful reviews of the field).

between the various referents of, for example, "tall," lead to the extraction of their common cues, and thus the boundaries of the concept are extended.

The meanings of spatial adjectives, according to this view, are acquired in a way similar to that in which the meanings of many other words are extended. Metaphorical extensions have already been dealt with in passing at the end of section 5.4. Let us look now at another example of extension, which appears to be fairly typical of some words, notably verbs.

Consider the verb "stand." The child at first probably takes this word to denote only "to support oneself on the feet in an erect position [Webster, 1970]." Later he has to learn that the word can also be used somewhat differently, as in:

> The tree stands near the house.
> The house stands on the hill.

Do such examples imply that for words like these different meanings must be acquired? That is, are there several protoverbal elements corresponding to a word like "stand"? At the first blush, there seems to be the following alternative. Learning the various uses of "stand" involves an adjustment of its cues. "Erect," in Webster's definition, still counts, but "on the feet" is found to be no longer indispensable: Anything in an upright position and not moving may be said to stand. It appears, however, that the meaning of "stand" may be stretched much further, as for instance in:

> The sun stands high.
> The machine stands still.

(That is, not to mention such metaphorical extensions as "This passage must stand" or "He stands in need of help.") Is there anything in common to all these uses of "stand"? It seems rather, that the relation between them is one of "family resemblances," and if so, the function defining category membership must involve a disjunction of properties (see section 5.3). That there are cases requiring further conceptual apparatus will become clear in section 6.3. At any rate, learning the various uses of "stand" involves the process of positive cue extraction: The child must note what is common to the situations described by "stand" in "Daddy stands near the table," "The tree stands near the house," "The sun stands high," and so on.

Note now that for positive cue extraction to occur, the referents in question must show sufficient resemblance to each other. In the absence of such similarities, two different protoverbal elements will crystallize around the word. This is what presumably happens, among others, in the case of homonyms or of homophones. "Tail" and "tale," for example, though they sound alike, will lead to the formation of two distinct protoverbal elements. There will hardly ever be any confusion in the process (*pace* Alice in Wonderland). In fact, it may take a child some time to discover that two words he knows really sound alike (Kaper, 1959, pp. 29-34).

Not only homonyms (which are, etymologically, separate words), but also a word having two different, though related, senses, may function for the child as two separate words. For instance, some words, like "warm," may be used to describe objects and also, metaphorically, persons. Children first learn the literal meaning of "warm" and other such "double function" words (like "bright," "hard," etc.) and when they later acquire their metaphorical meaning, they may be unaware for some time that they are really dealing with one and the same word (Asch & Nerlove, 1960). On our account the child first forms two separate protoverbal elements (e.g., for "warm" as describing objects and "warm" describing the nature of a person) and only later comes to notice the connection between these.[4]

Each protoverbal element is linked to a word in a lexical entry. As is seen in section 8.1, a lexical entry contains additional information pertaining to the use of words. There are various interrelations between lexical entries: "lead" is related to "follow," "eat" to "feed," and so on. These interrelationships are discussed in section 9.6.

The Course of Acquisition

Susan Carey (1978) has estimated that by age six the child has learned over 14,000 words. To penetrate the mystery of "the child's wizardry as a word learner [p. 265]" she and Elsa Bartlett conducted a study in which nursery school children were introduced to a new word in a play setting (see section 6.1). Their observations of how this word was used and understood indicate that already after one experience with it, or very few experiences, the child has a general idea of what it means. But after this initial, speedy process of acquiring a partial meaning, "protracted further experience was required before learning was complete [p. 274]."[5] If this is indeed the typical course

---

[4]One way of conceptualizing the process is to state that the two protoverbal elements then merge into one that covers a more extended meaning (e.g., that of "warm" both as applied to objects and as applied to persons). The outcome of this process would then be the same as when the meaning of a word (like "tall," in the earlier discussion) is gradually extended without temporarily functioning as a homonym. The decision between this conceptualization and one that assumes that the protoverbal elements (of "warm" referring to objects and "warm" referring to persons) remain separate will presumably have to await the development of a more detailed theory of protoverbal elements. It is my hunch that such a theory will involve various forms of relationships between protoverbal elements, among others, those ranging from differing degrees of overlap to complete independence.

[5]In some cases, when the boundaries between two concepts are fuzzy, it may take the child years to arrive at the mature form of the protoverbal element, even though he knows the corresponding words and can use them more or less correctly. Thus, Andersen (1975) has shown that it takes years to arrive at the distinctions that govern adult usage of "cup" and of "glass."

of acquisition, it leads to a surprising conclusion, namely that the child must learn hundreds of words at the same time. As Carey puts it, the child must "hold onto that fragile new entry in his lexicon [i.e., of the word and its rapidly acquired partial meaning] and keep it separate from hundreds of other fragile new entries [p. 275]." We may well marvel how the child accomplishes this stupendous feat, but let us remember that the child's uncanny abilities are displayed not only in the area of language acquisition: It is no less astounding how the child learns innumerable new facts and pieces together a coherent picture of the perplexing world around him.

A theory concerning the course of word acquisition that deserves to be mentioned here is the "cognitive pendulum" theory proposed by Nelson and Nelson (1978) for various domains of cognitive development. They suggest that in learning words, as in acquiring other "systems," the child passes through several stages. After an initial stage of a few unstable rules, he arrives at a "general rule stage," characterized by a few, usually broad, and very stable rules. This is superseded by a stage at which he develops a larger number of more narrowly applicable and rapidly changing rules. After this comes a period of "integration and consolidation" of the existing rules into a more stable system, which, finally, becomes flexible and adaptable to further contingencies. At the stage of broad rules, the child will overextend the use of words, whereas at the next narrow-rule stage "his naming behavior may become overrigid and inflexible [p. 231]." It appears that a test of Nelson and Nelson's interesting theory will have to wait until more extensive longitudinal data become available (see also section 5.2).

Children's Definitions

A methodological comment is in order here concerning the use of children's definitions in studying the development of word meaning. Such definitions no doubt can give us a clue to what the child knows about a word. It is very doubtful, however, whether we can conclude anything from children's definitions about what they *don't* know. When the child is asked about the meaning of a word, he does not play the investigator's game and gives him a full inventory of features, cues, or properties associated with that word; rather, he will come up with something worth telling about or, at least, salient to him. Suppose we ask a child what "daddy" means. We would hardly be surprised at his recounting some of daddy's latest feats (like, say, playing ball with the child) rather then proffer us the essential but vapid fact that daddy lives with the child and his mother in the same apartment, or such picayune information as that daddy is animate, human, and male.

Even when some type of information is systematically absent in his definitions, this does not imply that this is not part of what he knows. Children's definitions have been found to consist predominantly of functional information (Nelson, 1978). This may indicate nothing more than that it is more interesting to talk about what the definiendum does or what one does with it than about its shape or other perceptual aspects. That a dog brings the paper from the store is news; the pedestrian fact that he has four legs is not worth talking about.

What a child includes in his definition may also be determined by the linguistic resources available to him for the purpose of defining: Some things are difficult to express and may therefore be left unsaid. Note, for instance, that children—and most adults—know only very few words denoting shapes of objects, whereas they have a relatively large stock of words referring to actions. This may contribute to the preponderance of functional rather than perceptual information in children's definitions.

6.3 CONTEXT-DEPENDENT WORD MEANINGS

Our treatment so far has been based in part on the convenient fiction that the child acquires "the" meaning of a word in isolation. We should remember, however, that both linguistic and nonlinguistic context may determine word meaning. The implications of this fact for language acquisition is discussed in the following.

An example of the importance of nonlinguistic context is found in the case of so-called deictic terms: "I," "you," "here," "there," "this," "that," "before," "now," etc. The referent of each of these words depends on a variety of pragmatic factors: who is the speaker, whom he is speaking to, where they are located, and so on. The task of learning such words differs in some respects from that of learning words referring to a category of people, objects, or locations of fixed membership. The acquisition of these words has been the subject of several studies (e.g., Clark, 1977; see de Villiers and de Villiers, 1978, pp. 144-146, for a short review).

Linguistic context may determine not only the reference but also the sense of a word. In the previous section we have seen that the meaning of verbs like "stand" may depend on the word they are predicated of. The various alternative meanings of such a word must all be reflected in its protoverbal element. It was pointed out that membership in the category defined by such a word may depend on a disjunction of properties. We now analyze an example showing that this may be not enough, in some cases.

Observe the following uses of the word "run":

John is running to the store.
The train runs on wheels.
The fire ran along the street.
The street runs through the village.
The sea was running high.

In each of these sentences "run" describes a somewhat different activity or event. Suppose now that the cues—or disjunction of cues—pertaining to "run" are known. This would still not be sufficient for the proper use of "run" because it can be shown that there are other words with the same cues which can not be used in the above contexts, and conversely, there are situations involving similar cues and which can not be described by "run." What cue, for instance, would account for the fact that "run" is correctly ascribed to the fire in the aforementioned sentence, whereas a wildfire is said to "spread"? What is the difference in cues which leads us to say that fire "runs" along the street, but disease "spreads"? Why is the color of a dress said to "run" and not to "spread"? Or why does the street "run" through the village, whereas the river "flows" through it? Is there any non-linguistic motivation for our speaking of the sea running high but of the tide rising?

These examples should suffice to convince us that it is not the properties of the situation alone which determine whether, for example, "run" or "spread" is to be used. Rather, in certain verbal contexts "run" is appropriate (e.g., with "street" as subject), whereas in others "spread" must be used (e.g., with "disease" or "rumor"). Within our theoretical framework this can be conceptualized as follows. Whereas the protoverbal element is determined by the properties of the situation, the choice of word by which the protoverbal element is expressed depends on certain "stage directions" that are stored in the lexical entries of "run" and of "spread" along with the protoverbal element (see Schlesinger, 1977, p. 40; section 8.1) and that take into account the verbal context.

An alternative view would be as follows. "Run" and "spread" are realizations of two discrete protoverbal elements, each of which has "stage directions" stored with it (those for the protoverbal element of "run" for instance, state that the word applies to colors). The present stage of our theorizing does not provide a sufficient basis for deciding between these alternatives (see footnote 4). Further, it must remain an open question at the moment whether all senses of a word like "run" belong to the same protoverbal element, or whether there are perhaps some senses that are included in a separate protoverbal element.

We have seen that when a word has several somewhat different senses, these may all belong to the same protoverbal element. The latter contains cues—each with a different cue value (see section 5.4)—a disjunction of cues being sufficient for the various referents to be classified as belonging to it. On the other hand, when a word is used idiomatically, it belongs to a protoverbal element different from that corresponding to its literal meaning. "To harp" may express either one of two different protoverbal elements, depending on whether one speaks about playing a harp or about repeating something in a tiresome manner. Likewise, when a verb is followed idiomatically by a preposition, it expresses a different protoverbal element from that of the verb without that preposition: compare "run" with "run at" (in the sense of "attack") and with "run down" (in the sense of "chase").

We now come to the point where learning words becomes inseparable from learning grammar. Consider, first, function words, like "and," "which," "in," "of," etc., which do not mean anything in isolation; instead, they help to determine the meaning of the sentence in which they figure. To use these words appropriately, the child must master the realization rules that specify how certain underlying relations are expressed (cf. section 3.2).

The meanings of many other words, besides function words, can often also not be fully specified in isolation. The difference between "precede" and "follow," for instance, is dependent on the words preceding and following them:

> In the procession the coast guard preceded the Mounties.
> In the procession the Mounties followed the coast guard.

Many transitive verbs are like these. Suppose you explain to somebody what "catch" means, employing the word only in isolation. This will not enable your disciple to understand expressions of the form "A catches B," even if he knows English syntax and the meaning of A and B. To understand who does what—who catches and who gets caught—he has to learn something additional about "catch"—how it is used in sentences. This issue is taken up again in section 9.2.

Our discussion of how words are learned thus leads up to a discussion of how grammar is learned—a problem, or rather set of problems, that occupies us in the remainder of this book. At this point, however, an additional comment is in order. It is one thing to recognize that learning the use of certain words depends on learning grammar and quite another to claim that nothing about the meaning of these words can be learned without learning grammar. The child may have learned quite a lot about "catch," for instance, before he has command of even a single realization rule. He may be able, for instance, to sort a set of pictures into those that do and those that do not describe a catching event, and at the same time may not know yet how to indicate the various semantic roles (catcher and catchee) by syntactic structure (see Sinclair & Bronckart, 1972, for some data). Prepositions differ from verbs in that they seem to have no such substance: "before," "in," and "on," for instance, seemingly mean something only when used in a sentence. But even here it is possible for the child to grasp something of their import without mastering their use in the sentence. Conceivably, a child told to "put A on B" may respond promptly and reliably by putting A and B on one another, without knowing which is to be put on which.

This has been overlooked by Vendler (1972). He proposes that knowledge of word meaning "is to be explained in terms of understanding certain incomplete propositions [p. 130]." The adjective "fat," for instance, is understood if we understand what it is for somebody or something to be fat. We therefore "stipulate a minimal environment" for a word; for example, for adjectives, *N is fat*, and for adverbs, *N V (N) deliberately* (p. 131). From these observations Vendler goes on to argue that, because learning words presupposes the understanding of syntactically more complex expressions, language can not be learned from scratch, so to speak: There must be a previous native code into which language is coded. It is superfluous to dwell here on the fact that procuring such a nativist *deus ex machina* really gets us nowhere (see also Chapter 2). Such a move is merely an acknowledgment of—not a solution of—the puzzlement engendered by an a-developmental approach of language learning (and incidentally, some recent philosophic arguments concerning language reveal a penchant for an a-developmental view, which results in no end of confusion). Because understanding a word *ultimately* involves understanding it in a "minimal environment," it is held that from the beginning it must be either understood in this way or else not understood at all. The possibility is not even considered that there may be a gradual development of understanding from a global apprehension of what fat is like, to a full understanding of "fat" in a sentence frame. Which is after all mere common sense.

Let us take leave now from protoverbal elements and words and turn to underlying semantic relations and the rules governing their linguistic expression.

REFERENCES

Andersen, E. S. Cups and glasses: Learning that boundaries are vague. *Journal of Child Language*, 1975, *2*, 79-103.

Anglin, I. M. *Word, object, and conceptual development*. New York: Norton, 1977.

Asch, S. E., & Nerlove, H. The development of double function terms in children: An exploratory investigation. In B. Kaplan & S. Wagner (Eds.), *Perspectives in psychological theory: Essays in honor of Heinz Werner*. New York: International Universities Press, 1960.

Bartlett, E. J. Sizing things up: The acquisition of meaning of dimensional adjectives. *Journal of Child Language*, 1976, *3*, 205-219.

Bowerman, M. *Word meaning and sentence structure: Uniformity, variation and shifts over time in patterns of acquisition*. Paper presented at the Conference on Early Behavioral Assessment of the Communicative and Cognitive Abilities of the Developmentally Disabled, Orcas Island, Washington, 1976.

Bowerman, M. Systematizing semantic knowledge: Changes over time in the child's organization of word meaning. *Child Development*, 1978, *49*, 977-987.

Brown, R. How shall a thing be called? *Psychological Review*, 1958, *65*, 14-21.

Carey, S. The child as word learner. In M. Halle, J. Bresnan & G. Miller (Eds.), *Linguistic theory and psychological reality*. Cambridge, Mass.: MIT Press, 1978.

Clark, E. V. On the child's acquisition of antonyms in two semantic fields. *Journal of Verbal Learning and Verbal Behavior*, 1972, *11*, 750-758.

Clark, E. What's in a word? On the child's acquisition of semantics in his first language. In T. E. Moore (Ed.), *Cognitive development and the acquisition of language*. New York: Academic Press, 1973.

Clark, E. From gesture to word: On the natural history of deixis in language acquisition. In J. Bruner & A. Garon (Eds.), *Human growth and development*. Oxford, England: Clarendon Press, 1977.

Clark, H. H. Space, time, semantics, and the child. In T. E. Moore (Ed.), *Cognitive development and the acquisition of language*. New York: Academic Press, 1973.

Deutsch, W., & Pechmann, T. Ihr, dir, or mir? On the acquisition of pronouns in German children. *Cognition*, 1978, *6*, 155-168.

de Villiers, J., & de Villiers, P. A. *Language acquisition*. Cambridge, Mass.: Harvard University Press, 1978.

Gentner, D. Evidence for the psychological reality of semantic components: The verbs of possession. In D. A. Norman, D. E. Rumelhart, & the LNR Research Group, *Explorations in cognition*. San Francisco: Freeman, 1975.

Kaper, W. *Kindersprachforschung mit Hilfe des Kindes*. Groningen: Wolters, 1959.

Miller, G. A., & Johnson-Laird, P. N. *Language and perception*. Cambridge, Mass.: Harvard University Press, 1976.

Neimark, E. D. Natural language concepts: Additional evidence. *Child Development*, 1974, *45*, 508-511.

Nelson, K. Variations in children's concepts by age and categories. *Child Development*, 1974, *45*, 577-584.

Nelson, K. Semantic development and the development of semantic memory. In K. E. Nelson (Ed.), *Children's Language* (Vol. 1). New York: Gardner Press, 1978.

Nelson, K. E., & Nelson, K. Cognitive pendulums and their linguistic realization. In K. E. Nelson (Ed.), *Children's Language* (Vol. 1). New York: Gardner Press, 1978.

Osgood, C. E. *Method and theory in experimental psychology*. New York: Oxford University Press, 1953.

Saltz, E., Soller, E. & Sigel, I. E. The development of natural language concepts. *Child Development*, 1972, *43*, 1191-1202.

Schlesinger, I. M. *Production and comprehension of utterances*. Hillsdale, N. J.: Lawrence Erlbaum Associates, 1977.

Sinclair, H., & Bronckart, J. P. SVD—A linguistic universal. *Journal of Experimental Child Psychology*, 1972, *14*, 329-348.

Sinclair-de Zwart, H. Developmental psycholinguists. In D. Elkind & J. H. Flavell (Eds.), *Studies in cognitive development*. New York: Oxford University Press, 1969.

Vendler, Z. *Res Cogitans*. Ithaca, N. Y.: Cornell University Press, 1972.

Von Raffler-Engel, W. Some methodological problems in first-language acquisition. Paper presented in Symposium on Child Language, University of Belgrad, Yugoslavia, October 1972.

Webster's Seventh New Collegiate Dictionary. Springfield, Mass.: Merriam, 1970.

Werner, H. Change of meaning: A study of semantic processes through the experimental method. *Journal of General Psychology*, 1954, *50*, 181-208.

Werner, H., & Kaplan, E. The acquisition of word meanings: A developmental study. *Monographs of the Society for Research in Child Development*, 1950, *15*(1, Serial No. 51).

7

Acquisition of Relational Categories: The First Steps

with soft, uneasy steps
to pause and ponder.
Shelley

INTRODUCTION

To master his language, the child must acquire not only a knowledge of words but also rules determining how words are combined to express a given meaning: How they should be inflected and accorded positions relative to each other, what function words have to be used, what intonation contour is to be imposed on them, and what should be their phonological realization. The present chapter and the one that follows attempt to plot this development. To begin with, let us recapitulate some of the basic concepts introduced in Chapter 3.

The deep structure that underlies an utterance is a structure of elements and the relations between them. The elements, called protoverbal elements (section 5.4), are expressed by words. Relations fall into certain categories. For instance, in "John built the mobile" there is the Agent-Action relation between "John" and "built" (more pecisely, between the protoverbal elements underlying these words) and the Patient-Action (Object-Action) relation between "built" and "mobile"; in "Mary had a little lamb" there is the Possessor-Possession relation (between "Mary" and "lamb") and the attributive relation (between "little" and "lamb"). This structure of relations between protoverbal elements, which has been called I-marker, represents the meaning of the utterance.

The child must learn how to convert I-markers into utterances. This conversion takes place according to realization rules. One type of realization rules which will occupy our main attention in the following determines how relations are expressed (by means of word order, inflections, etc.). We will call these RELATION RULES. For example, one of the relation rules of

170

English determines that the word expressing the Agent precedes that expressing the Action of the Agent-Action relation. The child employs this rule in expressing this relation, saying things like "Johny build," and he may also employ it in construing an utterance made by someone else (although often he will have no need for this, the relation intended being self-evident, as in the example). In the mature linguistic system further realization rules are applied to the Agent-Action relation (such as the rule inflecting the third person singular verb in the present tense: "builds"), but these are later acquisitions (some of which are taken up again in the following chapter). Also, there may be various alternative relation rules for one and the same underlying I-marker relation (the choice between these alternatives depending on stylistic factors and others; e.g., interrogative sentences may have a different word order than declaratives). These, too, are not among the first rules learned by the child, and will be dealt with elsewhere (section 8.4). The present chapter concentrates on the child's earliest relation rules: those manifested at the two-word stage.

The plan of this chapter is as follows. The first section discusses the nature of rules which the child has mastered at the earliest stage. Then we raise the question how these rules are learned. This question is inextricably bound up with that of the origin of the relations that figure in the underlying I-marker, as it is these relations that are mapped into the surface string by the relation rules. Here the view is espoused that the relational categories are formed in the process of learning the rules of language, and the major part of this chapter is devoted to showing how such learning proceeds. Stages of language development are described which lead up to the final stage, in which two-word utterances have come fully under the dominion of relation rules. Then I propose a theory of how the formation of relational categories is part of the process of acquiring relation rules. The final sections deal with individual differences in learning relational categories and with their development. Later stages in the acquisition of relational categories and relation rules are the subject of the following chapters.

7.1   THE NATURE OF EARLY RELATION RULES

Word Order

I-marker relations may be realized in various ways. English and several other languages depend largely on word order. It is now well established that among the earliest rules acquired are those involving word order, and that these rules are defined in terms of the underlying relations expressed by the utterance (e.g., Bloom, 1970; Bowerman, 1973b; Brown, 1973; and

Chapter 3; on use of word order in comprehension, see de Villiers and de Villiers, 1973). Even children learning languages that, unlike English, have a relatively free word order (depending mainly on inflections to express the underlying relations), have been found to adhere at first to a rigid word order. This has been reported for children learning Russian (Slobin, 1966), Korean (Park, 1970b), Hungarian (MacWhinney, 1976, p. 406), and for some of the children learning Finnish studied by Bowerman (1973a).

Usually, the word order of children's early utterances conforms to that in the adult simple declarative sentence. Thus, in English-speaking children we find that the subject precedes the verb, which precedes the object. However, there are cases of children's speech deviating systematically from adult word order. Bates (1976, ch. 6) reports that in the earliest utterances of Italian-speaking children the subject tends to occur in final position. (The predominant word order in Italian is subject-verb-object; cf. Slobin, 1978). Bates explains this as due to pragmatic factors: The communicatively more important part of the sentence, the comment, is uttered before the topic. Deviation from adult word order has also been found in several German-speaking children, who in their early utterances put the action word (the verb) in final position (Miller, 1975; Park, 1970a). A possible explanation for the latter finding would be in terms of perceptual factors. The child tends to put first words that stand for salient and vivid concepts, and the concepts denoted by nouns are on the whole more salient and vivid than those denoted by verbs.[1] Gvozdev's reports on word order in his son learning Russian (Slobin, 1966) accords well with this explanation. In Russian there is no one prescribed word order, but adults normally prefer the subject-verb-object order. Zhenya, however, first used the subject-object-verb order. Likewise, Seppo, who learned Finnish, in which word order is also relatively free, at first adhered to the subject-object-verb order (Bowerman, 1973a), and the same has been reported for Susin, learning Korean, where word order is quite free (Park, 1970b). The tendency to put nouns first can be observed occasionally even in the corpora of children learning English (Schlesinger, 1976).

Taken singly, each of these explanations seems plausible. The trouble is that, together, they appear to engage in a tug of war. Why should pragmatic factors play a role only in children learning to speak Italian and not in those learning German? And why should the latter be more susceptible than the former to the influence of saliency? The fact of the matter is that at least some of the children speaking Italian tend for a while to put the subject in final position, whereas at least some of the German-speaking children tend

---

[1]The influence of the child's affect and of vividness in sequencing his first words has been discussed by Stern and Stern (1928/1968, pp. 217-224).

to put the subject and the object before the verb. This difference suggests that the explanation may lie in part in the different structures of the languages in question. For instance, in German the child is likely to hear sentences with the verb in final position after the object, like "Willst du den Teddy holen?" (Do you want to get the teddy bear?) or "Geh den Teddy holen!" (Go and get the teddy bear)[2]. On the other hand, in Italian the subject may be moved into final position for special emphasis, and Bates (1976, p. 188) suggests that the parent may have used such a construction frequently in talking to the child so as to make himself understood. However, the subject-final construction in adult speech was not so frequent as to render this a sufficient explanation, and, as Bates points out, there is presumably an interaction of factors—frequency of adult input and pragmatic factors—which determine the word order adopted by the child (see also Brown, 1973, pp. 156-158).

To the extent that the child's fixed word order is due to the operation of saliency and vividness, he may be said to arrive at it by himself; but to the extent that it affects the word order of adult language it must of course be learned. How such learning proceeds is a problem taken up in the following sections. Here it should be pointed out that learning can not be expected to be immediate; it may often be a piecemeal affair. Occasionally one even finds a child who for a while shows no evidence of having learned any word order at all; a phase of completely free word order in some children has been reported by Braine (1971a) and by Bloom, Lightbown, and Hood (1975, p. 39). More usual are short periods during which the child uses a free word order for a particular construction. For instance, the child may observe word order rules for most of his utterances but not for locatives, using "Entity + Location" alongside of "Location + Entity." Braine (1976) has studied several such instances, which he calls "groping patterns." This is a good descriptive term, but it should not be taken to imply that the child is necessarily trying consciously to follow the adult model and failing part of the time. Instead, he may be nonchalantly uttering words in whatever order is convenient at the moment; and only eventually he falls into the habit of using the order predominant in his environment. Conceivably, he may also at times be intent on emulating adult speech. On other occasions

---

[2]An effect of relative frequency of adult word order on the child's word-order preferences has been reported by Bowerman (1973a). In German, subordinate clauses also have the verb in final position, but it is not clear to what extent adults use such constructions when addressing the child; Park (1970a), at least, claims that these were infrequently used in the case of the child he reports on as using the verb-final order. The Sterns observed some utterances with "nonstandard" word orders in their daughter Hilde, which they explained as imitations of adult constructions (Stern & Stern, 1928/1968, p. 218).

he may even be actively exploring the rules of his language; as we see further on, some investigators believe there may be cases where he utters a few words and only subsequently tries to figure out how they are related.

Intonation And Stress

Word order is not the only means of signalling relations which the child must learn. Quite early, even before the first words appear, the infant begins to distinguish between demands and questions by intonation contour (Bloom, 1973, pp. 19 [note], 59-61; Menyuk, 1971, pp. 61-62; 1977, pp. 33-35, 44; Morse, 1974, pp. 39-41; see, however, Miller & Ervin, 1964, pp. 28-29).

Stress patterns appear early in the child's multiword utterances, and at times may be more consistently applied than word order rules. In a study of children with Mean Lengths of Utterance (MLU) ranging from 1.3 to 2.4, Wieman (1976) found that in Action-Location constructions the word denoting the location was stressed, and this rule was observed more consistently than the word order rule (Action + Location), for example, in "rúg jumped" the rule prescribing the word order "Action + Location" was violated, but the stress is on the word denoting the location. Further, the possessor was stressed in Possessor-Possession constructions ("rábbit house"), the object in Action-Object constructions, and the action in Agent-Action constructions (see also Miller & Ervin, 1964, pp. 22–23).

Inflections

Long before they use inflections meaningfully, children often modify the phonological form of words playfully, reduplicating words, adding syllables, usually those employed in diminutive and affectionate forms [Slobin, 1973, pp. 192-193]. The correct use of inflections, however, usually emerges later than the use of word order. Russian is an inflected language with relatively free word order, but Gvozdev's Zhenya, who learned this language, has been reported to adhere to a strict word order rule before mastering inflections (Slobin, 1966, p. 134). An interesting analogy to this can be found in the acquisition of American Sign Language. In this gestural language the agent and recipient of the action are usually incorporated into the sign for the action. Thus, "He gave her," differs from "She gave him . . ." in the direction in which the hand making the "give" sign moves (Namir & Schlesinger, 1978, p. 102). Children learning this language, however, tend, instead, to sign such sentences by separate signs in a fixed sequence (Newport & Ashbrook, 1977).

Why are inflections learned later than word order? Leopold (1949, p. 3) has suggested that this is because inflections are usually not stressed and are therefore not as readily attended to by the child. Schlesinger (1971b) has argued that a word order rule is easier to learn than a rule about an inflection because the latter involves remembering both an inflectional and an order rule: To which word must the inflectional morpheme be added, and in which position (prefix or suffix)? At any rate, when inflections are acoustically salient and systematically applied, as in Turkish, they can be mastered even before two years of age (Slobin, 1977, p. 190; see also Bowerman, 1973a, p. 114). Evidence for the importance of saliency in the acquisition of inflections has been reviewed by Slobin (1973, pp. 202-203).

Part of the difficulty in mastering inflections may be due to the semantic notions expressed by them. In English a concept like tense, for instance, which is expressed by inflection is presumably more advanced developmentally than, for example, the Agent-Action relation, which is expressed by word order. Further, some inflections, such as the third person singular present "s," are redundant, in the sense that they are not needed to make the speaker's meaning clear, and may therefore be acquired later (Schlesinger, 1971b, pp. 81-82). In some languages some of the rules governing inflections are semantically arbitrary (e.g., the phenomena of gender agreement in the case of nouns denoting inanimates, in French, German, and Hebrew), and may therefore be more difficult to master (Slobin, 1973, pp. 206-208). Brown (1973) has devoted the second half of his book to the problem of the determinants of the order in which various inflectional morphemes emerge in the child's speech. He found order of acquisition to be influenced by both semantical and grammatical complexity but to be unrelated to relative frequency in parental speech.

Grammatical Word Classes

The child must learn not only to place words in proper sequence and to inflect them appropriately but also to select words belonging to the appropriate grammatical category. "Knife," a noun, can not be used to refer to the action of cutting with a knife but only for the object used in cutting. Now, it is precisely such mistakes that one finds in the early multiword utterances of children (the earlier example of the erroneous use of "knife" being due to my Hebrew-speaking son at the age of 23 months). Errors like "more wet" and "all gone sticky" were reported by Braine (1963a) at a time when the child has already mastered some rules of word order. Schlesinger (1971b, pp. 80-81) therefore suggested that rules pertaining to word classes are acquired after those pertaining to word order, but Brown (1973, pp. 118-120), on the basis of more data at his disposal, showed that both types of errors appear at the early two-word stage, and argued that no conclusion as to the precedence of either kind of rule could be drawn. Again, Schaerlaekens (1973) has reported on a study of two sets of Dutch-speaking triplets, and stated that "some categories were used without error where the word order was not yet fixed or where it deviated from adult word order [p. 186]."

More recently, Braine (1976, pp. 76-77) has taken up the question again. On the basis of an examination of several corpora he argues that, to the extent that the child is found to use word classes in accordance with the grammar of his language, this can be accounted for by considering what the child speaks about. For instance, if the child almost always puts a noun after adjectives like "big" or "hot," this is simply because these attributes pertain only to entities which are referred to by nouns in English. Braine concludes therefore that there is no evidence for the child having mastered *grammatical* categories at this early stage. A discussion of the problem of how word classes are acquired will be postponed to the following chapter (section 8.1).

7.2   THE PROBLEM OF THE ORIGIN OF RELATIONAL CATEGORIES

Before the child can learn to produce multiword utterances in accordance with the grammar of his language, he must of course be able to understand the relations expressed by these utterances. He must be cognitively mature enough to interpret his environment before he talks about what happens in it.

This is a truism but one that may lead to disregarding an important distinction that needs to be made. Sometimes insufficent attention has been paid to the distinction between what I have called (section 4.2) the "interpretation problem" and the "categorization problem." The fact that the child has tackled the former task, that he knows particular objects, and can recognize them and makes sense of particular situations and events, does not ipso facto mean that he has formed the corresponding categories. In section 5.6 this point was made in regard to the categories underlying the use of words and the same reasoning applies to the categories underlying relation rules. The child may apprehend what we may call PARTICULAR RELATIONS without having formed a RELATIONAL CATEGORY.[3] For instance, he may realize at a certain moment that a person approaches him,

---

[3]Terminological note: The term "particular relation" might jar those who view "relation" as implying a category. One might suggest therefore a term like "link" or "connection," but what I want to bring out here is the contrast between particular relations and relational categories, that is, between instances and the class they are instances of. Perhaps the word "relation" in the term "particular relation" had better be put between quotes, but to adopt such a practice throughout would look rather too pedantic. Henceforward, "relation" will often be used for "relational category," when the context makes the meaning clear.

at another moment that this person hands him something, and later on again, that the person picks him up. Each of these events involves a particular relation between that person and an action. Moreover, the events have something in common: We say that they all embody the "Agent-Action" relation. But it is *we* who say so, and it does not follow that the child views things in the same manner. "Agent-Action" is a relational category that subsumes an indefinitely large number of particular relations: x approaches, x hands (something to y), x picks up (y), and so on (see section 3.4). The problem we must deal with is how—and when—does the child abstract from such particular relations and form a relational category.

Because abstract he must. It would be impossible to master a system of relation rules such that each particular relation is paired with a rule. The large number of particular relations the child encounters and may wish to talk about is much too large for such particularistic learning. Language would be unthinkable if relation rules would apply to particular relations rather than to relational categories, just as words do not apply to particular objects (attributes, events) but only to categories. But where do relational categories come from?

Several answers to this question are possible (see also Bowerman's [1976a] discussion). One possibility is that those relational categories which language operates with belong to our innate cognitive equipment. Years ago, in advocating the semantic approach to language learning, I suggested that these relations are "part and parcel of our way of viewing the world . . . part of our intellectual outfit [Schlesinger, 1971b, p. 98]." Alternatively, one might hold that the child forms relational categories by interacting with his environment (Nelson, 1973, p. 116 f.). What these two approaches have in common is that relational categories are held to precede the acquisition of language.

In contrast to this, it was proposed in Chapter 4, that the acquisition of relational categories occurs in the process of acquiring language. Conceivably, the child comes to the language-learning task with nothing but the ability to interpret the environment in terms of *particular* relations. In addition, he notices resemblances between different situations and events: He is aware of what we have called the texture of the world around him (section 5.6). But noting such resemblances, and even responding to them (as, in sorting tasks, for instance, cf. section 5.6), neither presupposes categories nor impels the child to form such categories. Categorization sets in as a result of a demand posed by language. As stated, the linguistic system requires that rules be defined in terms of relational categories, and to acquire language the child must note the uniformities in the linguistic expression of various particular relations and subsume several of the latter under one relational category. That the world has texture facilitates the attainment of relational categories. But the nature of these categories—how broad they are and where the boundaries between categories lie—is determined by the language learned. And, as pointed out before (section 4.2), languages may differ in the way they delimit these relational categories (see also sections 9.3 - 9.5).

Empirical evidence on this issue is hard to come by, and so far seems to be nonexistent. The findings of Golinkoff and Kerr (1978) on the child's perception of Agent and Recipient (Patient) roles are interpreted by these authors, tentatively, as showing that the child develops "cognitive categories of action initiation and action recipience" before he learns to express these notions in two-word utterances. In their experiment, 15-18-month-old infants who had not yet reached the two-word stage, were presented films portraying simple events, such as a man (A) pushing another man (B), or a man (A) pushing a chair (B). After several presentations of A pushing B the roles were reversed: B pushed A. These reversals were found to have measurable effects on cardiac deceleration and visual fixation (and, by varying the position of the actor, these effects could be shown not to be due to a change in the direction of the movement). These are interesting results, which are relevant to the way children at that stage solve the interpretation problem. The experiment does not address itself to the categorization problem, however, for by showing that a child perceives a difference between A pushing B and B pushing A, nothing has been established concerning a possible category to which *all* "pushers" belong (vs. one to which all those being pushed belong), not to mention a category including "pusher," "kickers," "eaters," etc. The point I am making here is similar to that made in section 5.6 where it was argued that sorting does not constitute evidence for a category having been formed. Likewise, perceiving a difference does not depend on categorization. (A similar argument concerning nonlinguistic behavior has been presented by de Villiers and de Villiers [1978, p. 77].)

It may turn out to be feasible to show how those relational categories that will eventually play a role in language are acquired by the child through his interaction with the environment, but this has so far not been done. What some writers did attempt was to show how the child learns to interpret his environment in terms of particular relations that, from the vantage point of adult language, may be viewed as belonging to categories like Agent-Action, Possessor-Possession, etc. (See, e.g., Brown [1973, pp. 178-201] who traces the relational categories underlying early child speech to the achievements of the sensorimotor period.) But this, again, is relevant to the child's interpretation of his environment and not to his categorization of the various particular relations observed in the course of this interpretation.

According to the alternative approach proposed earlier, then, relational categories are formed in the course of learning language (just as the concepts underlying words are acquired in the course of learning words, as argued in Chapter 5). In favor of this approach I would argue that it accords with sound scientific methodology. Little progress will result from taking relational categories for granted. Instead, it is incumbent on the theorist to show how they are formed, or else to provide positive evidence for their being innate. At present, it is not clear how such evidence for innateness might be found (cf. Chapter 2). Further support for the present conception of particular relations comes from an examination of the nature of the adult linguistic system and is presented in the final chapter (see especially section 9.5).

Without ruling out the other possibilities discussed earlier, I try therefore to show in the following how relational categories may be acquired in the course of learning relation rules. It becomes clear that such an account meets with a difficulty, which was not encountered in our previous account of how concepts are formed in the course of learning words. Words are relatively well-defined points around which various experiences of referents crystallize into a protoverbal element (as shown in Chapter 5); a linguistic construction is by comparison much more evanescent, and hence the process of categorization into I-marker relations has much less to hold on to. Further on this difficulty and ways of overcoming it are discussed. But first let us look at some stages in the child's early linguistic development that are precursors of the stage at which he expresses relations productively by means of two-word utterances. These stages, it is seen, may contribute to the formation of relational categories.

7.3   STEPS IN THE ACQUISITION OF RELATION RULES

One-Word Utterances

In the beginning was the word. Single words are what we hear from children when they first begin to talk. Only a few children represent an exception to this rule: They refrain from speaking until they are able to produce word combinations (Greenfield & Smith, 1976, p. 220). Most children go through a one-word stage, that may last as long as 12 months (Stern & Stern, 1928/1968, pp. 179-181; Leopold, 1949, p. 45). A single word is enough to get the child's meaning across to the adult who interprets it as standing for a statement or a demand. This was recognized already in 1893 by Stevenson (quoted in Dore, 1975, p. 22), who stated that these words are "equivalent to whole sentences." More recently Von Raffler-Engel (1964, p. 31) remarked that the child tries to imitate the adult discourse as a whole and not only a phrase or a word.

Although the facts have not been disputed, differences of opinion have arisen about their interpretation. The Sterns speak of "one-word sentences" (Stern & Stern, 1928/1968, pp. 179-181), and this raises the question in what sense one-word utterances may be regarded as *sentences*. Bloom (1973, pp. 32-64, 109) maintains that at this stage the child merely names aspects of the global situation. He is aware of the relations in this situation, but because he lacks the linguistic means to express these relations he uses only single words. A label is not a sentence, and for Bloom, then, the beginning of grammar is to be found at a later stage.

A different approach is that advocated by Greenfield and Smith (1976). These authors observe that the child usually utters a single word as an accompaniment to a gesture, such as pointing at a thing, looking at it, or reaching for it. At other times the child reacts to something given in the situation by the use of a single word, as when "Lauren, at 15 months, 5 days, said *Baba* (Barbara) upon hearing footsteps where Barbara (her babysitter) lived [p. 28]." It is the word used in combination with a nonlinguistic event, and not the word in isolation, which expresses a sentence, according to Greenfield and Smith (cf. also Ingram, 1971). In addition to referential meaning, then, the word has what they call "sentential" or "combinatorial" meaning. This distinction is overlooked, they claim, by those who speak about the flexibility of the child's word meanings. Thus, when Piaget (1962) notes that "papeu" (gone away) was used for "people going out of the room, vehicles going away, matches that were blown out [p. 217]," this does not constitute evidence for any fluidity of meaning, as he suggests; rather, it shows that the word must be interpreted in relationship with the situation as expressing a proposition (cf. "the people have gone away," "the car has gone away"; Greenfield & Smith, 1976, pp. 22, 215). Apparently, these authors would regard the child's overextensions on the basis of contiguity (see section 5.2) as his having the correct referential meaning, but using the word to express a proposition.

A major part of Greenfield and Smith's book is devoted to showing how the child progresses, selecting different terms of the proposition at different stages of his development. They view the one-word stage, therefore, as providing the basis for the child's subsequent syntactic development (p. 173 f.).

Greenfield and Smith, then, attribute to the child's speech more structure than is manifestly apparent in his utterances (and other writers have gone even further in this respect; see sections 3.4-3.5). Their approach has been subject to criticism by Bloom (1973, pp. 133-141), which has in turn been refuted by them (Greenfield & Smith, 1976, pp. 214-217). The controversy that ensued is to be found in the writings of Clark (1975); Miller (1975, pp. 164-165); Brown (1973, pp. 154-155); Howe (1976); see also Bates (1976, pp. 79-84), and the summary by de Villiers and de Villiers (1978). The issue is also discussed by Dore (1975), who presents a proposal of his own, which, as Greenfield (1978) argues, is similar in its essentials to that of Greenfield and Smith. The pros and cons of the various positions are not reviewed here, but it should be pointed out that the controversy is of interest only if it is assumed that the child at this stage has at his disposal relational categories. Then there is a point in asking to what extent these categories are involved in the child's one-word utterances. However, if, as has been argued earlier, the child comes to the language-learning task with only the ability to discern particular relations, there is little to dispute. The question then boils down, at most, to the degree of the child's awareness of the particular relations involved in the situation in which he utters the word (i.e., to the way he interprets this situation). And concerning this we all have very little evidence. On this account, therefore, it is questionable whether the one-word stage advances the formation of relational categories, and hence whether it makes a serious contribution to the acquisition of relation rules.

Successive One-Word Utterances

When the child begins to utter several words at a time he usually does so by making several starts, with pauses between the words. This has been noted years ago by several investigators (Jespersen, 1922, p. 135; Leopold, 1949, pp. 20, 24; Stern & Stern, 1928/1968, p. 199). Examples given by Bloom (1970, p. 11) include:

> car. ride
> girl fish. fish
> car. see

Bloom (1973, pp. 39-53) characterized such utterances as occurring without shift of topic, on the one hand, and without the intonation contour of a single sentence, on the other. Because there is no shift of topic, such sequences should not be viewed simply as several one-word utterances uttered shortly one after another. However, the lack of a single intonation contour shows that we do not have here a single sentence planned in advance by the child.[4]

Bloom distinguishes two substages in the stage of successive one-word utterances:

---

[4]In a subsequent study by Branigan (reported in de Villiers and de Villiers, 1978, pp. 50-51), using spectographic analysis of the speech of two children, it was found that the two successively spoken words in fact do have a single frequency contour, similar to that of sentences. As the de Villiers point out, it remains to be seen whether this finding holds up in a larger sample of children. The successive single-words stage may occur in some children, whereas others proceed directly to more sentence-like two-word utterances.

1. *Chained* successive utterances. For example, at 16 months, 3 weeks, Bloom's daughter Allison picks up a toy cow, saying "cow, cow. cow," tries to put it on the chair, saying "chair. chair," turns to her mother for help and says "Mama." Bloom comments: "Each of the utterances accompanied a particular movement relative to the total event [1973, p. 48]." The utterances were related to each other only through these movements.

2. *Holistic* successive utterances. Here the utterances are related to the total event that the child seems to have in her mind at the outset. At the age the above chained utterance was observed, Allison uttered in succession "Mama" and "baby" several times each, and from her behavior and the context "it was clear that she wanted [her mother] to put the doll into the truck [Bloom, 1973, p. 48]." Bloom views this as a development dependent on what Piaget calls "interiorization of action": The child attains the ability to represent to himself actions prior to their interiorization. McNeill (1975), also holds that this type of successive utterances, is controlled by action schemas. Holistic successive utterances were also found by Miller (1975, pp. 162-163) in two German-speaking children, and by Greenfield and Smith (1976, pp. 181-183, 211), who suggest that they may originate in internalized dialogue.

Successive one-word utterances do not necessarily reflect adult word order. Bloom suspects that the order in which the various words are mentioned depends on "factors of focus, salience or relative importance" (1973, p. 53). Greenfield and Smith (1976, pp. 211-213), show that order in successive one-word utterances is predictable to an extent by the principle of informativeness. Taking their lead from Veneziano (1973), they argue that at the one-word stage the child tends to select from the total underlying proposition that word that is most informative. In the successive one-word stage the more informative word is uttered first.

In what way does the successive one-word stage prepare the way for learning the rules governing multiword sentences? Bloom suggests that successive one-word utterances give the child an opportunity to learn about the relations encoded in speech. Prior to the onset of speech the child has "cognitive categories," that are holistic networks of relations (1973, 119-121). He then discovers the semantic relations that function in language (1) by hearing adults use word combinations that refer to the events he has represented conceptually by such networks; and (2) by using such combinations himself: "The child comes to discover the semantic relations that can exist between words by hearing such words in relation to each other, in relation to the events in which they occur, and using such words successively in the same kinds of situations, and noticing that different words mean the same thing relative to other words" [Bloom, 1973, p. 120]; see Clark, 1975, pp. 175-178 for an analysis of Bloom's views on this issue. Later on he learns the rules that govern the order of words standing for the semantic categories developed during the stage of successive one-word utterances (Bloom, 1973, p. 121).

Whereas our distinction between particular relations and relational categories is nowhere drawn explicitly in Bloom's book, it seems that her account of the role of successive one-word utterances presupposes that the child at this stage already has relational *categories*, structured in a holistic network. As Bloom (1973) states, "his cognitive categories are mental representations of the entire relation in experience between agent-action-object or person affected-affecting state, etc. [p. 121]." The task of successive one-word utterances, then, is to analyze the "holistic network" and to isolate the various relational categories. The latter then figure in the language learned by the child. But, as urged previously, we should not take relational categories for granted; rather we should start from the assumption that prior to learning language the child views the world in terms of yet uncategorized relations. According to this approach, the function of successive one-word utterances can merely be to focus on certain *particular* relations inherent in the situation and to make the child aware of them. This leaves us with the question how these particular relations later come to be categorized.

Patterns With Empty Forms

When the child begins to speak, his utterances are often partly unintelligible. Usually the reason will be his limited skill of enunciation: He tries to say a word he has heard and does not quite succeed. Sometimes, however, this is not the whole story. Bloom (1973, p. 33), for instance, describes at length the use of widə, a two syllable "word", by her daughter from the age of 16 months, 1 week on. Widə was unlike a word in that there was no apparent commonality in the situations in which it was used—it did not seem to have a fixed meaning. There was however a syntactic regularity in its use: Almost without exception it appeared in first position. Bloom calls it therefore an "empty" or "archetypal pivot." Dore, Franklin, Miller, and Ramer (1976) provide an additional example of the use of such an empty form by the children they studied, and also report on the use of monosyllables like ə and *te* preceding a word (the former also appears in the corpora of the children reported on by Bloom, Lightbown, & Hood [1975];[5] *cf.* also Peters [1977]). A further example is to be found in Leonard (1975).

---

[5]Conceivably, ə may be the result of the child's imitating the adult's use of the indefinite article. But even if this is so, ə presumably neither differentiates meanings, nor serves to organize the structure of the sentence in the manner of function words. It may therefore be viewed as an empty form.

Dore et al. observe that such empty forms occur in combination with meaningful words alongside of regular utterances, but that with the increase of patterned speech the use of empty forms tends to decrease. They call empty forms (and rote-learned patterns, which are discussed in the following section) "presyntactic patterns", and hold that their function is to provide the child with an opportunity to practise uttering two items with a single intonation contour (just as in their first year some children use "jargon" for a short period, employing meaningless syllables to produce the prosodic pattern of adult speech). The function of these "presyntactic patterns," then, is complementary to that of successive one-word utterances; the latter, conversely, represent combinations of meaning without the usual prosodic pattern.

Empty forms are not universally found among children at the two-word stage. Ramer (1976, p. 49) made a longitudinal study of the grammatical development of seven children and divided them into "rapid" and "slow" syntactic developers. She found that rapid developers used empty forms either not at all or only for a very short time and to a limited degree, or prior to the onset of syntactic constructions. Empty forms appeared mainly in slow developers, and Ramer suggests that because these children experience more difficulty in acquiring syntax, they may have more need of this means of mastering prosody.

It seems reasonable to speculate that not only meaningless sound sequences but also some of the child's earliest words may function as fill-ins in order to practice intonation contours. Words like "it," "is" and "this," for instance, are often found in the child's earliest two-word utterances that are usually held to express the relations of "Nomination" or "Ostension." Now, to name something or to point it out the child might just as well have uttered the name in isolation: Instead of saying "this doggie," just saying "doggie" might have been sufficient. Thus, "introducer" words like "this," "is," "it," etc. are often redundant, and perhaps their main function is to round out the utterance so that it can be given an appropriate intonation contour. The Swedish-speaking girl Embla frequently used the pattern "och + _____" (also + _____) at 23-25 months (Lange & Larsson, 1973, pp. 90-91). In adult speech "och" serves of course, among others, to connect utterances to previous ones, but for Embla this connection "may be more or less clear, and sometimes it is impossible to say what the child is connecting the utterance to [p. 90]." Eventually, Embla will of course learn to employ "och" for its proper purpose, and already at that time we find utterances in her corpus in which the word conjoins nouns or sentences (Lange & Larsson, 1973, p. 91).

Rote-learned Patterns

Some two-word utterances are learned and stored as a unit and are therefore not productive. Burling (1959) reported on the appearance of such rote-learned patterns in a child speaking Garo and English. Examples of such patterns include "no more," used by a child who would use both "more" and "no" in isolation but neither word in combination with any other word (Dore, et al., 1976, p. 28); "what's dat?" used frequently by the children studied by Brown (1968, pp. 282-283), which, he argues, was an unanalyzed form learned as such and not the result of applying a transformation rule. These stored patterns would be presumably analyzed by the child subsequently. Such a process was hypothesized also by Cazden (1968, p. 43). Several utterances of a 15-month-old girl in Nelson's (1973) study, such as "want a drink of water" (p. 107), were almost certainly rote-learned. Braine (1976, pp. 8-9, 13) also gives examples of two-word utterances that he holds to be delayed imitations of adult utterances and not productive patterns. Peters (1977) describes an unusual case of a child who very early tried to produce rather complex multiword utterances, some of which were presumably delayed imitations.

It seems that rote-learned patterns are fairly widespread. Examples can be found also in data published by writers who do not comment on the phenomenon. For instance, Peter, at Mean Length of Utterance (MLU) 1.75, is reported to have said "I turn the light on" and "turn it over" (Bloom et al., 1975, p. 68), and Eric at MLU 1.69—"turn light off [p. 42]," Because it is unlikely that children at that stage have mastered the rules responsible for discontinuous constituents (turn . . . on, turn . . . over, turn . . . off), these utterances presumably made use of rote-learned "prefabricated" routines (in Brown's, 1973, phrasing). A similar argument applies to the utterances of a German-speaking girl, Meike, who at MLU 1.75 said "grosse Nüsse" (big nuts), "grosser Tisch" (big table), using the correct inflections: masculine, plural and singular, respectively (Miller, 1975, p. 234). She could hardly have had learned the rules of gender and number agreement at that age; and in fact, she made errors of inflection at the same period: "gross turm" (big steeple) and "gross kaffee" (big coffee). It is also unlikely that in the former instances she had hit on the correct form by mere chance (five different inflectional endings being used for adjectives in German). Presumably, therefore, these expressions were rote-learned.

To what extent is the child aware of the structure of a rote-learned pattern? Dore et al. (1976) claim that the child does not use such "presyntactic devices" to indicate any relations holding between the words. Rather, the rote-learned pattern functions as a one-word utterance: "Since the forms are not recombinable, there is no true construction and thus there can be no structural meaning [p. 24]." But does this follow? Dore et al. argue from the fact that these forms are not recombined in actual practice to the conclusion that they are not recombinable. But it is conceivable that the child is aware of the relation holding between two words and yet does not recombine any one of them with others, because, when the occasion arises, he prefers a single-word utterance. Dore et al.'s argument is, in effect, that if the child were aware of the relation between the words in a pattern, he would generalize this relation: He would be able to substitute a new word for one of the constituent words, preserving the relation holding in the original pattern. Such generalization is in fact the only obtainable evidence that the structure of the pattern was perspicuous to the child; however, generalization need not immediately follow on its becoming perspicuous. For instance, the pattern may fail to be remembered in a situation where generalization would be appropriate. Further, according to the argument developed previously, the child may be aware only of particular relations at that period; he has not yet developed relational categories. Consequently, he may refrain from generalizing the pattern to any but very closely similar situations.

A possible way of viewing the function of rote learned patterns follows a discussion by Ruth Clark (1974). She reports on sequences of utterances at a somewhat later stage of the child's linguistic development, which are "taken over as unopened packages from the previous adult utterance . . . which were quite clearly copied as incompletely analyzed units, and given a global interpretation with reference to the situation [pp. 3-4]." This characterization may be applicable also to the earlier rote-learned patterns: They are given a "global interpretation" and are "incompletely analyzed." If this is so, they are a step taken by the child toward clarifying to himself the relations holding between words, just as successive one-word utterances serve, in Bloom's opinion, a step in that direction.

Pivot Patterns

The renewed interest in the grammar of child language in the early 1960s led to a spate of studies which revealed a peculiarity of the child's two-word utterances: For a given child's corpus, it is possible to identify a small set of words that appear over and over again in combination with various words from a much larger set of less frequently occurring ones. Furthermore, it was noted that each of the high-frequency words tended to occupy a fixed position in the two-word utterance (Braine, 1963a; Brown & Fraser, 1963; Miller & Ervin, 1964). The occurrence of such "pivot words," as he called them, led Braine (1963b) to propose that the child begins to learn the grammar of his language by noting the relative position of a limited number of words, and he showed experimentally that preschoolers were indeed capable of such position learning. He also maintained that pivot words would not combine with other pivot words (Braine, 1963a), and has been understood —or rather misunderstood, as he claims (Braine, 1976, p. 10)—to hold that pivot words do not occur alone. Subsequently, McNeill (1966) has developed the pivot theory further.

The proposal that the child's two-word utterances can be described by a pivot grammar has since been refuted by other investigators on the basis of more extensive data than those at Braine's disposal (Bloom, 1970; Bowerman, 1973a; Brown, 1973, pp. 97-104; Schaerlaekens, 1973, pp. 29-37; Van der Geest, 1974). Braine (1976, pp. 13, 88) now admits that his theory was erroneous because data from too few children were then available. It now appears that many, perhaps most, corpora are not adequately described by a pivot grammar. Moreover, Bloom (1970) has shown that even for those children in whose early speech pivot words are evident such a grammar fails to describe the knowledge that the child possesses at that stage. The child must be credited with knowing rules that determine how semantic relations are expressed. The fact that some words occur in a wide variety of combinations does not show that the positions of these words have been learned; instead, this may be due to their versatility and usefulness for expressing the child's semantic intentions (Brown, 1973, pp. 169-172). The reason a description in terms of pivots appeared plausible is that such an account and one in terms of semantic relations "converge on the same set of data, because pivot words tend to appear in combinations exhibiting certain relations and, hence, in certain positions. Thus, 'more' is a modifier, and . . . [therefore] comes in the first position. Pivot theory states the same fact by saying the 'more' is a P_1 (i.e., a first position pivot [Schlesinger, 1971b, p. 79])."

The fact remains, however, that the child's early speech often evinces the pronounced frequency imbalance described by Braine (Brown, 1973, p. 103). Typically, there are a few frequent words, each in a fixed position, and many infrequent ones, and this holds true not only for children learning English but also for those learning such widely differing languages as "Bulgarian, French, German, Japanese, Luo (Kenya), Russian, Samoan, and Serbian" (Slobin, 1971, p. 46), Finnish (Bowerman, 1973a) Egyptian Arabic (Omar, 1973), Polish (Smoczyńska, 1976) Swedish (Brown, 1973, p. 103), and Dutch (Klein, 1974, p. 320; Schaerlaekens, 1973, p. 32). What has been refuted by the data is only the claim that these few frequent words always meet the criteria for pivot words set down by Braine (1963a) and McNeill (1966). What needs to be noted, and was previously not appreciated, is that when these frequent words combine with other words they serve to express semantic relations. Hence there are constraints on such combinations: A pivot word cannot combine with just any word but only with those with which it stands in a semantic relation (Brown, 1973, pp. 99-100; Schaerlaekens, 1973, p. 34).

It appears, therefore, that one of the characteristics of early child speech is the occurrence of what we call PIVOT PATTERNS. We speak of a pivot pattern whenever there are a number of utterances in a child's corpus which have the following in common: (1) all of the utterances include the same word (the pivot word); (2) in a fixed position; (3) which stands in the same (or in a very similar) relation to the other word or words in the utterance. (Note that this definition does not include certain distributional criteria previously associated with pivots: nonoccurrence of a pivot word with another pivot word or in isolation.)

Accordingly, we may have two different pivot patterns whenever a word appears repeatedly but stands in different relation to the other word. Thus, Miller (1975, p. 255 f.) recorded 16 utterances with "auch" (also) in first position and 41 utterances with this word in second position, for Meike at an MLU of 1.14 - 1.75; and for another girl, Simone at MLU 1.09 - 1.46, 35 times "auch" in first and 14 times in second position. Miller shows that the different positions correspond to different semantic relations expressed by the combination. The word "auch," then, participated in two pivot patterns. In principle it would be possible to have two pivot patterns differing in the relations expressed but where the common word appears in the *same* position.

We thus take over the old notion of pivots and add to it the requirement that a given semantic relation be expressed. This new look, I believe, may contribute to an understanding of grammatical development. Pivot patterns are productive: The pivot word can enter additional combinations involving similar semantic relations. Moreover—as is shown later on—the pivot pattern may be generalized to other combinations not involving the pivot word. But before going on to show how this leads to the formation of relational categories, I would like to document the fact that pivot patterns are indeed ubiquitous.

Tables 7.1 - 7.5 list pivot patterns found in the corpora of children speaking different languages, arranged according to the semantic relations expressed. An arbitrary criterion was adopted: a minimum frequency of four occurrences of a pattern. This criterion probably entails an under-representation of pivot patterns, in particular for small corpora (see Bowerman, 1975, pp. 81-83). Also, the most frequent type of pivot patterns are not included in the tables, namely, those expressing relations of ostension, recurrence, and disappearance (Bloom's, 1973, p. 23, "functional categories") and involving pivot words like "here," "there," "see," "it," "more," "other," "all gone," "no," "no more," "auch" (in the German study

TABLE 7.1
Pivot Patterns Exhibiting The Agent-Action Relation

Pivot Argument	Name of Child	MLU or Age in Months	Language	Source	Examples
Agent	Gia	1.58-1.79	English	Bloom et al. (1975, Appendix)	Gia writing Gia push
	Peter	1.33-1.41	English	do.	I did it I get them
	Eric	1.42-1.69	English	do.	I fix it I do
	Åsa	1.72-1.82	Swedish	Lindhagen (1976, p. 144)	Åsa åka (Åsa go) Åsa sitta (Åsa sit)[1]
	Embla	1.52	Swedish	Lange & Larsson (1973, p. 94)[2]	Mamma bygga (mother build) Mamma hjälpa (mother help)[3]
	Kendall	1.10	English	Bowerman (1973a, p. 237)	Kendall sit Kendall read[4]
	Seppo	1.42	Finnish	Bowerman (1973a, p. 247)	tipu laulaa (chick sings) tipu katsoo (chick watches)[5]
	Rina	1.83	Finnish	Bowerman (1973a, p. 276)	Rina pelleilee (R. clowns) Rina avaa (R. opens)
	Meike	1.14-1.35	German	Miller (1975, p. 215)	Mone weint (Simone weeps) Mone klingelt (Simone rings)
Action	Jonathan	24 m.	English	Braine (1976, p. 34)	Andrew walk daddy walk
	Meike	1.14-1.35	German	Miller (1975, p. 215)	Teddy schläft (teddy bear sleeps) puppe schläft (doll sleeps)
	Tofi	1.6	Samoan	Kernan (1969, p. 130-131)[6]	pa'u: mea (fall thing)[6] pa'u: teine (fall girl)[6]

[1]The same child had similar pivot patterns with "Mamma" and "Karin" as agent terms.
[2]Cited in Braine (1976, p. 49).
[3]The same child had a similar pivot pattern with her own name as agent term.
[4]Pivot patterns with "Mommy" and "Daddy" as agent terms were also found for this child.
[5]Another pivot pattern with "pupu" (bunny) as agent term was also found for this child.
[6]Note that in case grammar the argument of "fall" is classified as "Object".

TABLE 7.2
Pivot Patterns Expressing Their Action-Object Relation

Pivot Argument	Name of Child	MLU or Age in Months	Language	Source	Examples
Action	Gia	1.34-1.58	English	Bloom et al. (1975, p. 50)	ride Dumbo ride dis
	Meike	1.14-1.34	German	Miller (1975, p. 216)	Teddy holn (get teddy bear) buch holn (get book)[1]
	Simone	1.04	German	Miller (1975, p. 218)	Stiefel aus (boots off) Strümpfe aus (socks off)
Object	Gregory	from 18 m. on	English	Braine (1963b)	push it move it[2]
	Eric	1.19-1.42	English	Bloom et al. (1975, p. 42)	ə find it play it
	Peter	1.37-1.41	English	do.	pull it turn it

[1]The same child had also a pivot pattern with "suchen" (look for) in first position.
[2]But Braine (1976, p. 13) believes these to be rote-learned patterns.

cited earlier), etc., as well as those expressing wishes and demands, with pivot words like "want" and "give me." This is because these relations do not seem to function as relational categories in the linguistic system of the mature speaker (where ostension, recurrence, demands, etc. are expressed by words functioning as terms in other relations). It is therefore not clear whether these pivot patterns serve as a basis for the formation of relational categories. We limit ourselves therefore to pivot patterns exhibiting the following relations, which presumably figure in the adult language system: Agent-Action (Table 7.1), Action-Object (Table 7.2), Action-Locative and Entity-Locative (Table 7.3), Possessor-Possession (Table 7.4), and Entity-Attributive (Table 7.5). (This classification is the one given in Brown [1973, p. 173]. The term *Patient* seems to be preferable to *Object*, because the latter is used as a syntactic term, but in the following *Object* will often be used.) The tables present ample evidence that pivot patterns expressing these relations are indeed widespread.

The tables give the MLU of the child at the time the utterance was recorded (or the range of MLUs, where data from a number of sessions were com-

TABLE 7.3
Pivot Patterns Expressing Action-Locative And Entity-Locative Relations

Pivot Argument	Name of Child	MLU or Age in Months	Language	Source	Examples
Action	Embla	1.52	Swedish	Lange & Larsson (1973, pp. 95-96)[1]	gå Martin (go [to] Martin) gå Moderna (go Modern [Museum])
	Patrik	1.59-1.69	Swedish	Lindhagen (1976, pp. 129, 133)	sitta där (sit there) sitter traktorn (sit in the tractor)
	Åsa	1.93	Swedish	Lindhagen (1976, p. 147)	ligga där (lie there) ligga soffa (lie sofa)
Location (of Action)	Tofi	1.61	Samoan	Kernan (1969, Appendix A)[2]	alu lea! (go there!) mai lea! (bring there!)
Entity	Kendall	1.48	English	Bowerman (1973a, pp. 241-242)	Kendall innere Kendall bed
Location (of Entity)	Simone	1.75	German	Miller (1975, p. 222)	karre rein (wheelbarrow innere) becher rein (cup innere)

[1]Cited in Braine (1976, p. 49).
[2]Cited in Braine (1976, p. 29).

bined to reach the criterial frequency of four utterances for a pattern). When information about MLU is missing, age to the nearest month is indicated in the table. These data are given for the earliest appearance of the pattern, and sometimes the same pattern continued to occur in later sessions.

Open Relational Patterns

Pivot patterns are productive, but their productivity may be restricted to combinations that include the pivot word. Eventually the child reaches a stage at which he can combine *any* two words expressing a given semantic relation in accordance with a relation rule involving word order or inflections. For example, Jonathan (see Table 7.1) learns to express the Agent-Action relation not only with the pivot word "walk," as in:

> Andrew walk
> daddy walk

but also with other words, as in:

> Elliot sleep
> mommy sit
> daddy work

(see Braine, 1976, p. 34). Productivity is now unrestricted. The place of the pivot word is taken by an open class of words standing in the same relation to other words. Let us therefore call such a pattern OPEN RELATIONAL PATTERN. As far as can be judged from the published corpora, such patterns occur at about the same time as pivot patterns, or shortly after the first pivot patterns appear but overlapping with the pivot pattern stage.

TABLE 7.4
Pivot Patterns Expressing The Possessor-Possession Relation

Pivot Argument	Name of Child	MLU or Age in Months	Language	Source	Examples
Possessor	Jonathan	23 m.	English	Braine (1976, p. 31)	daddy shoe daddy car
	Åsa	1.37-1.43	Swedish	Lindhagen (1976, p. 138)	Åsa blöja (Åsa diaper) Åsa mössa (Åsa hat)
	Sipili	1.52	Samoan	Kernan (1969, pp. 26-27)[1]	va'a a'u (boat me) lole a'u (candy me)[2]
	Meike[3]	1.13-1.34	German	Miller (1975, p. 223)	Mone löffel (Simone spoon) Mone stock (Simone stick)
	Simone[3]	1.09-1.10	German	Miller (1975, p. 224)	Mone sand (Simone sand) Mone brei (Simone pap)
	Kathryn	1.86	German	Park (1974, p. 85)	Bela bett (Bela bed) Bela bahn (Bela train)

[1]Cited in Braine (1976, p. 25 ff.).

[2]The same child also had a pivot pattern with " 'oe" (you) in second position, expressing possession.

[3]Meike and Simone used to spend much time together and Miller's detailed records evoke the impression of many similarities in their utterances.

A commonly held view concerning the acquisition of relational patterns is that when the child hears adults talking about a certain event or situation, he notices the relations holding between the referents of the words used and how these relations are expressed linguistically, for example, by word order. Then he tries to imitate the adult. Production, thus, is based on previously occurring comprehension. This order of events is reversed by Clark, Hutcheson, and Van Buren (1974). They suggest that instead of attempting to produce two-word utterances expressing previously comprehended relations, the child's production of utterances may lead to the formation of relations. The child, they argue, concatenates words, and by doing so frequently, he becomes aware of the relations that hold between them: "Through manipulating combinations of words and reflecting on them the child comes to the realization that various relationships can be expressed by means of language [p. 51]." Thus, the child may pick out two salient aspects of the situation, utter the words denoting these aspects, and subsequently notice that the aspects thus highlighted are related as location and entity located.

Various observations are cited by Clark et al. in support of their intriguing hypothesis. First, during the early two-word stage word order is not yet quite stable; in Braine's (1976) term—"groping patterns" are frequent.

TABLE 7.5
Pivot Patterns Expressing The Entity-Attributive Relation

Pivot Argument	Name of Child	MLU or Age in Months	Language	Source	Examples
Attribute	Jonathan	23 m.	English	Braine (1976, p. 32)	big plane big book[1]
	Eve	25.5 m.	English	Brown & Fraser (1963, p. 172)	two Bobby two chair
	Eve	25.5 m.	English	Brown & Fraser (1964, p. 64)	carriage broken chair broken[2]
	Meike	1.75	German	Miller (1975, p. 234)	gross turm (big tower) gross kaffee (big coffee)
	Kathryn	2.24	German	Park (1974, pp. 98-99)	grosse messer (big knife) grosse turm (big tower)

[1]The same child also had a pivot pattern with "little" in first position. One month later, the records show, in addition, pivot patterns with "hurt" "old" and "hot" and "two," expressing attributes.

[2]See comment in text.

There is no evidence at that time, then, that the child realizes in his speech the relations of adult language. Instead, he may just have concatenated two words—perhaps with the intonation contour of a sentence—which name various aspects of the situation. This suspicion that the child is not yet expressing relational categories is strengthened by the fact that the corpora contain many two-word utterances that do not seem to express any one of the semantic relations known to operate in adult language. Thus Clark's son, Adam, was playing with his toy car when his father left the room; Adam dropped the car and followed him, saying "daddy car." What could, conceivably, be the relation between "daddy" and "car"? Apparently, only a very indirect one. Another example, quoted by Clark (1975), is due to Allison, with an MLU of 1.73, who said "man empty" when pushing her finger in the window of an empty toy truck cab (Bloom, 1973, p. 250). In these instances the uttering of word pairs will presumably contribute little to the development of those relational categories that function in the adult system. Often, however, the child will fixate on more intimately connected aspects of the situation, the relation between the corresponding words will be one that functions in the mature linguistic system, and this may be conducive to developing the relevant relational category.

Another fact which may be adduced in favor of Clark's theory is that two-word utterances are often regarded as uninterpretable by the investigators (e.g., Bowerman, 1973a, Appendices C and G; Brown, 1973, p. 178; Leonard, 1976, pp. 155-156). Clark et al. refer us also to the "seemingly nonsensical concatenations found among the utterances" made by children engaged in substitution drills (Weir, 1962) and in replacement sequences (Braine, 1971a), and they report on an amusing anecdote showing that "there comes a point . . . when the child begins to notice when he is producing nonsense and be disturbed by it [p. 50]." All this seems to suggest, according to Clark et al., that the child may be learning by doing: He puts words together and then ponders the result.

Clark et al. also question the seemingly common-sensical assumption that production of sentences is more difficult for the child than their comprehension. First, they show that comprehension may often be overestimated, because successful communication with the child is assisted by contextual cues and certain redundancies in the language and the messages transmitted. They go on to argue that because the situation plays a major part in communication, speaking enjoys a relative advantage over understanding speech as far as the child is concerned. In speaking the child will remark on those aspects of the situation which are prominent to him, whereas in listening to someone else he must adjust himself to the other's viewpoint and redirect his attention to what is prominent to another person and is not so to himself. Production being easier, one may expect that it plays a leading role in language learning, much more so than comprehension, which is more difficult.

It should be noted that Clark et al.'s proposal does not deal with what we have claimed to be the main problem of the early acquisition of relation rules, viz. the problem of how relational categories are formed. According to the position outlined at the beginning of this chapter that the child does not come to the language learning task with relational categories, their hypothesis is relevant only to the question of how particular relations are explored and more clearly recognized. In reflecting on the relations between words he has haphazardly concatenated, the child interprets the situation to himself. Such interpretation, as we have seen, may be carried out in terms of particular relations. Hence, successive one-word utterances may, on Clark's et al.'s account, serve as a preparatory step toward the eduction of relational categories from particular relations, but it still remains for us to explain the latter process.

There is one difficulty with their account, however. If the child always starts out by producing combinations of words the relation between which he does not yet understand, we would expect the first two-word utterances not to obey any linguistic rules. The word order in the earliest utterances would be random, that is, correct about half the time. Almost all records of child speech, however, show that this is not so. The child adheres to the adult word order most of the time, and Braine's groping patterns are the exception rather than the rule. (Our hypothesis concerning the acquisition of relational categories, which will be proposed later on, explains this finding as well.) It appears, therefore, that Clark et al.'s description may be appropriate, at most, for *some* of the instances in which the child produces two-word utterances. Often the child understands already the relations he talks about and expresses these according to a relational rule he has acquired.

This ends our survey of the steppingstones leading up to the expression of semantic relations in the two-word stage. These stages are summarized, together with the terminal stage of open relational patterns, in Table 7.6. No strict sequence is implied by the enumeration of stages in the table; they are presented there in the order discussed in the previous sections. Little is known, for instance, about the time at which rote-learned patterns tend to appear relative to, say, pivot patterns or patterns with empty forms.

It should be clear from the discussion in the preceding sections that each of these steps presumably contributes something to the learning of relational rules. However, the process whereby the child acquires relational categories has so far not been elucidated. Before we take up this problem, a few remarks are in order concerning the way children learn language.

7.4   ACTIVE AND PASSIVE LEARNING

Several mechanisms of learning grammar have been discussed in the literature. It is now fairly clear that overt reinforcement and corrections are

TABLE 7.6
Characterization Of Various Stages In The Acquisition Of
Relation Rules According To Three Criteria

	Relation Between Linguistically Expressed Element	Order of Elements	Productivity
One-word utterances			
Sequences of one-word utterances			
chained	?	no rule	
holistic	yes	no rule	
Patterns with empty forms.		rule determined	restricted
Rote learned patterns	sometimes	fixed	none
Pivot patterns	yes	rule determined	restricted
Open relational patterns	yes	rule determined	full

Note: Where the criterion is inapplicable the cell has been left empty.

not indispensable for language acquisition (Braine, 1971b, pp. 159-161; Brown, 1973, pp. 410-412). Evidence is accumulating that the child's imitations may have an important role to play (e.g., Bloom, Hood, & Lightbown, 1974; Braine, 1971a, pp. 65-66; Clark, 1977; Nelson, 1973; Whitehurst & Vasta, 1975, cf., however, Leonard & Kaplan, 1976). For a long time the idea has been around that the acquisition of syntax is facilitated by the adult's repeating the child's rudimentary sentences in a fuller, more "expanded" form (Brown 1973, p. 411), but only recently some evidence for this has been found (Newport, Gleitman, & Gleitman, 1977). Another interesting proposal is that of Greenfield and Smith (1976, pp. 174-181, 201), who argue that dialogues between adult and child may contribute to the emergence of rule-governed two-word utterances. In answer to questions posed by the adult, the child at first utters only one word. This word is semantically related to a word contained in the question. Later, the child in a sense internalizes the role of a questioner and forms such question-answer word pairs himself.

The foregoing mechanisms have this in common that they rely on the child's active use of language. Without detracting from their importance, we may here state with confidence that they are not indispensable to language learning. Children have been known to learn language without themselves ever uttering a word. The classic example is the case of the dysarthric boy, who could comprehend speech without ever having been able to talk. He therefore must have learned the language just by listening passively (Lennenberg, 1962). There are also reports on autistic children who never spoke, but learned language even to the point of expressing themselves in writing.[6] In a laboratory experiment with college students Braine (1971b) showed that syntactic rules of an artificial language constituted of nonsense words could be learned from listening to tape recordings (see, however, section 3.3). That such artificial languages can be learned by visual observation has been shown by Reber and Allen (1978). Language, then, can be attained by passive learning.

This conclusion has an important bearing on the function of the processes discussed in the preceding sections. It implies that the child does not necessarily have to *produce* any of these types of utterances in order to learn language. Sequences of one-word utterances and patterns with empty forms may facilitate the learning of relation rules and may be operative in the normal child under normal conditions, but they are certainly not indispensable. Likewise, concatenating words and contemplating the result may clarify for the child the relations expressed in language, as argued by Clark et al. (1974); but if this strategy would be indispensable, a child who has to fall back on passive learning would never learn language.

Children who, due to some abnormality, never use language productively thus provide us with a test case that may reveal the minimal conditions for language learning. Presumably, they avail themselves of some of the steppingstones in Table 7.6 in a passive manner—by observing patterns occurring in adult speech. Specifically, it seems reasonable to assume that there is opportunity to acquire two kinds of patterns by listening to adult speech: rote-learned patterns and pivot patterns. A sequence of words can be learned by rote through merely listening, without ever uttering them. Likewise, a child may learn a pivot pattern without producing it in his speech. It will of course be hard to come by any evidence that the child has learned such a pattern unless it turns up in his speech, as it is bound to do sooner or later in the normal course of events. But active use is not a prerequisite for learning such patterns, and frequency of occurrence in the child's speech is therefore not an infallible guide to the strength of the patterns learned. (It is generally true that production data may lead to an underestimation of a child's knowledge; see Limber, 1976.) These considerations seem to suggest strongly that rote-learned patterns and pivot patterns may fulfill a crucial function in the attainment of relational categories. In the next section we follow this lead.

---

[6]I owe this information to Avigail Schlesinger, who has taught several such children to write. It is also of interest that Genie, the girl who was reared in isolation up to the age of fourteen, also could comprehend much more language than she ever produced (Curtiss, 1977).

7.5 FORMATION OF RELATIONAL CATEGORIES

In a previous section we advanced the working hypothesis that the child perceives only particular relations in the world around him before he starts learning language. In the course of acquiring the rules by which words are combined into sentences he must group those particular relations into categories to which these rules apply. In the following, we take up the question of how these relational categories are formed.

The Problem Of Nonuniqueness Of Linguistic Expression

In section 3.4 it was proposed that the child observes regularities in the way various particular relations are expressed linguistically and on the basis of a common linguistic expression groups these into categories. Note the analogy between this process and the one suggested in Chapter 5 to account for the formation of protoverbal elements. The common linguistic expression, the word, was claimed to be the cement that held together the internal representations of the various referents. The situation is far less simple, however, in the case of relational categories. The word is a relatively salient linguistic element associated with each of the instances of referents belonging to the same protoverbal element and unique to them. By contrast, there may be no linguistic expression common and unique to a given relational category. The English-speaking child hears various utterances exhibiting the Agent-Action relation in all of which the word representing the agent precedes the one representing the action; but he likewise hears utterances in which the possessor precedes the possession, the entity precedes the place it is located, and so on (see also Howe, 1976). There is therefore no linguistic characteristic unique to any one of these relations which can serve to delimit them from each other. Children learning inflected languages, in which the various relations have different inflectional endings, may be somewhat better off in this respect, but we must find a mechanism of learning which deals adequately also with the achievements of children learning uninflected languages, who seem to attain their goal just as fast and as effectively.

However, the lack of unique linguistic expressions for relational categories presents much less of an obstacle than might appear at the first blush. This becomes clear by considering the way words are learned. It was pointed out that we cannot assume that the child remembers all the occasions on which a word was uttered and then proceeds to compare the corresponding referents and to abstract what is common to all of them. Such a procedure would impose far too great a strain on the child's limited memory capacity. Instead, it has been argued that the child generalizes from a referent paired with a word on one occasion to a similar referent encountered on another occasion. Such generalization may be active—the child produces the word—or passive—he hears the adult producing it (section 5.3). Similarly, the child can not acquire a relational category at one go, by comparing instances of a certain word order pattern; as stated, the various particular relations exhibiting such a pattern are much too mixed a lot. Rather, a relational category is formed, as in the case of protoverbal elements, by moving from one instance to another. The child may observe a certain word order being used in expressing a particular relation, and on the next occasion he generalizes this word order to a very similar particular relation. Thus, through successive accretions, a relational category is built up. He will not generalize to a quite unsimilar particular relation that in the adult system may belong to a different relational category, and hence the various relational categories will be held separate.

This explanation is based on the assumption that the child's relational categories are quite distinct from each other on purely semantic grounds. This is not true for the adult system in which rather broad categories function, and boundary cases abound, so that the membership of any particular relation in a category is determined by the form of the appropriate linguistic expression (see sections 9.3-9.5). As will be shown in detail in section 7.6, however, the child starts out with much more narrowly circumscribed categories. Particular relations cluster closely around certain prototypes and these prototypes are very easily distinguishable from each other. Take, for example the Agent-Action relation. For many children the prototype of this relational category involves an animate actor performing an overt movement (see de Villiers, 1979). The earliest Agent-Action constructions of these children will therefore appear in utterances like "daddy walk," "Johnnie push" and "baby eat" (and only later on will this narrow category be extended to include particular relations less similar to the above prototype). This prototype will not tend to be generalized to the quite unsimilar Possessor-Possession relation or to any one of the other early relational categories.

The lack of uniqueness of linguistic expression thus does not obviate the formation of categories. There are different, semantically distinct particular relations that serve as prototypes around each of which various instances cluster. A fictitious analogy would be the learning of homonyms. Imagine a language in which for some reason apples and dogs are referred to by two homonymous words. This would not debar the child from forming the corresponding concepts (say, fruit and quadruped). The perceptual distance between apples and dogs would safeguard the two concepts from merging: Instances of apples (and perhaps some similar referents) would accrue to the paired referents of "apple" and instances of dogs—to those of "dog" (see section 6.2 on this point). Admittedly, the distinctions between situations to which various relational categories apply may at times be much less salient cognitively than those between apples and dogs, but then we do not know how broad the child's early relational categories are; as is discussed in the following section, he may at first lump together two categories that are somewhat similar and only later on differentiate these. Furthermore, the child's task of keeping two categories apart may be facilitated if one of them has become well established before he begins to form the other (e.g., if he learns the word for apple before finding out that a homonymous word applies to dogs). Presumably, such successive acquisition is typical in the case of relational categories.

Patterns Forming The Basis Of Generalization

Here one might raise the following objection. The above proposal presupposes that the utterance forming the basis for generalization to an open relational pattern is in some sense remembered from one occasion to another. The child who has heard an Agent-Action relation expressed on one occasion, and perhaps imitated it as, say, "mummy come," must remember the precise form of this utterance—including word order—as well as the particular relation expressed thereby at the time he generalizes from it to an utterance exhibiting a similar particular relation, such as, for instance, "baby cry." Can we credit the child with such memory feats? A one-time occurrence of an utterance seems rather too transient an event to serve as a basis for generalization.

But there are two-word utterances that are well enough established to form such a basis: rote-learned patterns. The child may have learned "mummy come" as a fixed prefabricated form that he uses on various occasions, and he may moreover be aware of the particular relation holding between what is denoted by "mummy" and by "come" (as argued in our previous discussion of rote-learned patterns). Subsequently he may interpret another situation in terms of a particular relation that resembles that in "mummy come"—for example, the baby cries—and he may generalize from that well-entrenched pattern and produce a new combination: "baby cry."

The greater the similarity between perceived particular relations the more likely will generalization be to occur. The relation expressed in "daddy come" presumably appears to the child to be more similar to that in "mummy come" than the relation in "baby cry"; the relations perceived in two acts involving coming resemble each other more than those in an act of coming and in one of crying. Not surprisingly, therefore, pivot patterns tend to be formed, each of which is built around particular relations resembling each other very much, such as those involving "walk"(or "ride," "big," "broken"; see Tables 7.1, 7.2, and 7.5). Pivot patterns are also easy to form because generalization has a particular word to hold on to. It is the position of the *word* "big" or "walk" that is generalized, in addition to the more evanescent attribute-of-being-big or action-of-coming-executed-by-an-agent. The relative position of a specific word is presumably easier to generalize than the relative position of an argument of a relation (say, attribute) which can take the form of a variety of words ("big," "little," "hot," "broken," etc.).

Once a pivot pattern has been attained, the child may generalize from it to an open relational pattern (Schlesinger, 1971b, pp. 79-80): from "_____ + walk" (Table 7.1) he may generalize to "doggie jump," and later—gradually expanding the category—perhaps to "baby cry"[7]. Such generalization may be facilitated, if a child has in his repertoire several pivot patterns for a given relational category. This appears to be often the case, as can be seen from Tables 7.1, 7.2, 7.4, and 7.5, and footnotes.

We do not know how similar the particular relations have to be for generalizations to occur, or how the strength of tendency to generalize varies with the degree of perceived similarity. Presumably there are individual differences between children in this respect. Some may start out from a rote-learned pattern (say, "mummy come") and immediately proceed to utterances bearing some similarity in respect to the relation exhibited (e.g., "baby cry"). Others, more conservative, may stay at first within the confines of a pivot pattern (situations with relations involving walking, for the pattern "_____ + walk"), and only when this pattern is firmly established, venture forth into the realm of relations that are perceived of as less similar. This may partly explain differences between children in the extent to which their corpora include pivot patterns (more on this further on).

The degree of homogeneity of the relations encompassed by a pivot pattern differs from pattern to pattern. On the one hand we have "_____ + walk" ("Andrew walk," "daddy walk"—Table 7.1) and "ride + _____" ("ride Dumbo," "ride dis"—Table 7.2) with rather narrowly circumscribed scope of particular relations. On the other, there are patterns including a much wider range of particular relations, such as "_____ + it" ("push it," "move it"—Table 7.2). Again, the relations in "carriage broken" and "chair broken" (Table 7.5) intuitively seem to be more similar to each other than those in "Gia writing" and "Gia push" (Table 7.1). Children may differ in their acquisition strategies, and although some may start out with a pattern of narrowly circumscribed relations, others may tend to start out with a pivot pattern incorporating a wide range of parti-

---

[7]A similar suggestion has been made by Bowerman (1973), who mentions the possibility of relational rules being preceded by "different rules based on the individual lexical items involves (e.g., the name for one who rides (goes, jumps) precedes the name of the action of riding (going, jumping))" (Bowerman, 1974, p. 201). Braine (1976) discusses "limited-scope formulae," of which pivot patterns seem to be a special case (see later discussion).

cular relations. Such a broad-spectrum pattern may be more difficult to form, but once it has been formed it will presumably be a more convenient starting point for further generalizations leading to an appropriately broad relational category.

It is proposed therefore that rote-learned patterns and pivot patterns are levers for learning relation rules and forming relational categories. The occurrence of pivot patterns exhibiting five relations prevalent in early speech is substantiated in Tables 7.1 - 7.5. In view of the central role accorded in this proposal to pivot patterns, one might expect such patterns to be still more widespread; after all, not every relation is represented by a pivot pattern for every child in these tables. But, as argued earlier, the criterion adopted for inclusion in Tables 7.1 - 7.5, and other factors, probably have led to underrepresentation of pivot patterns. Similarly for rote-learned patterns, many more of these may exist than can unequivocally be identified in the corpora. Further, each of the corpora investigators managed to record and which were searched for pivot patterns and rote-learned patterns (like those corpora on which these tables are based) includes only a small subset of the child's speech. Brown (1973, p. 103) suspects that pivot patterns are universal at the very beginning of the two-word stage. Finally, as pointed out in the section on active and passive learning, the child may have knowledge of a pivot pattern or a rote-learned pattern acquired passively, without actually using such patterns in his speech. Taken together, these considerations make it appear very plausible that such patterns are sufficiently widespread to allow us to regard them as the basis for the development of open relational patterns.

The present hypothesis also accounts for the fact that the stage of pivot patterns normally begins before that of open relational patterns but overlaps with it (or else begins simultaneously with it). The latter develop out of the former. We now also understand why violations of adult word order are infrequent in two-word utterances (which, as we have seen in section 7.3, presents a problem for Clark et al.'s [1974] account of the two-word stage). Conformity of word order is to be expected if the child generalizes from a rote learned pattern or a pivot pattern.

Another factor that may contribute to this conformity is the child's disposition to utter words in a sequence corresponding to their relative salience (Goldin-Meadow, 1978; Schlesinger, 1976), which may often correspond to the order in adult speech (see also section 7.1). McNeill (1975) has proposed that the sequence of words in the child's early utterances corresponds to that of his action schemas, and this may also result in conformity with the adult sequence. The finding that two-word utterances preserve the word order of adult language therefore need not always be the outcome of a learning process, and hence inspection of the corpora may lead to an overestimation of the degree to which the child has mastered relation rules.

Conversely, the very fact that the rules governing order of words in adult speech dovetail with the child's natural tendencies may facilitate the acquisition of these rules.

Deviations From Adult Word Order

Occasionally, of course, the child will produce utterances with "incorrect" word order. He may lack, at a certain point in time, a rote-learned pattern and a pivot pattern from which he might generalize. In such a case we may hardly expect him to refrain from expressing himself for lack of such a model. The result may be a "groping pattern" (Braine, 1976): The child tries out various word orders. Occasionally there occur utterances with words not standing in any one of the relations regularly expressed in adult speech, such as "man empty" (see earlier section on "Open Relational Categories"), or he produces two words—either in the "correct" word order or not—such that we may discern one of the relational categories appearing in adult speech, but which does not appear in the child's speech at that time. In all these cases he may be doing no more than uttering two isolated words labeling two aspects of the situation, or he may be expressing some particular relation he has in mind. At any rate, he will not be expressing one of his relational *categories*: In the absence of evidence for a regularity in his speech he cannot be credited with a relation rule, and according to the approach advocated in this chapter, the formation of a relational category is dependent on the learning of such a rule. Much current writing concerns itself with the relations a child may be said to "have" at a certain stage, without making this distinction between particular relations and relational categories (see also section 7.7).

But even when the child already has formed a relational category he may occasionally run foul of the relation rule expressing it. Whether through carelessness, excitement, or due to stress, the words may be blurted out in the wrong order. The result may be such strange utterances as that of Kathryn (Park, 1974, p. 39), who, with an MLU of 1.86, blithely unconcerned with word order, said: "Kata Eis geb Kata Mama" (Kathryn ice-cream give Kathryn mummy; i.e., mummy gives Kathryn ice-cream). The sequence of words in this case was presumably determined by momentary factors of saliency and attention. Eventually, of course, Kathryn's speech, like that of all children, will fall into the grooves of adult usage.

Distinctiveness Of Pivot Patterns

It will be remembered that by definition all utterances belonging to a given pivot pattern exhibit the same or very similar semantic relations. Thus, a number of two-word sequences sharing the same word in the same position may belong to different pivot patterns; namely, when different relations are involved. Ideally, such externally similar pivot patterns should not appear in the child's repertoire if he is to use pivot patterns as a steppingstone to open-relational patterns, because they might lead to confusion between different relational categories. However, as shown in our earlier discussion of homonyms, a one-to-one mapping of linguistic expressions into underlying categories is not a prerequisite to learning; it only makes the task easier.

It is hardly to be expected that things should always work out as smoothly as one would wish for the child. Externally similar pivot patterns in fact do occur. Let us examine a few such cases. For Åsa his own name served in two pivot patterns: one for the Agent-Action relation (Table 7.1) and one for the Possessor-Possession relation (Table 7.4). However, the "Åsa +_____" pattern appeared first—at MLU 1.37 − 1.43—for the Possessor-Possession relation, and at that time there were in his corpus hardly any utterances expressing the Agent-Action relation. A few weeks later—at MLU 1.72 − 1.82—"Åsa +_____" expressed the Agent-Action relation, and a large number of Agent-Action utterances began to appear (Lindhagen, 1976, pp. 144-145). In this case, then, the two pivot patterns were separated in time. Although Possessor-Possession constructions continued to appear during the later period, there was presumably little interference because by that time this relational category had already become well established and the child was ready to tackle the Agent-Action relation. Likewise, Kendall's name appears in first position in two pivot patterns at a few weeks' interval (Tables 7.1 and 7.3).

By contrast, there was no separation in time for the Agent-Action pivot pattern and the externally similar Possessor-Possession pattern of Meike (Tables 7.1 and 7.4), who used her friend's name in first position for both relations. There is the possibility, however, that we have misinterpreted here the Possessor-Possession constructions. Thus, "mone löffel" (Simone spoon) might mean Simone takes the spoon or holds the spoon, not Simone's spoon; that is, it might be an Agent-Object construction (see section 3.6 for an explanation of such constructions). A similar reinterpretation is possible also for Åsa's utterances in Table 7.4 discussed earlier ("Åsa hat" might mean that he puts on his hat). In Åsa's corpus at that time (Lindhagen, 1976, p. 146) there are three more utterances in which, presumably, the action term was represented by a noun (e.g., "Karin vatten," Karin water). At any rate, even if there are cases where such an explanation does not apply, that is, in which two externally similar patterns serve for the expression of two different relations during the same time period, this would not present an insurmountable obstacle to learning relation rules, for the reasons stated earlier.

Take now the converse case: the appearance, in one child's corpus, of two (or more) pivot patterns for what we would classify as one and the same relational category. This occurs several times in the corpora represented in Tables 7.1-7.5, and if the two pivot patterns imply the same relational rule they might be mutually supporting. Not so in the case of Eve, whose two pivot patterns for the Attributive relation were "two + _____" and "_____ + broken" (Table 7.5). It seems implausible that, at the age of 25.5 months Eve might be credited with one rule for attribution (adjective + noun) and one for predication (noun + "is" + adjective). Generalizing from the foregoing two patterns, therefore, she might arrive at two conflicting relation rules. Presumably, one of the two patterns turned out to be more powerful—through being more frequent, for instance—and served as the main source of generalization. Whatever the way in which such a conflict is resolved, it should be clear that the problem raised here is not peculiar to our present hypothesis concerning the role of pivot patterns; the conflict between different constructions exists according to any account of learning.

That a pivot pattern may sometimes fail to be generalized can be seen in the corpus of Åsa (Lindhagen, 1976, p. 136). At MLU 1.37 − 1.43 there appears a pivot pattern with "aka " (go) or "åker" (goes) in first position: "aka bat" (go boat), "åker häst" (goes horse), etc. At that time he had very few other constructions that we would classify as Agent-Action, and in those few the word order was unstable[8]. About two weeks later, with MLU 1.72 and up, Agent-Action constructions begin to be frequent, but their word order differs from that in the "aka + _____" pattern: The word for the Agent now almost invariably precedes that for the Action. Apparently, the boy has generalized from a conflicting pivot pattern appearing at that period: "Åsa + _____" (see Table 7.1). The predominant adult word order may have contributed to the latter pattern's gaining the upper hand. At any rate, the "aka + _____" pattern did not seem to influence word order. This is all the more interesting because this pattern remained unaffected by the newly acquired open relational pattern (Agent + Action): "aka + _____" continued to be used concurrently with it. The reason for this was perhaps that "aka + _____" continued to express for this child a *particular* relation that for the time being existed outside its "appropriate" relational category (into which it later, presumably, became absorbed).

This Swedish-speaking boy, then, did not let the potentially misleading pattern confuse him. The German-speaking girls studied by Miller (1975), by contrast, seemed to have generalized from the "Object + Action" pivot pattern (see Table 7.2) and used for a time this word order, which differs

---

[8]Lindhagen (1976) following case grammar, classifies the previously discussed constructions with "aka" as Action-Object. It seems to be justified, however, to interpret boats, horses, and other vehicles and animals as Agents.

from the order in the German simple, declarative sentence. Earlier (at the beginning of our section on "The Nature of Early Relation Rules") an explanation for this deviation has been offered. Eventually, of course, these children must have mastered the standard "Action + Object" order.

Some years ago I proposed an explanation of how relation rules are learned via "generalized pivots" (Schlesinger, 1971a; see section 3.2). The child observes that several pivot words in a given position refer to a certain relational notion (e.g., several pivot words in first position refer to agents), and thereby forms a generalized pivot (e.g., Agent, a first position generalized pivot). This proposal has some affinities to the one presented in the present chapter. In fact, the formation of a generalized pivot might be viewed as a special case of the process described here: Only one word is focused on and generalized from, with the result of a rule being formed pertaining to the position of only one of the two terms of the relation. The generalized pivot concept had the advantage of providing an explanation of the occurrence of Agent-Object constructions (see section 3.2). However, now that Braine (1974) has offered a different, very plausible explanation of these constructions (see section 3.6), there seems to be no longer any need to postulate the special process involved in the formation of generalized pivots.

7.6   THE SCOPE OF EARLY RELATIONAL CATEGORIES

Earlier it has been argued that the child generalizes from rote-learned patterns and pivot patterns to open relational patterns. Such a generalization need not occur at one go; there may be intermediate stages. Bowerman (1976a) has suggested that the child may form narrowly circumscribed categories. Thus she reports on her daughter Christy that the words "up," "down," "on," "off," "back," "all began to combine at about the same time with a word for the person or object undergoing the indicated directional motion [p. 160]." This pattern was thus broader than a pivot pattern in that it was not based on a single pivot word but on a set of words perceived to be semantically similar to each other. However, it was more restricted than an Entity-Locative or Action-Locative pattern, into which it would have to be expanded eventually. It may therefore have been an intermediate stage between a pivot pattern and an open relational pattern.

Another example is from the corpus of a Samoan-speaking girl, Tofi, who at MLU 1.6 combined words like "go," "fall," "take," "put," "set," and "bring" (translated) with words indicating to which location the movement takes place (Braine, 1976, pp. 28-30). Braine points out that, at that period, she produced no utterances indicating where something is located, and he calls this pattern "Movement-to-Locatives." At this stage, then, the full locative pattern had not yet been acquired.

Braine believes that, in general, the child's early categories are more nar-row than has been previously supposed. Children at first learn "limited-scope formulae," each being "concerned with a specific, often quite nar-row, range of relational conceptual content [Braine, 1976, p. 69]." The term "limited-scope formula" is used by Braine for patterns such as Tofi's "Movement-to-Locatives," but sometimes he uses this term for patterns which may be pivot patterns, in our terminology. Thus, he reports that Jonathan, at 23-24 months, had utterances with "big" and "little" in first position. He argues that because at that time "wet" in two-word utterances did not appear in a fixed position, the child could not be credited with a "Property + _____" formula (i.e., the open relational pattern "Attribute + _____") but only with the more limited "Size + _____" formula. There is no evidence, however, that Jonathan can be credited with a "size" category, because "big + _____" and "little + _____" may have been just two different pivot patterns (see Table 7.5). The same reasoning applies to Jonathan's "eat + _____" and "bite + _____," which, he sug-gests, are "conceivably . . . some minor pattern [p. 36]," and to Embla's "eat + _____ [pp. 53-54]." However, a genuine case of an underextended relational category is that of Zhenya, who used the Russian accusative to mark objects that were transferred and relocated, but not for the direct ob-jects of verbs like "read" or "draw" (Bowerman, 1973a, p. 191). Braine (1976, p. 67) suspects that the same may be true of other children as well, but as he points out, it is difficult to determine in each particular case how broad the Action-Object category really is.

Other investigators, too, have noted the gradual broadening of the scope of relational categories. Edwards (1973) observes that in early child language the possessive apparently signifies a very restricted relation: privileged access to a thing (e.g., "Mommy's shoes," "Daddy's TV"). Adult use of this construction then shows the child that other relations, too, belong in this category (e.g., those expressed in "John's nose" and "John's sister"). McNeill (1975) also discusses such a process, which he calls "semiotic extension." More recently, de Villiers (1979) has studied ex-perimentally the hypothesis that the child's relational categories are built around prototypes (see also sections 9.3 - 9.4).

The situation is summed up by Brown (1973, p. 196), who states: "The productive acquisition of a syntactic construction seldom at first entails us-ing it over the full semantic range to which it applies." The "syntactic con-structions" Brown talks about may be pivot patterns, which as argued earlier serve as a ubiquitous steppingstone to mature relational categories; and they may also be intermediate patterns expressing a more narrow rela-tional category. The latter have not been observed for all children. For in-stance, Bowerman (1976a) reports that, unlike Christy, her other daughter Eva used for some time pivot patterns like "more + _____" and "want + _____" without apparently generalizing from these to relational categories, and then switched without apparent transition to broad categories. There was no evidence for categories of intermediate scope. May one conclude from this that children may somehow manage to leap from the very limited relational category expressed in a pivot pattern directly into a category that exactly corresponds with that in adult use? I do not think so. Children presumably differ in respect to the rate at which they solve the delimitation problem (see also the following section). The process of finding the boundaries of the adult category may have been very fast in the case of Eva, and there may have been very short-lived intermediate categories that it was not possible to spot by inspection of her corpus. Alternatively, Eva may at first have overxtended her relational categories. Such overextensions would be difficult to detect in a corpus; likewise, it would be difficult to reject this possibility by examining a corpus. Anyhow, some investigators believe that overextensions occur, as we will see presently.

The suggestion has been made by Braine (1976, pp. 24-25; 52-53; 67-68) that children at first do not have an Agent-Action and an Action-Object relation, but what he calls an Actor-Action relation. He observes that in regard to actions like driving or breaking it may be difficult for the child to distinguish between the agent of the action and the patient. The object involved in the event is affected by the action, but at the same time it is also an actor. In English this dual role is reflected in two constructions: "He drives the car" and "The car drives" (see Lakoff [1977, pp. 248-254] for an analysis of "patient subjects" like that in the latter example). In line with this, Braine found "groping patterns," in which word order is unstable, to be especially frequent in utterances involving actions. He proposes that in the early stage such utterances are best regarded as belonging to an Actor-Action category, for, at least as far as linguistic expression goes, the child has at first only an "Actor" category that is undifferentiated between the Agent and the Patient. When no Patient is involved in the event (i.e., when there is only one "Actor"), the child may follow an Actor + Action rule and word order may be fixed, whereas when there are two candidate "Actors"—an Agent and a Patient—the child, who has no rule involving two Actors, will be uncertain as to word order.

A more radical position is that of Howe (1976), who claims that in early child speech there is so far evidence for only three broad categories: Action of concrete object (regardless of whether the object is Agent or Patient), State of concrete object (including Attribute, Location and Possession), and Name of object (as in utterances expressing "Ostension"). (But see section 3.5, on "Inferring Relational Categories.")

So far we have discussed underextensions and overextensions. In principle there is also a third possibility: the child categorizes according to a classificatory principle different from that employed in the adult system. This may be the case with a relational category that makes its appearance somewhat later than those discussed in this chapter: the past tense. Past, like Plurality, and various other notions usually expressed by inflection, may be viewed as a relation having one argument (and not two, like Possessor-Possession, for instance). Now, Antinucci and Miller (1976) showed that when children first add "-ed" to verbs, they do so not to refer to actions prior to the utterance, but to express various aspectual notions. Specifically, the English data show that the first productive past tense forms are of verbs describing events resulting in a presently perceived end-state, like "falled," "spilled," and "covered." At that time, verbs like "walk," "play," "sleep," which describe events that have no clearly perceived end-state, are not inflected for the past. Similar results were found in a study of Italian children. This could be a case of an underextended relational category. However, in other studies quoted by Slobin (1977, p. 206), the past inflection was first used to express aspects of the action, such as its duration, inception, or repetition. In these cases, considerable reclassification must have occurred so that the child's relational category would finally converge with that of the adult.

There is still another finding that might seem to point to the prevalence of a dimension of categorization in child language which differs from that in adult language, and which would therefore have to be discarded subsequently. It has been observed that the Agents in early child utterances are usually animate beings, whereas Patients (direct objects) are inanimate (section 3.2, Brown, 1973, p. 212). De Villiers and de Villiers (1974, p. 14) found this to be the case in 87% of the instances occurring in the speech of eight children having an MLU of up to 1.5. It seems not very plausible, however, that the child's first relation rules should be formulated in terms of animate and inanimate entities because this would mean either one of the following: (1) the system is redundant and both the animate-inanimate distinction and the notions of Agent and Patient figure in it; or else (2) the child fails to take into account the relations holding between Agents, Actions, and Patients. The latter is unlikely, because at least at the cognitive level, the child is certainly aware of these relations. Some data that are incongruent with the possibility that children's rules are based on the animate-inanimate distinction are adduced by Brown (1973, p. 212). What seems much more likely is that the process of forming relational categories is facilitated by the fact that those Agents the child cares to speak about and listens to adults speaking about are usually animate, whereas the Patients are typically inanimate.

To the extent that children overextend relational categories they will subsequently have to narrow them down by discrimination learning. In cases of underextension, the child will eventually notice that the same relation rules are being applied by the adult in various other situations involving particular relations not yet included by the child in the relational category in question. As a result, his attention will be drawn to similarities between these particular relations and those included in the category. This is the process of positive cue extraction described in section 5.3. Its consequence is that these particular relations will be subsumed under the category to which they are similar. The boundaries of the category will thus be drawn somewhat wider, and ultimately, as a result of several such extensions, they will coincide with those effective in the adult system. (The gradual extension of a relational category to include not quite so similar relations is discussed in sections 9.3-9.5.)

The present proposal fits in well with Bowerman's (1974, pp. 203-204) suggestion that cases be analyzed into semantic features. Basically, the process of acquiring relational categories resembles therefore that of acquiring the concepts underlying words. There is no need for the assumption that the child comes to the task of language learning with a set of ready-made relational categories into which he classifies utterances, any more than there is a need to assume that he approaches the task of learning words with a set of ready-made concepts. Instead, his categories develop through his experience with language.

7.7   INDIVIDUAL DIFFERENCES IN
THE ACQUISITION PROCESS

Earlier it has been pointed out that children may differ in the rate at which they explore the boundaries of relational categories. One of the factors which may be at work here is suggested by a study of Ramer (1976), which has already been mentioned in connection with patterns with empty forms. Ramer found marked differences among the children she studied—4 girls and 3 boys—in the rate at which they acquired syntax. Interestingly, the "rapid developers", to which belonged all 4 girls and none of the boys, made more word errors than the "slow developers". Ramer suggests that this difference may be due to the greater inclination of the former to take risks. It is plausible to assume that such differences in risk taking also account partially for differences in the scope of relational categories entertained by children on their way to mastery: Some children may be prone to underextend for a relatively long time because they are reluctant to risk being wrong (by operating with too broad a category).

The tendency to underextend may also lead to the prolongation of the pivot pattern stage. Bloom (1970, 1973) observed that only some children use many pivot words, whereas others appear to adopt what she calls a "categorical" strategy, rarely or never using pivot words. As argued previously, pivot patterns may be much more prevalent than appears from a cursory examination of the corpora (at least if the stringent definition of pivot is abandoned). But there seem indeed to be differences between children in regard to the number of pivot patterns used, and probably also in regard to length of time the patterns are used. (A possible artifact here is that the longer a pivot pattern is being used, the greater the probability of its being detected by the investigator.) As stated, children differ in their tendency to underextend and in the time it takes them to explore the boundaries of the relational category. Bloom, Lightbown, and Hood (1975) also report that some children tend to use pronouns and other proforms, such as "it," "this one," or "that" for patients, and "here" or "there" for locations. They emphasize that this is not due to lack of the relevant vocabulary because the names for the people, things or places referred to by "this one," "here," etc. were often known to the children, and were used by them in their one-word utterances or in combination with "no" or "more." The use of pronouns and proforms must have been otherwise motivated. Bloom et al. suggest that these forms permitted the children to talk about a variety of patients and locations without having to venture forth into the use of relation rules that are defined in terms of general concepts, like Patient and Location. Instead, they avail themselves of single words, like "it" and "there." It is simpler to learn the relative position of a single word; so why not stay put with a few pronouns and proforms in pivot patterns?

Bloom et al. classify children into those who use pronouns and proforms and those who use a different strategy, called by them the "nominal strategy," which involves hardly any use of pronouns and proforms in the early two-word stage (cf. also Nelson, 1975). Reviewing data from other sources, however, Bowerman (1976b) concludes that there is actually a continuum in respect to the use of these two strategies. Bowerman also refutes Bloom et al.'s proposal that the pronominal and nominal strategies develop from "pivotal" and "categorical" strategies, respectively.

As suggested earlier, the "pivotal" and "categorical" strategies presumably reflect differences in learning rate and in tendency to underextend. Another possible factor may be the differential interests of children. A large proportion of pivot patterns involves demands ("want + _____") and the relations of recurrence ("more + _____") and disappearance ("allgone + _____", "no + _____"). Some children may be more interested in demanding and commenting on the fulfillment of their demands, whereas others may prefer to comment on states of affairs (as Gruber [1973, pp. 442-443] has suggested; see also Miller & Ervin [1964, p. 30] on the occurrence of the pivot words "on" and "off" reflecting the interests of the child studied). This would be in line with Nelson's (1973) classification of children with low MLUs into "expressive"—whose language expressed feelings, needs, and personal interactions—and "referential," whose language is more object-oriented. Her findings were replicated by Starr (1975).

Piaget's (1951, p. 222) remark that the child at first expresses mainly orders and desires was presumably made on the basis of his observing children who leaned more to the "expressive" pole of the continuum rather than others who had different preferences. At any rate, his observation has not been confirmed in Greenfield and Smith's (1976) study of one-word speech.[9]

Differences in interest may also have a part to play in determining the sequence in which various relational categories emerge in children's speech. The findings on this issue have been equivocal. Braine (1976) found considerable variability between children in the order of emergence of semantic notions, whereas Bloom et al. (1975) found much uniformity. The sequence reported by Braine differs from that of Bloom et al.; that reported by Wells (1974) is similar in part to that of Bloom et al. Bowerman (1976a) has shown that these divergent findings can be accounted for in part by methodological differences between the three studies but that there were some differences that remained which cannot be laid down to methodology. The methodological differences pointed out by Bowerman pertain to the way semantic notions were defined and classifed and to the criterion adopted for crediting the child with a semantic notion. A comment is in order here about the latter. Whereas Braine determined sequence according to the emergence of productive patterns exhibiting a fixed word order, Bloom et al. and Wells did not require fixed word order. It appears that, on our account of the formation of relational categories, this is not merely a difference of stringency of the criterion adopted; instead, these investigators are in fact looking at different things: If one intends to study relational categories one must, with Braine, concentrate on productive patterns with a fixed word order. If, on the other hand, one is interested in the semantic notions the child talks about, one should look instead at the intentions underlying the child's utterances, as Leonard (1976) in his recent book did. But then one is dealing with particular relations, not with relational categories.

The topic of this chapter has been the formation of the child's earliest relational categories and relation rules. These are both acquired together through one and the same learning process. Subsequent stages in the acquisition of relation rules are treated in the following chapter, and in the final chapter I return to relational categories and discuss how these develop.

---

[9]Additional evidence for interindividual variability comes from Park (1974, p. 31), who points out that the English corpora differ from the German ones in respect to the sequence of emergence of attributive and predicative objectives. There seems to be no evident explanation of this in terms of a difference in the grammar of the two languages. In addition to differences between children speaking one language, there are also interlingual differences. As reported by Slobin (1978), the acquisition patterns of children learning an inflected language may differ from those of children learning languages relying more on word order.

REFERENCES

Antinucci, F., & Miller, R. How children talk about what happened. *Journal of Child Language*, 1976, *3*, 167-189.

Bates, E. *Language and context: The acquisition of pragmatics*. New York: Academic Press, 1976.

Bloom, L. *Language development: Form and function in emerging grammars*. Cambridge, Mass.: MIT Press, 1970.

Bloom, L. *One word at a time: The use of single-word utterances before syntax*. The Hague: Mouton, 1973.

Bloom, L., Hood, L., & Lightbown, P. Imitation in language development: If, when, and why. *Cognitive Psychology*, 1974, *6*, 380-420.

Bloom, L., Lightbown, P., & Hood, L. Structure and variation in child language. *Monographs of the Society for Research in Child Development*, 1975, *40* (2, Serial No. 160).

Bowerman, M. F. *Early syntactic development*. Cambridge: Cambridge University Press, 1973. (a)

Bowerman, M. Structural relationships in children's utterances: syntactic or semantic? In T. E. Moore (Ed.), *Cognitive development and the acquisition of language*. New York: Academic Press, 1973, (b).

Bowerman, M. Development of concepts underlying language: Discussion summary. In R. L. Schiefelbusch & L. L. Lloyd (Eds.), *Language perspectives: Acquisition, retardation, and intervention*. Baltimore: University Park Press, 1974.

Bowerman, M. Commentary [to Bloom, L., Lightbown, P., & Hood, L., Structure and variation in child language]. *Monographs of the Society for Research in Child Development*, 1975, *40*, (2, Serial No. 160).

Bowerman, M. Semantic factors in the acquisition of rules for word use and sentence construction. In D. Morehead & A. Morehead (Eds.), *Directions in normal and deficient child language*. Baltimore: University Park Press, 1976. (a)

Bowerman, M. *Word meaning and sentence structure: Uniformity, variation and shifts over time in patterns of acquisition*. Paper presented at Conference on Early Behavioral Assessment of Communicative and Cognitive Abilities of the Developmentally Disabled. Orcas Island, Washington, May 1976. (b)

Braine, M.D.S. On learning the grammatical order of words. *Psychological Review*, 1963, *70*, 323-348. (a)

Braine, M.D.S. The ontogeny of English phrase structure: The first phase. *Language*, 1963, *39*, 1-13. (b)

Braine, M.D.S. The acquisition of language in infant and child. In C. Reed (Ed.), *The learning of language*. New York: Appleton-Century-Crofts, 1971. (a)

Braine, M.D.S. On two types of models of the internalization of grammars. In D. I. Slobin (Ed.), *The ontogenesis of grammar*. New York: Academic Press, 1971. (b)

Braine, M.D.S. Length constraints, reduction rules, and holophrastic processes in children's word combinations. *Journal of Verbal Learning and Verbal Behavior*, 1974, *13*, 448-456.

Braine, M.D.S. Children's first word combinations. *Monographs of the Society for Research in Child Development*, 1976, *41*, (1, Serial No. 164).

Brown, R. The development of Wh questions in child speech. *Journal of Verbal Learning and Verbal Behavior*, 1968, *7*, 279-290.

Brown, R. *A first language: The early stages.* Cambridge, Mass.: Harvard University Press, 1973.

Brown, R., & Fraser, C. The acquisition of syntax. In C. N. Cofer & B. S. Musgrave (Eds.), *Verbal behavior and learning: Problems and processes,* New York: McGraw-Hill, 1963.

Brown, R., & Fraser, C. The acquisition of syntax. In U. Bellugi & R. Brown (Eds.), The acquisition of language. *Monographs of the Society for Research in Child Development,* 1964, *29* (1, Serial No. 92).

Burling, R. Language development of a Garo and English speaking child. *Word,* 1959, *15,* 45-68.

Cazden, C. B. The acquisition of noun and verb inflection. *Child Development,* 1968, *39,* 433-438.

Clark, R. Performing without competence. *Journal of Child Language,* 1974, *1,* 1-10.

Clark, R. Review of L. Bloom, *One word at a time.* The Hague: Mouton, 1973. *Journal of Child Language,* 1975, *2,* 169-183.

Clark, R. What's the use of imitation? *Journal of Child Language,* 1977, *4,* 341-358.

Clark, R., Hutcheson, S., & Van Buren, P. Comprehension and production in language acquisition. *Journal of Linguistics,* 1974, *10,* 39-54.

Curtiss, S. *Genie: A psycholinguistic study of a modern-day "wild child,"* New York: Academic Press, 1977.

de Villiers, J. The process of rule learning in child speech: A new look. In K. E. Nelson (Ed.), *Child Language* (Vol. 2), 1979.

de Villiers, J. G., & de Villiers, P. A. Development of the use of word order in comprehension. *Journal of Psycholinguistic Research,* 1973, *2,* 331-341.

de Villiers, J. G., & de Villiers, P. A. Competence and performance in child language: Are children really competent to judge? *Journal of Child Language,* 1974, *1,* 11-22.

de Villiers, J. G., & de Villiers, P. A. *Language acquisition.* Cambridge, Mass.: Harvard University Press, 1978.

Dore, J. Holophrases, speech acts and language universals. *Journal of Child Language,* 1975, *2,* 21-40.

Dore, J., Franklin, M. B., Miller, R. T., & Ramer, A. L. H. Transitional phenomena in early language acquisition. *Journal of Child Language,* 1976, *3,* 13-28.

Edwards, J. Sensory-motor intelligence and semantic relations in early child grammar. *Cognition,* 1973, *2,* 395-434.

Goldin-Meadow, S. Structure in manual communication system developed without a conventional language model: Language without a helping hand. In H. Whitaker & H. A. Whitaker (Eds.), *Studies in Neurolinguistics* (Vol. 4). New York: Academic Press, 1978.

Golinkoff, R. M., & Kerr, J. L. Infants' perception of semantically defined action role changes in filmed events. *Merrill-Palmer Quarterly,* 1978, *24,* 53-61.

Greenfield, P. M. How much is one word? *Journal of Child Language,* 1978, *5,* 347-352.

Greenfield, P. M. & Smith, J. H. *The structure of communication in early language development.* New York: Academic Press, 1976.

Gruber, J. S. Correlations between the syntactic constructions of the child and of the adult. In C. A. Ferguson & D. I. Slobin (Eds.), *Studies of child language development.* New York: Holt, Rinehart, & Winston, 1973.

Howe, C. J. The meanings of two-word utterances in the speech of young children. *Journal of Child Language*, 1976, *3*, 29-48.

Ingram, D. Transitivity in child language. *Language*, 1971, *47*, 888-910.

Jespersen, O. *Language: Its nature, development and origin*. New York: Holt, 1922.

Kernan, K. T. The acquisition of language by Samoan children. Unpublished doctoral dissertation, University of California, Berkeley, 1969.

Klein, E. Review of T. van der Geest, *Evaluation of theories on child grammars*. The Hague: Mouton, 1973. *Journal of Child Language*, 1974, *1*, 317-323.

Lakoff, G. Linguistic Gestalts. In W. A. Beach, S. E. Fox, & S. Philosoph (Eds.), *Papers from the 13th Regional Meeting, Chicago Linguistic Society*. Chicago: University of Chicago Press, 1977.

Lange, S., & Larsson, K. *Syntactic development of a Swedish girl Embla, between 20 and 42 months of age. Part I, Age 20-25 months* (Report No. 1). Stockholm: Stockholms Universitet, Institutionen för Nordiska Språk, 1973.

Lenneberg, E. Understanding language without the ability to speak: A case report. *Journal of Abnormal and Social Psychology*, 1962, *65*, 419-425.

Leonard, L. On differentiating syntactic and semantic features in emerging grammars: Evidence from empty form usage. *Journal of Psycholinguistic Research*, 1975, *4*, 357-363.

Leonard, L. B. *Meaning in child language*. New York: Grune and Stratton, 1976.

Leonard, L. B., & Kaplan, L. A note on imitation and lexical acquisition. *Journal of Child Language*, 1976, *3*, 449-455.

Leopold, W. F. *Speech development of a bilingual child: A linguistic record* (Vol. 3). *Grammar and general problems in the first two years*. Evanston, Ill.: Northwestern University Press, 1949.

Limber, J. Unravelling competence, performance and pragmatics in the speech of young children. *Journal of Child Language*. 1976, *3*, 309-318.

Lindhagen, K. *Semantic relations in Swedish children's early sentences*. Acta Universitatis Upsaliensis: Studia psychologica Upsaliensa. Uppsala, 1976.

McNeill, D. Developmental psycholinguistics. In F. Smith & G. A. Miller (Eds.), *The genesis of language: A psycholinguistic approach*. Cambridge, Mass.: MIT Press, 1966.

McNeill, D. Semiotic extension. In R. L. Solso (Ed.), *Information Processing and cognition: The Loyola Symposium*. Hillsdale, N.J.: Lawrence Erlbaum Associates, 1975.

MacWhinney, B. Hungarian research on the acquisition of morphology and syntax. *Journal of Child Language*, 1976, *3*, 397-410.

Menyuk, P. *The acquisition and development of language*. Englewood Cliffs, N.J.: Prentice-Hall, 1971.

Menyuk, P. *Language and maturation*. Cambride, Mass.: MIT Press, 1977.

Miller, M. H. *Zur Logik der frühen Sprachentwicklung*. Deutsches Seminar der Universität Frankfurt am Main, 1975.

Miller, W., & Ervin, S. M. The development of grammar in child language. In U. Bellugi & R. Brown (Eds.), The acquisition of language. *Monographs of the Society for Research in Child Development*, 1964, *29* (1, Serial No. 92).

Morse, P. A. Infant speech perception: A preliminary model and review of the literature. In

R. L. Schiefelbusch & L. L. Lloyd (Eds.), *Language perspectives—acquisition, retardation, and intervention*. Baltimore: University Park Press, 1974.

Namir, L., & Schlesinger, I. M. The grammar of Sign Language. In I. M. Schlesinger & L. Namir (Eds.), *Sign language of the deaf: Psychological, linguistic, and sociological perspectives*. New York: Academic Press, 1978.

Nelson, K. Structure and strategy in learning to talk. *Monographs of the Society for Research in Child Development*, 1973, *38* (1-2, Serial No. 149).

Nelson, K. The nominal shift in semantic-syntactic development. *Cognitive Psychology*, 1975, *7*, 461-479.

Newport, E. L., & Ashbrook, E. F. The emergence of semantic relations in ASL. *Papers and Reports on Child Language Development*, 1977, *13*, 16-21.

Newport, E. L., Gleitman, M., & Gleitman, L. R. Mother, I'd rather do it myself: Some effects and non-effects of maternal speech style. In C. E. Snow & C. A. Ferguson (Eds.), *Talking to children*. New York: Cambridge University Press, 1977.

Omar, M. K. *The acquisition of Egyptian Arabic as a native language*. The Hague: Mouton, 1973.

Park, T. Z. *The acquisition of German Syntax*. Unpublished manuscript, University of Münster, West Germany, 1970. (a)

Park, T. Z. *Language acquisition in a Korean child*. Unpublished manuscript, University of Münster, West Germany, 1970. (b)

Park, T. Z. *A study of German language development*. Psychological Institute, Berne, Switzerland, January 1974.

Peters, A. M. Language learning strategies: Does the whole equal the sum of the parts? *Language*, 1977, *53*, 560-573.

Piaget, J. *Plays, dreams and imitation in childhood*. New York: Norton, 1951.

Ramer, A. L. H. Syntactic styles in emerging language. *Journal of Child Language*, 1976, *3*, 49-62.

Reber, A. S., & Allen, R. Analogic and abstraction strategies in synthetic grammar learning: A functionalist interpretation. *Cognition*, 1978, *6*, 189-221.

Schaerlaekens, A. M. *The two-word sentence in child language development*. The Hague: Mouton, 1973.

Schlesinger, I. M. Learning grammar: From pivot to realization rule. In R. Huxley & E. Ingram (Eds.), *Language acquisition: Models and methods*. London: Academic Press, 1971. (a)

Schlesinger, I. M. Production of utterances and language acquisition. In D. I. Slobin (Ed.), *The ontogenesis of grammar*. New York: Academic Press, 1971. (b)

Schlesinger, I. M. Is there a natural word order? In W. von Raffler-Engel & Y. Lebrun (Eds.), *Baby talk and infant speech*. Amsterdam: Swets & Zeitlinger, 1976.

Slobin, D. I. The acquisition of Russian as a native language. In F. Smith & G. A. Miller (Eds.), *The genesis of language: A psycholinguistic approach*. Cambridge, Mass.: MIT Press, 1966.

Slobin, D. I. *Psycholinguistics*. Glenview, Ill.: Scott, Foreman, 1971.

Slobin, D. I. Cognitive prerequisites for the development of grammar. In C. A. Ferguson & D. I. Slobin (Eds.), *Studies of child language development*. New York: Holt, Rinehart & Winston, 1973.

Slobin, D. I. Language change in childhood and in history. In J. Macnamara (Ed.), *Language learning and thought*. New York: Academic Press, 1977.

Slobin, D. I. *Universal and particular in the acquisition of language*. Paper prepared for workshop conference on "Language Acquisition: State of the Art." University of Pennsylvania, May 19-22, 1978.

Smoczyńska, M. Early syntactic development: Pivot look and pivot grammar. *Polish Psychological Bulletin*, 1976, *1*, 37-43.

Starr, S. The relationship of single words to two word sentences. *Child Development*, 1975, *45*, 567-576.

Stern, C., & Stern, W. *Die Kindersprache: Eine psychologische und sprachtheoretische Untersuchung*. Darmstadt: Wissenschaftliche Buchgesellschaft, 1968. (Originally published 1928.)

Van der Geest, T. *Evaluation of theories on child grammar*. The Hague: Mouton, 1974.

Veneziano, E. *Analysis of wish sentences in the one-word stage of language acquisition: A cognitive approach*. Unpublished Master's thesis, Tufts University, 1973.

Von Raffler-Engel, W. *Il prelinguaggio infantile*. Brescia: Paideia, 1964.

Weir, R. *Language in the crib*. The Hague: Mouton, 1962.

Wells, G. Learning to code experience through language. *Journal of Child Language*, 1974, *2*, 243-269.

Werner, H., & Kaplan, B. *Symbol formation: An organismic-developmental approach to language and the expression of thought*. New York: Wiley, 1963.

Whitehurst, G. J., & Vasta, R. Is language acquired through imitation? *Journal of Psycholinguistic Research*, 1975, *4*, 37-59.

Wieman, E. A. Stress patterns of early child language. *Journal of Child Language*, 1976, *3*, 283-286.

8 The Developments of Relation Rules

In the preceding chapter the child's first steps in acquiring the grammar of his language were discussed. It was shown how he begins to form the relational categories that figure in the underlying I-marker, and how he learns to express these by the simplest type of relation rules: those that accord relative position in the two-word utterance. The relation rules governing language are of course much more elaborate. They determine, among others, what word classes (parts of speech), function words (auxiliaries, articles, prepositions, relative pronouns, etc.), and inflections appear in the utterance. Here we discuss (in section 8.1) only the formation of word classes. Inflections and function words are a somewhat later development, which are dealt with only in passing (see Brown, 1973, for a comprehensive discussion, and see also section 7.1).

The preceding chapter took us as far as the two-word stage. When the child's utterances become longer than two words, he expresses more than one relation in an utterance. In sections 8.2 and 8.3 we examine the question of how several relation rules may apply jointly to a more complex underlying structure of relations. In the final section, we discuss the acquisition of alternative relation rules applicable to a given underlying relational structure, which are responsible for variations in focus, emphasis, and for other stylistic effects.[1]

---

[1]I am indebted to Michael Maratsos with whom I had an interesting discussion that led to my making some changes in the first section.

8.1 WORD CLASSES

Word Class in Relation Rules

The child must learn not only in which sequence words are to be uttered if they are to express a given relation, but also which words are eligible for each position in the utterance. Thus "The food is good" is an acceptable sentence, whereas "The eat is good," although its meaning may be clear, is unacceptable; "People eat" is all right, but "People food" is not. The correct use of inflections also presupposes the formation of word classes, because each inflection is appropriate only to a certain part of speech; for instance, "-ing" and "-ed" may be added only to verbs, "-er" and "-est" to adjectives; and so on. But even before he uses inflections, the child may acquire relation rules of the following form:

$$\text{AGENT--ACTION a, b} \quad \rightarrow \quad a^N + b^V$$

Left of the arrow we have an expression consisting of the name of the relation and its arguments, represented here by the variables a and b. In the I-marker, the arguments of the relations are protoverbal elements, that is, concepts that are realized as words when the relation is expressed in speaking (see section 5.4). The formula right of the arrow shows how the relation is to be expressed. The capitalized superscripts N and V are CATEGORY MARKERS, standing for 'noun' and 'verb,' respectively. The rule states that if a is the Agent of Action b, the relation is expressed by a followed by b, and a is to be expressed by a noun, and b by a verb. (This is an example of a relation rule in English. A child learning a language with free word order may acquire relation rules that do not accord any order to a and b; see, however, section 7.1.) When this relation rule is applied to the I-marker AGENT-ACTION people, eat (where 'people' and 'eat' stand for protoverbal elements), we obtain:

$$\text{AGENT-ACTION people, eat} \quad \rightarrow \quad \text{people}^N + \text{eat}^V$$

To the right of the arrow we have two protoverbal elements, which must now be lexicalized (for the purpose of exposition we have, of course, no choice but to present also the protoverbal elements as words). For the protoverbal element 'people' a word must be substituted that is marked in the lexicon as being a noun, and for 'eat' one that is marked as a verb. The lexical entry for the protoverbal element 'eat' will include, among others, the *word* "eat" with a category marker showing that it is a verb and hence eligible for substitution in the above formula. However, we cannot substitute for this protoverbal element the word "food", for instance, because it is marked in the lexicon as a noun. (And besides, we can imagine an occurrence of food without a simultaneous occurrence of eating, and hence "food" and "eat" presumably do not belong to the same protoverbal element: They express somewhat different, though related, concepts.)

The task of the child, then, is two-fold. He must acquire relation rules that introduce (among others) category markers, as in the foregoing example, and he must learn the correct lexical entries, which include category markers that indicate the part of speech membership of each word.[2]

Word Class Errors

In the majority of his early two-word utterances the child already selects words of the correct part of speech. This does not imply, however, that he has already mastered this two-fold task. As Braine (1976) has pointed out, the fact that no errors of word class are made in early utterances may be due to semantic constraints, which obviate his using words from an inappropriate word class. Thus, the agents the child talks about are almost invariably persons and things, and the words he has available for referring to these are usually nouns (see section 7.1, and the later section on "Semantic Correlates").

Occasionally, however, children do select a word from an incorrect form class, even at later ages. Examples reported for various children and by various writers are given in Table 8.1. Further examples can be found in most of the references cited in the table, in Smith (1933), Chukovsky (1971, pp. 4–7), and in Clark and Clark (1979). There are two possible sources for these errors: (1) the child may have failed to master (or he infringes) the appropriate relation rule; and (2) he may have an incorrect (or missing) category marker in his lexical entry (or he disregards the category marker). Table 8.1 is arranged in roughly chronological order. In the later examples (from the age of 30 months on), the incorrectly chosen word tends to have an inflectional ending appropriate for the slot in the sentence frame in which it appears. When at 31 months "sore" is used as a verb, for instance, it receives the ending of a verb: "soring." It appears, therefore, that in this particular case the child did apply the correct relation rule, which determined that in this construction a verb is called for (cf. Menyuk, 1969, p.

---

[2]In addition to relation rules there are other realization rules that have to be learned by the child: concord rules, which are responsible for phenomena like grammatical agreement, phonological rules, and intonation rules (Schlesinger, 1977a, ch. 2); but these are not dealt with in detail in this book.

40). Where he went wrong is in classifying "sore" as a verb. At earlier ages, by contrast, the incorrectly chosen words are uninflected (with only one exception among the examples given in the table), and there is no evidence, therefore, that the child **has** mastered the pertinent relation rules. The 19-month old child who said "piece it" instead of "break it," for example, possibly did not have a rule of the form:

$$\text{PATIENT-ACTION a, b} \quad \rightarrow \quad b^V + a^N,$$

but rather a more primitive rule containing no category markers and only according relative positions to the arguments of the relation:

$$\text{PATIENT-ACTION a, b} \quad \rightarrow \quad b + a$$

But what about lexical entries at these earlier ages? Could these children already have had the correct category markers in their lexical entries, their errors being due only to a deficiency in relation rules? Or were the relevant lexical entries incomplete, failing to indicate, for instance, that "piece" and "page" are not verbs, and "bye-bye," "write," "sticky," and "wet" are not nouns? This question can only be answered by examining another one: How are word classes acquired? Let us address ourselves now to the latter problem.

Semantic Correlates

The first point to consider is that parts of speech have semantic correlates. Most nouns in the speech of young children refer to persons or objects, and most verbs, to actions (Brown, 1957). Now, long before the two-word stage the child presumably learns to recognize objects and to interpret ongoing events. The fact that he makes these interpretations means that for him (just as for the adult) objects differ from actions. This may suggest that the child learns word classes via this nonlinguistic distinction. In a small informal experiment, Braine (1971a, pp. 55-56) taught his 21-23-month-old daughter two nonsense words by simple ostension. He pointed to a certain kitchen utensil and called it "niss"; and he made his fingers walk, accompanying this with "seb." Braine reports that "both words were rapidly taken up into her speech [p. 56]." She said, for instance, "more niss," "this niss," using the new word in a context where a noun was required. Apparently, the fact that the word was used to refer to a thing was sufficient for her to classify it as a noun. If word classes are indeed formed in this manner, the process is independent from that of the acquisition of relation rules. Formation of word classes may accordingly even precede the formation of relation rules,

TABLE 8.1
Examples Of Errors In Word Class

Approximate Age in Months	Language	Source	Example
19	English	K.E. Moore (quoted in Wundt, 1904, p. 282)	piece it
20	English	Bloom (1970, p. 113)	air-conditioner noise[1] 'nother wet
22	bilingual: English & German	Leopold (1949, p. 59)	bye-bye dunkel (bye-bye dark; = outside it is dark)
22	German	Stern & Stern (1928/1968, p. 407)	Scheischeibe (write; = pencil)
22	German	Preyer (1900, p. 330)	messen (cut)[2]
19-25	English	Braine (1963, pp. 5, 10)	allgone sticky allgone outside (when the door was shut) bye-bye dirty more high more wet more page (= read more)
26	bilingual: English & Hebrew	Braine (1971a, p. 56)	nafal didn't hurt (fell didn't hurt; = the fall didn't hurt)
27	English	Braine (1971a, p. 33)	more outside (= I want to go outside)
27	English	Bowerman (1974, Table 1)	Full it up! (= fill)
29	bilingual: Korean & German	Park (1970, pp. 12–13)	throw (translated = ball)
undated	German	Park (1970, p. 15)	zwei aufblase (two blow up; = two balloons)
30	German	Stern & Stern (1928/1968, p. 410)	hauer (hitter[3]; = hammer)
30	German	Stern & Stern (1928/1968, p. 410)	es glockt (it bells[4])
30	English	Carlson & Anisfeld (1969, p. 573)	a louding plane
31	English	Carlson & Anisfeld (1969, p. 573)	it's still soring (= hurting)
33	English	Carlson & Anisfeld (1969, p. 573)	I'll stomach you (= push you in the stomach)
32-34	English	Braine (1971b, p. 173)	Daddy, why don't it wind your hair this big wind? (= ruffle your hair)

(Continued)

TABLE 8.1 (continued)

33	German	Stern & Stern (1928/1968, p. 409)	
			klaviert (pianoed)[5]
34	German	Stern & Stern (1928/1968, p. 409)	
			schneide (cut)[6]
35	English	Bowerman (1974; Table 1)	How would you flat it? (= flatten)
36 and later	English	Menyuk (1969, p. 40)	He's a bigger I want the blue
42	English	Bowerman (1974; Table 1)	I'm gonna sharp this pencil (= sharpen)
60	English	Kuczaj (1977)	You axed the wood
68	English	Kuczaj (1977)	rocked (= threw a rock)

[1]This was probably not a shortened version of "air conditioner make noise," because in the latter expression "make" has no independent semantic content, but serves merely to supply the verb required by the rules of grammar.

[2]The German noun "Messer" (knife) has been turned here into a verb by a suffix.

[3]The German verb "hauen" (hit) has been turned here into a noun by a suffix.

[4]The German noun "Glocke" (bell) has been turned here into a verb by a suffix.

[5]The German noun "Klavier" (piano) has been turned here into a verb by a suffix.

[6]The German verb "schneiden" (cut) has been turned here into a noun by a suffix.

and if so, the errors at the earlier ages in Table 8.1 may have to be accounted for by incomplete mastery of relation rules.

There are arguments against such an interpretation of the experiment, however. Braine reports that although his daughter usually treated "seb"—the word referring to an action—as a verb (saying, for instance "Daddy seb Teddy"), there were two utterances in which she used it as a noun ("more seb"). Another observation is of his daughter at 26 months (see Table 8.1), who used the Hebrew word "nafal" (fell) correctly as a verb in "hu nafal" (he fell), but immediately afterwards used it as a noun: "nafal didn't hurt." The hypothesis that a nonlinguistic distinction determines the use of a word as a noun or as a verb seems to lead to the prediction that no such errors would occur. Braine therefore raises the possibility that "perception of the ontological distinction" between thing and action is really not prior to that of the corresponding grammatical distinctions.

One need not go as far as this, however. First, Braine does not take into account the possibility that while "seb" and "nafal" were categorized correctly, infringement of relation rules may have led to errors. Further, one might credit the child with perceiving his environment in terms of things and actions, without inferring from this that he will use this distinction in classifying words. There are various ways of classifying the world around us, and the thing-action distinction is only one of them. If a word, say "piece," is used as a name of a thing, there is nothing to prevent the child from using it subsequently to refer to an action associated with it. This would be, then, a case of overextension, of the kind discussed in connection with the acquisition of words in section 5.2, and does not provide any evidence for perceptual confusion. As argued in section 5.6, a distinction must be made between the child's ability to respond to differences (discriminate, sort) and his forming categories. The former is relevant to the 'interpretation problem,' and the latter to the 'categorization problem.'

Now, this argument cuts both ways. Errors of word class cannot be taken as evidence of the child's being incapable of making the necessary perceptual distinctions, but neither does the ability of making these distinctions entail that word classes have been formed which are used in the application of relation rules. Braine's observations on "seb" and "nafal" also confirm this and, as he says, "argue against the idea that 'thingness' is the implicit characteristic of the noun class around the time this first develops [p. 56]." If his daughter learned that "niss" was a noun from its nonlinguistic correlate, this does not show that this is the usual way part-of-speech membership is learned. At the two-word stage, most words are presumably already introduced in a linguistic context ("This is a niss," "I am sebbing"), rather than by ostension, and it may be that normally the child learns to which class a word belongs primarily by the way it is used. This is the proposal that is spelled out below. Meanwhile it should be recognized that there is no convincing argument for the thesis that word classes are formed by merely noting correlations with a nonlinguistic classification into things, actions, attributes and so on.

In fact, there is a good argument against it. As Brown (1957) has pointed out, it is only in the speech of young children that word classes are semantically fairly consistent; in adult language the correspondence between noun and thing, verb and action, etc. is much more tenuous than in child language, and even in child language it is far from perfect. "A trip" is not any more thing-like than "to travel"; if it 'feels' differently (cf. Flavell, 1958) this is a *result* of the way the word is used in the language, not the reason. Nor is there any ontological difference between what is denoted by "the rain" and "to rain," "a long sleep" and "to sleep long." Hence, even if it be granted, for the sake of the argument, that the part-of-speech membership of words is often registered on the basis of their semantic correlates, there must be an additional mechanism for learning the membership of words for which no such cue is provided by their meaning (and many abstract words also belong to this type). Now, such a mechanism may explain the formation of word classes for other words as well, and thus renders unnecessary the earlier proposal of a mechanism that notices correlations with things, actions, and attributes. At most, the latter may have an auxiliary role to play. Let us consider now what process would be adequate for learning the word class membership of all kinds of words.

Distributional Evidence

Recently, Kiss (1973) proposed that the child learns that words of a given word class belong together because they share associative links to the same words. Nouns, for instance, tend to appear after "a" and "the," and verbs share other distributional characteristics. A mechanism that takes account of such distributional evidence is capable of forming certain word classes, according to Kiss, who has tested this claim by simulating the acquisition of word classes by a computer program that utilizes such evidence. (His theory thus is an extension of Jenkins and Palermo [1964], but contains various sophisticated features to which I cannot do justice here; see Maratsos & Chalkley, [1979] for a related approach.) In the following I propose a process that seems to be more powerful than that described by Kiss and makes use of all the information that his model is assumed to take into account.

Acquisition Based On Relation Rules

My proposal, which has been hinted at in Schlesinger (1975; see also Sinclair, 1971, p. 29), is that the formation of word classes is dependent on the acquisition of relation rules. As we have seen earlier, the child event ually acquires relation rules that specify not only the relative position of words but also word classes. When the child begins to acquire relation rules, however, he does not yet have such word classes. He presumably starts out with noting the relative positions of the arguments of the expressed relation, and—possibly simultaneously with this—notes which specific words are eligible for the expression of each argument. For each word, then, the child registers the relational arguments it may express. For instance, he learns about certain words that they can express the Attribute, and these words thus constitute the class of adjectives (which, as he finds out later, have certain other characteristics in common, such as their having comparative and superlative forms). Some word classes may express arguments of several relations. Thus, the class of nouns is that class of words that can function as Agent and as Patient—that is, the a-terms in the rules AGENT-ACTION a, b $\rightarrow$ $a^N + b^V$, and PATIENT-ACTION a, b $\rightarrow$ $b^V + a^N$ —and as Possession in the POSSESSOR-POSSESSION relation, and so on. A word class will thus be defined by the total set of relation rules in which it may figure (see also section 9.2).

Some doubts might be raised as to whether verbs can be defined in this manner. Many verbs do not denote actions (e.g., so called stative verbs, like "think," "remain," etc.). But, as is shown in section 9.3, relational categories like AGENT-ACTION are gradually extended and instances involving such verbs are assimilated into it. Due to semantic assimilation, the relational categories operating in I-markers are fewer in number than classification of the relations expressed in sentences by a purely semantic criteria might lead one to think (see section 3.4). The fact that the number of relational categories is thus limited may greatly facilitate the formation of word classes on the basis of I-marker relations.

Word classes are not necessarily acquired at one go. Possibly there will be intermediate stages at which the child has somewhat more narrow or more wide classes. One such possibility was discussed in section 7.6: The child may at first have two classes of nouns: animate and inanimate.

Because membership in a word class must be registered for each word separately, it should not surprise us that errors continue to occur for a long time. The later-occurring errors in Table 8.1 may have been due to incomplete entries in the child's lexicon. The word "wind," for instance, may not yet have been marked as a noun; and in the absence of such a category marker there was no constraint on its use: It would figure as an all-purpose word, both in contexts in which a noun and in those in which a verb was required. Or else, if it was so marked, Braine's daughter may have failed to remember this when she said "wind your hair" (for: ruffle your hair). It seems at least as plausible, however, to assume that the child was in command of the full lexical entry but extended the use of the word, generalizing from the observation that English nouns are used as verbs. After all, "gossip," "drive," "work," "climb," and many others, are used both as verbs and as nouns—so why not use "wind" that way, too? (see also Clark & Clark, 1979).

Evidence that children can classify words into word classes without any cue from their nonlinguistic correlates comes from an experiment by Brown (1957). He presented children with a picture showing an action being performed by a strange tool on a strange substance (e.g., kneading a spaghetti-like mass), and described the picture by a nonsense word, say, "sib," in one of the following ways:

> Here's a picture of sibbing.
> Here's a picture of a sib.
> Here's a picture of some sib.

Note that the picture did not give any clue as to whether "sib" was a verb denoting the action (kneading), a count noun referring to the instrument, or a mass noun referring to the substance on which the action was performed, because it described all three aspects. The only clue was the sentence that went with the picture. This clue was indeed found to be effective when Brown subsequently ascertained, by means of different pictures, whether the child took "sib" to be a verb, a count noun, or a mass noun.

These results might be accommodated by the model proposed by Kiss, because in each case the word appeared in a different linguistic environment. They can equally well be accommodated by my proposal, because in each case a different relation rule, requiring a different word class, is involved. (There must be two different rules, one for count nouns and one for mass nouns, specifying which determiners—"a," "the," "some," etc.—may be used for each.) Typically, when evidence for word class membership is provided by the linguistic environment, as required by the model of Kiss, there will also be such evidence provided by the relational argument expressed by the word (i.e., whether it expresses the Agent, the Action, an Attribute, and so on). Conversely, there may often be evidence from the relational argument expressed, while the evidence from the preceding and following words (qua words, and not expressions of relational arguments) is not clear-cut. A noun, for instance, may be preceded not only by an article or other determiner ("a," "the," "some," "any"), but also by a whole range of adjectives, verbs, prepositions, and other words; determiners may precede not only nouns, but also adjectives; verbs need not be followed by nouns, etc. Kiss was of course aware of this, and his model was therefore designed to take care of probabilistic information. It seems to be an advantage of the present proposal that it requires much less dependence on such probabilistic information. A proposal based both on distributional data and on the relations expressed has been advanced by Anderson (1977).

The explanation proposed here seems to be sufficient as far as major word classes are concerned. There are various subclasses of these, however, which cannot be defined in terms of the relations into which the respective words may enter. Take, for instance, the gender distinction, which has grammatical consequences in a number of languages. Except for a minor proportion of nouns that may be assigned "natural" gender, there is no semantic correlate to a noun's gender (the word for sea is masculine in Hebrew, feminine in French, and neuter in German). Nor does the gender distinction affect the I-marker relations the word can enter into. The distinction must therefore be acquired solely on the basis of distributional evidence. Maratsos and Chalkley (1979) have presented some speculations concerning the way such distributional evidence is utilized in the acquisition of subclasses of the major parts of speech.

The fact, commented on earlier, that word classes used by the child early in his linguistic career are semantically consistent, may be a facilitating factor in learning to classify them correctly. Later on, the noun class grows and absorbs nouns that do not refer to things, the verb class absorbs verbs that do not refer, strictly speaking, to actions, and so on. We note in passing that the core of a word class, which does have a semantic correlate, may continue to exert an influence on the way we view what is referred to by it. Thus, when we learn a noun that does not refer to a thing, we may tend to view what is denoted by it as being in some way thing-like (Brown, 1958, pp.

244–245, 253). The fact that "soul" is a noun made it possible to ask questions about the organ in which it resides. The question of how far this influence extends is an unsettled issue, which we cannot pursue further here.

The nonlinguistic correlates of word classes, then, may assist learning. Another facilitating factor, which presumably operates at a somewhat later stage, is the shape of a word, which often betrays its part-of-speech membership. English has endings typical of nouns (e.g., "-ation"), verbs ("-ate"), adjectives ("-est"), and adverbs ("-ly"). Although these cannot be depended on fully (see "to ration," "a debate," "contest," and "flee"), they may serve as supplementary cues for classification.

Word Class In The Lexical Entry

To conclude our discussion of word classes, let us illustrate the form of a lexical entry that the child eventually arrives at in the way described earlier. The lexical entry for the protoverbal element that may be realized by the word "good", for instance, will include the following information:

$$\text{good}^A$$
$$\text{well}^{ADV}$$
$$\text{goodness}^N$$

(The latter item will probably be acquired at a much later date than the two preceding ones.) These three words differ only in the way they have to be used in sentences; beyond that there seems to be little that can be said about differences in meaning between them. Therefore, they should be regarded as belonging to the same protoverbal element. Notice that on the one hand etymologically unrelated words, like "good" and "well," may belong to the same protoverbal element, and on the other hand, words of the same root need not belong to the same protoverbal element: consider "goodly," for instance, which means comely, handsome, and because it expresses a different idea than "good," belongs to a different protoverbal element.

In addition, the lexical entry contains information as to how words are to be inflected. Thus, it will indicate that from both "good" and "well" we may form "better" and "best" to express degrees of comparison, and that "goodness" does not have a plural. The lexical entry contains also "stage directions" specifying in what contexts a word may be used (section 6.3), and dealing with certain pragmatic aspects of word use—which word is appropriate to formal situations and which is to be used only colloquially, which one is polite, and which is vulgar (Schlesinger, 1977a, p. 40). Further, the lexical entry must contain information pertaining to the use of the word in a sentence, see section 9.2. We return to lexical entries in the next chapter, in which the organization of the lexicon is discussed.

8.2   UTTERANCES RESULTING FROM MORE THAN ONE RELATION RULE

For a few months, at most, the child limits himself to two-word utterances alongside one-word utterances. Then longer utterances begin to appear (Leopold, 1949, pp. 45–46). Whether this progress occurs because of the need to make himself better understood or because of the intrinsic satisfaction gained from exercising the language function and approaching the adult model is an open question.

Types of Multiword Utterances

The greater length of an utterance does not necessarily involve greater complexity. Several kinds of multiword utterances require of the child no more than the application of a single relation rule or the repeated application of such a rule. The following types of utterances occur at the early multiword stage:

1. Repetitions of two-word utterances. At the age of 20 months, Hildegard said "this brush. this brush" to indicate two brushes (Leopold, 1949, p. 43). (Here and in the following, a period mark will be used to indicate a longer pause in the child's utterance, usually after terminal intonation.)
2. Juxtaposition of two-word utterances. At 22 months Hildegard is reported saying "Dada's hat. this mine [Leopold, 1949, p. 43]."
3. Addition of the name of the person addressed to the two-word utterance, so as to attract the person's attention; for example, "Papa, push me [Hildegard at 23 months; Leopold, 1949, p. 35]."
4. Conjoining of words. At MLU 1.10 Kendall said, "Kendall mommy walk (Bowerman, 1973, p. 237)." Here we do not have to credit the child with a relation rule expressing the Comitative. The child does not have to learn any new rule; rather, the two names are uttered one after another, in accord with a natural tendency to utter together things thought of as being together. In this case the girl wanted to report what both she and mommy were doing, and so the two corresponding words tumble out together. The relation rule resulting in Agent + Action is applied to both these words as a unit. Another example is "Marion Joey away [Hildegard at 20 months; Leopold, 1949, p. 37]." It was once thought that such reduced coordinations appear only after complete sentences joined by "and" are mastered. But there are also cases where this sequence is reversed (de Villiers & de Villiers, 1978, pp. 110–111).

By contrast, a syntactically more complex utterance is one in which more than one relational category is expressed, where the regularity in word order suggests that this is effected by the application of more than one relation rule. Kendall's corpus at MLU 1.48, for instance, contains several utterances of the pattern Agent + Action + Location, e.g., "Kendall play bed [Bowerman, 1973, p. 242]." Because all these utterances followed the word order that corresponds to that in adult speech, it is reasonable to assume that Kendall used two relation rules in producing each such utterance, one for the Agent–Action relation and one for the Location–Action relation. How two such relation rules can apply in unison and converge on a single utterance is a question that concerns us in a moment. But first we consider some types of utterances involving more than one relation, which parallel some of those described in section 7.3 as a transition from the one-word to the two-word stage.

First, we note that some of the early multiword utterances are rote learned patterns. Leopold (1949) reports that three months before three-word utterances appeared regularly in her speech, Hildegard had two patterns in her linguistic repertoire—"I see you" and the German "da ist es"—and both were "achieved by mechanical imitation [p. 33]." There may also be cases where one word pair of the three-word utterance is a rote learned unit (so that the child puts together, in effect, two elements). A longer utterance that most probably was in its entirety a routine formula is: "and there's one for Kathryn", uttered by Kathryn at MLU 1.89 (Bloom, Lightbown, & Hood, 1975, p. 61). Further examples were given in section 7.3. As was pointed out there, such rote-learned patterns may be incompletely analyzed, or unanalyzed "unopened packages." However, to the extent that the child then analyzes them and becomes aware of the relations figuring in them, these patterns may fulfill a learning function: They may provide him with an opportunity to observe and practice the application of two (or more) relation rules in combination.

Pivot patterns were found to fulfill an important function in the transition from one-word to two-word utterances (section 7.5). They may also play a role in the transition to three-word utterances. Thus we find that the earliest three-word utterances of David, at MLU 1.7, were constituted of the "pivot" word "want" in first position, followed by a two-word combination (Braine, 1976, p. 44). The latter could express any one of a number of relations:

> want my hat
> want more cookie
> want open door
> want baby sister

The corpus presented by Braine contains 18 such patterns with "want," and these constitute almost all the three-word utterances occurring at that period (except for an utterance in which the name of the person addressed precedes the two-word utterance). This child, then, seems to have approached the task of combining two relation rules warily, limiting himself for a while to a single type of pattern. A similar strategy was observed by Ruth Clark (1974) in her son, whose earliest three-word utterances had his nickname as the first word. Sometimes this name served merely as a place holder, having no meaningful relationship to the rest of the utterance. Smoczyńska (1976) also describes the fusing of two different pivot patterns into multiword utterances in a Polish-speaking child. However, because word order in Polish is relatively free, her definition of pivot did not require its appearance in a fixed position.

Just as successive one-word utterances were found often to precede the two-word stage, we find children who try to make their meaning clear by successive two-word (or two-word and one-word) utterances. The following examples, by different children, are from Schaerlaekens (1973, pp. 182–183), translated from the Dutch:

> more flowers. more vase
> (Brings in flowers and wants them put in the vase).
> more nun. more make. more doll
> (When mother dresses doll like nun)
> cupboard closed. closed. Joost
> (= Joost has closed the cupboard)
> pants Karel. dirty pants. dirty pants. Karel

In each of these sequences the child expressed, one at a time, several relations. At a later stage he would have expressed all the relations in a single three- or four-word utterance, but for the time being he is tied down to shorter utterances. A somewhat more advanced stage is that in which two-word utterances serve as building blocks for more complex ones. The child starts out with several short utterances like the aforementioned and then ties them together into a longer utterance expressing more than one relation. This phenomenon has been called REPLACEMENT SEQUENCE by Braine (1971a, p. 16). A simple example is:

> want more. some more. want some more

(Braine, 1971a, p. 17). More elaborate examples are given in Table 8.2. The first items of the sequence serve as a take-off run; from there the child rises into more articulate utterances.

TABLE 8.2
Examples Of Progressive Replacement Sequences

Name of Child	MLU or Age in Months	Source	Example[1]
Anthony	30m.	Weir (1962, pp. 80-82)	block. yellow block. look at all the yellow block
Anthony	30m.	Weir (1962, pp. 80-82)	sit down. sit down on the blanket
Steven	undated	Braine (1971 a, p. 17)	want more. some more. want some more
Steven	undated	Braine (1971a, p. 16)	Stevie gun. Tommy, Stevie gun. Tommy give gun. Gun. Tommy gun. Tommy, give Stevie gun.
Gia	2.30	Bloom et al, (1975, p. 55)	my cookies. my cookies down there
Eric	1.69	Bloom et al, (1975, p. 46)	I see. I see train
Gia	2.30	Bloom et al, (1975, p. 54)	sit over dere. man sit over dere
Gia	2.30	Bloom et al, (1975, p. 51)	read book. man read book
Steven	25-26 m.	Braine (1971a, p. 33)	build house. Cathy build house
Andrew	27 m.	Braine (1971a, p. 33)	all wet. this shoe all wet
Jonathan	26-27 m.	Braine (1971a, p. 33)	on table. wine on table
Gregory	undated	Braine (1971a, p. 16)	man. car. man, car. man, in car. man, in the car

[1]A period indicates a pause. a comma, a mid-utterance intonation break.

Sometimes a little parental help is needed. The adult may first show the child how to put the building blocks together. The following is an interchange between Allison, at MLU 1.73, and her mother (Bloom, 1973, p. 234):

>   *Allison*: baby eat. baby eat. cookies
>   *Mother*: O.K. Baby eat cookies. O.K.
>   *Allison*: (getting down from chair): baby down chair
>   (walking towards bag): baby eat cookies

Once the adult model has been followed, Allison can go through the whole sequence by herself. A little later (p. 235), trying to open a box of cookies, she says:

>   baby eat. baby eat. cookie

and holding the box out to mother:

> baby eat cookie

It is suggested, then, that rote-learned patterns, pivot patterns, successive two-word utterances, and replacement sequences may provide the child with opportunities to practice and observe the application of more than one relation rule in a given situation. They may prepare him for the stage at which he combines two or more relation rules freely for the expression of one I-marker. What we have to look at now is the mechanism that permits such a joint operation of relation rules to converge on the same utterance.

Joint Operation Of Relation Rules

In the following we consider how the application of two relation rules results in a three-word utterance. Later on, we consider how these rules are learned.

Relational categories are sometimes expressed by inflections and affixes (e.g., the relational category "Plural" in English); hence utterances expressing two relations may be shorter than two words. But, as noted in section 7.1, children learning English as a native language acquire inflections later than word order, and therefore we concentrate here on relation rules detemining word order. How do two relation rules operate jointly to determine the relative position of three words?

In some cases this may seem to be a simple feat. For instance, to produce "Adam kick ball," the child has (1) to put "Adam" *before* "kick" (according to the relation rule that says that the Agent comes before the Action); and (2) to put "ball" *after* "kick" (according to the rule that the Action precedes the Object, or Patient). Or, as Brown (1973, p. 183) puts it, he must apply the Agent + Action rule, resulting in "Adam kick," the Action + Object (Action + Patient) rule, resulting in "kick ball," and to delete the repeated element "kick."

This process would be appropriate indeed for the production of some three-word utterances. The upper part of Table 8.3 gives examples of utterances that can be produced by such simple combination. Also, some of the replacement sequences of Table 8.2 may be cases where we can observe this process in operation: a relational argument, such as the Agent is added to a previously uttered relational pattern (e.g., "build house. Cathy build house"). But, as Brown points out, this procedure will not work with, for example, "sit Adam chair" (= sit on Adam's chair), for here the relation rules result in "sit chair" and "Adam chair"; that is, "chair" is established in final position, but the question remains of how "Adam" is to be positioned relative to "sit."

TABLE 8.3

Examples Of Early Three-Word Utterances

Name of Child	MLU or Age in Months	Source	Example	Outputs of the Two Relation Rules Involved
Adam	2.06	Brown (1973, p. 205)	tractor go floor	Agent + Action Action + Location do.
Kendall	1.84	Bowerman (1973, p. 242)	Ben swim pool	
Kendall	1.84	Bowerman (1973, p. 241)	Kendall turn page	Agent + Action Action + Patient do.
Hildegard	23 m.	Leopold (1949, p. 39)	Papa reads book	do.
Gia	1.79	Bloom et al. (1975, p. 50)	Mommy change sheets	do.
Hildegard	22 m.	Leopold (1949, p. 34)	wash baby's dress	Agent + Patient possessor + possession do.
Adam	2.06	Brown (1973, p. 209)	hit Adam ball	
Adam	2.06	Brown (1973, p. 209)	sit Adam chair	Action + Location possessor + possession do.
Hildegard	22 m.	Leopold (1949, p. 33)	ride Papa's neck	
Hildegard	23 m.	Leopold (1949, p. 36)	where my ball?	Location[1] + Entity possessor + possession do.
Gia	1.79	Bloom et al. (1975, p. 51)	read orange chair	Action + Location Attribute + Entity

[1] as a Question

Clearly, a somewhat different process must be at work here. The locative results in "sit + ____", and the construction "Adam chair", resulting from the relation rule for possessive constructions, must be *embedded* in the position indicated by the blank. (Or, as Brown puts it, the locative term [in "sit" + ____"] must "unfold".) It is the thing referred to by the expression "Adam chair" on which someone sits. (Later we present a more formal treatment of the operation of relation rules). The second part of Table 8.3 (below the line) presents some examples of three-word utterances that require embedding of a possessive or attributive construction. Other constructions that are often embedded at the early three-word stage, according to Brown (1973, p. 209), are those expressing recurrence (e.g., "more + ____"), and in my son I frequently observed embedding in the construction "not + ____" (in Hebrew).

What are the relations expressed in the three-word stage? In the earlier discussion, several relations appearing already at the two-word stage have been mentioned. Brown (1973, pp. 185–187) has formulated a "law of cumulative complexity," according to which any relation that the child can express in the more complex three-word utterances will be expressed also in his two-word utterances; but the converse need not be the case, that is, relations expressed in two-word utterances will not necessarily be combined with others in three-word utterances. As we have seen, the child often approaches the task of combination haltingly, by route of rote-learned patterns, pivot patterns, successive two-word utterances, and replacement sequences.

But once he has mastered the principles of combination, he need not confine himself to two relation rules. Although, as we have seen, the transition from the two-word to the three-word stage may take months, there is often no such time lag between the three-word stage, resulting from the application of two relation rules, and the first four-word utterances, resulting from three such rules. In fact, Leopold (1949, p. 45) reports that the first four-word utterance of his daughter even antedated her three-word utterances. In my son, I observed four-word utterances only a few weeks after the first three-word utterances.

However, the expression of more than two relations may impose an additional load on the child's production mechanism, which may lead to errors in word order. Thus, Leopold's daughter had the Agent + Action + Patient pattern well established at 23 months (Leopold 1949, p. 40), but in a four-word utterance this pattern broke down: "watch bake cake Mama [p. 42]."

This should not be taken to mean, of course, that word order in the three-word utterance always follows the adult model. Not only do occasional errors occur, but there may be relations for which the child does not yet have relation rules at the two-word stage. (Note that our thesis that relational categories are formed in the course of acquiring relation rules, section 7.5, implies that in this case the child cannot be credited with a relational category.) At MLU 1.48 Kendall had no fixed word order for the Patient-Action relation in two-word utterances, and among her three-word utterances we find 'Kimmy change here" and "Kimmy kick there,'' where it is "Kimmy" who is changed and kicked (Bowerman, 1973, pp. 241–242). For most children some relational categories apparently are formed much later than the early multiword stage, and therefore no fixed word order should be expected at that stage. Thus, "all sticky candy" was said by the 23-month-old Hildegard when her hands were sticky *from* the candy (Leopold, 1949, p. 38), and at that period she presumably had not yet any relation rule bearing on this relation (see also section 7.3 on "Open Relational Patterns").

We must consider now in a somewhat more formal fashion how two relation rules may result in a three-word utterance. Let us take as an example "wash baby's dress" (Table 8.3). Underlying this utterance is an I-marker including two relations: PATIENT–ACTION and POSSESSOR–POSSESSION. The two relation rules needed for deriving this utterance are:

$$\text{PATIENT–ACTION } a, b \;\longrightarrow\; (b^V + a^N)^V$$

$$\text{POSSESSOR–POSSESSION } a, b \;\longrightarrow\; (a^N + s + b^N)^N$$

The output of these rules has some features which have not been dealt with in the preceding section. First, note the genitive s in the second rule. This is italicized, because, unlike the terms a and b, it is not a protoverbal element, but indicates the way the relation is actually realized in speech (after the application of a phonological rule which determines whether s is to be voiced or unvoiced). Second, not only the individual terms a and b, but also the entire expressions to the right of arrows bear category markers. This is needed so as to permit the operation of additional relation rules, as becomes clear in a moment. These category markers may perhaps be learned in the same way as the category markers of single protoverbal elements are learned, namely, by observing how relation rules operate to produce utterances (see section 8.1). But further on we see that, given the category markers of the single elements, the category marker of the entire expression can be easily determined.

To return to "wash baby's dress," let us see how the above two rules may be applied to the I-marker underlying the utterance. The I-marker here is:

PATIENT–ACTION (POSSESSOR–POSSESSION baby, dress), wash

(Baby's dress is the patient of the action of washing). One way of deriving the utterance is by letting the possessive rule apply first:

Step 1: The POSESSOR-POSSESSION relation rule (above) is applied to the parenthesized term of the I-marker, which results in:
$$(\text{baby}^N + s + \text{dress}^N)^N$$

Step 2: The PATIENT-ACTION rule is applied, and the output of Step 1 serves as patient term. The result is:
$$(\text{wash}^V + (\text{baby}^N + s + \text{dress}^N)^N)^V$$

Note that because the output of Step 1 is an expression marked N, it satisfies the condition imposed by the PATIENT-ACTION rule that says that the a-term must be marked N.

An alternative way of producing this utterance is by applying the two rules in the reverse order:

Step 1: Apply the PATIENT-ACTION rule to the I-marker, leaving the parenthesized expression unanalyzed. This results in:
$$(\text{wash}^V + (\text{POSSESSOR-POSSESSION baby, dress})^N)^V$$

Step 2: Apply to the parenthesized expression in the output of Step 1 the POSSESSOR-POSSESSION rule, and obtain, again,
$$(\text{wash}^V + (\text{baby}^N + s + \text{dress}^N)^N)^V.$$

It seems to be generally the case that the various relation rules can be applied to an I-marker in any sequence, and that the sequence does not affect the form of the utterance. Also, more than one relation rule may be applied simultaneously (Schlesinger, 1977a, section 3C).

The terms in the output of Step 2—which, it will be remembered, are pro-toverbal elements, and not words—must now be lexicalized. Words belonging to the word class indicated by the category marker have to be substituted for them, as described in section 8.1.

The full relation rules are actually somewhat more complicated than those presented here. The output of a rule includes information as to the relation that has been realized; this permits the subsequent operation of intonation and concord rules (see footnote 2). Relation rules may also introduce auxiliaries, prepositions, and other function words. A detailed presentation of the form of relation rules and their mode of operation is to be found in Schlesinger (1977a, sections 2C and 3A), where I also discuss the problem of context sensitivity, which arises with the present conception of relation rules (see also section 8.4). For a shorter discussion see Schlesinger (1977b). (Note that in the latter presentations the term *Goal* was used for what I now prefer to call *Patient*. Discontinuous constituents may require relation rules of a more complex format.)

Relation Rules In Comprehension

The relation rules learned by the child serve him not only in production but also in comprehension. Suppose the phrase "baby's dress" is heard (and suppose further that the words have been analyzed out of the sound sequence—no mean task this, but one that cannot be dealt with here). The comprehension process then involves two phases:

1.   Assigning of category markers to the words in the input string. This can be on the basis of either (a) a lexical look-up (recall that in the lexical entry each word is associated with a category marker); or (b) the morphological form of the word (see section 8.1, at the end of subsection "Acquisition Based on Relation Rules"). The result of this assignment may be formalized as:

$$baby^N + s + dress^N$$

2.   Applying to the result a relation rule in reverse. In the present case, the relation rule the output of which would fit the above formula is:

$$POSSESSOR\text{-}POSSESSION\ a, b \longrightarrow (a^N + s + b^N)^N$$

Applying this rule in reverse we obtain:

$$baby^N + s + dress^N \dashrightarrow POSSESSOR\text{-}POSSESSION\ baby,$$
dress

(where the dotted arrow stands for the application of a relation rule in reverse).

Now note that the expression left of the dotted arrow does not match exactly the output of the aforementioned relation rule: The category marker N, that characterizes the parenthesized expression $(a^N + s + b^N)$ as a whole is missing. An important feature of the comprehension model discussed here is that relation rules may operate on such partial information. Even if not all the relevant information has been retrieved in Phase 1—with the result of, say, $baby + s + dress^N$—the relation rule may be applied. The comprehension mechanism is probabilistic: It makes guesses that may be disconfirmed by further analysis in which larger constituents of the I-marker are retrieved (see Schlesinger [1977a, Chapter 6] for a presentation of this comprehension model).

Relation rules, then, figure in comprehension as well as in production. But whereas converting an I-marker into an utterance in production involves only relation rules and other realization rules, the reverse process of retrieving an I-marker from an utterance involves, in addition, strategies that make use of the hearer's knowledge of the world and of the situational and verbal context. These strategies—we may call them semantic strategies—interact with the application of relation rules described above on every level of the analysis; for a detailed treatment see Schlesinger (1977a, Chapter 10).

This fact may be part of the explanation why the child's production and comprehension of syntactic structures need not go hand in hand. Although it is commonly held that production lags behind comprehension, some writers (Chapman & Miller, 1975; de Villiers & de Villiers, 1973; cf. also Keeney & Wolfe, 1972) have reported that children may use a syntactic rule correctly in production and yet fail to apply the same rule correctly in comprehension. These are not necessarily conflicting claims. By using situational cues and knowledge of the world the child may comprehend an utterance correctly before he has learned the relevant relation rules and, hence, before he can produce similar constructions correctly (Bloom, 1974). However, when he has already begun to use a relation rule in production, he may still not have mastered it to such a degree that it can compete successfully with semantic strategies in comprehension. One finds therefore that 3-year olds tend to construe sentences so that they accord with the most probable state of affairs, and in conflict with their syntactic structure (Strohner & Nelson, 1974).

The Acquisition Of Relation Rules

After having shown above how relation rules operate in comprehension, we can now turn to the question of how they are acquired. This problem has already been dealt with in the previous chapter, in connection with the child's first relation rules. Here we introduce some further detail so as to account for later stages of acquisition. Comprehension must be crucial to the acquisition of relation rules, as argued in section 7.4, because there are cases where language is learned without the child using it actively. It is proposed therefore that learning a relation rule involves:

1. Analyzing an input string.
2. Inferring the underlying I-marker, or part of an I-marker, from situational cues.
3. Formulating the output of both (1) and (2) as a rule.

An important qualification needs to be stated here concerning operation (2). It will often be the case that a relational category expressed in the input string has not yet been formed by the child. As shown in sections 7.2 and 7.5, the formation of relational categories may be part of the process of forming a relation rule. Let us illustrate this here again by the example of how the child might acquire the rule that the plural of nouns is formed by affix-ing *s*. This relation rule is one of the earliest morphophonological rules ac-quired by English-speaking children (Brown, 1973), but before its acquisi-tion the child presumably has had no occasion to form the I-marker relation expressed by the plural. (This is a monadic relation, that is, a relation hav-ing only one argument.) Consider that the use of the plural is appropriate in a variety of situations: when there is a heap of things (e.g., apples), when there are bunches of them (grapes, fingers), or when things stand in rows, like books on a bookshelf, or appear in pairs (hands, eyes), or in extended patches (trees, ants). The notion of plurality—being-more-than-one-of-a-kind—which all these have in common has become so familiar to us adults, partly through the influence of language, that we are apt to overlook the heterogeneity of the situations from which the child must factor out this no-tion. He does so presumably by noticing the uniformity of linguistic expres-sion: In all these situations the plural inflection is used.

Even such an elementary notion as plurality, then, is not a semantic primitive that we come equipped with to the task of language learning. True, to interpret the world around him the child must be able to distinguish between one and many. But, as we have had occasion to note time and again, interpretation does not entail any specific categorization of the inter-pretanda. In fact there are various logically possible categorizations, and the languages of the world differ among themselves in respect to the categorizations they adopt. Thus we find languages that distinguish between things that come in pairs and larger numbers of things, that is, between the dual and the plural, and others that have, in addition, a special form for three of a kind: the trial.

To return to the three processes that according to our proposal operate in learning relation rules, the example of the plural shows that not only (1) but also (2) requires analysis. Of course, once a relational category has been formed by means of such an analysis, it may be employed as such in the ac-quisition of further realization rules through operations (1)–(3). (A critical review of findings on the acquisition of the plural and other mor-phonological rules is presented in MacWhinney [1978].)

Typically, acquisition of the appropriate relation rule will pass through a number of stages. Suppose the child is at a stage where he does not yet have any relation rule for the possessive relation. When he then hears "baby's dress," he may:

1.   Analyze the input string as baby + dress (that is, disregard the genitive *s*).
2.   Judge from the situation that some sort of possessive relation is in-tended.

As a result he will:

3. Tentatively formulate a relation rule that apportions relative positions to the possessor and the possession. (Further experiences with possessives will presumably be needed to establish this rule.) This is typical of the two-word stage, when the child still has only word order rules (see chapter 7).

At a somewhat later stage, he may already pay attention to more details of the input string, and analyze it as:

$$\text{baby} + s + \text{dress}$$

The utterance can now be construed correctly as involving the possessive by means of the previously formed relation rule for the possessive (and possibly with the aid of situational context). Construing it thusly and pairing this construal with the analyzed input string will lead (perhaps only after sufficient experience with similar constructions) to augmenting the previous rule, which now becomes:

$$\text{POSSESSOR-POSSESSION a, b} \quad \rightarrow \quad a + s + b$$

Next the child will come to the stage where his analysis of the input string determines also the category markers of the individual words (through lexical look up, or on the basis of other cues—see the previous subsection). The output of the analysis will then be:

$$\text{baby}^N + s + \text{dress}^N$$

Such analyses will eventually lead to reformulating the relation rule as:

$$\text{POSSESSOR-POSSESSION a, b} \quad \rightarrow \quad a^N + s + b^N$$

So far so good. But how does the child ultimately arrive at the mature relation rule that accords a category marker to the whole expression right of the arrow, viz. $(a^N + s + b^N)^N$? There is no information in the individual *words* "baby" and "dress" that might lead to an analysis of the input string as:

$$(\text{baby}^N + s + \text{dress}^N)^N.$$

But the category marker of the parenthesized expression is essential for er-rorless functioning of the relation rules, as we have seen in our earlier treat-ment of relation rules in production.

There are two ways to deal with this problem. First, the very fact that these category markers are vital for the correct operation of the rules en-sures that eventually the child will have to take note of them. Thus, he will observe repeatedly that the realization of a given I-marker relation may in-clude not only a *word* that is marked as N in his internal lexicon but also a whole expression of a certain structure, for example, $a^N + s + b^N$. He will therefore register that this structure may function as an N. For instance by observing that "baby's dress," "daddy's chair," "mommy's glass," etc. may serve as Patient terms, he will learn that expressions having this struc-ture function as N. Alternatively, he may notice constraints in the use of such expressions. In adult language, expressions marked N cannot function as Action terms in the output of the AGENT-ACTION relation, but only such expressions are amenable to insertion as, for example, Patient terms in the output of the relation rule for the PATIENT-ACTION relation (as shown in "Joint Operation of Relation Rules"). Violations of this con-straint (either in the child's speech or in comprehending utterances of others) will sooner or later lead to negative feedback. The child will therefore have to adjust his rules in such a manner that errors are avoided.

Furthermore, the category markers of parenthesized expressions are largely, perhaps even entirely, determined for us by meaning. Intuitively, baby's dress is a kind of dress, and because 'dress' is marked N in the aforementioned expression, the whole parenthesized expression has to be marked N. Similarly, in $(\text{clean}^V + \text{baby}^N)^V$, which is an output of the PA-TIENT-ACTION relation rule, cleaning the baby is a kind of cleaning (just try to imagine "clean the baby" as denoting a kind of baby!), and because 'clean' is marked V, the whole parenthesized expression has to be so marked. In other words, *dress* and *baby* are what are sometimes called head terms in the earlier expressions, and the remaining terms are dependent on them; and the category marker of the head term determines that of the expression as a whole. As we have just seen, these dependencies are anchored in cognition. Hence, in finding out which category markers apply (given the category markers of the constitutive protoverbal elements) the child is steered by his apprehension of the situation talked about.

Note now that once a full relation rule, including the category marker, has been acquired, the output of one relation rule can be nested within that of another in the manner described earlier (see "Joint Operation of Rela-tion Rules"). Applying more than one relation rule thus presents no addi-tional problems in principle. (The requirements on the processing mechanism are of course larger than in the case of applying only one rela-tion rule, and hence smooth functioning may require a considerable amount of practice.)

We have barely touched here on the problems attendant on the acquisition of relation rules. Clearly, much more work on these remains to be done before we will be able to give even a cursory description of how the child learns the rules of his language. A particularly knotty problem is the child's attaining mastery of exceptions to rules. Here some important suggestions have been made by Maratsos and Chalkley (1979).

A final point has now to be made about the learning of relation rules. In the adult linguistic system the application of one rule is often a necessary condition for the application of another. For instance, for an active declarative sentence, the PATIENT–ACTION relation rule can be applied only if the AGENT–ACTION rule is applied to the same I-marker; consequently, if in an active sentence the Patient is expressed the Agent will be expressed as well. Not so in children's speech, where we often find agentless sentences, as in "put truck window" (Brown, 1973, p. 205), for example. Not only the Agent, but any one of the constituents obligatory in adult speech may be missing in early child speech (Brown, 1973, p. 207). The problem of missing constituents has been discussed in detail in section 3.6. Here it should be noted that this phenomenon shows that one of the things the child still has to learn about his language is which constituents are obligatorily expressed in the utterance; or in other words, what are the mutual dependencies of relation rules. These dependencies are discussed in section 8.4.

8.3   THE HIERARCHICAL STRUCTURE OF I-MARKERS

In the preceding section we have seen how relation rules operate on an I-marker and result in utterances. The relation rules are of course learned. Not so the I-marker that the relation rules operate on, which represents the way we perceive what is talked about and the various relations we apprehend in it. But as pointed out in section 3.4, I-markers are not identical with cognitive structures. They are affected by the language we learn and serve to filter our apprehension of the environment as we express it in our speech. There are the certain aspects of the I-marker which are the result of learning. Take the I-marker underlying "wash baby's dress," given earlier as:

PATIENT–ACTION (POSSESSOR–POSSESSION baby, dress), wash

This I-marker includes:

1.   The protoverbal elements 'baby,' 'dress,' and 'wash,' that is, those 'concepts' that will ultimately be converted into the words "baby,"

"dress" and "wash" (see section 5.4). As shown in chapter 5, these protoverbal elements are categories, and we form these categories in the course of learning to label referents with the appropriate words.

2.   The relational categories PATIENT–ACTION and POSSESS-OR–POSSESSION. As shown in section 7.5, these categories are formed in the course of acquiring relation rules. Independently of language, we probably interpret the world in terms of particular relations (section 7.2); only when language enters the picture, are these classified into categories like the aforementioned.

Now, the I-marker is not just a congeries of relational categories, but a hierarchical structure of these. Thus, in the earlier example, the Possessive relation is embedded in the Patient relation. Following the reasoning in the last section, we may say that this hierarchical structure may be largely unlearned. We cannot possibly conceive of the state of affairs described by "wash baby's dress' in any other way but that it is baby's dress that is being washed. The bracketing (wash, (baby, dress))—rather than, for example, ((wash, baby), dress)—is cognitively given. Similarly the attributive relation may be embedded in the agentive relation in just one specific way, for ex ample, ((white, smoke), rises); the alternative bracketing ((white, rises), smoke) just "doesn't make sense" (see also Braine, 1976, p. 13).

Here it may be objected that there are I-markers where the hierarchical structure is by no means as obviously determined by our cognitions as in this example. In particular this seems to hold for I-markers involving both the agentive and the Patient relation, as for instance the one underlying "Kendall turn page" (Table 8.3):

AGENT–ACTION Kendall, (PATIENT–ACTION page, turn)

Why could one not conceive of the bracketing here as being ((Kendall, turn) page)? That is, perhaps 'page' might be viewed as the Patient of the expression consisting of the AGENT–ACTION relation holding between 'Kendall" and 'turn.' Or, perhaps, following Bloom's (1973, p. 121) view that the child's "cognitive categories are mental representations of the entire relation in experience between agent–action–object . . ." we might have here *one* relation with three arguments: Agent, Patient, and Action. But most linguists are agreed that the verb and the direct object—not the verb and the subject—form one constituent, and their decision is dictated by the simplicity of the rule system. The system of realization rules will therefore be simpler if we follow them in this respect (and this is what we have done in the case of the foregoing I-marker).

There are two ways of dealing with this issue. One may start from the assumption that the way the agentive and patient relations are embedded one within the other is indeed only one of several possible ways these relations may be hierarchically organized. The child's I-markers may therefore be at first organized in a way which differs from that in which it is organized in the I-markers of adults speaking English. But because the bracketing suggested by the linguist is (presumably) the optimal one, making for the simplest rule system, there is pressure exerted by the system on the child learning language: In order to operate as efficiently as possible, he eventually reorganizes his I-markers in a way consonant with the adult—and most economical—organization. (His relation rules may also have to be reformulated accordingly.) For instance, the child may conceivably have at first two separate I-marker relations that are not embedded within each other: AGENT–ACTION a, b and PATIENT–ACTION c, b. He applies to each of these his newly acquired relation rules, one positioning the Agent before the Action and the other, positioning the Action before the Patient, in the way suggested earlier ("Joint Operation of Relation Rules" in section 8.2). But as soon as he attempts somewhat more complex utterances, this simple solution fails to work and he is thus led to organize the two relations hierarchically so that his relation rules will render the required output.

But maximum economy in the rule system is perhaps not of such overbearing importance in the human performance model. Certain kinds of organization first imposed on I-markers may possibly be retained, even though this results in a less than maximally efficient system. Now, the organization he first imposes on his I-markers may be determined by all sorts of chance factors operating at the time of speaking, which may cause some aspects of the situation to become more salient than others. Therefore, it is conceivable that different children happen to hit on different ways of organizing their I-markers, and their different tendencies may continue to be in effect for years, perhaps permanently. There seems to be no good argument against the proposition that there are individual differences in the internalized linguistic systems.[3]

There is also a possibility of quite a different approach. So far we have proceeded from the assumption that there is nothing that compels us to apprehend the hierarchical structures of relations in the way they appear in I-markers of the type AGENT–ACTION a, (PATIENT–ACTION c, b). However, we may have been wrong in assuming this. Conceivably, there is some cognitive factor, however elusive, which predisposes us to organize

---

[3]This suggestion has been made by the late Yehoshua Bar Hillel, but I cannot recall where it appears in his writings.

the I-marker in just this way. (Similar considerations may apply of course also to I-markers involving certain other relations.) Accordingly, one might hypothesize that our conceptual apparatus is such that we are bound to impose one particular hierarchical structure on a set of relations. This would be, then, an unlearned aspect of our I-markers.

An interesting proposal by Höpp (1970, pp. 12-17) concerning the phylogenetic development of hierarchical structures is relevant here. Höpp speculates that words and sentences originated in imperatives: People had to instruct each other to perform certain actions in fulfilling common tasks. The original imperatives were single words. Most of these single-word imperatives designated each a specific kind of action carried out on a specific kind of object ("bring-axe," "cut-wood," etc.). However, people could not fail to observe that often the same kind of action may be performed on different kinds of objects (bringing an axe, wood, food, etc.). As a result of such observations, a word that had hitherto been employed for an action-object complex would come to be used for the action itself, irrespective of the object on which it was carried out (e.g., the word "bring-axe," came to mean 'bring'). Similarly, observations that different actions may be carried out on the same object (e.g., wood is cut, burnt, stored away, etc.) would eventually lead to a single word being used for the object (e.g., the word "cut-wood" came to mean 'wood'). At this stage it may already require two words to designate an action-object complex (such as bringing wood). On Höpp's account, then, Action-Patient constructions developed out of a single word that served as an imperative. This single word was often accompanied by another one that served to indicate the person to whom the imperative was directed. Out of the latter, the sentence subject developed, as Höpp shows at length.

Höpp thus gives an account of the phylogenesis of the Agent (Action-Patient) hierarchy. His speculations are plausible enough, but like all speculations regarding the origins of language in the race can be neither empirically verified nor refuted. At any rate, they suggest a possible cognitive basis for the hierarchical organization of I-marker relations.

The view that hierarchical semantic structures are cognitively determined is supported by a study by Wexler, Culicover, and Hamburger (1975). These authors are interested in the problem of learnability of a grammar, and they start from the assumption that underlying the syntactic deep structure there is a universal hierarchical semantic structure that is not ordered from left to right. They obtained support for their model by a cross-linguistic study of the hierarchical structure (Determiner (Numeral (Adjective, Noun))), e.g., "the two old men." This bracketing, which is presented diagrammatically in Fig. 8.1, is endorsed by linguistic analysis. Wexler et al. now formulate an additional principle (which they call the "invariance principle"), according to which the hierarchical organization of the underlying semantic struc-

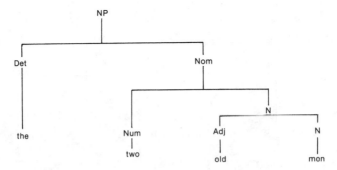

FIG. 8.1 The hierarchical structure of Determiner, Numeral, Adjective, and Noun (after Wexler et al., 1975). (By kind permission of the authors).

ture is retained in the syntactic deep structure. (A similar principle is postulated for an acquisition model by Anderson [1977], who calls it "graph transformation condition"). That is, while the left-to-right order[4] of elements in the deep structure may be expected to vary from language to language, the hierarchical structure should not be violated. The reader may familiarize himself with this notion by imagining that the diagram in Fig. 8.1 is a mobile, the branches of which are free to rotate around their axes. Thus, "Det" and "Noun," for example, can interchange their positions, and the order Numeral, Adjective, Noun, Determiner, accordingly, preserves the above hierarchy. By contrast, the order Numeral, Adjective, Determiner, Noun does not (it cannot be obtained by any rotation of branches). The "invariance principle" predicts that only an order that preserves the hierarchy will appear in the deep structure of any language. On the additional assumption that the hierarchical organization of the deep structure is retained in the surface structure, they predict for the above hierarchy eight possible orders in surface structures, out of 4! = 24 possible ones for four categories. Wexler et al. examined data from 218 languages and found only one exception to their prediction (and, they suggest, that this "must be a transformationally derived order"). There seems thus to be something cognitively compelling in the above hierarchical organization. "Old" and "men" are more strongly linked to each other than "two" and "men," for instance, and this represents not something language-specific, but a universal trait, which is presumably based on the way we conceptualize the world around us.

---

[4]Transformational theory postulates that the syntactic categories in deep structures are ordered, and this order is retained in the surface structure, unless it is permuted by transformations. By contrast, the protoverbal elements of our I-markers are not ordered in a left-to-right fashion (see Schlesinger, 1977a, section 1C). Wexler and Culicover's theory is discussed also in section 3.5.

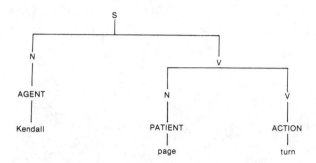

FIG. 8.2   Diagrammatic representation of the I-marker of "Kendall turn page"—AGENT-ACTION Kendall (PATIENT-ACTION page, turn)—with category symbols according to the applicable relation rules.

Let us see now whether a similarly good case can be made for the universality of the hierarchical organization of I-markers including AGENT–ACTION and PATIENT–ACTION relations, represented in Fig. 8.2. Following Wexler et al.'s line of reasoning, the deep structures of all languages may be expected to adopt various left-to-right interchanges of the three constituents, but the following two orders would be excluded because they do not preserve the hierarchical organization: Patient, Agent, Action and Action, Agent, Patient.

Data pertaining to the dominant surface order which might be used to test this prediction have been presented in a well-known paper on universals of grammar by Greenberg (1963). These do not seem to support the universality of the hierarchical organization, as six languages (out of the 30 examined) had a verb, subject, object (Action, Agent, Patient) order. However, this need not be taken as constituting conflicting evidence, because as stated these were data concerning surface structures and there is the possibility that the order has been transformed from an underlying deep structure that did *not* violate the hierarchical organization. Another possibility is of course that whereas the hierarchical organization in the semantic deep structure (our I-marker) is universal, Wexler et al.'s "invariance principle" does not hold; that is, for some kinds of hierarchical semantic structures, deformations may be introduced in the process of deriving the syntactic deep structures. It is reasonable to suppose that during the millenia of their evolution, languages did yield to pressures that changed their original, cognitively determined organization (see Schlesinger [1976] for a related discussion). These arguments are, of course, only defensive and do not come anywhere near proving the case for the universality of the hierarchical organization we are dealing with.

Suppose we approach this issue from a different angle and ask whether there is any evidence that the proposed hierarchical organization—(Agent

(Patient, Action))—is more 'natural' than other possible organizations. I think there is some support for a positive answer to this question. In a study of the sign language in use among the Israeli deaf we investigated the relative position of signs expressing various semantic relations (Namir & Schlesinger, 1978). As far as is known, the Israeli sign language has existed in its present form only for a few decades, having been developed by immigrants from various countries, who began to form a community of deaf signers. It also differs from some other sign languages, notably from the American sign language, in that it has remained relatively uninfluenced by spoken language. Such an unadulterated language, that in its short span of existence has not had time to pass through all kinds of historical processes that a language usually undergoes, may plausibly be expected to reflect in its sign order (note that we are talking here about surface structures!) any universal, cognitively determined underlying organization. This, in fact, seems to be the case. The order of signs in this language was found to be relatively free, but the hierarchy of the underlying I-markers seemed in general to be preserved. The two sign orders that would have destroyed the hierarchical structure of an I-marker like that described in Fig. 8.2 occurred only rarely.

Turning now from a young language to the language of the young, we find that in general the same constraints are observed. Among the deviations from adult word order we hardly find any instances of the Agent being inserted between the Patient and the Action (which would be a violation of the hierarchy of Fig. 8.2). However, two quotations of Bühler (1922/1971, p. 53) must be considered in this connection, which, although not pertinent to the I-marker of Fig. 8.2, involve violations of other hierarchical structures. The violator was a German-speaking boy, who said: "ich olol hoto wapa"—unintelligible German words that, according to Bühler, translate literally as "I Rudolph horse topple," meaning: Rudolph has toppled my horse. Note that "I" and "horse" are arguments of the possessive relation which should belong together, and the insertion of the Agent term, "Rudolph" between them is contrary to expectation. Another utterance by the same boy, whose name was Hans, was: "fallen tul bein anna ans," literally "fall chair leg Anna Hans," which was intended to say that Hans had fallen against Anna's chair and hurt his leg. Here, too, the arguments of the possessive relation, "chair" and "Anna" are separated, and so are "leg" and "Hans." A further case involving violation of this kind is (spelled according to normal adult pronunciation) "trousers Maria brother water," which was intended to mean "brother's trousers are wet, Maria" (Jespersen, 1922, p. 186).

These cases may seem to argue against the thesis that the child respects the cognitively determined hierarchical structure of the I-marker. But should we really expect no such deviation to occur? A child may be expected to respect the underlying hierarchical organization to the extent that he abides by the rules in producing his utterance. It should not surprise us, however, that occasionally the words come tumbling out without any constraint whatever being observed. Or take the case of a 22-month old Hebrew-speaking boy,[5] who would often repeat his utterances. Once he was recorded as saying: "I want wash hands. Hands I want wash." In the first sentence "wash" and "hands" appeared adjacently, reflecting the hierarchical I-marker organization (and, incidentally, this was a perfectly correct Hebrew sentence). In the second utterance, however, "hands" was pre posed, perhaps for emphasis. Such 'lapses' should not be taken as invalidating the thesis that the child's utterances, to the extent that they are planned, mirror the I-marker structure. And if this thesis is correct, the rarity of errors in which the Agent term is inserted between the Patient and the Action seems to be an argument in favor of a cognitively based hierarchical organization of these relations which is like that in Fig. 8.2.

Some support for this claim comes also from replacement sequences, which often consist of an Action + Patient construction to which the Agent is subsequently added (see some of the examples in Table 8.2). This seems to indicate that the Action and the Patient function as one unit vis à vis the Agent. There are exceptions, however, as in Eric's replacement sequence (at MLU 1.69; Bloom et al., 1975, p. 46) "I see. I see train."

Finally, the hypothesis that the hierarchical structure of Agent, Action, and Patient is cognitively determined is in line with Braine's (1974) explanation of the child's early noun + noun constructions (like "Mommy sock"). As stated in section 3.6, Braine accounts for these constructions by assuming that the child chooses one word to express the whole action event (e.g., "sock" for the event of putting on the sock). Accordingly, this action event will in a subsequent stage of his development be further differentiated. This, then, would be an account of the developmental history of the hierarchical structures discussed above.

It seems fair to conclude that, although the data are far from unequivocal, there may be some truth in the notion that, as far as the AGENT–ACTION and PATIENT–ACTION relations are concerned, the hierarchical structure of the I-marker (as described in Fig. 8.2) is cognitively based.

8.4   ALTERNATIVE SETS OF RELATION RULES

In our discussion of relation rules so far we have only dealt with those rules that are required for the production of simple declarative sentences. There

---

[5] I am indebted to Elisheva Goldschmidt for making notes on this boy available to me.

are other kinds of sentences, commonly called "transformations"—interrogative, negative, and passive sentences, and other sentence types that are stylistic variants of simple declarative sentences—each of which expresses some of the relations expressed by a corresponding simple declarative sentence. However, as illustrated presently, some of these relations may have to be realized by different relation rules. The child must therefore acquire these rules and learn when they are to be applied. This section attempts to outline the learning process involved here by means of examples from two types of interrogative sentences and one kind of stylistic variant. It is not intended to give a full description of the acquisition of transformations; the reader is referred to the detailed treatments of Klima and Bellugi (1967), Maratsos (1979), Maratsos, Kuczaj, and Fox (1979), Menyuk (1969), and de Villiers and de Villiers (1978).

Interrogatives

Consider the following relation rule for simple declarative sentences:

$$\text{AGENT--ACTION } a, b \quad \rightarrow \quad (a^N + b^V)^S$$

(The category marker S indicates that the output of the rule is a full sentence.) This rule will be employed in the production of utterances like "John eats," "Lions walk," etc. Usually, children know early how to employ the above rule, as evidenced by their frequent Agent + Action construction in which the two terms appear in the correct sequence. (They may omit the inflectional ending and say "John eat," because they still have incomplete command of the relevant concord rule—another type of realization rule [see Schlesinger 1977a, p. 21].) But this relation rule will obviously not lead to correct interrogative sentences, like "Does John eat?" or "Do lions walk?" because the latter sentences require the insertion of "do" or "does," not provided for by the above rule. The child's first yes-no questions are therefore typically constructed like simple declarative sentences, except that they have a question intonation; for example (Klima & Bellugi, 1967, pp. 200, 202):

> I ride train?
> You want eat?

Eventually he will learn additional relation rules for interrogative sentences. (Even for the AGENT-ACTION relation there are several such rules, but to simplify the discussion we do not deal here with the rules involved in sentences with auxiliaries, such as "can," "will," "must," and "be.")

Sentences like "Does John eat?" and "Do lions walk?" presumably require the following relation rule:

$$\text{AGENT-ACTION a, b} \quad \longrightarrow \quad (do + a^N + b^V)^S$$

After application of this relation rule, an intonation rule (Schlesinger, 1977a, section 2A) introduces the question intonation. This rule is resorted to whenever an element specifying that a question is to be asked is contained in the I-marker.[6] "Do" is italicized here to indicate that this is a word, not a protoverbal element that still has to be lexicalized (see the first section of this chapter). When the Agent term is in the singular, "do" is converted into "does" (unless the Agent term is a first or second person pronoun). This is effected by a concord rule. When the Agent term is in the plural, this will be indicated in the I-marker, where PLURALITY may figure as a relation with one argument, for example, AGENT-ACTION (PLURALITY lion), walk. A concord rule will then determine the realization "do": "Do lions walk?" When the PAST relation applies to the Action term—as in AGENT-ACTION Paul, (PAST cry)—a concord rule specifies the form "did" and the present tense form of the verb (e.g., "cry" rather than "cried"): "Did Paul cry?"

Usually the foregoing relation rule for yes–no questions is acquired before the relevant concord rules, with the result that "do" is inserted in the correct position, but does not yet have the correct form; for example (Klima & Bellugi, 1967, p. 204):

> does lions walk?
> Oh, did I caught it?

As Klima and Bellugi remark, "There seems to be a gradual development of rules and not necessarily the wholesale replacement of one set by another [p. 203]."[7]

Another type of question, called wh-question, requires preposing of a question word, like "why," "when," or "where." In addition to the relation rule that positions these question words at the beginning of the sentence, the rule given above for the AGENT–ACTION relation must apply and introduce "do": "Why does he eat?", "Where did they walk?," etc. Children seem to acquire the relation rule for the question word before that for "do" and produce utterances like:

---

[6]For convenience of exposition this element is being positioned here in the I-marker. In Schlesinger (1977a, section 4A) the underlying structure is divided up into two components: the I-marker, which contains the propositional content, and the component of communicative considerations responsible for choices between relation rules.

[7]Similarly, Maratsos, Kuczaj, and Fox (1979) found that children often do not "naturally and quickly arrive at certain kinds of general formulations [p. 44]," like that between "not" and the contracted form "n't."

where horse go?
why not he eat?

[Klima & Bellugi, pp. 200, 202]. Later, utterances resulting from the application of both relation rules will appear, but at first there may still be faulty operation of concord rules:

what did you does?

[p. 205]. The child must learn that the I-marker element that triggers off the relation rule introducing the question word must also trigger off the above AGENT–ACTION rule that introduces "do." Generally speaking, relation rules operate not singly but in sets, and a specific element in the I-marker will be responsible for activating the several rules in the set (see Schlesinger [1977a, section 4A], for a more detailed discussion). The child must therefore learn which *sets* of rules go with the making of statements, which with the asking of questions, and so on.

The foregoing should make it clear how one might deal with one of the problems raised by the proposed format of relation rules. Transformations in generative grammar are traditionally conceived of as taking an underlying structure as their input, and converting it, as a whole, into another structure. By contrast, each relation rule applies to only one I-marker relation. This departure from current theory has been motivated on the one hand by the need to account for the way the child learns relation rules—at the two-word stage he learns rules each of which applies to a single relation—and on the other, by considering how the production mechanism operates (see Schlesinger, 1977a, pp. 33-34). Now, as we have seen, there are several alternative relation rules for some of the I-marker relations, and the selection of a specific rule for one relation will often be dependent on the selection made (out of the set of alternative rules) for another relation. It is necessary, therefore, to account for the fact that relation rules operate in unison and do not get in each other's way, so to speak. One way of ensuring the smooth operation of the system is, as indicated earlier, by letting a given element of the I-marker (e.g., the element determining that a question is to be asked) make the selection (between alternative relation rules) for all relations in the I-marker.

Stylistic Variants

The production of stylistic variants is governed by essentially the same principles as that of questions. If, instead of "John eats" one says "It is John who eats," so as to achieve a different emphasis or focus, one must have activated a different set of relation rules, just as interrogative sentences require a set of relation rules which differs from that responsible for declarative sentences. Such stylistic variants of standard constructions are normally acquired rather late. It will be more difficult for the child to detect subtle differences in focus, or other determinants of stylistic variants, than to notice that a question is being asked. The process of learning the construction exemplified by "It is John who eats" will therefore differ somewhat from that of learning interrogatives.

What presumably happens is that the child first finds out that the two variants ("John eats" and "It is John who eats") mean the same. This would not be too difficult. At the age he learns the rules governing stylistic variants, he will probably not be dependent on hearing the sentence exhibiting such a variant in the situation described by it. Instead, he may utilize contextual clues to its meaning (see section 6.1). Due to the information he has about the topic that is being talked about and his knowledge of the world, he may figure out what, for example, "It is John who eats" means. Particularly so as this sentence is in some respects similar to "John eats"; for instance, in both sentences the "s" of "eats" indicates that this verb is the Action term and "John" is the Agent term. Usually stylistic variants will share not only some of the constituent words but also some structural features.

Inferring the meaning of a stylistic variant is a first step, which makes it possible for the child to educe, from a sufficient number of examples of the same construction, the relation rules that are responsible for the stylistic variant. This permits his using the variant productively in his own speech. It does not ensure, however, that he uses the variant for the same communicative purposes adults use it for (providing focus, etc.): The subtle effects achieved by using one stylistic variant rather than another construction are an additional thing he has to learn through observation.

Interim Stages

So far we have assumed that the child learns for each construction the appropriate relation rules. Conceivably, mastery of these rules may be pre ceded by an interim stage at which he operates with more primitive ones. This is suggested by some data reported by Leopold (1949) for his daughter, who already at 23 months produced utterances for which—in the adult system—a fairly complicated relation rule would be required: "put hat on [p. 33]," "pretty dress on [p. 36]," "ask Papa on (= to put this on)[p. 35]." "No, shoes, on [p. 39]," "water on [p. 23]"; and even one month before that we find "Papa this on (= turned this on)[p. 40]." It is quite implausible that the child had mastered already at this stage the relation rule that permits moving the preposition to a position after the Patient term (e.g., instead of "put on shoes"—"put shoes on"). What she presumably does learn is that "on" may serve as a sort of pivot word occurring in final position. This rule serves her for a while, but because it is inadequate for more complex sentences (cf. "Put your shoes on now!"), she will eventually have to learn more complex relation rules. We may speculate that before the child acquires the full set of relation rules appropriate for the production of wh-questions, she learns a primitive rule that puts a few specific question words—such as "who," "what," "when," "where"—in first position, as noted by Klima and Bellugi (1967; see earlier discussion).

The Passive

In the psycholinguistic and linguistic literature, passive sentences have been frequently discussed. One of the questions raised is whether the passive sentence is derived from the same deep structure as the corresponding active sentence (see, e.g., Chomsky, 1965; Bresnan, 1978). In the following, developmental data will be discussed which suggest that underlying the passive there may be an I-marker that differs from that of an active sentence.

Children at first do not use full passives, but passives without agents; for example, "John was pushed" may occur in their speech, but "John was pushed by Mary" does not (Horgan, 1978).[8] Watt (1970, pp. 179–189) argues that this shows that the agentless passive cannot have been derived by the child from the full passive (which is the derivation traditionally proposed in transformational grammars). Presumably, the child forms agentless passives in the same way as adjectival predicates (compare "John was pushed" with "John was happy" [see also Braine, 1965, p. 483]). It appears, therefore, that the child learns to use the agentless passive not as a realization of the Patient relation that is expressed by the active sentence. Now, it is quite unlikely, Watt goes on, that when the child has acquired the full passive he subsequently reorganizes his syntactic system and analyses the agentless passive, in line with the full passive, as a variant of the active sentence. According to Watt, then, the two types of passive continue to lead separate lives, only the full passive having a deep structure similar to that of the active.

---

[8]Maratsos and Abramovitch (1975) found no difference in comprehension of agentless and full passives in children 35–47 months of age. Watt (1970, p. 183) suggested that when presented with a full passive the child may concentrate only on the first part of the sentence (disregarding the by-phrase), but Maratsos and Abramovitch have ruled this out by supplementary experiments. However, Harris (1976) found that whereas 10 percent of her youngest subjects (mental age 34–53 months) passed her criterion for comprehension of full passives, none of them did so for agentless passives. (These results pertain only to reversible sentences, which do not provide any semantic clues [see her Table 2].) On the passive see also Langacker and Munro (1975).

It seems to me that we may go one step further. It appears plausible that when the child gradually learns the full passive, he construes it in accordance with the previously acquired agentless passive, that is, he forms relation rules linking the full passive to the same I-marker relation that figures in the agentless passive. The *by*-phrase of the full passive would then be viewed by the child as indicating the Source (of the state of the entity denoted by the subject noun) and not the Agent. Some indication that children interpret *by*-phrases in this manner comes from a study by Maratsos and Abramovitch (1957) (see also Horgan, 1978). The agentless and full passives would accordingly have a common I-marker relation, and the I-marker of neither of these constructions would be similar to that of the active. When the child subsequently becomes aware of the paraphrastic relationship between the active and corresponding passive, he might formulate this by a "paraphrase rule", of the kind proposed by Simmons (1973, p. 81).

In the preceding I have departed from my previous account of the functioning of the passive in the adult system (Schlesinger, 1977a, section 4A). Even if it should turn out that the present proposal is too far-reaching, and that in the adult system active and passive sentences have the same underlying I-marker, the foregoing might still be a valid description of the development of the passive *before* it is reorganized in terms of the active.[9]

REFERENCES

Anderson, J. R. Computer simulation of a language acquisition system: A second report. In J. Laberge & S. J. Samuels (Eds.), *Basic processes in reading: Perception and comprehension*. Hillsdale, N.J.: Lawrence Erlbaum Associates, 1977.

Bloom, L. *Language development: Form and function in emerging grammars*. Cambridge, Mass.: MIT Press, 1970.

Bloom, L. *One word at a time: The use of single-word utterances before syntax*. The Hague: Mouton, 1973.

Bloom, L. Talking, understanding, and thinking. In R. L. Schiefelbusch & L. L. Lloyd (Eds.), *Language perspectives—Acquisition retardation, and intervention*. Baltimore: University Park Press, 1974.

Bloom, L., Lightbown, P., Hood, L. Structure and variation in child language. *Monographs of the Society for Research in Child Development*, 1975, *40* (2, Serial No. 160).

Bowerman, M. F. *Early syntactic development*. Cambridge, England: Cambridge University Press, 1973.

Bowerman, M. Learning the structure of causative verb: A study in the relationship of

---

[9]An experimental study of the acquisition of the passive has been carried out by Horgan (1978). Her reconstruction of the acquisition process parallels in part the foregoing account but includes also further ramifications.

cognitive, semantic and syntactic development. *Papers and Reports on Child Language Development*. Stanford University Committee on Linguistics, 1974, *8*, 142-178.

Braine, M.D.S. The ontogeny of English phrase structure: The first phrase. *Language*, 1963, *39*, 1-13.

Braine, M.D.S. On the basis of phrase structure: A reply to Bever, Fodor, and Weksel. *Psychological Review*, 1965, *72*, 483-492.

Braine, M.D.S. The acquisition of language in infant and child. In C. Reed (Ed.), *The learning of language*. New York: Appleton-Century-Croft, 1971. (a)

Braine, M.D.S. On two types of models of the internalization of grammars. In D. I. Slobin (Ed.), *The ontogenesis of grammar*. New York: Academic Press, 1971. (b)

Braine, M.D.S. Length constraints, reduction rules, and holophrastic processes in children's word combinations. *Journal of Verbal Learning and Verbal Behavior*, 1974, *13*, 448-456.

Braine, M.D.S. Children's first word combinations. *Monographs of the Society for Research in Child Development*, 1976, *41* (1, Serial No. 164).

Bresnan, J. A realistic transformational grammar. In M. Halle, J. Bresnan, & G. A. Miller (Eds.), *Linguistic theory and psychological reality*. Cambridge, Mass.: MIT Press, 1978.

Brown, R. Linguistic determinism and the part of speech. *Journal of Abnormal and Social Psychology*, 1957, *55*, 1-5.

Brown, R. *Words and things*. Glencoe, Ill.: Free Press, 1958.

Brown, R. *A first language: The early stages*. Cambridge, Mass.: Harvard University Press, 1973.

Bühler, K. Vom Wesen der Syntax. In *Idealistische Neuphilologie, Festschrift für Karl Vossler*. Heidelberg, 1922. English translation in A. Bar-Adon & W. F. Leopold (Eds.), *Child language: A book of readings*. Englewood Cliffs, N.J.: Prentice-Hall, 1971.

Carlson, P., & Anisfeld, M. Some observations on the linguistic competence of a two-year old child. *Child Development*, 1969, *40*, 569-575.

Chapman, R. S., & Miller, J. Word order in early two and three word utterances: Does production precede comprehension? *Journal of Speech and Hearing Research*, 1975, *18*, 355-371.

Chomsky, N. *Aspects of the theory of syntax*. Cambridge, Mass.: MIT Press, 1965.

Chukovsky, K. *From two to five*. Berkeley, Calif.: University of California Press, 1971.

Clark, E. V., & Clark, H. H. When nouns surface as verbs. *Language*, 1979, *55*, 767-811.

Clark, R. *Aspects of psycholinguistics in the context of the symposium*. Paper presented at the UNESCO Symposium on Interaction between Linguistics and Mathematical Education, Paris, 1974.

de Villiers, J. G., & de Villiers, P. A. Development of the use of word order in comprehension. *Journal of Psycholinguistic Research*, 1973, *2*, 331-341.

de Villiers, J. G., & de Villiers, P. A. *Language acquisition*. Cambridge, Mass.: Harvard University Press, 1978.

Flavell, J. H. A test of the Whorfian theory. *Psychological Reports*, 1958, *4*, 455-462.

Greenberg, J. H. Some universals of grammar with particular reference to the order of meaningful elements. In J. H. Greenberg (Ed.), *Universals of language* (2nd ed.). Cambridge, Mass.: MIT Press, 1963.

Harris, M. The influence of reversibility and truncation on the interpretation of the passive voice by young children. *British Journal of Psychology*, 1976, *67*, 419-427.

Höpp, G. *Evolution der Sprache und Vernunft*. Berlin: Springer, 1970.

Horgan, D. The development of the full passive. *Journal of Child Language*, 1978, *5*, 65-80.

Jenkins, J. H., & Palermo, D. S. Mediation processes and the acquisition of linguistic structure. In U. Bellugi & R. Brown (Eds.). The acquisition of language. *Monographs of the Society for Research in Child Development*, 1964, *29*, (1, Serial No. 92).

Jespersen, O. *Language: Its nature, development and origin*. New York: Holt, 1922.

Keeney, T. J., & Wolfe, J. The acquisition of agreement in English. *Journal of Verbal Learning and Verbal Behavior*, 1972, *11*, 698-705.

Kiss, G. Grammatical word classes: A learning process and its simulation. In G. H. Bower (Ed.), *The psychology of learning and motivation: Advances in research and theory* (Vol. 7). New York: Academic Press, 1973.

Klima, E. S., & Bellugi, U. Syntactic regularities in the speech of children. In J. Lyons & R. J. Wales (Eds.), *Psycholinguistics papers: The proceedings of the 1966 Edinburgh conference*. Edinburgh: University Press, 1967.

Kuczaj, S. A. The acquisition of regular and irregular past tense forms. *Journal of Verbal Learning and Verbal Behavior*, 1977, *16*, 589-600.

Langacker, R. W., & Munro, P. Passives and their meaning. *Language*, 1975, *51*, 789-830.

Leopold, W. F. *Speech development of a bilingual child: A linguistic record* (Vol. 3). *Grammar and general problems in the first two years*. Evanston, Ill.: Northwestern University Press, 1949.

MacWhinney, B. The acquisition of morphophonology. *Monographs of the Society for Research in Child Development*, 1978, *43* (1-2, Serial No. 174).

Maratsos, M. How to get from words to sentences? In D. Aaronson & R. Rieber (Eds.), *Perspectives in psycholinguistics*. Hillsdale, N.J.: Lawrence Erlbaum Associates, 1979.

Maratsos, M. P., & Abramovitch, R. Children's understanding of the full, truncated, and anomalous passive. *Journal of Verbal Learning and Verbal Behavior*, 1975, *14*, 145-157.

Maratsos, M. P., & Chalkley, M. A. The internal language of children's syntax: The ontogenesis and representation of syntactic categories. In K. Nelson (Ed.), *Children's language* (Vol. 2). New York: Gardner, 1979.

Maratsos, M., Kuczaj, S. A., & Fox, D. M. C. Some empirical studies in the acquisition of transformational relations: Passives, negatives and the past tense. In W. A. Collins (Ed.), *Children's language: The Minnesota symposium on child psychology* (Vol. 12). Hillsdale, N.J.: Lawrence Erlbaum Associates, 1979.

Menyuk, P. *Sentences children use*. Cambridge, Mass.: MIT Press, 1969.

Namir, L, & Schlesinger, I. M. The grammar of sign language. In I. M. Schlesinger & L. Namir (Eds.), *Sign language of the deaf: Psychological, linguistic, and sociological perspectives*. New York: Academic Press, 1978.

Park, T. Z. *Language acquisition in a Korean child*. Unpublished ms. University of Münster, W. Germany, 1970.

Preyer, W. *Die Seele des Kindes* (5th ed.). Leipzig: Th. Grieben, 1900.

Schaerlaekens, A. M. *The two-word sentence in child language development.* The Hague: Mouton, 1973.

Schlesinger, I. M. Grammatical development: The first steps. In E. Lenneberg & E. Lenneberg (Eds.), *Foundations of language development.* New York: Academic Press, 1975.

Schlesinger, I. M. Is there a natural word order? In W. von Raffler-Engel & Y. Lebrun (Eds.), *Baby talk and infant speech.* Amsterdam: Swets & Zeitlinger, 1976.

Schlesinger, I. M. *Production and comprehension of utterances.* Hillsdale, N.J.: Lawrence Erlbaum Associates, 1977. (a)

Schlesinger, I. M. Components of a production model. In S. Rosenberg (Ed.), *Sentence production: Developments in research and theory.* Hillsdale, N.J.: Lawrence Erlbaum Associates, 1977. (b)

Simmons, F. R. Semantic networks: Their computation and use for understanding English sentences. In R. C. Schank & K. M. Colby (Eds.), *Computer models of thought and language.* San Francisco: Freeman, 1973.

Sinclair, H. Sensorimotor action patterns as a condition for the acquisition of syntax. In R. Huxley and E. Ingram (Eds.), *Language acquisition: Models and methods.* London: Academic Press, 1971.

Smith, M. E. Grammatical errors in the speech of preschool children. *Child Development,* 1933, *4,* 183-190.

Smoczynska, M. Early syntactic development: Pivot look and pivot grammar. *Polish Psychological Bulletin,* 1976, *1,* 37-43.

Stern, C., & Stern, W. *Die Kindersprache: Eine psychologische and sprachtheoretische Untersuchung.* Darmstadt: Wissenschaftliche Buchgesellschaft, 1968. (Originally published 1928).

Strohner, H. & Nelson, K. E. The young child's development of sentence comprehension: Influence of event probability, nonverbal context, syntactic form, and strategies. *Child Development,* 1974, *45,* 567-576.

Watt, W. C. On two hypotheses concerning psycholinguistics. In J. R. Hayes (Ed.) *Cognition and the development of language.* New York: Wiley, 1970.

Weir, R. *Language in the crib.* The Hague: Mouton, 1962.

Wexler, K., Culicover, P., & Hamburger, H. Learning-theoretic foundations of linguistic universals. *Theoretical Linguistics,* 1975, *2,* 215-253.

Wundt, W. *Die Sprache.* I. Teil. Leipzig: Engelmann, 1904.

9 Toward an Adult System

INTRODUCTION

The first steps of language were the focus of the preceding chapters; somewhat later developments were touched on only here and there. Although a writer on child language is entitled to limit the scope of his treatment in this fashion, the theory he proposes must stand the test of later stages of development. The theoretical approach of this book must be defended against the charge that it offers seemingly satisfactory explanation of only the early stages of language learning but will turn out to lead us up the garden path once it is attempted to explain how the adult linguistic system is acquired.

In this final chapter I try to show that the account so far provides a firm enough foundation for the adult system. Proposals are made regarding the type of relations in the adults' underlying structure and the form of lexical entries that enable the rule system to convert these structures into utterances. The approach here is eclectic, making use of several notions that have recently appeared in the writings of various linguists. It is not my purpose here to propose a conception of grammar that is either novel or comprehensive; instead, my objective is merely to show that nothing precludes, in principle, leading the young language learner from where we left him to the final stages of his linguistic development.

The central problem that has to be dealt with here is how the relational categories we assumed to have been formed in earlier stages eventually develop into those functioning in the adult system. Various possibilities of dealing with this problem are discussed in the first section. The solution that I advocate, semantic assimilation, is then expounded in the following sections. Much of the burden of this solution is borne by lexical entries, the form of which is discussed in section 9.2. Sections 9.3 and 9.4 treat of various forms of semantic assimilation. This treatment leads to the previously made distinction between I-markers and cognitive structures (see sections 3.4–3.5), which is further discussed in section 9.5. The two final sections are devoted to the problem of the organization of the lexicon. Among others I take issue with the extreme nativist thesis recently propounded by Fodor (1975) (section 9.7).

9.1   RELATIONAL CATEGORIES IN THE ADULT SYSTEM

In Chapter 7 it has been shown how the child acquires relational categories of a semantic nature, like Agent-Action, Possessor-Possession, and so on. The problem to be dealt with in the following is whether the fully mature linguistic system can be accounted for in terms of such semantic categories. Perhaps, as some have argued (see section 3.5), these categories function only in the first stages of language development and are subsequently replaced by more abstract, syntactic categories.

Take for instance the Agent–Action category. It is well known that what linguists call the subject is a much more comprehensive category than the Agent.[1] The subjects of the following sentences, for example, are not Agents, in the sense of instigators of action, or according to any other definition of "Agent" one might think of:

> This hall can seat 500 people.
> The old woman saw the first cherry blossoms on the tree.
> The hoary joke produced a few subdued yawns.

These sentences can all be passivized, just like sentences with Agents, so that the object phrase becomes the surface subject:

> Five hundred people can be seated in this hall.
> The first cherry blossoms were seen by the old woman.
> A few subdued yawns were produced by the hoary joke.

Similarly, they can all be paraphrased in the same way as follows:

---

[1]Terminological note: It will be convenient to refer not only to relations (relational categories), like Agent-Action, but at times also to the arguments (terms) of these relations, like Agent and Action. The latter will also be referred to as *categories*, when they are contrasted with abstract grammatical categories, like subject, etc. The term *subject* is used here only for the deep structure subject, and not for the surface structure subject.

It is the hall that can seat 500 people.
It is the old woman who saw the first cherry blossoms
on the tree.
It is the hoary joke that produced a few subdued yawns.

Because the terms Agent and Patient, taken in a strict sense, do not seem to be applicable to these sentences, one might argue as follows. If the rules responsible for the passive or for pseudocleft sentences were formulated in terms of Agent and Patient, they would not hold for the derivation of the foregoing sentences. Hence, in addition to the rules responsible for the derivation of Agent-Action-Patient, there would have to be parallel rules for the derivation of the foregoing sentences from their respective underlying semantic structures (whatever these might be). Such lack of economy is anathema to the linguist. The rules of syntax can be formulated most efficiently in terms of syntactic categories—like noun phrase, verb phrase (or, alternatively, subject, predicate, etc.)—which are apparently much broader in scope than the semantic ones. Thus, whereas "the hall," "the old woman," and "the hoary joke," in the earlier sentences do not seem to be Agents, they certainly are all subjects (i.e., noun phrases directly dominated by S). It seems therefore necessary for the child to change from his early semantic relational categories to more abstract syntactic ones.

But how is such a switch to be achieved? One possibility suggested by Bowerman (1973, 1974a; see also section 3.5) is that the child notes that some relations are linguistically similar, that is, they are realized by means of the same kinds of rules and result in similarly constructed utterances. "The old woman saw the first cherry blossoms on the tree" is constructed like "The old woman snipped the first cherry blossoms from the tree" (and they even have stylistic variants produced by the same relation rules, e.g., "It is the old woman who . . .," "It is the first cherry blossoms that . . ."). By observing such structural similarities between sentences involving the agentive relation and those involving the Experiencer relation (or Person Affected relation, as it is sometimes called), the child comes to classify these two relations together. Subsequently he adds to them other semantic relations, and thus the more general subject category is formed. (This process need not be fully conscious, of course.) Note that it is not necessary, on this account, to check for each semantic relation separately whether it observes *all* the relation rules that are applicable to the incipient subject category. It may be sufficient to observe *some* commonality in the linguistic behavior of the relations in order to classify them together. The process will be similar to that involved in forming a stimulus equivalence class (see, e.g., Jenkins & Palermo, 1964).

A different approach has been outlined in section 3.4 (see also Schlesinger, 1977, section 2A). Instead of several relations being *subsumed* under a more general one, they may be *assimilated* into one central relation. Let us illustrate this by a concrete (fictitious) example. Suppose a child's corpus contains utterances like the following:

> Mommy kiss Kathy.
> Kathy hug mommy.
> Kathy eat cooky.
> Daddy push chair.
> Mommy put block.

These utterances involve overt actions and they are all formed according to the same pattern—Agent before Action and Action before Patient. So she presumably has formed the Agent–Action and Patient–Action relations (by the process outlined in section 7.5) and the appropriate relation rules (section 8.2). Comprehending utterances like the aforementioned involves applying these relation rules in reverse (section 8.2). (The last three sentences may be understood without this because of semantic constraints, but understanding sentences like the first two examples requires application of relation rules.) As a matter of fact, most early utterances that include verbs involve such overt actions (expressing either the Agent–Action or the Patient–Action relation—see section 7.3, Tables 7.1 and 7.2—or both). But eventually the child hears, and understands, utterances built on the same pattern as those in the foregoing which do not describe any overt actions and do not involve an Agent—in the strict sense of instigator of an action. These will also be analyzed by the same relation rules. Thus, "Daddy hears the bell" will be construed as an Agent (daddy) performing an Action (hear) affecting a Patient (bell). Such a construction may be accepted by the child because some similarity may be perceived between the relations exhibited in "Daddy hears the bell' and those in other utterances with prototypical agents and actions, like "Daddy push chair." In other words, the *particular* relations (see section 7.2) underlying "Daddy hears the bell" are viewed as belonging to the previously formed relational *categories* Agent-Action and Action-Patient. When such constructions occur sufficiently often, those particular relations will be assimilated into these relational categories: The child has learned that—for the purpose of using language—hearing is a kind of Action, and the 'hearer' is the Agent of this Action. A more formal presentation of the results of this categorization is given in section 9.3. An interesting experimental procedure for following up these ideas is now being developed by de Villiers (1979), and her preliminary results can be interpreted in line with this approach.

At this point the suggestion might be made that because the assimilation hypothesis leads to the formation of broad categories, like those postulated in most grammatical systems, the standard linguistic nomenclature ought to be adopted. For instance, there is no reason why the Agent category, once extended by semantic assimilation, should not be renamed 'subject of.' However, the correspondence between linguistic categories and our semantic ones is not necessarily complete, as becomes clear further on. Besides, the semantic terminology has the advantage of being more revealing in respect to the ontogenetic origin of these categories. I propose therefore to retain this terminology also for the adult system, with the proviso that terms like "Agent" not be taken literally (as 'instigator of action' or the like), but in their extended sense, somewhat metaphorically, as all that is treated by the language as, for example, an Agent.

We have discussed here two explanations of how the child forms categories broader than those he starts out with. According to one of these, the child subsumes several relations under a more abstract and general one, and according to the other, several relations may be assimilated into a prototypical one. Let us clarify now in what respects these two hypotheses differ.

1. The abstraction hypothesis claims, as stated, that on observing that various relations are expressed in the same way, the child subsumes these under a more general one. This hypothesis is thus based on perceived similarity of linguistic expression; the assimilation hypothesis requires, *in addition*, that the child perceives the intended relations to be somehow similar. One advantage of this view is that it links up with an explanation of why a given language arrives at a certain system of "syntactic" categories, rather than at another, for classifying the various particular relations that speakers may perceive in their extralinguistic experience. What, for instance, is common to all the subjects of the sentences listed earlier? Unless we are ready to claim that the syntactic relations of a language were concocted in a completely arbitrary manner, we have to assume that the speakers of a given language noted some similarities between the notions expressed, which led to their being categorized in the same way (by speakers of that particular language). Now, it is precisely these similarities that the child capitalizes on when he learns language. He learns that certain notions that are similar to Agents are treated by language like Agents; and likewise for other relational categories.

2. Because according to the assimilation hypothesis there is a prototypical relation that assimilates others, we may expect that the resulting broad category retains characteristics of the prototypical relation. Specifically, it may be expected that what is usually called the *subject* category, being based on the Agent relation, will have certain connotations of agency. That this is in fact the case is shown

in the following sections. Among others, it is seen that semantic assimilation predicts certain constraints on possible structures, that cannot be predicted otherwise (section 9.4). By contrast, the abstraction hypothesis does not postulate that any one relation is more central or prototypical than others subsumed with it under the same syntactic relation, and hence does not make any of these predictions. The phenomena discussed in the following sections thus constitute support for the assimilation hypothesis.

3.   The two hypotheses may lead to somewhat different systems of adult categories. According to the abstraction hypothesis, *all* those relations that are treated similarly linguistically, will be subsumed under one general category. The assimilation hypothesis predicts this only for those relations that can be viewed as similar in some way to the prototypical relations; when this additional condition is not met, no assimilation can occur. How broad the final categories are conceived of under the assimilation hypothesis will therefore depend mainly on the intuitions of the theorist as to what relations may possibly be conceived of as similar to the prototype, but it seems likely that they will be less broad than those provided for by the abstraction hypothesis. In particular, it is shown in the following two sections that many types of subjects may be viewed as extended Agents in accordance with the assimilation hypothesis; many, but not all, for there seem to be certain subjects that—intuitively at least—resist such an interpretation (section 9.4, "Agents and Subjects"). The assimilation hypothesis does not purport therefore to explain *all* the regularities in the linguistic system. It claims that similarity of the notions expressed is a facilitating factor in many cases, but does not rule out the possibility that, in other cases, a number of relational categories may be subsumed under a broader category on the basis of merely linguistic similarity. To achieve greater economy of the system, therefore, it may be the case that the extended Agent category (arrived at by semantic assimilation) will eventually be classified with other categories, as far as applicability of relation rules is concerned.

A comment on terminology is in order here. The question may be raised whether the relations underlying language are syntactic or semantic. Bowerman (1973) has dealt with the nature of categories in early child language, and has argued forcefully (in line with the semantic approach advocated in this book) that children begin their linguistic career with semantic categories, and that at first there is no evidence for any syntactic ones (see section 3.5). This is an empirical issue concerning which she has marshalled compelling evidence. As far as adult language is concerned, however, the issue is, on the present account, largely terminological. One may wish to call the relational categories that, as I have claimed here, figure in adult grammar *syntactic*, because they are far more comprehensive than those the child starts out with. Alternatively, one may prefer the label *semantic* also for adult relational categories, thus drawing attention to their origin. It is this question of origin which is the main substantive issue. Further on the semantic assimilation proposal is presented in detail. But to do so, we must first clarify some aspects of lexical entries.

9.2   I-MARKER FRAMES AND SPECIFICATIONS

This section deals with the form of entries in our internal lexicon. This will enable us to conceptualize various phenomena of semantic assimilation, dealt with in the following section. It will also provide a conceptual framework for dealing with the problem raised in Chapter 6: Word acquisition involves not only learning to what a word refers but also how it is used in a sentence.

As stated in section 8.1, the lexical entry for a word contains its protoverbal element (i.e., the "concept" that has been formed in the course of learning the word; see section 5.4), and information concerning the way it may be realized, including the phonological shape of the word, its word class membership, and information as to how it is inflected. In addition, we now stipulate that the entry contains information concerning the relational arguments for which the protoverbal element is eligible. For instance, the protoverbal element for 'eat' can function as the Action term of the Agent–Action relation and of the Patient–Action relation, whereas it can not function as, for example, the Attribute term (for that would patently be nonsense). It is proposed that this information be formalized by an I-MARKER FRAME. For example, the lexical entry for 'eat' will include:

$$\text{eat: AGENT–ACTION x, (PATIENT–ACTION y,\_\_\_)}$$

This means that the protoverbal element for 'eat' may appear in the position indicated by the blank in the frame, that is, as an Action term (y is a variable standing for the Patient term; see the notation in section 8.2). The application of relation rules and substitution of a word for the protoverbal element then determine at which position in the sentence the *word* "eat" appears.

This protoverbal element can of course appear also in much more complex I-markers (e.g., one that contains, in addition, locative, possessive, and attributive relations). Because its sole purpose is to indicate the function the protoverbal element may fulfill in the I-marker, the I-marker frame will include only those I-marker relations in which the protoverbal element functions as argument.

The protoverbal element for 'eat' may at times occur in an I-marker without Patient term (e.g., the I-marker which underlies "Johnnie is eating"). The lexical entry must therefore include, among others, the information that in active sentences, y, the Patient term, is optional.

I-marker frames have obvious affinities to the lexical entries proposed by Katz (1972), Jackendoff (1976), and Bresnan (1978). But to suit our purpose, categories like Agent and Patient have been introduced here instead of syntactic categories like 'noun phrase.' I-marker frames also differ from the lexical entries proposed by these writers in that they pertain to protoverbal elements rather than to words. This is so, because I-markers, too, contain protoverbal elements (and words, it will be remembered, are introduced subsequently by lexicalization of protoverbal elements).[2]

Stemmer (1973) has also proposed that the child learns in which frame words are to be inserted. But his frames are idiosyncratic to each particular verb. For instance, he would stipulate that "eat" is preceded by the word standing for the person or animal that ingests the food, and followed by that standing for the food ingested. Stemmer would thus base the whole internalized rule system on such stipulations, without any abstractions like our I-marker relations, or like those in traditional grammars. Learning a system of rules without such generalizations appears to be a hopeless task, however (see Schlesinger [1975] for a discussion and Stemmer's [1975] reply).

The example of an I-marker frame just presented may give the impression that the information in the I-marker frame is redundant, because it is already included in the protoverbal element: Once the child knows what "eat" refers to, he does not have to learn that it is an action and that there is an Agent performing the action and a Patient on whom it is performed. The same seems to hold for many other verbs denoting actions involving overt movement (prototypical actions like "throw," "put," "break," etc.) But things are not always so simple. Consider the verb "lead." The child who learns this verb does so in a situation that involves one who leads and one who is led. But which one is to figure as the Agent of "lead"? Obviously, one might say, the one who goes in front and shows the way because he is more "active." Let us look now at "follow." This word will be learned in situations similar to those in which "lead" is learned; a scene described by "A follows B" will hardly differ from one describable by "B leads A." The

---

[2]In the following, however, I do not cling to this distinction pedantically; when convenient, I refer to I-marker frames of words.

protoverbal elements of the two words will therefore be very similar. But how will the child come to know how "follow" is to be used in a sentence: Who is to be referred to as Agent and who as Patient? If, following the above reasoning, the Agent is the more "active" entity, and the leader is viewed as more active, the leader should also figure as Agent in a sentence with "follow." But this is incorrect.

What we need therefore is, first, an I-marker frame:

follow: AGENT–ACTION x, (PATIENT–ACTION y, ____)

and, second, SPECIFICATIONS for this I-marker frame by means of which x and y can be identified. The protoverbal element 'follow' consists of internal representations of (roughly speaking) situations in connection with which the word "follow" was applied. In each of these situations there was one who followed and one who was followed. The specification of x links x with the protoverbal element and indicates which one of these dramatis personae is the Agent term in the above I-marker frame. Likewise, the specification of y links y to the protoverbal element and indicates which is the Patient term.

The I-marker frame in the lexical entry for "lead" will be identical to that for "follow," the difference between 'lead' and 'follow' being brought out by the specifications for this frame. These specifications will identify the Agent and Patient terms with certain aspects of the internal representation in the protoverbal elements. The one who follows will now be the Patient and the one who is followed—the Agent. 'Lead' and 'follow' thus have separate lexical entries, including separate protoverbal elements with separate (though very similar) internal representations. However, there are "cross-references" between these entries that show up the fact that 'lead' is the converse of 'follow.' The nature of these is discussed in section 9.6.

The specifications for some I-marker frames are very broad. In the frame for "own," for instance (which includes an Agent, Action, and Patient, like those for "eat," "lead," and "follow"), the Patient term can denote any alienable possession, and the Agent term—the owner of this possession. The type of semantic assimilation involved here is discussed further on (section 9.3).

A lexical entry, then, has an I-marker frame, which is anchored to the protoverbal element by means of specifications. To be able to use words in sentences, the child must acquire, through his experience with the word, the appropriate I-marker frame and specifications. For some lexical entries, such as 'eat,' the specifications are obvious; in others, such as 'lead' and 'follow,' they are far from that. Children will therefore have more difficulty in learning how "lead" and "follow" are used in sentences than in learning how "eat" is used. Other things being equal, the clearer the differentiation of Agent and Patient roles in the situations referred to by the verb (and hence, in the internal representation included in the protoverbal element), the easier it will be for the child to master the use of the word.

Some data relevant to this are provided by Sinclair, Sinclair, and De Marcellus (1971), who studied preschoolers' comprehension of several verbs appearing in active and passive sentences. They found that "follow" was the most difficult of the verbs studied, and was poorly understood even in active sentences. The other verbs studied were understood correctly in active sentences, but in passive sentences some mistakes were made. The verbs were, in decreasing order of difficulty: "push," "wash," "knock down," and "break." Sinclair et al. point out that "push," like "follow," involves only a change in position, which cannot be perceived unless one observes the action in progress, whereas the actions referred to by "wash," "knock down," and "break" have a clear result that is perceptible also after termination of the action. Consequently, the latter three words were easier to comprehend. "Break" was the easiest because of nonlinguistic constraints: The action in the context of the experiment was irreversible (A could break B, but "B breaks A" made no sense). In terms of our earlier discussion we might say that the internal representations pertaining to the latter group of verbs have more perspicuous structures, the various roles (Agent, Patient) being more clearly differentiated. Hence the specifications linking the I-marker frames to the protoverbal elements of these verbs were easier to master.

On first learning a word, the child presumably tends to use it in all situations resembling the learning situation (see section 5.2). "Follow" may be used where "lead" is appropriate, or vice versa, and "give" may not be clearly differentiated from "take" or "receive" (but see section 6.2). The constraints on the use of words have to be learned, and I-marker frames and their specifications are constructs introduced here to conceptualize what has been learned. Protoverbal elements pertaining to things (i.e., those usually expressed by nouns) are usually subject to fewer constraints than those pertaining to actions and states (expressed by verbs). The protoverbal element of "stone," for instance, may figure in the I-marker as Patient, Location, Instrument, or Possession, and presumably in various other roles. Such *lack* of constraints is presumably not something the child has to learn.

9.3 LEXICALLY BASED SEMANTIC ASSIMILATION

Some phenomena of semantic assimilation can be described as stipulations concerning the use of particular words: They are lexically based. It is proposed (following Brown, 1973, pp. 146, 237) that, as far as these phenomena of semantic assimilation are concerned, the child expands his relational categories by learning certain facts about the use of particular words. These facts can be described in terms of I-marker frames and their specifications, as is seen in the following. In section 9.4 we deal with other kinds of semantic assimilation.

Location

As a first example of lexically based semantic assimilation we consider so-called "Locatives." In the I-marker these may figure as Agent or as Patient terms, depending on the verb with which they appear. Take, for example:

> The road crossed the mountain pass.

If we define "Agent" by strict semantic criteria—as instigator of an action, for instance—the road here is not an Agent. However, the road may be viewed as if it were an Agent, much as a human being might be, as in:

> Hannibal crossed the mountain pass.

But note that he who utters the former sentence does not improvise a metaphor ad hoc; he just uses the verb "cross" as it is customarily being used. In our terms, there is an I-marker frame:

> cross: AGENT–ACTION x, (PATIENT–ACTION y, ____)

and specifications indicating that y, the Patient term, stands for the place across which something lies, and x, the Agent term, for what lies across that place. The entity located is assimilated by the Agent term and the location, by the Patient.[3] Note the departure here from case grammar, where "mountain pass" in the foregoing sentences would be treated as a Locative. Instead, I propose that these sentences be viewed as regular Agent-Action–Patient constructions.

Consider now the following sentences:

> This hall can seat 500 people.
> The barrel holds seven gallons of wine.

---

[3]Here and in the following, the names of relations and their argument appearing in the I-marker are written with initial capitals, whereas those pertaining to aspects perceived in the situation talked about, but assimilated by a differently named I-marker relation, are in lower case.

These examples differ from the foregoing one with "cross" in that the surface subjects—"this hall," "the barrel"—denote the location, not the entity located. According to the semantic assimilation approach, these sentences as well as the former have AGENT–ACTION and ACTION–PATIENT relations in the underlying I-marker. The difference between the sentences resides in the specifications to the I-marker frames for the respective verbs. Thus, although the I-marker frames for "seat" and "hold" are of the same form as that for "cross," their specifications differ: They indicate that the location is represented by x, the Agent term, and the entity located by y, the Patient term.

The child has to learn for each of these words how it is used; he must register the I-marker frames for "cross," "seat," and "hold" and their specifications. As suggested in section 9.1, in doing so he may rely not only on the similarities between sentences (i.e., between a sentence including "cross," on the one hand, and those including verbs like "pull," "eat," and "hug," on the other), but may also be aided by similarities between the relations described in these sentences. Imagination makes things come alive. Roads, halls, and barrels may be viewed (if only for a fleeting moment) as animate beings performing actions. The fact that the sentence "treats" a road like an Agent may suggest to the child that the road, like a person, travels across a mountain pass (while being quite aware that this is only a figure of speech). Likewise, "the barrel holds" may be construed as a metaphor of sorts, the barrel being very much like a person holding, say, a pile of books. I am not suggesting that the learner continues to become aware of these resemblances each time he uses the word but only that noting the resemblance may facilitate the learning process.

Once the child has learned constructions like "the barrel holds . . ." and "the hall seats . . .," he may perhaps tend to generalize from them to other instances in which a location is to be expressed. But soon he will find out that there is no general rule applying to all locations and to all entities located. In "the cat is on the mat," for instance, the location cannot be assimilated into another category; instead, the I-marker underlying this sentence contains a locative relation. Likewise, the location in sentences with "cross," as we have seen, behaves differently than that in sentences with "hold" (or "seat"). As far as locations are concerned, then, I-marker frames must be learned separately for each verb.

The situation is somewhat different in the case of alienable possessions. Here the child is somewhat better off because these can be assimilated across the board by using the verb "own" (see section 9.2). (That "Old Macdonald owns a cow," for instance, is an Agent–Action–Patient construction is shown by its being subject to all the stylistic variants these constructions are subject to: "It is old Macdonald who owns a cow," "It is a cow that old Macdonald owns," etc.)⁴. But the case of locations is more typical. In the following, the complexities of semantic assimilation are examined by an example of a different notion: the so-called Experiencer.

Experiencer

What is commonly called Experiencer (or Person Affected) may be assimilated into the Agent category. According to the specifications for "see" and "hear," for instance, the one who receives the sense impression is the Agent, and the thing seen or heard, the Patient. Rhodes (1977) has suggested that what characterizes the Agent is that it has control over the situation, and in the case of "see," she claims, "there is marginal control of the one doing the seeing [p. 510]." In "The old woman saw the first cherry blossoms on the tree," "the old woman" is therefore the Agent term. In Japanese, however, the object seen is the Agent (see Weisgerber, 1962, p. 311; the cherry blossoms are said to reveal themselves to the old woman, in the corresponding Japanese sentence). The specifications linking the I-marker frame to the protoverbal element thus are different in that language. The situations described by verbs like "see" are nonprototypical, as far as the agentive relation is concerned, and as argued by Rhodes, in such nonprototypical situations "there is some leeway for language specific choices in case assignment [p. 509]."

It will be apparent now that I-marker relations differ considerably from the cases of case grammar as traditionally conceived. The latter are supposed to be universal, but I-markers, as the preceding shows, may be language specific. Further evidence for the language specificity of I-markers is adduced in section 9.5 (see also Schlesinger, 1977, section 5C; and Chapter 4 herein).

I-markers also differ from the deep structures of case grammar and of generative semantics in being much closer to surface structures. Note that in the earlier examples what we have called Agent would be regarded as surface subject in those theories. The Agents expressed in the earlier examples are of course a mixed bag, including experiencers, locations, etc. But in the present framework these are cognitive distinctions, which do not pertain to the linguistic I-marker level. Collapsing of various cognitively distinct no-

---

⁴Possessive constructions with "have" are also subject to the above stylistic variants, but unlike those with "own" they cannot be passivized: "A cow is had by old MacDonald" is unacceptable (except in some dialects, where they may be the result of subsequent analogical formation). However, according to the suggestion made in section 8.4, the passive is not an Agent–Action–Patient construction at all, and so the inadmissability of passivization does not necessarily bar a treatment of "have" along the lines proposed here for "own." In our discussion of the Experiencer in section 9.3 it becomes clear why this treatment is preferable.

tions into one I-marker relation becomes possible by viewing notions like Agent and Patient as prototypes, as suggested by Rhodes and by de Villiers (1979).

The claim that a category has a prototypical structure entails that instances of the category vary in their degree of proximity to the prototype. Sentences with verbs denoting mental states and activities like "know," "recall," and "guess" seem, in fact, to lie along a continuum, some being closer to the prototypical Agent—the instigator of an overt action—than others (Schlesinger, 1977, p. 27). The following sentences seem to be ranged along this continuum:

> John knows the answer.
> John recalls the answer.
> John guesses the answer.
> John computes the answer.
> John writes down the answer.

Where should one draw the line between "Experiencer" and "Agent"? According to the approach advocated here, no such line is to be drawn. All these sentences have the same surface structure, and I propose that they are all realizations of Agent–Action and Patient–Action relations. The fact that these sentences seem to lie on a continuum, is a reflection of the way we interpret them at the cognitive level that underlies the I-marker level (see section 3.4), and not of their organization at the I-marker level. The experiencer and the stimulus (or source) of the experience are notions that pertain to the cognitive level. These are assimilated at the I-marker level into the Agent and Patient, respectively. (Further evidence for continua at the cognitive level is presented in section 9.5).

Some empirical evidence that children view the experiencer as Agent is provided by an experiment by Maratsos, Kuczaj, and Fox (1979). These investigators found that in their third year children tend to overregularize the past tense form "-ed" for nonaction verbs to the same extent as for action verbs, saying, for example, "seed" or "feeled." Now, the past tense is learned first for action verbs and is much more frequent with the latter. Sentences with nonaction words like "see" and "feel" involve what is commonly regarded as the experiencer relations. The fact that the past tense rule was applied to these sentences as readily as to sentences expressing more prototypical agent relations (i.e., those with action verbs) suggests that both these kinds of sentences have the same underlying I-marker.

Maratsos et al. also report on two experiments comparing the comprehension of these two kinds of sentences, viz. sentences with action verbs, like "shake" and "wash" and those with nonaction verbs like "forget," "know," "like," and "see." For active sentences, no differences in comprehension was found in 4–5 year old children, and this was shown not to be due to a ceiling effect. This is in line with our claim that these two sentence types include the same relational categories, to which the same relation rules are applied. In the case of passive sentences, however, performance was better for the action-verb sentences. Two possible explanations of this finding, which make it consonant with the assimilation hypothesis, are as follows.

1. According to the hypothesis, the prototypical Agent–Action relation involves overt actions, like those denoted by "shake" and "wash," performed by animate agents. Relations involving experiencers and experiences—denoted by nonaction verbs, like "forget," and "know"—are learned later and are assimilated into the Agent–Action relation. Now, realization rules resulting in passive sentences are relatively difficult to apply, and the difficulty will be greater when they are applied to I-markers containing peripheral rather than prototypical instances of the Agent–Action category. It is much easier to apply realization rules resulting in active sentences than those resulting in passive ones, and, we may assume, comprehending active sentences is so easy that the difficulty of processing peripheral instances (rather than prototypical ones) does not make itself felt. (This explanation parallels a prediction made by de Villiers [1979] which she tested in an experiment in which small children learned new rules—the passive and cleft sentence rules—and employed these in production. De Villiers' hypothesis was sustained.)

2. The second explanation is based on the proposal made in section 8.4 that, as far as child language is concerned, the I-marker underlying a passive sentence differs from that underlying the corresponding active sentence: Unlike the active sentence, which realizes the Agent–Action and Patient–Action relations, the passive sentence is presumably a realization of the attributive relation. Now, "forget," "know," and other nonaction verbs have been encountered by the child in active sentences, and the lexical entries for their protoverbal elements will therefore include I-marker frames with the Agent–Action and Patient–Action relations. They have these I-marker frames in common with action verbs and accordingly should not be expected to differ from the latter in respect to performance on active sentences. Where lexical entries for action and nonaction verbs presumably do differ is in respect to I-marker frames for the attributive relation. The latter will have been formed primarily for action verbs, as these have often been encountered by the child in passive sentences. By contrast, small children have little experience with passive sentences including nonaction verbs, as was

found by Maratsos et al., and consequently they have little opportunity for forming I-marker frames for the attributive relation for these verbs. This would explain why children are much worse in understanding passive sentences with nonaction verbs than those with action verbs.

Another observation of Maratsos et al. is of interest here. In their first experiment, children were asked after presentation of the sentence "Who did it?", and this question seems to have been found by them to be just as appropriate for experiencers as for agents. This suggests that for them experiencing is a kind of doing.[5]

Not all putative Experiencers are Agents at the I-marker level. For some words, like "glad" and "angry," the I-marker frame prescribes an attributive relation (cf. "I am glad"). Again, the experiencer may sometimes be viewed as Possessor, as, for instance, in:

> He has a toothache.
> He has a feeling that something terrible is going to happen.

(See also Braine, 1976, p. 27).

The latter examples pose a problem: How should we formalize these cases of semantic assimilation? It might seem that this can be done by means of the I-marker frame for the verb "have." Presumably, "have," like "own," is employed in Agent–Action–Patient constructions (see section on "Location," earlier, and footnote 4):

> have: AGENT–ACTION x, (PATIENT–ACTION y, ___)

Perhaps there is a specification that the *y*-term in this frame can be any feeling or malady? But this solution will not do, as becomes clear on considering the following examples:

> He has angina.
> He has a limp.

---

[5]Braine and Wells (1978) carried out a series of experiments designed to reveal the relational categories of preschoolers. In two of their experiments, conflicting evidence was found regarding the distinction between Experiencer and Agent, and they argue that animacy was a confounding factor. Because they set out to find support for the categories of case grammar they interpret their results to mean that, but for this confounding factor, the Experiencer is distinguished from the Agent, as shown in one of their experiments. One might just as well argue, however, that but for this factor, the Experiencer will not be distinguished from the Agent, as shown in the other experiment (see section 9.4 for a short description of their experiment).

*He has deafness.
*He has blindness.
*He has jealousy.

It is not at all clear according to what principle the line is to be drawn between states and feelings that can be "had" and those that cannot, and hence how the specification for the y-term might be formulated. In the foregoing cases it seems preferable therefore to assign I-marker frames to nouns (or, rather, to protoverbal elements expressed by nouns), unlike the I-marker frames discussed thus far, which were formulated for verbs. "Toothache," "feeling," "angina," and "limp"—but not "deafness," "blindness," and "jealousy"—may have I-marker frames with specifications stipulating that they may be "had". But exactly what I-marker frames? Let us try the following:

toothache: POSSESSOR–POSSESSION x, ____

and a specification that x is the one who feels the toothache. The following problem now remains. There are types of constructions involving the possessive relation that are not limited to words which can appear in constructions with "have," viz. constructions with possessive pronouns ("his deafness," "his jealousy"), and genitives ("John's deafness," "John's jealousy").

What we need therefore is two kinds of I-marker frames: (1) frames like the one in the foregoing with the POSSESSOR–POSSESSION relation that permit constructions with possessive pronouns and genitives ("John's deafness"); and (2) those that permit constructions with "have." The latter have the following form:

toothache: AGENT–ACTION x, (PATIENT–ACTION ____, have)

(i.e., toothache can be the Patient of 'have'). "Deafness," "blindness," and "jealousy" have only I-marker frames like (1), involving the POSSESSOR–POSSESSION relation, whereas "feeling," "angina," and "limp" are like "toothache" in having both kinds of I-marker frames.

Cross-linguistic comparisons of sentences with so-called "Experiencers" reveal again the language specificity of I-markers. Where English has an attributive relation, French employs the possessive relation:

I am thirsty.
J'ai soif.

But whereas in French the experiencer is the Possessor, in Moré it is the possession: "Thirst has me" (Nida, 1964, p. 214).

There are other instances in which the I-marker frame is like that for "see," "hear," and "know"—i.e., AGENT–ACTION x, (PATIENT–AC-TION y, ___)—but the specification states that the one who undergoes the experience is the Patient, not the Agent:

>   The play pleases me.

Sometimes, the lexical entry for one word denoting an experience includes a number of I-marker frames. Consider the following example (Sidney Greenbaum, personal communication, 1978):

>   John has worries.
>   John worries.
>   Something worries John.

In these sentences John is the Possessor, Patient, and Agent, respectively. This may be represented by three I-marker frames for 'worry':

>   worry: POSSESSOR–POSSESSION x, ___
>   worry: AGENT–ACTION x, ___
>   worry: AGENT–ACTION x, (PATIENT–ACTION y, ___)

Specifications then stipulate that the worrywart (John) in the first two I-marker frames is x, and in the third—y. There is, however, an alternative way of conceptualizing the relationship between "John worries" and "Something worries John," which is discussed in section 9.6.

The foregoing approach does away with the "Experiencer" category at the I-marker level. The reason that such a category has been proposed is that writers have formulated semantic categories on the basis of a *conceptual* analysis. From a conceptual point of view there is a wide gulf between "the instigation of events" and "the entity which receives or accepts or experiences or undergoes the effect of an action [Fillmore's (1971, p. 376) definition of Agent and Experiencer, respectively]." However, there are many more conceptual distinctions which might be made (see, for instance Nilsen's [1973], treatment of cases). What is at issue here is how the language categorizes the various conceptual distinctions at the I-marker level. And language, as we have seen, proceeds by means of semantic assimilation.

Choice Between I-markers

The "experiencer," then, can be assimilated by a number of I-marker relations. There may therefore be sentences that, according to the case grammar approach, have the same underlying structure, but not according to the semantic assimilation hypothesis. For instance, in "I like the play" the pro-toverbal element of "I" is Agent, whereas it is Patient in "The play pleases me." The same "content" has given rise here to different I-markers. In general, different paraphrases do not necessarily derive from the same I-marker (Schlesinger, 1977, section 5B). Which I-marker is chosen may de-pend on factors like response strength, but it may also reflect a selection made (not necessarily with full awareness) on the basis of various com-municative considerations. In the production model a special component must therefore be included which is responsible for this selection (Schles-inger, 1977, sections 5A and 5B).

9.4   SEMANTIC ASSIMILATION THAT IS NOT LEXICALLY BASED

In the following, two additional kinds of semantic assimilation are discussed, which unlike that dealt with in the preceding section, cannot be accounted for in terms of I-marker frames:

1.   Metaphorical extension of the Agent category to the aspect of the situation which is perceived as being most similar to the pro-totypical Agent.
2.   Assimilation of what is, in effect, a complete relational category into another, thus providing an alternative I-marker for expressing the same content.

Metaphorical Extension

Consider the following sentences:

> The situation justified taking drastic measures.
> Caution outweighed the need for action.
> The hoary joke produced a few subdued yawns.
> The news caused a drop in the stock market.
> Aunt Clementine's death sent the whole family into hectic
>   activity.

The first two examples are from Bowerman (1974a), who observed that "the subjects of many sentences resist interpretation as agents or even as ex-tended agents [p. 206]." She believes, accordingly, that such examples would be beyond the scope of the semantic assimilation hypothesis. Bower-man argues therefore that the child must at some point of time arrive at more formal categories, like subject and predicate, which are not seman-tically based.

But how is this feat to be accomplished? Bowerman's explanation that the child notes similarities in the relevant linguistic expressions is insufficient by itself, as becomes clear in a moment, and must be supplemented: There must be, in addition, similarities in the relations referred to. Let us see now how semantic assimilation might explain the foregoing examples.

What distinguishes verbs like "justify," "outweigh," and "produce" from those discussed in the preceding section is that their function in sentences seems to elude description by specifications for I-marker frames. Take "produce"; the following list shows various uses of this word:

> The farm produces butter and cheese.
> The salesman produced his passport for inspection.
> The composer produced a large number of light pieces last year.
> The defense could not produce the witness.
> The pancreas produces insulin.
> The university has produced some of the country's
>   greatest scholars.
> The hoary joke produced a few subdued yawns.

What do the farm, the salesman, the pancreas, and the hoary joke have in common? Very little; in fact, nothing, except of course the fact that they all produce something (in some sense, for "produce" is used in different senses in these examples). "Produce," when speaking of a passport, is only remotely similar to "produce" in "produce insulin," and these two uses of "produce" differ again from that in "produce scholars" or "produce a yawn." Once we give up the attempt of pinning it down by I-marker frames and specifications, the phenomenon seems to be perspicuous. Protoverbal elements always lend themselves readily to metaphorical extension (see section 5.4). Once the word "produce" has been understood in some contexts, it will be understood in all others. The foregoing list is open-ended: speakers of English, and hearers, are prone to generalize to further instances.

Similar comments are appropriate to the other examples at the beginning of this section (although "justify" and "outweigh" do not seem to be quite as productive as "produce"). There, the use of the verbs has been extended far beyond what might seem warranted by their literal meaning (and this is what usually happens when speaking about anything that is not concrete). It should come as no surprise therefore that a whole category, like the Agent category, has been extended metaphorically, as indeed it must be if we are to use these particular verbs metaphorically. In the example given, we cannot speak about "justifying," unless we are prepared to view "the situation" as an Agent of sorts (see also Schlesinger, 1977, pp. 30–31).

The type of semantic assimilation we have been discussing here is not lexically based. The process of metaphorical extension is not something particular to "produce," or "justify," but cuts across the various examples given at the beginning of this section and many others besides. All these have as much in common as the examples in the list of sentences with "produce," namely, that many "things" can figure as Agents by virtue of similarity in some aspect to the prototypical Agent (i.e., that expressed in sentences with "pull," "eat," and "hug," for instance). This aspect is perhaps best characterized by the term *responsibility*, as Van Oosten (1977) has proposed. We must not feel bound, then, by the definition of the Agent as "instigator of an action" nor by the name "Agent." Much wider boundaries of this category must be staked off. This becomes possible if we view the "Agent" category as having a prototype structure as suggested earlier.

It is not only the Agent category that has prototypical structure. An example given by McNeill (1978, p. 177) shows that the Location can also be metaphorically extended:

> They perceive various possibilities in the law.

(McNeill points out that one can paraphrase this by "within the limits of the law".) McNeill discusses this phenomenon under the term *semiotic extension*.

Assimilation Of Instrument Into Agent

As an example of the assimilation of a relational category into another, let us consider now the phenomenon that has been treated already in section 3.4. The instrument with which an action is performed may figure as an Agent:

> The pen is drawing thin lines.

> Ivory pieces move on the chessboard.

The same applies to what is sometimes called "Natural Force":

> The flood ravaged the area.

> The storm overturned the hut.

> The sun dried his clothes.

Here again, semantic assimilation is not lexically based. The phenomenon may occur with very many verbs. There are constraints, but they are of quite a different nature. As pointed out in section 3.4, agency can be granted to an inanimate instrument only for "low level" tasks. Thus, one cannot say:

*The pen is writing poetry.

*Ivory pieces play chess.

That it is not any particular verb which bars the assimilation of the instrument into the Agent category is shown by the following sentence pairs:

The chalk produced a few squeaks on the blackboard.

*The chalk produced a proof of the theorem on the blackboard.

The pen is scribbling fast.

*The pen is scribbling a poem.

The motivation for the constraint is intuitively quite clear: The agent metaphor is not yet quite dead and one cannot stretch it beyond endurance. If subjectivization of the instrument were a surface phenomenon (as currently held by case grammar), we would be at a loss for an explanation for this constraint. Again, if the terms we have called here Agent were merely semantically neutral subjects, there would be no explanation. Any explanation seems to hinge on the assumption that the subject (if you prefer that term) has not completely lost the character of Agent, the category out of which it grew through semantic assimilation. (An example of semantic assimilation by the Agent which is subject to a similar constraint is discussed in section 9.6.)

The phenomenon described here provides therefore evidence for our view that in the course of the child's linguistic development various relations have been assimilated by the Agent, as opposed to the thesis that various semantic relations that merely behave linguistically alike have formed an "alliance" for the purpose of the operation of syntactic rules. The ontogenetic process is presumably as follows. The child notices that adults sometimes speak about instruments as if they were Agents, and he then generalizes from these instances to others. He is helped here of course by his natural tendency to conceive of inanimate things as if they were animate. But no imprint will be left by this tendency on his linguistic system, unless it is reinforced by adult usage. If there is a language in which the Agent category cannot be extended to include the instrument, the child learning it will soon find out that—contrary to what his animistic world view might insinuate—subjectivization of the instrument is inadmissible: He would draw the boundaries of his Agent-Action category differently.

That the instrument may be viewed as a kind of Agent was also shown in an experiment by Braine and Wells (1978). Their objective was to find out what semantic categories are being entertained by preschoolers. The experiment was designed to show how children generalize from clear instances of a given category. The children were given tokens of different shapes and shown pictures exemplifying various semantic roles. They were taught to put each token on an object in the picture, according to the role played by the object, using for each role a token of a different shape. One shape of token was earmarked for the "actor" (a term Braine prefers to Agent; cf. Braine, 1976), another one for the location, and a third—for the object acted on. Among others, they used pictures and the following sentences describing them:

> The fan blows the curtain.

> The soda is cooled by the ice.

> The cake is cut with a knife.

They found that children put the "actor" token on the instrument—curtain, ice, knife. From this and similar findings these authors conclude that Instrument is a subcategory of Actor: "Actors are not necessarily animate, though the most prototypical Actor may be animate. The Actor category clearly embraces the subjects of large numbers of transitive verbs and includes the traditional Agent [p. 120]." Their findings thus confirm our hypothesis.[6]

Braine and Wells report that when both the Agent and the Instrument are expressed (e.g., "The hostess cut the cake with a knife"), children do make a distinction between Agent and Instrument. Semantic assimilation does not do away with the Instrument category (as it does away with the experiencer as an I-marker category; section 9.3). The instrument of an action may appear in the I-marker either as INSTRUMENT-ACTION, in which case it is realized by a "with"-phrase, or as AGENT-ACTION, and then it appears as surface subject, as in the examples given earlier. When he intends to describe a situation in which an action is performed with an instrument, the speaker therefore has to choose between the above two possibilities[7] (see section 9.3).

---

[6]The theoretical framework of these authors differs from mine, however, as they do not share my view that categorization of relations is achieved through language learning, but hold that they are "cognitive categories that are natural to the perception of events and states [Braine & Wells, 1978, p. 100]. Their results on the Experiencer were less clearcut (see footnote 5).

[7]The instrument can also be expressed by sentences with "use," and then it is best viewed as having been assimilated by the Patient (compare "I use a knife" with "I take a knife").

Agents And Subjects

In this and the preceding sections we have seen that in many instances what transformational grammarians regard as deep structure subject is really an Agent in disguise. Semantic notions, like "experiencer," are often assimilated into the Agent category, the Agent may be metaphorically extended, and whole categories, like the Instrument (and possibly also some other categories), may be assimilated into the Agent. But one should not rashly conclude from this that *all* subjects are Agents extended through semantic assimilation. One prevalent type of sentence in which, intuitively, the subject does not seem to be an extended Agent is that with adjectival predicates. It would be stretching our imagination too far to regard, for instance, "the girl" in "The girl is pretty" as expressing an Agent of sorts and being pretty as the Action of this Agent. Rather, this seems to be an instantiation of the attributive relation, like "pretty girl" (the syntactic context determining whether the Attribute is realized as predicate or not [see Schlesinger, 1977, section 4C]). Semantic assimilation must stop somewhere. Further, as argued in section 8.4, passive sentences ("The girl has been married") are presumably also realizations of the attributive relation rather than of the Agent–Action relation.

The notion of subject is thus broader in scope than that of our I-marker category Agent–Action. It is also possible that additional cases of subjects will turn up which are not to be analyzed as Agents. This means that there are generalizations in the syntax of English that cannot be captured by positing an extended Agent category; for instance:

Mary Anne is skating.

It is Mary Anne who is skating.

Mary Anne is pretty.

It is Mary Anne who is pretty.

Mary Anne has been married.

It is Mary Anne who has been married.

As these examples show, the relation rules responsible for pseudocleft sentences apply both to the Agent–Action relation and the Entity–Attribute relation.

There is, then, room for an abstract "subject" category that comprises both the Agent and the Entity having an Attribute. The child must have learned the abstraction under discussion by observing that these two semantic categories are realized by means of the same relation rules (see section 9.1). But in this case he is guided only by the similarity in linguistic expression, and not—as in instances of semantic assimilation—by similarity of the relations expressed.

Not only the Agent category is extended by semantic assimilation but other relations as well. In our discussion of locations and experiencers we saw that certain notions become assimilated into the Patient. In the following we discuss the extension of the instrument category through semantic assimilation.

Assimilation Of Manner Into Instrument

Consider the following sentences:

> John did his homework with intelligence.

> John did his homework with enthusiasm.

The manner of the action is expressed here by a *with*-phrase, which is typical of the way the INSTRUMENT-ACTION relation is realized, as for example, in:

> John did his homework with a slide-rule.

One might argue that two underlying relations, MANNER-ACTION and INSTRUMENT-ACTION, happen to be realized by the same linguistic structure, but this raises the question why the English language should have adopted such an equivocal way of expression. A preferable explanation is therefore one which parallels that given earlier of the subjectivization of the instrument. There are two ways of expressing the manner of the action: (1) by means of the MANNER-ACTION relation, and then it is realized by an adverb ("intelligently," "enthusiastically"); (2) through semantic assimilation, by means of the INSTRUMENT-ACTION relation, and then it is realized by a *with*-phrase. Thus, in these examples, intelligence and enthusiasm are viewed as a kind of instrument with which the task was performed.

As in the case of the assimilation of the instrument by the Agent relation, there are certain constraints on the assimilation of manner by the instrumental relation. Thus, we cannot say:

> *John did his homework with laziness.

> *John did his homework with slowness.

Laziness and slowness, for whatever they are worth, cannot be imagined as instruments for doing something; that would be stretching the metaphor too far. Here our choice is limited to the MANNER–ACTION relation and we must resort to the use of adverbs: "lazily," "slowly."[8]

9.5 COGNITIVE STRUCTURES AND I-MARKERS

In sections 3.4 and 3.5 we introduced the distinction between two levels: cognitive structures and I-markers. The preceding sections lend additional support for this view. Languages differ in the relational categories by which a given state of affairs is expressed, and the I-marker level is the only plausible locus of this difference. Thus, if speakers of English, French, and Moré differ in the relations employed in saying that they are thirsty (section 9.3), one need not invoke any far-reaching explanations involving different ways of viewing their thirst, but may attribute this simply to the various ways of expression imposed by their respective languages (see Schlesinger [1977], section 5B for additional examples). Such cross-linguistic comparisons show that a given cognitive structure can often be crystallized into different I-markers constituted of different relations. A parallel intralinguistic phenomenon is the occurrence of paraphrases that do not have identical deep structures; in these cases the locus of sameness of meaning is therefore to be found at the cognitive level (Schlesinger, 1977, section 5B).

The process of speaking is accordingly not a conversion of cognitive structures directly into utterances; there is (at least) one intermediate level, namely the level constituted of protoverbal elements and relational categories formed in the process of learning language. That there must be such an intermediate level is also the conclusion independently arrived at by Pinker (1977). After reviewing some recent formal models of language acquisition, he concludes that there must be a level "sufficiently language specific that all the rules of syntax are learnable, but not so language specific as to be inconsistent with a plausible theory of perception and thought [p. 59]." I-markers answer this description. They are "consistent" with what we know about perception and thought; in fact, they originate in perception and thought, but impose on them a language specific categorization for the purpose of speaking or writing. Bloom (1973) also distinguishes between two levels: "The categories AGENT-OF-ACTION or PERSON

---

[8]Matters are more complicated, though, for we can say that something is done "with cowardice," "with stupidity," "with folly," etc. But note that the corresponding positive expressions, "with courage," "with cleverness," "with prejudice" sound less awkward, which suggests that the former constructions are parasitic on the latter.

AFFECTED, for example, are linguistic categories . . . They are not cognitive categories [p. 121; see also section 7.3]."

The need for distinguishing between these two levels is also accentuated by our discussion of semantic assimilation in the preceding sections. Semantic assimilation phenomena are a good starting point for clarifying how the three levels—cognitive structures, I-markers, and utterances—map into ech other, a topic which we now turn to.

The Relationship Between Levels

Consider the following sentences:

> Logs are being cut with an axe.

> A statue is being carved with a chisel.

> The theorem was proved with a piece of chalk on the blackboard.

All three sentences exhibit the Instrument relation at the I-marker level. At the cognitive level, however, we do not have just one relation: There are three distinguishable ways in which the instrument relates to the action. In fact, as argued in section 7.2, there are subtle differences between the relations perceived in any two situations, and the relations figuring in our cognitive structures are therefore what we have called *particular* relations. In mapping cognitive structures into I-markers we categorize these particular relations. Thus, the relation between the axe and the action of cutting can be categorized in two ways at the I-marker level: as the IN-STRUMENT-ACTION relation (as in the above sentence), and as the AGENT-ACTION relation, as in:

> The axe is cutting the logs.

By contrast, the particular relation between the chisel and the action of carving, and that between the chalk and that of proving, can only be categorized as INSTRUMENT-ACTION, and not as AGENT-ACTION (for reasons discussed in the preceding section). For each of the relational categories in the I-marker there are, again, various alternative mappings into utterances. The one-to-many mappings from cognitive structures into I-markers and from I-markers into utterances are represented schematically in Fig. 9.1.

In Fig. 9.1 the R at the cognitive structure level is a particular relation; relational categories appear only at the I-marker level. The rules of mapping from the cognitive level into the I-marker level are in part imposed by the

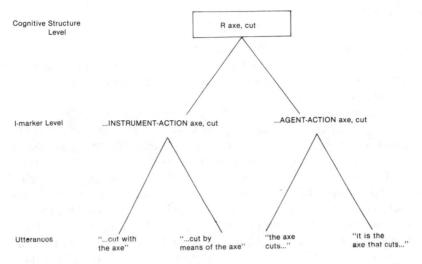

Cognitive Structure
Level

R axe, cut

I-marker Level

...INSTRUMENT-ACTION axe, cut

...AGENT-ACTION axe, cut

Utterances

"...cut with
the axe"

"...cut by
means of the axe"

"the axe
cuts..."

"it is the
axe that cuts..."

FIG. 9.1 Relationships between cognitive structures, I-markers, and utterances. (Only a section of each I-marker and utterance is presented.)

way we view reality. Thus, we can view the axe cutting logs as an Agent of sorts, but we do not apprehend the chisel as an Agent in the situation in which a statue is being carved. In other cases, these rules must be learned, one for each protoverbal element, as when we learn how "see," "worry," "cross," and "seat" are linked to their various relational arguments (section 9.3). Because they are learned, they may differ from language to language. The rules mapping I-markers into utterances, viz. relation rules and other realization rules, are of course all learned (see Chapter 8).

The conception of particular relations that are classified at the I-marker level into relational categories parallels the account given in chapter 5 of experiences at the cognitive level that are categorized into protoverbal elements at the I-marker level. As I have tried to show, there is no convincing evidence for categorization prior to the acquisition of language, either of elements (section 5.6) or of relations (section 7.2). The world may be said to have texture (section 5.6): We apprehend things and events and relations as more or less similar to each other. But to be able to speak about it at all, this infinite variety of phenomena must be organized into categories. I therefore postulate a level at which those aspects of cognitive structures that "are systematic and play special semantic and syntactic roles within language are recognized, retained, sharpened and organized in relation to each other [Bowerman, 1974b]."

There will be those who find it hard to reconcile themselves with the notion of cognitive structures without relational categories. What I have called particular relations would, in their view, fall naturally into a number of more or less clearly delimited categories. Granted that the relation between the axe and cutting differs somewhat from that between, say, a pen and writing, they might be deemed sufficiently similar to each other to constitute a category (which one may choose to baptize "Instrumental"). After all, this is what all case grammarians are looking for: a universal set of relational categories. And if they are universal, they may be assumed to be part of our innate cognitive equipment.

The semantic assimilation phenomena discussed in the preceding section are of course an embarrassment to this alternative hypothesis. But it is not my purpose at the moment to show why I think this alternative is untenable (evidence against it will be presented further on). Here I want to point out that, even if one grants for the sake of the argument that cognitive structures comprise relational categories and not particular relations, this does not enable us to do away with the intermediate I-marker level. There would still be a need for the two-stage mapping exemplified in Fig. 9.1, from cognitive structures into I-markers and from I-markers into utterances, because a direct mapping from cognitive structures into surface structures would result in an unwieldy system of rules. Suppose that according to the present system there are m rules for mapping the relations in cognitive structures into relational categories figuring in I-markers (including all the rules expressed in the form of I-marker frames and specifications, as well as those of semantic assimilation that are not lexically based, discussed in the preceding section), and n relation rules mapping I-marker relations into surface structures. Then, a direct mapping would require $m \times n$ rules, instead of the $m + n$ rules, that must be acquired by the child according to the present system. Because n, and especially m, are large numbers, this would be an exorbitant price to pay for a "simplification" of the system which would reduce the number of levels by one. In fact, the task of learning language, according to such a revision, would probably be beyond human capacity.

This may be illustrated by Fig. 9.2, which summarizes some of the mappings discussed in the preceding sections. For the sake of the argument, the relations at the cognitive level have been labeled in this figure as if they were relational categories. As stated, I hold that at this level there are mainly particular relations; but the point the figure intends to illustrate does not depend on this assumption. Further, the figure has been simplified by omitting from it the counterpart of "experiencer" (the "experience" or "stimulus") and that of the possessor ("possession"), so as to avoid having another six intersecting lines cluttering up the figure; and for the same reason the mappings entity located—ENTITY LOCATED, location—LOCATION, and patient—PATIENT have been omitted. Even so, the figure may give some idea of the complexity of the mappings, and of the need for postulating an I-marker level. Without this level, all relation rules applicable to the agentive relation, for instance, would have to be duplicated for each of the eight cognitive notions in the figure that map into the Agent.

This discussion suggests that one of the main considerations in defining relational categories for the I-marker level should be economy of the rule

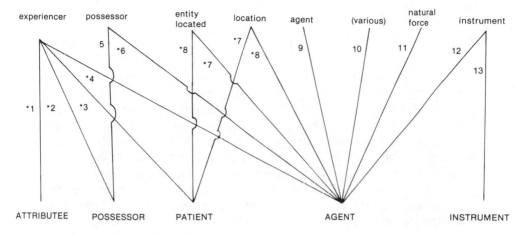

FIG. 9.2 The mapping of some types of arguments of particular relations in cognitive structures (lower case) into arguments of relational categories in the I-marker (capitalized). Digits refer to the examples that follow, in which the relevant argument is italicized. Asterisks indicate lexically based assimilations.

*1. *Ophelia* was sad.
*2. *I* have a toothache.
*3. The play pleases *me*.
*4. *I* like the play.
 5. *The farmer*'s cow ran off.
*6. *Old MacDonald* owns a cow.
*7. *The road* crossed the *mountain pass*.
*8. *This hall* can seat *500 people*.
 9. *Hannibal* paved the *mountain pass*.
10. *The situation* justifies taking drastic measures.
    The hoary joke produced a few subdued yawns.
    etc.
11. *The flood* ravaged the area.
12. *The chalk* produced a few squeaks on the blackboard.
13. He developed the proof *with paper and pencil*.

system. The details remain to be worked out but the principle to be followed is that an I-marker relation is one that makes a linguistic difference (see section 3.4). Two notions that, in a given language, result in the same surface structure are not to be treated as separate I-marker relations, but should be regarded as having merged into one through semantic assimilation (unless no similarity at all can be detected between them). Consequently, the system of I-marker relations is language specific, as shown earlier (see also Schlesinger, 1977, sections 1A and 5C). Cognitive structures, by contrast, may for all we know be universal. We note in passing that the reason why the extreme Whorfian hypothesis that we are at the mercy of our language is an exaggeration, if not outright wrong, is that we have always our cognitive structures to fall back on.

The Relations In Cognitive Structures

Let us return now to the issue raised earlier: whether one might posit relational categories at the cognitive structure level. We have already seen that this would not render the I-marker level superfluous, so that this proposal does not commend itself for contributing to parsimony in the theory. Further, the claim that there are relational categories in cognitive structures is not supported by the fact that some relations are very similar to each other, whereas others are not. As we have seen in our discussion of prelinguistic concepts (section 5.6), similarity enables us to categorize experience but does not categorize it for us: We are left free to determine where the boundaries lie. Now, the foregoing shows that there is no corroborating evidence for categories at the cognitive level. But we can go further and adduce arguments for particular relations at this level. One such argument, discussed in section 9.4, is based on certain constraints on semantic assimilation (see also the constraints discussed in section 9.6). A further argument is advanced in the following.

As shown in section 9.3, there is at the cognitive level a gradual transition from the notion of agent to that of the experiencer. Such a transition does not mesh well with the conception of clearly delimited categories, but rather suggests that we have to do here with various particular relations arranged along a continuum. Now, as argued elsewhere (Schlesinger, 1979), such continua seem to be the rule rather than the exception at the cognitive level. Here one example is given for which some experimental evidence has been obtained.

Consider the notions of accompaniment and instrumentality, as expressed in "John goes to the movies with his wife" and "John cuts the cake with his knife." It can be shown that there is a continuum of relations between the two poles exemplified by these two sentences. A high degree of agreement has been found between judges in ranking the following sentences, from those expressing most clearly accompaniment to those expressing most clearly instrumentality (Schlesinger, 1979):

1. The pantomimist gave a show with the clown.
2. The acrobat performed an act with an elephant.
3. The blind man crossed the street with his dog.
4. The prisoner won the appeal with a highly paid lawyer.
5. The Nobel prize winner found the solution with a computer.
6. The sportsman hunted deer with a rifle.
7. The hoodlum broke the window with a stone.

(The set used in the experiment included three additional sentences.) A supplementary experiment showed that this consistency in ranking could not be attributed to some sentences being viewed as ambiguously describing different situations.

The rankings of these sentences reflects a continuum of particular relations at the cognitive level. In many languages these sentences fall into two (and sometimes more) groups, differing in the relational category realized, as shown by the different prepositions or suffixes used in their translation. Significantly, though, languages differ in the point along the continuum at which they make a break between the groups of sentences—those with prepositions or suffixes indicating the Comitative (i.e., denoting accompaniment) and those with prepositions or suffixes indicating the Instrumental. Thus Korean distinguishes between (1) and the rest of the sentences, in Japanese the break occurs between (2) and (3), and so on. Each possible dichotomization in the set was observed in at least one of the 12 languages for which data were obtained, except for that between sentences (4) and (5) [Schlesinger, 1979]. It appears, then, that I-marker relations are partly language-specific.

We note in passing that English also distinguishes between the Instrumental, which can be realized among others, by "by means of" (sentences 5-7) and the Comitative, which can be realized by "together with" (sentences 1-3; sentence 4 seems to be a special case, and possibly expresses still another relation). That both these relational categories can also be realized in the same way by "with" seems to be a reflection of their presenting two poles of a continuum at the cognitive level.

Implications For Language Acquisition

Some of the implications of the present model have already been spelled out. Contrary to the strong claim that the child comes to the language-learning task with a set of relational categories, it has been proposed that no such assumption need be made. Instead, these categories are formed in the course of learning the rules governing their linguistic expression (sections 7.2 and 7.5). A parallel proposal has been made above (section 5.6) regarding the formation of categories underlying words.

The present conception of the relationship between I-markers and cognitive structures leads us to view in a critical light some recent attempts at specifying the relations evident in child language (e.g., Edwards, 1973; Wells, 1974). In these writings the focus of the inquiry usually is the content expressed by the child, and not the regularities evident in his speech (for a notable exception see Braine, 1976). What can be revealed thereby is, at most, the relations in the child's cognitive structure, and this leaves us with the question of what are the relational categories formed by the child for the purpose of linguistic performance (see also section 7.7). Further, one may doubt the value of any particular taxonomy for relations at the cognitive level, because many alternative taxonomies are possible and there seems to be no principled way of deciding between them. There are many alternative ways of perceiving the world's texture, of describing it, and categorizing it. Why should one, therefore, adopt any one categorization as having psychological reality, as long as one does not specify the purpose of the categorization? One of the purposes of such categorization which we know a little about is to learn the system of relation rules operating in language. To achieve this, the child must indeed classify the various particular relations in his cognitive structures into the relational categories operating in his I-markers.

Although I-marker relations have some affinities with the cases of case grammar (and, in fact, their original formulation had been influenced by case grammar [see section 3.1, footnote 1]), there are important differences between them. Cases are assumed to be universal, whereas I-marker relations, and as pointed out earlier, especially the boundaries between the relational categories in I-markers, may be language specific. Those universal notions that are represented by the cases of case grammar have been relegated here to the cognitive level (see Fig. 9.2). I-marker relations are the result of categorizing these cognitive notions in accordance with the way they are expressed linguistically. The I-marker is therefore much more similar to the surface structure than the deep structure of case grammar (Schlesinger, 1977, pp. 90–91).

Moving the deep structure closer to the surface structure is in line with some recent developments in transformational grammar. In the model proposed by Bresnan (1978) much of the burden of derivation is shifted to the lexicon. Deep structures consequently become more similar to surface structures, and the number of transformations is reduced drastically. Bresnan regards such a model as psychologically more realistic. The present theory, in agreement with Bresnan, allocates much of the information needed for processing to the lexicon (section 9.3). Furthermore, some of the tasks fulfilled by transformations in "classical" transformational models are now imposed on the mappings from cognitive structures into I-markers (see Fig. 9.2); this is the semantic assimilation phenomenon. The result is a simplification of the mapping from I-markers into utterances: A smaller processing load is imposed on relation rules.

Such a division of labor is to the advantage of the learner. Learning the facts of semantic assimilation is facilitated by the similarities in the situations referred to (i.e., those similarities which presumably gave rise to the semantic assimilation phenomena in the phylogeny of language [see section 3.4]). Relation rules, by contrast, are largely arbitrary; they lack the semantic motivation of assimilation phenomena. Therefore the less of them there are to be learned, the better off the language learner will presumably be.

9.6   MEANING RULES

I-marker frames, as we have seen, integrate words into sentences. Now, the child learns not only how words are to be strung together—that is, how relation rules operate—but also, how various words in his lexicon are related to each other. We all know how "lead" is related to "follow," "eat" to "feed," "steal" to "thief," and our acquaintance with words is such that we may become aware of a multitude of such links between words. In the following only one type of link is discussed, which seems to be particularly relevant to a theory of language acquisition (For a fuller treatment from the point of view of linguistic theory see Fodor [1977] and Miller [1978].) A possible adaptation of some notions developed in linguistic theory is presented here in outline, with the details remaining to be filled in. It should be pointed out that ultimately the merits of the present proposal should be judged according to criteria that differ from those appropriate for evaluating semantic theories, because the objective here is not to account parsimoniously for the facts of language as a system but primarily for their acquisition and for the way they function in a performance model (see also Watt, 1972).

The Operation Of Meaning Rules

As pointed out in section 9.2, "lead" and "follow" are closely related. Let us see now how this relationship may be formally represented. The I-marker frame for "lead" was given as:

lead: AGENT-ACTION x, (PATIENT-ACTION y, ____)

That for "follow" has the same form, and it is in their specifications that these two lexical entries differ. The link between the two words may now be established by including in the lexical entry for "lead," in addition to the above I-marker frame and its specifications, the following MEANING RULE:

AGENT-ACTION x, (PATIENT-ACTION y, lead)⟶ AGENT-ACTION y, (PATIENT-ACTION x, follow)

This rule states that if x leads y, then y follows x. Note that the reverse is not true: A may follow B without B leading A (and, in fact, even without B even knowing that he is being followed). There is therefore no converse of the above meaning rule (i.e., no similar meaning rule with the terms 'lead' and 'follow' interchanged). Instead, the lexical entry for "follow" will include the meaning rule given earlier, or (what amounts to the same) a cross-reference to the meaning rule in the entry for "lead."

As this example illustrates, meaning rules are not symmetrical: They state implications, not equivalences. This asymmetry is frequently found in the various links that exist between words. Consider the relation between "kill" and "cause to die." According to the generative semanticists, "kill" can be defined as "cause to die," that is, the relation is symmetrical. However, as Jerry Fodor (1970) has shown, "kill" has much less syntactic freedom than the latter phrase: There are many types of statements involving "cause to die" which do not imply corresponding statements involving "kill." Thus, one may cause somebody to die a month from now, but one cannot kill somebody a month from now. Or, to give another example, "cause to die" cannot be substituted for by "kill" in the following sentence:

John caused Mary to die and it surprised me that she did so.

For this and other reasons Fodor is skeptical of the attempt to represent words by definitions (see section 9.7 for a discussion of this issue), and adopts Bar Hillel's (1967/1970) proposal that entries of the internal lexicon have the form of Carnap's "meaning postulates." Thus, there is a meaning postulate—Bar Hillel uses the term "meaning rule"—"red" $\rightarrow$ "colored," but there is no way of defining "red" in terms of "colored" in conjunction with other predicates; that is, there is no way of explicating "red" by a statement of the form "x is red if x is colored and . . ." (Fodor, 1975, pp. 148–152; Fodor, 1977, pp. 144–155).

Similarly, Fodor's evidence against the derivation of "kill" from "cause to die" does not argue against "A killed B" entailing "A caused B to die," and hence we may state a meaning rule linking these phrases. To take an example closer to children's speech, the lexical entry for "feed" will include a meaning rule which we may tentatively formulate as:

AGENT–ACTION x (PATIENT–ACTION y, feed) → AGENT–AC-
TION x, (CAUSE (AGENT–ACTION y, eat))

(This rule might be expanded to accommodate a variable standing for the food eaten by y, but these details need not concern us here.)[9] There is no converse meaning rule; x may cause y to eat without feeding him (e.g., by

---

[9] As Mordechai Rimor has pointed out to me, there is an alternative formulation of the expression right of the arrow which treats 'cause' as an action term: AGENT–ACTION x, (PA-TIENT–ACTION (AGENT–ACTION y, eat), cause). A similar alternative exists for the relation INCHOATE (see the formula further on).

threats, by exposing him to a commercial for a new brand of food, etc.) CAUSE is an I-marker relation that can be realized in various ways, and a sentence stating that x feeds y can therefore be substituted for by a sentence including "eat," for example, "x causes y to eat," "x makes y eat." Suppose the speaker has forgotten for the moment the word for "feed" (the "tip-of-the-tongue" phenomenon). He can then resort to the above meaning rule and switch to an I-marker containing the protoverbal element 'eat.'

However, the meaning rule need not be invoked for all I-markers that include the protoverbal element 'feed.' We may realize 'feed' in our speech without activating 'eat,' and we may understand a sentence containing "feed" without partially decomposing this word into 'cause to eat' at any level. As Kintsch (1974, p. 240) concludes on the basis of his experimental studies, words "are not decomposed either in comprehending or in memorizing sentences" (see also Fodor, 1975, pp. 150–152; Schlesinger, 1977, pp. 99–102). Furthermore, learning the meaning of "feed" does not require noting its link with the word "eat"; the meaning rule linking the corresponding protoverbal elements may be learned at a later stage. (In principle, nothing even prevents learning "feed" before learning "eat".) In line with this, Bowerman (1974b) found that causative verbs at first function as unanalyzed wholes. Before discussing her study, we must take another look at the lexical entries of such verbs.

Verbs Used Both Causatively And Noncausatively

The verbs "eat" and "feed" have separate lexical entries. Now, there are meanings related to each other in the way those of "eat" and "feed" that are expresed by the same word. Compare:

> The door is open.

> John opens the door.

These two meanings of "open" can be distinguished by their I-marker frames:

> $open_1$: ATTRIBUTE x, _____
> $open_2$: AGENT-ACTION x, (PATIENT-ACTION y, _____)

A meaning rule linking these two frames may be tentatively formulated as:

AGENT–ACTION x, (PATIENT-ACTION y, $open_2$) $\longrightarrow$ AGENT-AC-
TION x, (CAUSE (INCHOATE y, $open_1$))

INCHOATE is taken here to be a subrelation of ATTRIBUTE.[10] In English it may be realized as "become." This meaning rule, then, states that if x opens$_2$ y, then x causes y to become open$_1$.

The I-marker frames for open$_1$ and open$_2$ are presumably linked to the same protoverbal element (and thus belong to the same lexical entry), as the child probably learns these two uses of "open" in the same situations. "Eat" and "feed," by contrast, will probably be learned in different situations and hence belong to different protoverbal elements. The child will have to learn the two uses of "open"—that is, incorporate the just mentioned two I-marker frames in his lexical entry—and the connection between them, that is, incorporate the above meaning rule.

A third use will probably be acquired later, namely, that in:

> The door opens.

The I-marker frame here is:

$$\text{Open}_3 : \text{AGENT–ACTION } x, \text{\_\_\_\_}$$

That is to say, 'open' can function like any action term in an agentive construction, as evidenced by the fact that this sentence can be paraphrased in the way other agentive constructions are, for example:

> It is the door that opens.

This is another case of lexically based semantic assmilation (see section 9.3).[11] Open$_3$ is linked to open$_1$ by the meaning rule:

$$\text{AGENT–ACTION } x, \text{open}_3 \quad \rightarrow \quad \text{INCHOATE } x, \text{open}_1$$

"The door opens" paraphrases as "The door becomes open."

A number of English words have I-marker frames like those for open$_2$ and open$_3$: "sell," "read," etc. The subject may denote either the person who sells, reads, etc. or what is sold, read, etc. Van Oosten (1977) shows

---

[10]It might perhaps be advisable to forego brevity for the sake of clarity and write instead CAUSE (INCHOATE (ATTRIBUTE y, open$_1$)), which makes the connection with the I-marker frame of open$_1$ more evident. Incidentally, in ergative languages, "door" would be nominative in both these sentences, and "John" ergative (Hockett, 1958, p. 235). Such languages thus have only one frame (instead of the two given here for English) with the ergative marked as optional.

[11]A similar kind of semantic assimilation is that of the location by the Agent in "The garden swarmed with bees." This implies "Bees swarmed in the garden," but not vice versa: The former, but not the latter, sentence states that the bees were all over the garden. This implication will be expressed by a meaning rule for "swarm."

that "the choice of subject depends on what the speaker sees as most responsible for the successful occurrence of the action of the verb [p. 466]." This is because the Agent is characterized by some notion of responsibility. As evidence of this she presents, inter alia, the following sentence pairs, where the second sentence of each pair is unacceptable:

> A good tent puts up in about two minutes.

> *The tent puts up in my back yard.

> The clothes wash with no trouble, because
> they are machine washable.

> *The clothes wash with no trouble, because I have
> lots of time.

> The book is selling like hot cakes.

> *The book is buying like hot cakes.

The construction of the tent is partly responsible for the fact that it can be put up in a short time, but there is no apparent connection between its construction and the place it is put up. Likewise, the rate at which a book sells is due to some characteristics of the book, whereas in talking about buying a book one ascribes the responsibility to the buyer. Note that the semantic constraint that rules out the second sentence in each pair is in some ways similar to the constraint preventing assimilation of some instruments into the Agent category (section 9.4). There is something odd about a tent being viewed as partly responsible for the place it is put up at, just as there is something odd about the pen being responsible for writing poetry. The moral is that although the Agent can be made to do many jobs, it should not be stretched too far.

Let us digress for a moment and look at an interesting parallel to these phenomena, found in Navaho. In that language a subject–object inversion is possible in some cases but not in others. Translating sentences with subject–object inversion by the passive, the following are acceptable in Navaho:

> The girl was killed by the water.

> The man was kicked by the horse.

but the following are unacceptable:

The water was drunk by the girl.

The horse was kicked by the man.

The explanation given by Witherspoon (1977) is that the water is less in a position of control of the situation than the girl, and can therefore not be said to "let itself be drunk" (this being a closer approximation to the sense of the Navaho sentence). Similarly, animals, being less intelligent than men, are viewed to be less in control than men. The latter can let themselves be kicked by horses (i.e., cause this to happen, perhaps by careless behavior), but not vice versa. Hence it is also acceptable to say:

The girl drank the water.

The man kicked the horse.

but not:

The water killed the girl.

The horse kicked the man.

In other words, in Navaho the word denoting the entity which is more able to control the behavior in question must appear in the subject position.

Turning to quite a different culture, we find that the Talmud (Mesopotamia, first to sixth century C.E.) interprets the surface subject of a passive sentence as having control of the situation.[12] This, again, parallels the phenomenon commented on by Van Oosten: There are constraints on what can serve as subject, that is, as Agent, in our terms. (Note that on this view the passive sentence is derived from a different underlying structure than the corresponding active one [see section 8.4]).

The Acquisition Of Causatives

To return to open₁ and open₂, it should be noted that several English verbs are like "open" in having both a causative and a noncausative sense. Compare for instance:

---

[12]In discussing a text concerning marriage, which formally constitutes an acquisition, the Talmud explains: "Were it taught '*he acquires*,' I might have thought, even against her will, hence it is stated '*a woman is acquired*' implying only with her consent, but not without [The Babylonian Talmud. Seder Nashim. Rabbi I. Epstein (Ed.), London: Soncino Press, 1936, p. 2]." Quite a different conception of the passive is found in Old Irish (see section 4.4).

The water was warm.

John warmed the water.

In other cases the causative is etymologically related to the noncausative verb: "rich"-"enrich," "sharp"-"sharpen," "lie"-"lay."

The acquisition of causative verbs has been studied by Bowerman (1974b). When her daughter Christy was just over two years old, she began to use noncausative verbs in a causative sense; "flat" for "flatten," "down" for "push down," "full" for "fill," etc. For instance, when her mother was preparing to feed her sister Christy said:

No, mommy, don't eat her yet, she's smelly.

A similar phenomenon has also been observed for other children (see the examples quoted in Bowerman, 1974b, footnote 2). Thus, a 32–34 month old girl is reported by Braine (1971, p. 173) as saying:

I don't want any more grapes; they just cough me.

And the same child also used "reach over" for "make reach over" and "ride" for "make ride." These children had apparently noted that some verbs, like "open," can be used both noncausatively and causatively and had formed the relevant meaning rules. Then they overgeneralized these rules to other verbs (like "eat" and "cough").

Interestingly, these productive errors of Christy coincided with her first utterances expressing the causative by overt constructions, like "I got her wet" and "I made it warm." As argued earlier, these originate in an I-marker including the relation CAUSE. Bowerman suggests that mastering the latter type of constructions leads to the child's noticing the relationship between these constructions and those in which the verb is used causatively, for example, between "I made it warm" and "I warmed it." As a result, she forms a rule that, as mentioned earlier, is then overgeneralized. It took Christy years to trim down these overgeneralizations and to find out to which verbs a meaning rule linking the causative to the noncausative use applies.[13]

But verbs like "open" are used causatively even at the two-word stage ("open it," "give cookie," etc.). Bowerman argues persuasively that the child understands these words correctly. When Christy used "give," for instance, she knew very well who was giving what to whom. However, at that

---

[13]In Turkish and Serbo-Croatian, inflected languages that mark the causative clearly by special particles, this construction is acquired much earlier than in English (Slobin, 1978).

stage the causative aspect had not yet been partialled out; in other words, Christy had already formed the protoverbal elements for words like "open" and "give," but not yet the meaning rules that go with them.[14]

9.7   THE PROBLEM OF LEXICAL DECOMPOSITION

What is a knife—the fork's husband?
Child quoted in Chukovsky, *From two to five.*

Complete Lexical Decomposition Versus Meaning Rules

As shown in the previous section, some of our knowledge about the relationships between words can be captured by meaning rules that establish links between the corresponding protoverbal elements. The relationship between "eat" and "feed," for instance, is recorded in the internal lexicon by a meaning rule. In addition to the meaning rules discussed in the previous section, there are those that link a word to its superordinate: If something is a table, it is a piece of furniture. But usually we know more about a word than its superordinate; we know in what way it differs from other words having the same superordinate. To bring out the relationships between "table" and words denoting other pieces of furniture, a definition is needed. Definitions, in the classical sense, are not unidirectional implications, like meaning rules, but are bidirectional: Everything that answers the definition of "table" is a table. The definition of "table" specifies not only its superordinate term, but also what distinguishes a table from a chair, a sideboard, and a desk, among others. In semantic theory such definitions take the form of what has been called COMPLETE DECOMPOSITION into semantic elements (Fodor, 1977).[15]

Consider for instance the case of "kill" discussed in the preceding section. There is a meaning rule connecting "kill" to "cause to die" (killing someone implies causing him to die), but "cause to die," as Jerry Fodor (1970) has shown, does not imply "kill" (one can cause someone to die without killing him, e.g., by hiring an assassin). "Kill" is thus richer in

---

[14]However, already as soon as the child employs the word consistently according to adult word order, we must credit him with the appropriate I-marker frame and specification because these are a prerequisite for the correct application of relation rules.

[15]Conversations with Jerry Fodor, Stephen Kosslyn, George Miller, and Hilary Putnam have helped me formulate the ideas in this section. Benny Shanon made invaluable comments on a draft of this section. I am grateful to all these persons, none of whom I expect to be very happy with the results of their investment.

meaning than "cause to die"; it has many additional meaning components, as Wierzbicka (1975) has shown. And because these components are part of our knowledge of the word, they should in some way be represented in the lexical entry. Several linguists have attempted lexical decompositions of words in various domains (e.g., Bierwisch, 1967), and there is a widely held view that in principle all words of the language can be completely decomposed into a set of primitive meaning elements.

That the child, like the linguist, may engage in some kind of decomposition becomes strikingly evident in those instances where he comments on relations between words. For example, I once heard a little boy improvise the paraphrase "elbow of the leg." Apparently, he had momentarily forgotten the word "knee", and proceeded to analyze the intended concept into at least one of its components. Note also that analogies also presuppose such decomposition. Take a very simple one, of the type children also are capable of solving:

foot — shoe

hand — ?

To arrive at the correct answer, one must find out how "shoe" is related to foot; that is, one must analyze "shoe" into 'apparel worn on the foot,' or into some such components. The question we are faced with, however, is whether the acquisition of words entails their *complete* decomposition—that is, whether it is stored in the form that usually goes under the name of definition.

Suppose a child who knows the word "walk" subsequently learns the word "stroll." Let us assume that 'stroll' can be decomposed completely into 'walk' and 'in a leisurely manner.' The child has learned the use of "stroll" when he has recorded the fact that this word refers to a special kind of walking, namely to walking leisurely. Should we say that his lexical entry for "stroll" must contain this complete decomposition? There seems to be a possible objection to this account which runs as follows. Presumably, the child does not yet know the word "leisurely" when he learns the meaning of "stroll." It seems to be quite often the case that a child learns a word before learning names for its components. Hence the definitions of such words cannot be represented in the child's internal lexicon in the form of words of his native language. This objection can be seen to have no meat to it, however. By comparing the use of "walk" and "stroll" the child may have isolated a semantic component, viz. the component that he may eventually learn to express by "leisurely". His lexical entry may therefore contain lexical decompositions that are couched, at least in part, in terms of such semantic components.

But this is only one possibility. We are not forced to assume that the lexical entry of a word always contains its decomposition from the outset. As noted in the previous section, some words are first learned as unanalyzed wholes. Bowerman, (1976) has reported that her daughter first used correctly each of a number of words close in meaning to each other—"put," "take," and "bring"—but later on confused these words with each other. Eventually the child will have learned to avoid such confusion, and this will have been achieved by her discovering those facets of meaning in which these words differ; that is, she must have in some way decomposed the words that previously functioned as unanalyzed wholes.

The child, then, does not necessarily start out with a complete decomposition of the word he learns. But, we must ask now, does he invariably arrive at a complete decomposition of all words he learns? Is there some subconscious level at which the linguist's ambitious program of complete decomposition is actualized?

Fodor's Thesis

An extremely skeptical view concerning the decomposition program has recently been voiced by Jerry Fodor (1975). His thesis is diametrically opposed to current trends in semantic theory and in Artificial Intelligence, which view all words (or concepts), as ultimately analyzable into a limited set of semantic primitives (called components, features, etc.). Fodor argues that there remains little hope that such a program is realizable, even in principle. He arrives at the conclusion that "there is no psychologically real level of representation at which definable terms are replaced by their definitions [p. 131]." Words cannot be constructed out of their elements. They are unanalyzable wholes, and only some of the relationships between them can be represented in the form of meaning rules. Here Fodor is opposed to the whole tradition of empiricism. If his arguments are conclusive, they pull the rug out from under all empiricist theories of word acquisition, including that proposed in Chapter 5. So far no detailed response to his attack on empiricism has been made, to my knowledge, and this is perhaps because—unadvisedly, in my opinion—it has not been taken seriously enough. In the following I intend to examine Fodor's thesis critically. First, let me try to present his thesis and the arguments marshalled in its support as objectively and impartially as I am able to.[16]

---

[16]My presentation of Fodor's thesis follows not only Fodor (1975) and Fodor (1978) but also a discussion with him in which he clarified his views for me. I hope I have not misrepresented his approach in any way. In the following I indiscriminately refer to decomposition of concepts and of words as nothing in the issues discussed hinges on this distinction.

The thesis that all our concepts are constructed out of a small set of primitive concepts has held its sway for centuries, argues Fodor, but no evidence has been forthcoming that such a constructionist approach is feasible (Fodor, 1978, p. 237). According to Fodor, there are good reasons (some of them to be discussed below) to regard the constructionist program as a failure. Consider now what this implies for the prospect of an empiricist explanation of the acquisition of words and concepts. If complete lexical decomposition were feasible, then a learning account of concept acquisition would be possible, too. Lexical decomposition would provide (at least in principle) a list of primitive elements into which all concepts can be decomposed. (These primitive elements would then either be assumed to be innate, or else one might attempt to show how they themselves are acquired.) The learning theorist would then have to show how the child, so to speak, reverses the decomposition process, that is, how he concocts his concepts out of the set of primitive elements, with the help, of course, of guidance from language. This is obviously a big order, but not one that is in principle beyond the scope of an empiricist account. Fodor's case against empiricism thus stands and falls with his arguments against lexical decomposition. We examine these arguments further on. First, let us consider Fodor's alternative.

According to the decompositional (or constructionist) program there is an innate "vocabulary" of primitive terms of a very limited size, and all the words of a natural language are analyzable into (or constructible from) this set of terms. In view of the failure of the constructionist program, Fodor proposes to consider seriously its logical alternative, namely that the set of primitive terms, rather than being of limited size, is of very large proportions; in fact, it is of the same order of magnitude as the vocabulary of a natural language, since decomposition can play only a relatively minor role (an example of complete decomposition given by Fodor is that of "airplane" into 'flying machine'). This has important implications for a theory of language learning. Instead of constructing words out of a small set of primitive elements, the task of the child, according to this alternative, is to map the words of the language learned into the vast set of concepts already available to him. Now, on pain of infinite regress, the latter set must itself be unlearned. Fodor thus arrives at the staggering conclusion that there is an innate lexicon of a richness comparable to that of the natural language we learn.

To the objection that it is implausible to postulate such a large innate component, Fodor replies that the empiricist approach, which assumes a very narrow base of primitive innate terms, in fact also has to assume an enormously complex innate component (Fodor, 1975, p. 97). This is so because to master a word means to master a concept and the ability to categorize various disparate referents (objects, actions, states, etc.) as belonging to this concept. Such categorization is carried out on the basis of the tendency of perceiving greater or lesser similarity between things and to categorize them on the basis of similarity. Now, similarity is a far from simple notion: Things can be similar to each other in many ways. The multidimensional similarity space involved here must be innate; an empiricist like Quine (1969) explicitly concedes this.

Instead of this enormously complex innate equipment required by empiricism, Fodor proposes a rich innate stock of concepts. Accordingly, the task of the psychologist is not to account for how concepts are formed out of the data of experience on the basis of similarity, but for the way innate concepts are triggered off by experience. Fodor would thus exchange the promissory note for a learning theory—unrealized so far, and unrealizable, in his opinion—for a program for a much less complex triggering theory. He feels that triggering theory holds promise of eliminating the perennial problems attendant on accounts of how concepts are attained. As is made clear further on, such hopes are unfounded; triggering theory does not buy us anything. But before going into the reasons for this, we must take a closer look at Fodor's arguments concerning the prospects for lexical decomposition.

The Argument From Processing

One of Fodor's arguments against the decompositional approach is based on evidence (or, rather, the lack of it) concerning the way words are processed in comprehension. This argument can be shown to be inconclusive, and I will deal with it first. If words were represented in the form of a definition, Fodor argues, certain predictions concerning relative processing difficulty should follow. For instance, if "bachelor" were internally represented as "unmarried male", then "John is unmarried" should be psychologically simpler than "John is a bachelor." There is no evidence for such differences in difficulty; if anything, the opposite may be true, as coining of new terms for linguistically complex phrases (e.g., "id" for "the source of instinctual impulses striving for immediate gratification") is done precisely with an eye to facilitating mental operations (Fodor, 1975, pp. 146–148). Hence, "bachelor" is best regarded s a primitive concept connected with "unmarried" by a meaning rule. Unlike definitions, which analyze words into primitive terms—that is, into constructs at a more basic level—meaning rules establish relations between entities at the same level. They are resorted to only as the need arises, for example, for establishing inferences, but are not integrally involved in the comprehension process. Accordingly, no differential behavioral complexity may be predicted: Other things being equal, it may be as easy to move from "unmarried" to "bachelor" as in the opposite direction. Some support for Fodor's claim concerning processing comes from an experimental study by Kintsch (1974, Chapter 14), who showed that words need not be decomposed in comprehension (see also Holyak, Glass, & Mah, 1976), and although this evidence has not remained uncontested (see Schank, 1976), the view seems to have plausibility on its side so that the burden of the proof seems to lie with those who would argue that to understand a word is to decompose it completely.

This argument, however, applies only to processing by the performance mechanism, and nothing follows from it necessarily about the way words and concepts are acquired. The word "bachelor" may have been acquired by construction out of "unmarried" and "male," but once it has been acquired it may function as an unanalyzed whole in comprehension. Facts about performance thus cannot provide evidence concerning the stock of concepts that must be presumed to be innate.[17] Furthermore, the argument is not even compelling as far as the mature processing mechanism is concerned. It ignores the possibility that just as meaning rules may be invoked only as the need arises, so a definition stored along with a word need not be invoked invariably but only when the need arises. Comprehension, it is true, does not entail activating the definition, but the latter may be at our beck and call whenever relationships with other words need to be established.

The Failure Of The Decompositional Program

More convincing than Fodor's argument from processing discussed in the preceding, is his insistence that the decompositional program has not realized the hopes set on it. Consider the successes of the program so far. Traditionally, kinship terms have been submitted to componential analysis. These concepts are in fact ideally suited for decomposition: The term "maternal uncle," for instance, signified nothing but a male sibling of the mother, because that is the meaning for which the term was introduced, all other attributes of the concrete uncle being irrelevant. In addition feature analysis has been carried out in certain restricted, well-regimented areas; see, for instance, Bierwisch's (1967) analysis of spatial adjectives, Miller and Johnson-Laird's (1976, pp. 526-558) and Ikegami's (1969) analyses of verbs of motion, and Lehrer's (1969) analysis of verbs for various ways of preparing food by heat ("cook," "boil," "simmer," etc.). The semantic components revealed in any one of these areas are usually inapplicable to others. The results of this sample of investigations suggest, then, that with

---

[17]I owe this point to George Miller, with whom I discussed this topic. A further possibility, which faults Fodor's argument, is that there may be different levels of processing (see Miller, 1978, p. 93, for a short discussion).

each new area analyzed one must start afresh and arrive at a new set of components. If this is so, there seems to be no hope of arriving at a reasonably small set of primitives; instead, the set of components will be of a large order of magnitude, which is precisely what Fodor's thesis states.

Moreover, the areas from which these examples are drawn seem to be of a very specific kind; more concrete concepts seem to be resistant to this mental chemistry approach. This seems to be tacitly acknowledged by workers in the field of Artificial Intelligence. Schank (1975), for instance, has developed a system for analyzing conceptual structures of words. But, tellingly, he provides us only with analyses of verbs. Nouns remain unanalyzed, presumably because their meaning is more concrete. Consider what it would take to provide an exhaustive analysis into semantic components for, for example, breeds of dogs, species of fruit, and the like. It seems unlikely that these not too well delineated concepts can be defined without residue. They are too full-blooded for that.

Here one might object that after all dictionaries do just this job of defining words—all words, nouns included. The fact that it was possible to contrive a language like Basic English even suggests that all words can be defined by means of a very limited primitive vocabulary. But this objection rests on an erroneous conception of dictionary entries. True, dictionaries attempt to give full definitions wherever these are within their reach, but often they remain content with pointing out the referent of a word so that the user can identify its meaning. In these cases the dictionary fulfills a role similar to that of the pointing finger, except that the referent pointed at is not actually present; instead, it is in the user's stock of information. Such vicarious ostension differs from a definition: It can be achieved with much less than the full list of components—if such a list exists (see also Miller & Johnson-Laird, 1976, pp. 267–268). "A carnivorous animal, long domesticated and kept by man as a pet for catching rats and mice" is a perfectly good way to help the user of *Webster's Seventh New Collegiate Dictionary* to identify a cat, but is it a good decomposition of the concept? The insufficiency is even more apparent in "a highly variable carnivorous domesticated animal," the dictionary's entry for "dog," which would hardly even help to identify the animal without the accompanying line drawing. It is an easy exercise to pick out a dictionary "definition" of a concrete noun and think up a possible but nonexisting object answering the description but nevertheless not meriting the name that has been defined thereby. Our success at this game shows that the dictionary entry does not achieve a complete decomposition of the word described by it. Dictionary entries are nevertheless useful, because to indicate something it is sufficient to single it out only from those alternatives that are likely to present themselves, not from all possible alternatives. It appears, therefore, that Fodor can uphold his claim that the decomposition program has failed in the face of the fact that dictionaries exist and seem to do their job successfully.

Fodor counsels us, then, to leave the trodden path of empiricism and explore a nativist alternative. But note that his argument for adopting this course, the alleged failure of empiricism, has the weakness of any argument by default. Previous failures may presage, but do not constitute proof of, future lack of success. Perhaps more ingenuity, more effort, and above all, new ideas are required to implement the program. In the present case such an optimistic antidote to skepticism has more to commend it than that it points to a logical possibility. After all, the semantic components of a word are responsible for its various relationships with other words, and because we may become aware of these relationships, these components form part of our knowledge about the word. And, tautologically, what is known relies on information internally represented in some way.

It seems to me, therefore, that the fact that little headway has so far been made in complete decomposition merely reveals the poverty of our analytic tools; no conclusions follow concerning the nature of our internal representations. There seem to be two possibilities deserving consideration. One is that more powerful tools of analysis can be developed, and the other, that our ability to *formulate* our analyses is subject to inherent limitations. Let me explain.

Recently, a view of concepts is being advocated that differs radically from the traditional analyses into necessary and sufficient components. According to this alternative proposal, concepts may be chracterized as fuzzy sets of meaning components (see Hersh & Caramazza, 1976). In a fuzzy set of components there need be no subset that is either necessary or sufficient for the definition of the concept, and furthermore, the components need not all have equal weights. Transition from membership in the set to nonmembership is gradual. This approach is also being pursued in experimental studies by Rosch and her colleagues (e.g., Rosch & Mervis, 1975). In line with this, the acquisition of protoverbal elements has been described in section 5.3 as the gradual incorporation of cues, each of which may have a different cue value.

This approach seems to come closer to the truth of the matter than the traditional one of defining concepts or words in terms of necessary and sufficient conditions. Does this mean that it will eventually be possible to implement a program of decomposing concepts of the type described earlier? Not necessarily. There is no assurance that the *formulation* of decomposition along these lines will turn out to be feasible. Verbal formulations, and perhaps also other kinds of symbolic formulations, may prove to be too unwieldy a tool for getting at the intricacies of the structure of concepts. The fact that *some* aspects of a word's denotation can be pinpointed by verbal formulation may mislead us into assuming that the residual aspects of denotation can be formulated by similar means. Verbal formulations may not be fine-meshed enough to capture the residual meanings of "kill," for instance, after 'cause to die' has been partialled out (witness the tortuous formulas that had to be resorted to by Wierzbicka, 1975). Of course, all that philosophers or linguists have ever attempted is to analyze concepts verbally. If they have failed for centuries, as Fodor insists, this is telling only in so far as the tools of analysis are concerned. To analyze the composition of a concept verbally is somewhat like attempting to perform neurosurgery with a bread knife: Centuries of failure with this method do not imply that neurosurgery is impossible.

The hoary saying that a picture is worth a thousand words seems pertinent here. We need not take a stand on the problem whether internal representations employ a perceptual code or not (a question that is far from settled [see Anderson, 1978; Kosslyn & Pomerantz, 1977]). Even if it should be incorrect that internal representations *are* images, the fact is that the meanings of many words *appear* to us as best captured by images or pictures. This indicates that the task of verbally describing internal representations has some affinities with the notoriously difficult task of giving a faithful and exhaustive verbal definition of a picture.

Now, even if it should turn out that no satisfactory formulation of decompositions is attainable, it may be unwarranted to draw from this fact conclusions concerning the nature of internal representations: These representations may be composed of elements of our experience (whatever the code in which they are stored). Ultimately, all experience can be decomposed into elementary sensations. One can, if one chooses to, call these primitive; they are certainly innate and universal. On the other hand, more molecular, global components—like 'human,' 'male,' 'four-legged,' 'striped,' and many other features that have been suggested or may be serviceable for decomposition—are not innate.[18] They are extracted by the learner ad hoc from his experience with the referents of words. This is essentially the proposal made in sections 5.2–5.4. It may turn out, however, to be the case that, due to inherent limitations of our descriptive apparatus, we may be unable in practice to implement the program of describing these elements in any detail. Now, if our internal representations are composed of elements, then, as already stated, they can be constructed by the child out of these elements. Fodor's allegation that empiricism has gone bankrupt is therefore unfounded. His nativism has not won by default.

---

[18]The distinction made here needs sharpening. By "elementary sensations" I do not intend to exclude the results of innate perceptual organization ('vertical,' for instance, is presumably a primitive notion). Further, the need for the distinction may be acknowledged without taking a stand on such, undoubtedly important, questions as whether 'cause,' for instance, is an innate notion or acquired by experience.

The Credibility Of Fodor's Nativism

Let us now evaluate Fodor's proposal in its own right. On what grounds might his nativist approach be preferable to an empiricist approach?

A nativist approach makes fewer demands on the child learning language, because it assigns some of what has to be mastered to his innate endowment. The child's task in learning the vocabulary of his language does seem stupendous, and any proposal that lessens it might seem to offer a definite advantage over one that does not. But this cannot be a serious consideration in evaluating alternative approaches. No definitive statement about the size of the demands made on the child can be made on the basis of impressionistic judgments. Only after stating a theory that specifies the processes of acquiring command of the vocabulary can one examine the question whether these processes impose on the child a load exceeding his capabilities (cf. section 5.6). So far no rival theory to Fodor's nativism has been spelled out in sufficient detail and evaluated in this respect. And as argued in the previous subsection, it is not the case that such rival theories can be ruled out in principle.

Turning now to arguments that can be made against Fodor's proposal, the most obvious one is the argument from implausibility; it is extremely unlikely that a vast stock of concepts are inborn and genetically transmitted. Now, as we have seen, Fodor has countered the charge that his proposal assumes too much that is innate by observing that the empiricist approach also presupposes a vast innate endowment of the organism: a highly intricate learning mechanism that attains concepts on the basis of a complex similarity space. The assumption of a rich innate internal language does not require such a learning mechanism. Instead of a learning theory that makes strong assumptions about an innate similarity space (henceforward to be called simply 'learning theory'), it requires a triggering theory, based on a less complex mechanism, which shows how the items of the innate language are activated by experience. There is no a priori reason for preferring an innate complex machinery over an innate set of concepts, according to Fodor.

On closer examination, however, this argument turns out to be faulty. A triggering theory must be based on a mechanism that is just as complex as that on which a learning theory must be based. To see why this is so, one has merely to compare the requirements from a learning theory to those from a triggering theory. A learning theory must show how a concept underlying a word is formed on the basis of various instances which bear some similarity to each other (or each of which is in some way similar to a prototype). This, as we have seen, presupposes a complex similarity space. A triggering theory does not have to explain how such a concept is formed, because it is assumed to be innate. What it does have to explain, however, is how the various instances of a concept are recognized as belonging to this concept, that is, how they trigger the concept off. Evidently, this requires just as complex a similarity space as is required by a learning theory.

Consider in what way it might be possible to avoid this conclusion. Obviously, it cannot be avoided by claiming that not only the concept but all instances belonging to it are innate because each concept may have an infinite number of possible instances, all differing from each other in some respect. Instead, one might argue that the innate concept is such that it carries within it the instructions necessary for recognizing instantiations of it in the outer world. In this case the innate concept would no longer be an unanalyzed whole but a very complex structure, including, in fact, semantic components, each of which is to be compared to an aspect of reality. Semantic decomposition, the alleged impossibility of which was Fodor's prime motive for proposing a nativist approach, would then return by the back door. (Furthermore, the innate similarity space presupposed by learning theory, would still be required by triggering theory: Each property in the experienced instance would be similar to some degree to the corresponding component of the concept.) Triggering theory would thus be quite similar to learning theory in respect to the assumptions made about innate equipment.

Here the nativist might object that triggering theory would still have an edge over learning theory because it would drastically reduce the number of components to be considered in the case of each concept. To form the concept of 'chair' out of various experiences of instances of chair, so the argument might run, the learner has to scan all the properties of these instances because any one of them may possibly turn out to correspond to a component of the concept. By contrast, to find out what is an instance of the innate concept 'chair,' the learner would merely have to check on those properties that correspond to the innate components of the concept. This would entail a considerable saving of labor in the acquisition process.

There are two points to be made concerning this argument. First, it does not bear on the observation made earlier, namely that to assume that each innate concept is fitted out with a mechanism for detecting its own instantiations means in effect to embrace the semantic decomposition program. Fodor exhorts us to abandon empiricism because semantic decomposition is impossible, but if this is so, there can also be no satisfactory analyses of innate concepts into innate components. And without the latter no detection mechanism is possible, and triggering theory can not survive as a viable alternative to learning theory.

Now suppose we shelve this problem of semantic decomposition, or admit that semantic decomposition is possible after all. Would not triggering theory commend itself as a labor saving strategy in concept acquisition? Is it not definitely advantageous to have a limited list of properties to be scanned rather than an indefinitely large list? But now consider that it has never been shown that we really *need* such a labor saving strategy for our acquisition theory. As pointed out earlier, only when a theory has been developed in fairly complete detail can one evaluate it as to whether it makes excessive demands on the learner. Further, as shown in chapter 2, sweeping our problems under the nativist carpet is not a fruitful research program, at least at the present stage of our knowledge. We should therefore consider what price we are asked to pay for the labor-saving device.

And the price is exorbitant indeed. According to Fodor's nativist thesis, the child would have to be born with an internal lexicon including items corresponding to "dog," "horse," "cat," "cow"—in fact, for every species of animal (as there seems to be no prospect for an explicit decomposition of any animal concept, in the sense that "airplane" permits a decomposition into "flying machine"). According to one of the possibilities considered earlier, each such concept would have to be equipped with a detection mechanism permitting the child to recognize dogs, horses, cats, cows, etc. and to distinguish them from each other. He would also have to be equipped from birth with the concepts of subspecies—schnauzer, spaniel, collie, terrier, and poddle—because these are no more decomposable than the concepts of the species (and each of these concepts would have to comprise a complex detection mechanism). The child who has no interest in dogs and will never learn the names of those breeds is of course not exempt from carrying around with him this innate information, nor is the child who grows up in the Amazonas jungle where no such breeds are known. Furthermore, all of us would have to be equipped with concepts of breeds of animals—various subvarieties of dogs, fish, butterflies, and lizards—which have become extinct and which will be discovered in the future. But, no, the nativist might object, it is only concepts at a certain level in the hierarchy that are innate; the lower-order concepts are subsequently constructed from the former on the basis of experience. However, once this is acceded, the whole case against empiricism collapses. For, if any one of the lower-order concepts can be constructed out of experience, then the concepts of 'dog,' 'cat,' 'horse'—in fact, any concept—can be so constructed. There is no principled way of deciding where this invasion of innate ideas is to stop.

It is tempting, of course, to ridicule Fodor's thesis on this account. This would not be quite fair, however, because Fodor did not advance his proposal on the ground of its plausibility, but because he believed that the empiricist program has had its chance of proving itself for a couple of centuries and failed to realize the hopes set on it. He offers his nativism as a way out of an impasse and suggests that it is an alternative worth exploring. However, as I have tried to show in the preceding subsection, there is no such impasse. To be sure, there are practical difficulties with semantic decomposition, but even if it should turn out that these cannot be overcome in practice, this does not entail that our concepts are not constructed out of elementary components. And even if, mysteriously, this were the case, a nativist triggering theory, as we have seen, offers no way out of the predicament.

There is no need therefore to accept Fodor's counsel of despair and embrace an utterly implausible nativistic hypothesis. Let us brace ourselves, instead, for the task of figuring out how the child succeeds in forming the concepts underlying words out of his encounters with the world.

REFERENCES

Anderson, J. R. Arguments concerning representation for mental imagery. *Psychological Review*, 1978, *85*, 247–277.

Bar Hillel, Y. Dictionaries and meaning rules. *Foundations of Language*, 1967, *3*, 409–414. (Reprinted as Chapter 31 in Y. Bar Hillel, *Aspects of Language*, Jerusalem: Magnes Press, 1970.) (a)

Bierwisch, M. Some semantic universals of German adjectives. *Foundations of Language*, 1967, *3*, 1–36.

Bloom, L. One word at a time: The use of single word utterances before syntax. The Hague: Mouton, 1973.

Bowerman, M. Structural relationships in children's utterances: Syntactic or semantic? In T. E. Moore (Ed.), *Cognitive development and the acquisition of language*. New York: Academic Press, 1973.

Bowerman, M. Development of concepts underlying language: Discussion summary. In R. L. Schiefelbusch & L. L. Lloyd (Eds.), *Language perspectives: Acquisition, retardation, and intervention*. Baltimore: University Park Press, 1974. (a)

Bowerman, M. Learning the structure of causative verbs: A study in the relationship of cognitive, semantic and syntactic development. In E. Clark (Ed.), *Papers and Reports on Child Language Development, No. 8*. Stanford: Linguistics Committee, 1974. (b)

Bowerman, M. *Word meaning and sentence structure: Uniformity, variation and shifts over time in patterns of acquisition*. Paper presented at the Conference on Early Behavioral Assessment of the Communicative and Cognitive Abilities of the Developmentally Disabled, Orcas Island, Washington, 1976.

Braine, M.D.S. On two types of models of the internalization of grammars. In D. I. Slobin (Ed.), *The ontogenesis of grammar*. New York: Academic Press, 1971.

Braine, M.D.S. Children's first word combinations. *Monographs of the Society for Research in Child Development*, 1976, *41*, (1, Serial No. 164).

Braine, M.D.S. & Wells, R. S. Case-like categories in children: The Actor and some related categories. *Cognitive psychology*, 1978, *10*, 100–122.

Bresnan, J. A realistic transformational grammar. In M. Halle, J. Bresnan, & G. A. Miller (Eds.), *Linguistic theory and psychological reality*. Cambridge, Mass.: MIT Press, 1978.

Brown, R. *A first language: The early stages*. Cambridge, Mass.: Harvard University Press, 1973.

de Villiers, J. The process of rule learning in child speech: A new look. In K. E. Nelson (Ed.), *Child Language* (Vol. 2), 1979.

Edwards, D. Sensory-motor intelligence and semantic relations in early child grammar. *Cognition*, 1973, *2*, 395–434.

Fillmore, C. J. Types of lexical information. In D. D. Steinberg & L. A. Jakobovits (Eds.), *Semantics: An interdisciplinary reader in Philosophy, Linguistics and Psychology.* Cambridge, England: Cambridge University Press, 1971.

Fodor, J. A. Three reasons for not deriving "kill" from "cause to die." *Linguistic Inquiry*, 1970, *1*, 429–438.

Fodor, J. A. *The language of thought.* New York: Crowell, 1975.

Fodor, J. A. Tom Swift and his procedural grandmother. *Cognition*, 1978, *6*, 228–247.

Fodor, J. D. *Semantics: Theories of meaning in generative grammar.* Hassocks, Sussex; Harvester Press, 1977.

Hersh, H. M., & Caramazza, A. A fuzzy approach to modifiers and vagueness in natural language. *Journal of Experimental Psychology: General*, 1976, *105*, 254–276.

Hockett, C. F. *A course in modern linguistics.* New York: Macmillan, 1958.

Holyak, K. J., Glass, A. L., & Mah, W. A. Morphological structure and semantic retrieval. *Journal of Verbal Learning and Verbal Behavior*, 1976, *15*, 235–247.

Ikegami, Y. *The semiological structure of the English verbs of motion.* Linguistic Automation Project, Yale University, 1969.

Jackendoff, R. Toward an explanatory semantic representation. *Linguistic Inquiry*, 1976, *7*, 89–150.

Jenkins, J. H., & Palermo, D. S. Mediation processes and the acquisition of linguistic structure. In U. Bellugi & R. Brown (Eds.), The acquisition of language. *Monographs of the Society for Research in Child Development*, 1964, *29* (1, Serial No. 92).

Kintsch, W. *The representation of meaning in memory.* Hillsdale, N.J.: Lawrence Erlbaum Associates, 1974.

Katz, J. J. *Semantic theory.* New York: Harper & Row, 1972.

Kosslyn, S. M., & Pomerantz, J. R. Imagery, propositions, and the form of internal representations. *Cognitive Psychology*, 1977, *9*, 52–76.

Lehrer, A. Semantic cuisine. *Journal of Linguistics*, 1969, *5*, 39–55.

Maratsos, M., Kuczaj, S. A., & Fox, D.M.C. Some empirical studies in the acquisition of transformational relations: Passives, negatives, and the past tense. In W. A. Collins (Ed.), *Children's Language: The Minnesota Symposium on Child Psychology (Vol. 12).* Hillsdale, N.J.: Lawrence Erlbaum Associates, 1979.

Miller, G. A., & Johnson-Laird, P. N. *Language and perception.* Cambridge, Mass.: Harvard University Press, 1976.

McNeill, D. Speech and thought. In I. Markova (Ed.), *The social context of language.* Chichester: Wiley, 1978.

Miller, G. A. Semantic relations among words. In M. Halle, J. Bresnan, & G. A. Miller (Eds.), *Linguistic theory and psychological reality.* Cambridge, Mass.: MIT Press, 1978.

Nida, E. *Toward a science of translating.* Leiden: Brill, 1964.

Nilsen, D.L.F. *The instrumental case in English.* The Hague: Mouton, 1973.

Pinker, S. *Formal models of language learning.* Unpublished paper, Harvard University, 1977.

Quine, W. *Ontological relativity and other essays.* New York: Columbia University Press, 1969.

Rhodes, R. Semantics in a relational grammar. *Papers from the 13th Regional Meeting, Chicago Linguistic Society.* Chicago, Ill.: University of Chicago Press, 1977.

Rosch, E. Mervis, C. B. Family resemblances: Studies in the internal structures of categories. *Cognitive Psychology,* 1975, *7,* 573–605.

Schank, R. C. *Conceptual information processing.* Amsterdam: North-Holland, 1975.

Schank, R. C. Memory represented (Review of *The representation of meaning in memory* by W. Kintsch). *Contemporary Psychology,* 1976, *21,* 326–328.

Schlesinger, I. M. On semantic approaches to language acquisition. *Language Sciences,* 1975 *34,* 5–8.

Schlesinger, I. M. *Production and comprehension of utterances.* Hillsdale, N.J.: Lawrence Erlbaum Associates, 1977.

Schlesinger, I. M. Cognitive and linguistic structures: The case of the Instrumental. *Journal of Linguistics,* 1979, *15,* 307–324.

Sinclair, A., Sinclair H., & De Marcellus, O. Young children's comprehension and production of passive sentences. *Archives de psychologie,* 1971, *41,* 1–20.

Slobin, D. I. *Universal and particular in the acquisition of language.* Paper prepared for workshop conference on "Language acquisition: State of the art", University of Pennsylvania, May 1978.

Stemmer, N. *An empiricist theory of language acquisition.* The Hague: Mouton, 1973.

Stemmer, N. On semantic approaches to language acquisition. *Language Sciences,* 1975, *34,* 8–11.

Van Oosten, J. Subjects and agenthood in English. *Papers from the 13th Regional Meeting, Chicago Linguistic Society.* Chicago, Ill.: University of Chicago Press, 1977.

Watt, W. C. *Competing economy criteria.* Working paper School of Social Sciences, University of California, Irvine, 1972.

Weisgerber, L. *Von den Kräften der deutschen Sprache. Grundzüge der inhaltsbezogenen Grammatik* (Vol. 1). Düsseldorf: Schwann, 1962.

Wells, G. Learning to code experience through language. *Journal of Child Language,* 1974, *2,* 243–269.

Wierzbicka, A. Why "kill" does not mean "cause to die": The semantics of action sentences. *Foundations of Language,* 1975, *13,* 491–528.

Witherspoon, G. *Language and art in the Navajo universe.* Ann Arbor: University of Michigan Press, 1977.

Author Index

Page numbers in italic indicate complete reference information

Subject Index